The Left Academy

Marxist Scholarship On American Campuses

Volume III

Edited by
Bertell Ollman and
Edward Vernoff

PRAEGER

New York
Westport, Connecticut
London

Grateful acknowledgment is made to the following for permission to reprint passages from previously published material:

Mayfield Publishing Company: Excerpts from David F. Greenberg, ed., *Crime and Capitalism: Readings in Marxist Criminology* (1981).

Academic Press: Excerpts from David Black, ed., *Toward a General Theory of Social Control – Vol. 2* (1984).

Library of Congress Cataloging-in-Publication Data

The Left academy.

Bibliography: v. 3, p.
Includes index.
1. Communism and education. 2. Education, Higher – United States. I. Ollman, Bertell. II. Vernoff, Edward.
HX526.L38 1986 335.4'07'1173 86-9321
ISBN 0-275-92116-6 (v. 3 : alk. paper)
ISBN 0-275-92117-4 (pbk. : v. 3 : alk. paper)

Library of Congress Catalog Card Number: 86-9321
ISBN: 0-275-92116-6
0-275-92117-4 (pbk.)

First published in 1986

Praeger Publishers, 521 Fifth Avenue, New York, NY 10175
A division of Greenwood Press, Inc.

Printed in the United States of America

The paper used in this book complies with the Permanent Paper Standard issued by the National Information Standards Organization (Z.39.48-1984).

10 9 8 7 6 5 4 3 2 1

To Lynda Sharp, our editor at Praeger,
for her creative efforts in helping to bring the ideas of
the left academy to the American public.

CONTENTS

INTRODUCTION

Copernicus could have been speaking about the modern academy instead of the astronomers of his day when he said, "With them it is as though an artist were to gather the hands, feet, head and other members for his images from diverse models, each part excellently drawn, but not related to a single body, and since they in no way match each other, the result would be a monster rather than man."[1] The existing breakdown of knowledge into mutually indifferent and often hostile academic disciplines, each with its own range of problematics and methods, has replaced the harmonious enlightenment we had been promised with a raucus cacophony of discordant sounds. In the confusion, the age-old link between knowledge and action has been severed so that scholars can deny all responsibility for their wares while taking pride in knowing more and more about less and less.

A major effort to criticize this state of affairs and to provide an integrated body of knowledge about human beings, society, and nature, particularly as they effect and are effected by the conditions of capitalism, has been undertaken by Marxist scholars operating out of universities in the capitalist world. The amount of serious Marxist scholarship already produced in the United States alone is prodigious, but most of it is of very recent origins and hence not very well known, even to most students of Marxism. To display the rich and varied work being produced by Marxists working in American universities, to compare the Marxist approach in its different variants with those used by mainstream scholars, and in the process to serve as an introduction to how Marxism unifies the knowledge now divided up according to academic disciplines are the main aims of *The Left Academy*.

In Volume 1 of *The Left Academy* (McGraw-Hill, 1982) most of the articles dealt with the social sciences. The disciplines covered were sociology, economics, political science, psychology, philosophy, history, and anthropology. The focus in Volume 2 (Praeger, 1984) was on the humanities. Besides articles on literature, classics, and art history, this volume contained pieces on education, law, geography, and biology. In Volume 3, we take account of new divisions of the academy along lines of gender, race, and ethnicity with articles on women's studies, Black studies, Puerto Rican studies, Mexican American studies, and Asian American studies, to which we have added articles on health, criminology, communications, and social work. As a group, these disciplines also deal with topics that have been the focus of some of the more important political struggles of recent years.

With the completion of this volume we have surveyed Marxist scholarship in twenty-three different disciplines. To our knowledge, there is no comparable survey of Marxist works in any other country. Nowhere in the American academy is Marxism the dominant theory or approach, but neither is it ignored anywhere. In practically every discipline, its scholarly achievements are winning support and being taken more and more seriously, even by its mainstream opponents. As we indicated in our Introduction to Volume 1, how far this can develop and where it will all lead is far more dependent on events in society outside the university than on anything Marxist scholars are doing or can do. Yet, in a period generally known for its conservative retrenchment, what our labors have managed to piece together represents an exceptional, albeit modest, radical success story.

As in the earlier volumes, we asked each contributor to concentrate as much as possible on American Marxist scholars and on work done in the last decade, to deal not only with debates between Marxists and non-Marxists in their discipline but with some of the important debates within Marxism, and to account for what has influenced these works as well as what they seem to have influenced. The contributors, who were chosen because of their standing as major Marxist scholars in their respective fields, were given considerable leeway in how they chose to respond to our requests. The result is a work that illustrates the different tendencies within Marxism every bit as much as it describes them. With its extensive bibliographies, reports on current debates, state of the art summaries of what has been achieved, and directional pointers to problems that still need to be treated, *The Left Academy* serves to document an ongoing project, one that is proceeding very fast in a variety of directions. Marxist orthodoxy, whatever that may have meant, is clearly behind us. What remains is an exhilarating effort on the part of several thousand scholars using the tools and theories of Marxism—developing and sharpening them, often revising them—to uncover the workings of our society on behalf of a liberatory purpose.

The Left Academy does not try to present a Marxist interpretation of the university, or an account of what it feels like to be a radical working in higher education; nor does it examine the major contributions to pedagogy and curricular reform of various non-Marxist radicals and progressives, or even how the Marxist ideas that are discussed here can be applied to concrete political struggles. These are all extremely important subjects, and material relating to them can be found in each of our volumes. However, in this work we have chosen to draw attention to the amount, variety, and quality of Marxist scholarship actually being produced in the hope of aiding others who are trying to make just these connections.

In the Introduction to Volume 1, we made a modest attempt to account for this surge of Marxist scholarship along with its precarious, though increasingly secure, position on American campuses. In the Introduction to Volume 2, we offered a brief summary of Marx's major theories—including the theory of alienation, the materialist conception of history, and the labor theory of value—as a framework in which to place most of the research that goes on in this tradition. Here, in the Introduction to Volume 3, we would like to supplement that summary with an equally brief account of Marx's dialectical method. As is evident from the articles throughout *The Left Academy*, there is no clear consensus among Marxists on how to interpret either Marx's theories or his method; nor is there agreement on how dialectics should be used. Still, it is our view that Marx's dialectics, his approach to the study of problems (despite the different emphases and interpretations to which it has been subjected), is as responsible for the impressive achievements of the left academy as are his theories, which are general conclusions based on what he finds using this approach. Given, too, the caricature of dialectics that is invariably put forward by its critics, even a very brief introduction to this subject may be of some value.

MARX'S DIALECTICAL METHOD

With all the misinformation conveyed about dialectics, it may be useful to start by saying what it is *not*. Dialectics is not a rock-ribbed triad of thesis-antithesis-synthesis that serves as an all-purpose explanation; nor does it provide a formula that enables us to prove or predict anything; nor is it the motor force of history. The dialectic, as such, explains nothing, proves nothing, predicts nothing, and causes nothing to happen. Rather, dialectics is a way of thinking that brings into focus the full range of changes and interactions that occur in the world. As part of this, it includes how to organize a reality viewed in this manner for purposes of study and how to present the results of what one finds to others, most of whom do not think dialectically.

The main problem to which dialectics is addressed is set out clearly in Marx's retelling of the Roman myth of Cacus.[2] Half man, half demon, Cacus lived in a cave and came out only at night to steal oxen. Wishing to mislead his pursuers, Cacus forced the oxen to walk backwards into his den so that their footprints made it appear that they had gone out from there. The next morning when people came looking for their oxen, all they found were footprints. Based on the evidence of these footprints, they concluded that starting from the cave their oxen had gone into the middle of a field and disappeared.

If the owners of the oxen had taken a methodology course at an American university, they might have counted the footprints and measured the depth of each step—but they would have arrived at the same conclusion. The problem here arises from the fact that reality is more than appearances, and that focusing exclusively on appearances, on the evidence that strikes us immediately and directly, can be extremely misleading. How typical is the error found in this example? According to Marx, rather than the exception, this is how most people in our society understand the world. Basing themselves on what they see, hear, and bump into in their immediate surroundings—on footprints of various kinds—they arrive at conclusions that are in many cases the exact opposite of the truth. Most of the distortions associated with bourgeois ideology are of this kind.

To understand the real meaning of the footprints, the owners of the oxen had to find out what happened the night before and what was going on in the cave that lay just over their horizon. In a similar way, understanding anything in our everyday experience requires that we know something about how it arose and developed and how it fits into the larger context or system of which it is a part. Just recognizing this, however, is not enough. For nothing is easier than slipping back into a narrow focus on appearances. After all, few would deny that everything in the world is changing and interacting at some pace and in one way or another, that history and systemic connections belong to the real world. The difficulty has always been how to think adequately about them, how not to distort them and how to give them the attention and weight that they deserve. Dialectics is an attempt to resolve this difficulty by expanding our notion of anything to include, as aspects of what it is, both the process by which it has become that and the broader interactive context in which it is found. Only then does the study of anything involve one immediately with the study of its history and encompassing system.

Dialectics restructures our thinking about reality by replacing the common sense notion of "thing," as something which *has* a history and *has* external connections with other things, with notions of "process," which *contains* its history and possible futures, and "relation," which *contains* as part of what it is its ties with other relations. Nothing that didn't already exist has been added here. Rather, it is a matter of where and how one draws boundaries and establishes units (the dialectical term is "abstracts") in which to think about the world. The assumption is that while the qualities we perceive with our five senses actually exist as parts of nature, the conceptual distinctions that tell us where one thing ends and the next one begins both in space and across time are social and mental constructs. However great the influence of what the world is on how we draw these boundaries, it is ultimately we who draw the boundaries, and people coming from different cultures and from different philosophical traditions can and do draw them differently.

In abstracting capital, for example, as a process, Marx is simply including primitive accumulation, accumulation, and the concentration of capital, in sum its real history, as part of what capital is. While abstracting it as a relation brings its actual ties with labor, commodity, value, capitalists and workers—or whatever contributes to its appearance and functioning—under the same rubric as its constituting aspects. All the units in which Marx thinks about and studies capitalism are abstracted as both processes and relations. Moreover, the terms "process" and "relation" each express, with only a difference in emphasis, what is ordinarily meant by both. Hence, in criticizing the ideological consequences of adopting what we've called the common sense approach, Marx says: "The economists do not conceive of capital as a relation. They cannot do so without at the same time conceiving of it as a historically transitory, i.e. a relative, not an absolute form of production."[3] This is not a comment about the content of capital, but about the kind of thing it is, its form, how one should conceive of it. To grasp capital, as Marx does, as a complex and developing relation is said to be equivalent to grasping it as an historical event, as something that emerged as a result of specific historical conditions and that will disappear when these conditions do. Based on this dialectical conception, Marx's quest—unlike that of his common sense opponents—is never for why something starts to change, but for the various forms this change assumes and why it may *appear* to have stopped. Likewise, it is never for how a relation gets established, but again for the different forms it takes and why aspects of an already existing relation may *appear* to be independent. Marx's critique of the ideology which results from an exclusive focus on appearances, on the footprints of events separated from their real history and the larger system in which they are found, is also of this order.

Besides a way of viewing the world, Marx's dialectical method includes how he studied it, how he organized what he found, and how he presented these findings to his chosen audience. But how does one inquire into a world that has been abstracted into mutually dependent processes? Where does one start and what does one look for? Unlike non-dialectical research where one starts with some small part and through establishing its connections tries to reconstruct the larger whole, dialectical research begins with the whole, the system, or as much of it as one understands, and then proceeds to an examination of the part to see where it fits and how it functions, leading eventually to a fuller understanding of the whole from which one has begun. Capitalism serves Marx as his jumping-off point for an examination of anything that takes place within it. As a beginning, capitalism is already contained, in principle, within the interacting processes he sets out to investigate as the sum total of their necessary conditions and results. Conversely, to begin with a supposedly independent part or parts is to assume a separation with its corresponding distortion of meaning that no amount of later relating can overcome. Something will be missing, something will be out of place, and, without any standard by which to judge, neither will be recognized. What are called "interdisciplinary studies" simply treat the sum of such defects coming from different fields. As with Humpty Dumpty, who after the fall could never be put together again, a system whose functioning parts have been treated as independent of one another at the start can never be reestablished in its integrity.

The investigation itself seeks to concretize what is going on in capitalism, to trace the means and forms through which it works and has developed, and to project where it seems to be tending. As a general rule, the interactions that constitute any problem in its present state are examined before studying their progress over time. The order of inquiry, in other words, is system before history, so that history is never the development of one or two isolated elements with its suggestion, explicit or implicit, that change results from causes located inside that particular sphere (histories of religion, or of culture, or even of economics alone are decidedly undialectical). In Marx's study of any specific event or institutional form, these two types of inquiry are always interwoven. The fuller understanding of capitalism that is the major result of such a study is now ready to serve as a more effective starting point for the next series of investigations.

Given an approach that proceeds from the whole to the part, from the system inward, dialectical research is primarily directed to finding and tracing four kinds of relations: identity/difference, interpenetration of opposites, quantity/quality, and contradiction. Rooted in his dialectical conception of reality, these relations enable Marx to attain his double aim of discovering how something works or happened while simultaneously developing his understanding of the system in which such things could work or happen in just this way.

According to Marx,

> It is characteristic of the entire crudeness of "common sense," which takes its rise from the "full life" and does not cripple its natural features by philosophy or other studies, that where it succeeds in seeing a distinction it fails to see a unity, and where it sees a unity it fails to see a distinction. If "common sense" establishes distinction determination, they immediately petrify surreptitiously and it is considered the most reprehensible sophistry to rub together these conceptual blocks in such a way that they catch fire.[4]

In what Marx calls the common sense approach, also found in formal logic, things are either the same/identical (the sense in which Marx uses "unity" above) or different, not both. On this model, comparisons generally stop after taking note of the way(s) any two entities are either identical or different, but for Marx this is only the first step. Indeed, the fire that comes from rubbing together identity and differences results from remarking identity where most others have seen only differences and with noting differences where others are content with simple identity.

Unlike the political economists, for example, who stop after describing the obvious differences between profit, rent, and interest, Marx goes on to bring out their identity as forms of surplus value (that is, wealth created by workers that is not returned to them in the form of wages). As relations, they all have this quality, this aspect that touches upon their origins, in common. The interest Marx takes in delineating the special features of production and of the working class (what makes them different) without neglecting all they have in common with other economic processes and other classes respectively are good examples of his approaching identity and difference from the side of identity. The relations that stand in for things in Marx's dialectical conception of reality are sufficiently large and complex to possess qualities that—when compared to the qualities of other similarly constituted relations—appear to be identical and others that appear to be different. In investigating what these are and, especially, in paying extra attention to whichever half of this pairing is currently most neglected, Marx can arrive at detailed descriptions of specific phenomena without getting lost in one-sidedness.

While the relation of identity/difference treats the various qualities that are examined with its help as given, the interpretation of opposites is based on the recognition that to a very large degree how anything appears and functions is due to its surrounding conditions. These conditioning factors apply to both objects and the persons perceiving them. As regards the former, for example, it is only because a machine is owned by capitalists that it is used to exploit workers. In the hands of a consumer or of a self-employed operator, that is, conditioned by another set of factors, operating under different imperatives, it would not function in this way. As regards the latter, when a capitalist looks at a machine, he sees a commodity he has bought on the market, perhaps even the price he has paid for it, and something that is going to make him a profit. A worker, on the other hand, looking at the same machine sees an instrument that will determine all his movements in the production process.

The perspectival element—recognizing that things appear very different depending on who is looking at them—plays a very important role in dialectical thought. This doesn't mean that the truths that emerge from viewing reality from different vantage points are of equal value. Involved as they are in the work of transforming nature, workers enjoy a privileged position from which to view and make sense out of the developmental character of the system, and with his interest in the evolution of capitalism this is the vantage point that Marx most often adopts for himself.

The notion of the interpenetration of opposites helps Marx to understand that nothing—no event, institution, person, or process is simply and solely what it seems to be at a particular place and time, that is situated within a certain set of conditions. Viewed in another way or by other people, or viewing them under drastically changed conditions may produce not only a different but the exact opposite conclusion or effect. Hence, the interpenetration of opposites. A losing strike in one context may serve as the start of a revolution in another; an election that is a farce because one party, the Republicrats, has all the money and the workers' parties none could, with an equalization of the conditions of struggle, offer a democratic choice; workers who believe that capitalism is an ideal system when they have a good job may begin to question this when they become unemployed. Looking for where and how such changes have already occurred and under what set of still developing conditions new effects are likely to occur helps Marx gauge both the complexity of the part under examination and its dependence on the evolution of the system overall.

What is called quantity/quality is a relation between two temporally differentiated moments within the same process. Every process contains moments of before and after, encompassing both build-up (and build-down) and what that leads to. Initially, movement within any process takes the form of quantitative change. One or more of its aspects—each process being also a relation composed of aspects—increases or decreases in size or number. Then, at a certain point—which is different for each process studied—a qualitative transformation takes place, indicated by a change in its appearance and/or function. It has become something else while, in terms of its main constituting relationships, remaining essentially the same. This qualitative change is often, though not always, marked by the introduction of a new concept to designate what the process has become.

Only when money reaches a certain amount, Marx says, does it become capital, that is, can it function to buy labor power and appropriate surplus value.[5] Likewise, the cooperation of many people becomes a new productive power that is not only more but qualitatively different than the sum of individual powers that compose it.[6] Looking for quantity/quality change is Marx's way of bringing into single focus the before and after aspects in a development that most nondialectical approaches treat separately and even causally. It is a way of uniting in thought the past and probable future of any ongoing process at the expense (temporary expense) of its relations in the broader system. And it is a way of sensitizing oneself to the inevitability of change, both quantitative and qualitative, even before research has helped us to discover what it is. While the notion of quantity/quality is in no sense a formula for predicting the future, it does encourage research into patterns and trends of a kind that enables one to project the likely future, and it does offer a framework for integrating such projections into one's understanding of the present and the past.

Of the four major relations Marx investigated in his effort to make dialectical sense out of capitalist reality, contradiction is undoubtedly the most important. According to Marx, "in capitalism everything seems and in fact is contradictory."[7] He also believes it is the "contradictory socially determined features of its elements" that is "the predominant characteristic of the capitalist mode of production."[8]

Contradiction is understood here as the incompatible development of different elements within the same relation, which is to say between elements that are also dependent on one another. What is remarked as differences are based, as we saw, on certain conditions, and these conditions are constantly changing. Hence, differences are changing; and given how each difference serves as part of the appearance and/or functioning of others, grasped as relations, how one changes affects all. Consequently, their paths of development do not only intersect in mutually supportive ways, but are constantly blocking, undermining, otherwise interfering with and in due course transforming one another. Contradiction offers the optimal means for bringing such change and interaction as regards both present and future into a single focus. The future finds its way into this focus as the likely and possible outcomes of the interaction of these opposing tendencies in the present, as their real potential. It is contradiction more than any other notion that enables Marx to think accurately about the organic and historical movements of the capitalist mode of production, how they effect each other and develop together from their origins in feudalism to whatever lies just over the horizon.

The common sense notion of contradiction is that it applies to ideas about things and not to things themselves, that it is a logical relation between propositions ("If I claim 'X', I can't at the same time claim 'not X' "), and not a real relation existing in the world. This commonsense view, as we saw, is based on a conception of reality divided into separate and independent parts—a body moves when another body bumps into it. Whereas non-dialectical thinkers in every sphere of scholarship are involved in a nonstep search for the "outside agitator," for something or someone that comes from outside the problem under examination that is the cause for whatever occurs, dialectical thinkers attribute the main responsibility for all change to the inner contradictions of the system or systems in which it occurs. Capitalism's fate, in other words, is sealed by its own problems, problems that are internal manifestations of what it is and how it works and are often parts of the very achievements of capitalism, worsening as these achievements grow and spread. Capitalism's extraordinary success in increasing production, for example, stands in contradiction to the decreasing ability of the workers to consume these goods. Given capitalist relations of distribution, they can buy ever smaller portions of what they themselves produce (it is the proportion of such goods and not the actual amount that determines the character of the contradiction), leading to periodic crises of overproduction/underconsumption. For Marx, contradiction belongs to things in their quality as processes within an organic and developing system. It arises from within, from the very character of these processes (it is "innate in their subject matter"), and is an expression of the state of the system.[9]

In the movement of quantity into quality, Marx approaches change by focusing on a single process, treating other elements in the relation as its dependent aspects. While in the movement of contradiction, the interaction of two or more processes (and there can be more than two) are brought into the same focus and given equal status, though research may reveal one process to be dominant. The buildup of pressure on either side of the contradiction, however, can still be viewed as an instance of the transformation of quantity into quality. This is one of the many ways these different dialectical relations, which can also be grasped as processes, intersect with one another.

Contradictions exist in capitalism as broken up in different ways, on a variety of axes, and into a number of overlapping parts. Hence, it is not only capital and wage labor that are seen to be in contradiction, but also the overlapping relations of capitalists and workers, and of wealth and poverty. Capital and labor, each viewed on its own, are also seen to contain contradictions between their constituting aspects, likewise conceived of as processes in relation of mutual support. It should be no surprise, therefore, if the main contradictions Marx finds in capitalist society are often given slightly different formulations.

Without a conception of things as relations, non-dialectical thinkers have great difficulty focusing on the different sides of a contradiction at the same time. The result is that these sides are examined, if at all, in sequence, with one invariably receiving less attention than the other, their mutual interaction often mistaken for causality. A frequent criticism Marx makes of political economists is that they try to "exorcise contradictions" by recognizing only one side at a time, by not seeing their internal relations.[10] By viewing capitalist forces of production and capitalist relations of distribution separately they miss the contradiction. A lot of effort of bourgeois ideology goes into denying, hiding, or otherwise distorting contradictions. Bad faith and interest politics, however, account for only a small part of these practices. For non-dialectical thinkers, operating out of a commonsense view, real contradictions can be understood only as differences, paradox, opposition, strain, tension, dislocation, imbalance, or, if accompanied by open strife, conflict. But without the dialectical notion of contradiction, they seldom see and can never adequately grasp the underlying forces responsible for these appearances. And, of course, they can never grasp the development or gauge the force of these tendencies before they have made their way to the surface of events. For Marx, on the other hand, the study of capitalist contradictions is also a way of discovering the main causes of *coming* conflict.

While any contradiction involves directly only a few processes in their particular relation to one another, the ramifications of a contradiction may extend throughout the system. Consequently, the resolution of a major contradiction, the moment when the uneasy equilibrium of forces gives way to the growing pressure for restructuring, calls into question the very existence of society in its present form. In Marx's eyes, such major contradictions are "so many mines to explode" capitalism.[11] *Contra* reports in the bourgeois media, it is not Marx who plants these mines. Capitalism does. Marx simply finds them—and would have us plan and act accordingly.

On the basis of what he uncovers in his study of identity/difference, the interpenetration of opposites, quantity/quality, and contradiction—a study that starts with the whole and proceeds inward to the part, and which conceives of all parts as processes in relations of mutual dependence—Marx reconstructed the working of capitalist society. Organizing reality in this way, he was able to capture both the organic and historical movements of capitalism in their specific interconnections. The still unfinished results of this reconstruction are the particular laws and theories we known as Marxism.

It is clear that Marx could not have arrived at his understanding of capitalism without dialectics, nor will we be able to develop this understanding further without a firm grasp of this same method. No treatment of dialectics however brief, therefore, can be considered complete without a warning against some of the more common errors and distortions associated with this way of thinking. For example, if non-dialectical thinkers often miss the forest for the trees, dialectical thinkers just as often do the opposite, that is, play down or even ignore the parts, the details, in deference to making generalizations about the whole. But the capitalist system can be grasped only through an investigation of its specific parts in their interconnection. Dialectical thinkers also have a tendency to move too quickly to the bottom line, to push a germ of a development to its finished form. In general, this error results from not giving enough attention to the complex mediations, both in space and over time, that make up the joints of any social problem.

There is also a related tendency to overestimate the speed of change along with a corresponding tendency to underestimate the barriers to change. Relatively minor cracks on the surface of capitalist reality are too easily mistaken for gaping chasms on the verge of becoming earthquakes. If non-dialectical thinking leads people to be surprised whenever a major change occurs, because they aren't looking for it and don't expect it, because it isn't an internal part of how they conceive of the world at this moment, dialectical thinking—for just the opposite reasons—can lead people to be surprised when such change takes so long in coming. In organizing reality for purposes of grasping change, relative stability does not always get the attention that it deserves. These are all weaknesses inherent in the very strengths of dialectical method. Ever present as temptations, they offer an easier way, a quick fix, and have to be carefully guarded against.

Nothing that we have said in our account so far should be taken to deny the empirical character of Marx's method. Marx does not deduce the workings of capitalism from the meanings of words or from the requirements of his theories, but like any good social scientist he does research to discover what is the case. And in his research he made use of the entire range of materials and resources that were available in his time. Nor do we wish to claim that Marx was the only dialectical thinker. As is well known, most of his dialectic was taken over from Hegel, who merely (?) filled in and systematized a way of thinking and an approach to studying reality that goes all the way back to the Greeks. And in our time there are non-Marxist thinkers, such as Alfred North Whitehead and F. H. Bradley, who have developed their own versions of this approach. Despite its heavy ideological content, common sense, too, is not without its dialectical moments, as is evidenced by such maxims as "Every cloud has its silver lining" and "That was the straw that broke the camel's back." Elements of dialectics can also be found in other social science methods, such as structural functionalism, systems theory, and ethnomethodology, where it constitutes most of what is of value in these approaches.

What stands out about Marx's dialectical method is the systematic manner in which he works it out and uses it for the study of capitalist society (including—because the dialectic requires it—its origins and probable future), the united theory of knowledge (set out in the still incomplete theories of Marxism) to which it leads, the sustained critique of non-dialectical approaches (suggested in our remarks on ideology throughout) that makes it possible and begins to develop, and —perhaps most striking of all—its emphasis on the necessary connection posed by dialectics itself between knowledge and action.

As regards this last, Marx claims, the dialectic "is in its essence critical and revolutionary."[12] It is revolutionary because it helps us to see the present as a moment through which out society is passing, because it forces us to examine where it has come from and where it is heading as part of learning what it is, and because it enables us to grasp that as actors, as well as victims, in this process in which everyone and everything are connected we have to power to affect it. In keeping in front of us the simple truth that everything is changing, the future is posed as a choice in which the only thing that cannot be chosen is what we already have. Efforts to retain the status quo in any area of life never achieve quite that. Fruit kept in the refrigerator too long goes rotten; so do emotions and people; so do whole societies (where the proper word is "disintegration"). With dialectics we are made to question what kind of changes are already occurring and what kind of changes are possible. The dialectic is revolutionary, as Brecht points out, because it helps us to pose such questions in a manner that makes effective action possible.[13]

The dialectic is critical because it helps us to become critical of what our role has been up to now. In Marxist terms, one doesn't advocate class struggle or choose to participate in it (common bourgeois misconceptions). The class struggle, representing the sum of the contradictions between workers broadly defined and capitalists, simply is, and in one way or another we are all already involved. On learning about it and where we fit into it, however, we can decide to stop acting as we have been (the first decision to take) and what more or else we can do to better serve our own interests. What *can* be chosen is what side to take in this struggle and how to conduct it. A dialectical grasp of our socially conditioned roles and the equally necessary limits and possibilities that constitute the present provides the opportunity for making a conscious and intelligent choice. In this manner does knowledge of necessity usher in the beginnings of real freedom.[14]

By helping to reconstruct the complex relations that make up capitalist society, relations that are broken up and distorted in the academy along lines of discipline, Marx's dialectical method enabled him to develop a unified theory of knowledge and a conscious political practice that integrates what we do with who we are and what we know. *The Left Academy* is intended both as a testimony to this knowledge (and to the vitality of the school that strives to apply and extend it) and as an instance of this practice.[15]

FOR UPDATE ON ACADEMIC REPRESSION

Readers interested in following the trials and tribulations of radical professors in the academy should consult *ZEDEK*, the newsjournal of the Social Activist Professors Defense Foundation, 19329 Monte Vista, Detroit, Michigan (48221); subscription rate: $10/year. *Guarding the Ivory Tower: Repression and Rebellion in Higher Education* (1985), by Philip Meranto, Oneida Meranto, and Matthew Lippman, offers an excellent survey of some of the more blatant cases of academic repression in the recent period. The book is available from Lucha Publications, P.O. Box 12671, Denver, Colorado (80211) for $10. The latest threat to the presence of Marxists and Marxist ideas on American campuses comes from a radical right group misnamed "Accuracy in Academia." Periodical bulletins on the activity of this group, which received an enormous amount of publicity during the school year 1985-1986, are available from Scholars Against the Escalating Danger of the Far Right, P.O. Box 133, New York, New York (10011).

Finally, the editors would like to thank Mrs. Sylvia Dunkelblau for her help in typing parts of the manuscript for this volume.

FOOTNOTES

1. Quoted in Thomas Kuhn, *The Structure of Scientific Revolutions* (Chicago: University of Chicago Press, 1962), p. 83.
2. Karl Marx, *Theories of Surplus Value*, Vol. III, ed. S. W. Ryazanskaya and R. Dixon; trans. Jack Cohen and S. W. Ryazanskaya (Moscow, 1971), pp. 536-7.
3. Ibid., p. 274.
4. Karl Marx, "Die Moralisierende Kritik," in Karl Marx and Frederick Engels, *Werke*, Vol. IV (Berlin, 1961), p. 339.
5. Frederick Engels, *Anti-Duhring*, trans. Emile Burns (London, n.d.), p. 140. It is Engels who gives this as an example of the transformation of quantity into quality, but it comes, he says, from Marx's work.
6. Ibid., p. 142.
7. Karl Marx, *Theories of Surplus Value*, Vol. I, ed. S. W. Ryazanskaya, trans. Emile Burns (Moscow, 1963), p. 218.
8. Marx, *Theories of Surplus Value*, Vol. III, p. 491.

9. Ibid., p. 137.

10. Karl Marx, *Theories of Surplus Value*, Vol. II, ed. S. W. Ryazanskaya, no trans. (Moscow, 1968), p. 519.

11. Karl Marx, *Grundrisse*, trans. Martin Nichlaus (New York, 1973), p. 159.

12. Karl Marx, *Capital*, Vol. I, trans. Samuel Moore and Edward Aveling (Moscow, 1958), p. 20.

13. Quoted in *Literature, Science, Ideologie*, No. 1 (Paris, May-June, 1972), p. 1.

14. See Engels's discussion of the dialectical relationship between freedom and necessity in *Anti-Duhring*, pp. 128-9.

15. Besides the works of Marx and Engels, writings that we have found particularly useful in elucidating the dialectical method include Ira Gollobin's *Dialectical Materialism: Its Laws, Categories and Practises* (1986); Carol Gould's *Marx's Social Ontology* (1978); Henri Lefebvre's *Sociology of Marx* (1968); George Lukacs' *History and Class Consciousness* (1971); Karel Kosik's *Dialectics of the Concrete* (1976); Scott Meikle's *Essentialism in the Thought of Karl Marx* (1985); John Mepham and David Ruben's (eds.) *Issues in Marxist Philosophy*, Vol. I (1979); Mao Tse Tung's *On Contradiction* (1952); Bertell Ollman's *Alientation: Marx's Conception of Man in Capitalist Society* (1976); Derek Sayer's *Marx's Method* (1979); John-Paul Sartre's *Search for a Method* (1963); and Jindrich Zeleny's *The Logic of Marx* (1980).

1

FEMINIST SCHOLARSHIP: THE IMPACT OF MARXISM

Lise Vogel

INTRODUCTION

Over the past two decades, the modern women's movement has provided the context for the development of a rich variety of feminist research and scholarship. Some of the best of this work has been produced by scholars who view themselves as part of the socialist-feminist wing of the women's movement, and who have therefore been involved to some extent with Marxism. Against the background of the oppositional ferment of the late 1960s, socialist feminists conceived of women's liberation as a revolutionary project and they committed themselves to developing theory and practice that were simultaneously socialist and feminist. By this effort, they distinguished themselves from liberal feminists, on the one hand, and radical feminists, on the other.[1] At first, socialist feminists hardly differentiated between Marxist and non-Marxist socialisms; this was especially characteristic of socialist feminism in the United States, where left traditions have been extremely weak. As the socialist-feminist movement evolved, disagreements concerning the relevance and interpretation of Marx and Marxism arose, but it is nonetheless currently not possible to demarcate some Marxist-feminist trend distinct from socialist feminism. This chapter will focus, then, on scholarship produced from within the socialist-feminist perspective.

For editorial and bibliographical suggestions, graciously provided on short notice, the author would like to thank Lourdes Benería, Renate Bridenthal, Norma Chinchilla, Miriam Frank, and Robert Shaffer.

With respect to the Marxist legacy, socialist feminists share several important underlying premises. They recognize that Marx and Engels paid serious attention to the so-called woman question, and made significant contributions in their attempts to answer it. They note the need to use historical and dialectical materialist approaches in confronting issues of women's oppression. But they also agree that neither Marx nor Engels nor the subsequent Marxist socialist tradition provided adequate theoretical or historical accounts of women's situation, much less practical guidance in the struggle for women's liberation. They differ, often widely, on the interpretation of these inadequacies as well as on just which of the tradition's elements remain useful and how to develop more adequate analyses and practice. It is socialist feminism's collective willingness to challenge certain tenets of so-called traditional Marxism while retaining a commitment to some sort of Marxist socialism that marks it as a distinct and highly innovative trend. Not surprisingly, the attempt to steer this difficult course often earns socialist feminists criticism from more traditional socialists, on the one hand, and liberal and radical feminists, on the other.

In its nearly twenty-year history, socialist-feminist scholarship has developed in a number of ways. In particular, North American socialist feminists have become more aware of new directions in Marxist thought in Europe and elsewhere. Socialist feminism is also inevitably being affected by the harsh economic, social, and political climate of the 1980s. This is the background for understanding the popularity of some recent socialist-feminist analyses that make a sharper distinction between the Marxist and other socialist traditions than heretofore, with an implied or occasionally explicit rejection of the former. There is a potential, then, for a future demarcation between Marxist-feminist and socialist-feminist scholarship, although many would still argue that "socialist feminism is in fact the most consistent application of Marxist method and therefore the most 'orthodox' form of Marxism" (Jaggar, 1983:125).

Within the academy, feminist scholars have explored the musty sexist corners of virtually every traditional discipline, and participated as well in the development of a broad range of women's studies courses, programs, journals, associations, and conferences. Reflecting its origins in the contemporary women's movement, feminist scholarship exhibits a variety of political perspectives, among them socialist feminism. Much socialist-feminist research falls within conventional disciplinary boundaries, and references to this literature can be found in other review articles.[2] What will be examined here is a portion of that socialist-feminist scholarship that explicitly addresses questions Marxists should ask concerning, for example: the material basis of women's oppression; the relationship between Marxism and feminism; the role of families in capitalist social reproduction; the interplay of sexuality, consciousness, and ideology; women as workers and as militants; and the politics of women's liberation. This is a vast literature, only some of which can be considered below. The discussion will emphasize recent contributions from the United States, although it is difficult to isolate this work from that of Canadian and English socialist feminists.

ROOTS OF WOMEN'S OPPRESSION

Perhaps the most urgent question socialist feminists have attempted to address is that of the source of women's subordination. The answer to this question is crucial, because it necessarily shapes strategic orientations to achieving women's liberation. The socialist-feminist movement analyzes the basis of female oppression in a manner that distinguishes it from other trends within feminism as well as from most versions of socialism. In contrast to liberal feminism, for instance, socialist feminism recognizes that women's subordination rests on more than irrational prejudice and differential sex-role socialization. In contrast to much of the Marxist tradition, it notes that male supremacy cannot be fully explained as an ideology enabling capital to divide the working class politically while simultaneously exploiting superprofits from women. Socialist feminism, like radical feminism, instead maintains that the oppression of women has a material root involving women as sexual beings and as childbearers, but it wishes to go beyond radical feminism's simplistic materialism to be both dialectical and historically specific.[3] To accomplish this task, socialist-feminist theory theory initially sought to "fit" women directly into the existing Marxist critique of political economy.

Early socialist-feminist efforts to use Marx's theory and method identified domestic labor as the material root of women's oppression. In an extensive controversy that came to be called the domestic labor debate, unpaid household labor was analyzed in terms of what were thought to be traditional Marxist categories, drawn mainly from *Captal*. (For samples, summaries, and further bibliography, see Malos, 1980, especially the introduction and the articles by Benston, Morton, and Dalla Costa; as well as Himmelweit and Mohun, 1977; Molyneux, 1979; Holmstrom, 1981.) The debate, which began in the late 1960s, was the first modern attempt to provide a materialist analysis of women's oppression by means of a feminist critique of Marx's critique of political economy.[4] Participants sought to put into theoretical context the contemporary feminist insight that childbearing, child care, and housework are material activities resulting in products. At the same time, they directed attention to the issues of women's position as housewives and of domestic labor's contribution to the reproduction of social relations. In this way they expected to be able to demonstrate that women's domestic labor constitutes the key link between female subordination and societal reproduction. Various analyses of domestic labor corresponded, more or less closely to a variety of political and strategic perspectives on the relationship of women's oppression to class exploitation and to revolutionary struggle, although theorists rarely stated these implications clearly, leaving political and strategic issues unconfronted.

The burgeoning literature of the domestic labor debate confirmed, for socialist feminists, the central role of women's activity in the so-called private sphere. Despite the debate's initial accomplishments, however, it was plagued by a number of weaknesses. First, it focused mainly on capitalist societies; the obvious subordination of women in other types of societies remained without explanation. Second, it concentrated almost exclusively on domestic labor and women's oppression in the working class, thereby leaving the subordination of women in other classes unexamined. Third, it generally restricted its analysis to theoretical questions at the economic level. Fourth, it tended to identify domestic labor with housework and child care, leaving the status of childbearing unspecified. Fifth, it failed to explain why it is that domestic labor seems universally to fall to women. Some, if not all, of these limitations might have been defended as preliminary steps in the development of a complex theoretical argument, but they rarely were. Although the discussion of domestic labor had been launched in response to the need for a materialist analysis of women's position, its promise remained unfulfilled. Many socialist feminists, especially in the United States, soon dismissed the debate as an irrelevant and essentially scholastic exercise that was not producing the kinds of concrete answers needed by the movement.

By the mid-1970s, socialist feminists dissatisfied with the domestic labor literature were exploring other conceptual categories. Among the concepts that seemed more capable than domestic labor of encompassing the broad range of phenomena involved in women's oppression was the division of labor according to sex. These divisions exist in every known society—women and men do different types of work—and their existence has in fact long been an object of attention for Marxists. Ordinarily, women tend to be responsible for work in the area of childrearing, as well as other types of labor in the household. Women may also be involved in production, usually in activities distinct from those of men. Generally speaking, sex divisions of labor represent stubborn barriers to women's full participation in every society, and within every layer of a given society. Socialist-feminist scholars examined the relationship of these sex divisions of labor to women's oppression in families and in society at large in articles that were and remain influential. For example, Gayle Rubin (1975) conceptualized sex divisions of labor as "sex/gender systems" and called for a "Marxian analysis" of them that would establish the "political economy of sex." Joan Kelly-Gadol (1976) pointed to the importance of using sex as an analytical category in historical research. Alice Kessler-Harris (1975a) underscored the role of the sex division of labor in the workings of the labor market.

Once the division of labor by sex became a central category in socialist-feminist research, the problem of causality had to be addressed. Heidi Hartmann made explicit what many had begun to assume when she argued that sex divisions of labor constitute the material basis for women's oppression, and linked her analysis to strategic considerations:

> It is my contention that the roots of women's present social status lie in this sex-ordered division of labor. It is my belief that not only must the hierarchical nature of the division of labor between the sexes be eliminated, but the very division of labor between the sexes itself must be eliminated if women are to attain equal social status with men and if women and men are to attain the full development of their human potentials (Hartmann, 1976:137).

In the past ten years, numerous empirical studies by anthropologists, economists, historians, and sociologists have documented the nature and dynamics of sex divisions of labor in a wide variety of circumstances. Implicit in most of this work is an identification of the division of labor by sex as the root of female subordination. Although this fairly unexamined assumption is still dominant within the socialist-feminist movement, some theoretically self-conscious modifications and exceptions have appeared. For example, several authors have made analytical distinctions among various aspects of the sex division of labor in order to explore differential linkages to surplus production and social reproduction (Edholm, Harris, and Young, 1977; Middleton, 1979; Benería, 1979). The assumption of a universal causal role for the sex division of labor in establishing women's subordinate position has been challenged. Carmen Diana Deere and Magdalena Léon de Leal (1981), for instance, emphasize the historical specificity of the sex division of labor, and argue that it is often a symptom, not a cause, of women's oppression; see also Quick (1977) and Sen (1980). Anthropologists have been especially sensitive to the historical malleability of sex divisions of labor, and they have persistently confronted the stubborn problem of situating both the origins of sex divisions of labor and the perpetuation of women's oppression within a dynamic understanding of societal evolution (for example, Reiter, 1977; Leacock, 1983; Leibowitz, 1983).

Alongside their investigation of sex divisions of labor, socialist feminists developed the concepts of reproduction and patriarchy. The concept of reproduction seemed to offer a means to link women's oppression to the Marxist analysis of production and the class struggle, not only in capitalist but in other types of societies. Socialist feminists conceptualized processes of reproduction as comparable to, but relatively independent from, the production that characterizes a given society. Often they talked in terms of a mode of reproduction, analogous to the mode of production (for example, Harrison, 1973; Larguia, 1975; O'Laughlin, 1975; Landes, 1977-78). These was little agreement, however, on the substantive meaning of the term "reproduction." Some simply identified reproduction with what appear to be the obvious functions of the family. Despite the empiricism of this approach, it clarified the analytical tasks that socialist feminists confronted. In Renate Bridenthal's (1976:5) words, "the relationship between production and reproduction is a dialectic within a larger historical dialectic. That is, changes in the mode of production give rise to changes in the mode of reproduction," and this dialectic must be analyzed. Several participants in the domestic labor debate postulated the existence of a "housework" or "family" mode of production alongside the capitalist mode of production, but subordinate to it. The concept of a mode of reproduction converged, moreover, with suggestions by some Marxist anthropologists that families act as a perpetual source of cheap labor power in both third world and advanced capitalist countries (see the reviews of Meillassoux, 1975, by Mackintosh, 1977; O'Laughlin, 1977; Rapp, 1977). A similar concept of the mode of reproduction was often implicit in the work of socialist feminists who studied the relationship between imperialism and the family (for example, Caulfield, 1974; Deere, 1976).

The notion of patriarchy was taken over from radical feminism, and it required appropriate transformation. Radical feminists used the term to indicate a multilevel system of political, economic, ideological, and above all, psychological structures through which men in all societies subordinate women. They suggested, furthermore, that such patriarchal cultures could provoke the emergence of oppositional female cultures; radical-feminist theories of patriarchy thereby continually posed questions of power, resistance, and revolution, albeit in an ahistorical manner. Socialist feminists attracted to the concept of patriarchy had to develop a version capable of being linked with Marxist theory, which posits each mode of production as an historically specific system of structures through which one class exploits and subordinates another. In general, socialist feminists suggested, as Heidi Hartmann and Amy Bridges (1975:14) put it, that "Marxist categories, like capital itself, are sex-blind; the categories of patriarchy as used by radical feminists are blind to history." From this point of view, the concept of patriarchy provided a means for discussing social phenomena that seemed to escape Marxist categories. Some suggested that a theory of patriarchy could explain why certain individuals, men as well as women, are in particular subordinate or dominant places within the social structure of a given society. Others believed that issues of interpersonal dominance and subordination could best be addressed by a theory of patriarchy. Socialist-feminist theorists were not in agreement, moreover, on the meaning of the concept patriarchy. For some, it represented a primarily ideological force or system. Many argued that it has a major material foundation in men's ability to control women's labor, access to resources, and sexuality. Different approaches emerged also to the problem of the relationship between patriarchy and the workings of a particular mode of production.

Early and influential socialist-feminist discussions of patriarchy in the United States include Hartmann and Bridges (1975), Rubin (1975), and Kelly-Gadol (1976). Hester Eisenstein (1983) provides a socialist-feminist analysis of the evolution of the concept of patriarchy within contemporary feminist thought. The most sophisticated considerations of patriarchy come out of England; for a sampling of this work, see Kuhn and Wolpe (1978); and for useful critical reviews of the literature, see Barrett (1980) and Sayers (1982).

These various discussions of patriarchy, reproduction, and the sex division of labor indicated a shift in the socialist-feminist focus. Socialist feminists had initially expected to be able simply to extend Marxist analysis to cover the relatively unexamined questions of women's oppression (for example, Mitchell, 1966, 1971; Guettel, 1974; the domestic labor debate), but they had encountered numerous difficulties. In response, they introduced concepts and theoretical frameworks whose relation to Marxism could be interpreted in several ways. To some, the new developments represented an authentic elaboration of the best in a revitalized Marxist tradition. To others, they constituted the transcendence of an inheritance that was by its very nature limited. The problem of the relationship between Marxism and feminism quickly became itself an explicit object of controversy.

MARXISM AND FEMINISM

In the United States, the controversy over the relationship between Marxism and feminism generally proceeded in isolation from the renaissance of Marxist thought that had been flourishing in Europe since the early 1960s. Faced with the impossibility of fitting women neatly into existing Marxist critiques of political economy, and stimulated by ongoing dialogue and joint practical work with radical feminists, socialist feminists in the 1970s were conceptualizing women's position in terms of a systematic mechanism of subordination, variously termed the sex/gender system, the mode of reproduction, and, most frequently, patriarchy. They emphasized how the systems of sex subordination and class oppression were inextricably intertwined, and they claimed a relative autonomy for patriarchy. Contemporary society could be described, then, as made up of the interacting systems of patriarchy and capitalism, requiring analysis by feminism, on the one hand, and Marxism, on the other. Implicit in this approach was a series of correlated oppositions–reproduction/production, sex/class, patriarchy/capitalism, and feminism/socialism–awaiting dialectical resolution in both theory and practice. In Zillah Eisenstein's (1977:3) influential formulation,

> the synthesis of radical feminism and Marxist analysis is a necessary first step in formulating a cohesive socialist feminist political theory. . . . To define capitalist patriarchy as a source of the problem is at the same time to suggest that socialist feminism is the answer. My discussion uses Marxist class analysis as the thesis, radical feminist patriarchal analysis as the antithesis, and from the two evolves the synthesis of socialist feminism.

In the course of achieving the synthesis, deficiencies in both Marxist and feminist theory were to be rectified. The synthesis was expected to provide, furthermore, an adequate theoretical foundation for developing analysis and strategy with respect to the relationship between feminism and socialism—a relationship with a long history of difficulty.

The capitalist-patriarchy approach seemed promising to most socialist feminists; see, for example, Kelly (1979) and Z. Eisenstein (1979). Many, however, were less optimistic than Eisenstein, as the popularity of the widely circulated article entitled "The Unhappy Marriage of Marxism and Feminism" indicated (Hartmann and Bridges, 1975; revised version published as Hartmann, 1979; reprinted and discussed in Sargent, 1981). In practice, the projection of a synthesis offered a way to simultaneously retain an abstract allegiance to Marxism as an account of production and the economy, yet be free of the necessity of directly confronting and transforming Marxist theory. Interestingly, this approach to investigating women's oppression reinforced the sex division of intellectual labor. Socialist feminists, virtually all of them women, were to analyze the workings of patriarchy, while others, mostly men, could continue to use Marxism to examine the workings of capitalism.

Analytical frameworks based on the capitalist-patriarchy model have recently been subjected to sharp criticism for their dualism (Beechey, 1979; Vogel, 1979; Barrett, 1980; Young, 1980, 1981; Burris, 1982). Although the proposal to create a synthesis of Marxism and feminism was intended to enable socialist feminism to overcome the shortcomings of each theory, the results have generally not gone much beyond mechanical juxtaposition. Socialist-feminist revisions of the radical feminist concept of patriarchy have not sufficiently freed it from its ahistorical and psychologistic origins. Marxist theory as used by socialist feminists has not been rescued from economic reductionism and functionalism. The unified framework sought by so many has not materialized. Indeed the dualism of socialist-feminist analysis often recapitulates the opposition between feminism and Marxism that the proposed synthesis had been expected to transcend.

For those socialist feminists who remain committed to constructing an integrated framework for the analysis of women's oppression, current efforts focus on developing more sophisticated critiques and elaborations of Marxism as well as feminism. The goal is being pursued along several paths.

One approach is to incorporate feminist philosophical perspectives into the understanding of the relationship between Marxism and feminism. For example, an important accomplishment of the modern feminist movement is its constitution of a variety of hitherto veiled phenomena—above all, sexual and procreative (or reproductive) activities—as objects of central theoretical and practical interest. This ability to see what had earlier been veiled is being analyzed by feminist scholars as an epistemological breakthrough of great import. For socialist feminists, the epistemological shift suggests a means by which a feminist transformation of Marxist theory can be initiated. Nancy Hartsock, for instance, speaks of using women's experience as the basis for achieving a "feminist standpoint," just as the working class's experience offers the possibility of a proletarian standpoint; she considers her own work to be a contribution toward a "feminist historical materialism that could adopt Marx's method and take over much of his analysis of class domination" (Hartsock, 1983a:259; see also Hartsock, 1983b, and the collection edited by Harding and Hintikka, 1983). Alison Jaggar argues that a Marxism reconstructed through feminist insight offers the most adequate approach to understanding human nature and developing feminist politics; in her view, "the socialist feminist method is fundamentally Marxist, [although] the way in which it utilizes this method results in a transformation of some central Marxist categories" (Jaggar, 1983:134; see Chapter 11 for discussion and bibliography on socialist-feminist epistemology). Whether these philosophical and methodological prescriptions will prove sufficient to prevent the socialist-feminist project from succumbing once again to dualism remains to be seen.

Other attempts to develop a unitary socialist-feminist framework are arising from the convergence of the critique of dualism with two other concerns: the need to investigate the role of biological differences in the construction of women's oppression, and a renewed interest in theorizing domestic labor. Male supremacists have traditionally used the existence of physiological sex asymmetry as a weapon in the battle to keep women subordinate, and feminists have generally hesitated to subject the phenomenon to open scrutiny. With the recent intensification of controversy over sociobiology, abortion, reproductive rights, and homosexuality, however, socialist feminists have developed positions on the specific issues and on their theoretical and political implications (for example, Breines, Cerullo, and Stacey, 1978; Sayers, 1982; Stacey, 1983a; Petchesky, 1984). Questions about the role of biology have also been raised in the context of a revival of discussion of domestic labor (for example, the collection edited by Fox, 1980). These various themes are being joined together in a series of articles appearing on both sides of the Atlantic. In England, Johanna Brenner and Maria Ramas's lengthy review (1984) of Michèle Barrett's *Women's Oppression Today* suggests that despite Barrett's insightful critique of the literature on the relationship between Marxism and feminism, she in fact falls into a version of the dualism she deplores; Brenner and Ramas propose instead a historical account of the inextricable involvement of sex subordination in capitalist social relations, with emphasis on the role of childbearing and lactation. In Canada, meanwhile, Pat and Hugh Armstrong's ambitious critical survey of the domestic labor literature, "Beyond Sexless Class and Classless Sex: Towards Feminist Marxism" (1983), argues that despite flaws, the domestic labor debate laid the basis for the theoretically precise and historically nuanced discussion of women's oppression.

The articles by Brenner, Ramas, and the Armstrongs have launched a lively dialogue about the roles of biology and domestic labor that is sensitive to such problems as dualism, functionalism, idealism, economism, and biological reductionism (Connelly, 1983; Miles 1983; Barrett, 1984; J. Lewis, 1985; see also the reply by Armstrong and Armstrong, 1984). This developing debate over how to be simultaneously feminist and Marxist in one's understanding of women's oppression suggests that in a decade marked by reaction and retrenchment, the socialist-feminist movement is nevertheless capable of measurably advancing the analysis. It is only a matter of time before the debate is taken up in the United States; see, for example, J. Smith (1983), Vogel (1983), and Himmelweit (1984).

FAMILY, SEX, AND WORK

The preceding discussion reviewed the socialist-feminist research that analyzes the roots of female subordination in terms of women's special position within the overall structure of societal reproduction. The specific institutional arrangements that underpin the perpetuation of women's oppression have also been the object of socialist-feminist attention. Chief among them is the family, and researchers have studied, for example, how families function in the context of the system of patriarchy or the mode of reproduction. Such work has sometimes tended to use the concept of the family as if it were unproblematic and without internal contradictions, and even to romanticize family life (for example, Zaretsky, 1976). There is, however, no single form of "the family"—only a variety of both conflictual and supportive relations that coalesce in the range of institutions socially recognized as families. Moreover, "the family" is in part a normative, or ideological, construct, which can operate in powerful and emotionally charged contradiction to lived experience. A number of socialist-feminist scholars have endeavored to disassemble the social institution known as "the family" and study its component elements over time and within and across different cultures.

One element in particular has been the focus of a great deal of socialist-feminist research: sexuality. In her pioneer article, "Women: The Longest Revolution" (1966), Juliet Mitchell analyzed the family as made up of relatively independent structures, and proposed that sexuality is the structure that today constitutes the strategic weak link. Issues of sexuality and the construction of gendered subjectivity have since become important topics in socialist-feminist scholarship. Among questions socialist feminists have examined are: how sexuality interacts with other forces in the formation of consciousness; the usefulness of Freud's work and, more generally, of the psychoanalytic tradition in developing a materialistic feminist understanding of gender and sexuality; class differences in the construction of subjectivity; the history of sexual experience, behavior, and identity, with sensitivity to variation based on class, race, and ethnicity; heterosexism and homophobia as social control mechanisms in capitalist societies; the state and sexuality; how the various socialist movements of the past century and a half have treated sexual matters; current trends within the left concerning the politics of sexuality; current controversies within the women's movement concerning pornography, prostitution, censorship, and sadomasochism.

Over the past decade and a half, then, socialist-feminist interest in the changing realities and ideologies of family, sexuality, and subjectivity has produced an extensive literature. For reviews and a sampling, see Rapp (1978), Rapp, Ross, and Bridenthal (1979), Cott and Pleck, (1979), Barrett (1980), Hirsch (1981), Flax (1982), Barrett and McIntosh (1982), Thorne and Yalom (1982), S. Eisenstein (1983), and Jones (1985). On issues and controversies in the area of sexuality, see also Vicinus (1982), Snitow, Stansell, and Thompson (1983), Vance (1984), and Caulfield (1985).

Socialist-feminist scholarly energies initially focused on women as domestic laborers, family members, and sexual beings because it was beneath these roles that socialist feminists located the material basis of women's oppression. Since the mid-1970s, however, the subject of women as workers has been equally under consideration. The topic is not, of course, entirely new. Labor historians have sometimes studied women workers, economists and sociologists have been aware of sex inequality in the labor market, and anthropologists recognize that in many cultures women participate in society's productive life. The rise of the modern women's movement provided the context for more intensive and systematic investigation of women workers by feminist scholars. Socialist-feminist researchers have brought to this effort their particular theoretical perspectives on the issue of women's oppression as both family members and workers, and, more generally, on the relationship between work and family in class societies. Socialist-feminist scholars also tend to put special emphasis on women workers in the nonelite sectors of the society they are studying: serfs, slaves, farmworkers, servants, industrial workers, clerical workers, and so forth.

Most socialist-feminist scholarship on women as workers falls within disciplinary boundaries and therefore will not be considered here; for useful overviews and bibliography, see Tilly and Scott (1978), Amsden (1980), Sokoloff (1980, 1981), Kessler-Harris (1982), Strasser (1982), and Sacks and Remy (1984). Socialist-feminist theorists have been important in posing questions and developing conceptual frameworks for this research. Veronica Beechey was among the first to emphasize socialist feminism's relative neglect of the problem of investigating female wage labor in capitalist society. Beechey argues that *Capital* provides a basis for such investigation, but that Marx was

> unable to relate his analysis of the forms of the labour process to an analysis of the sexual division of labour. It is a pressing task for feminists to integrate a feminist analysis of the sexual division of labour with a marxist analysis of the labour process, re-reading theorists such as Marx and asking specifically feminist questions (Beechey, 1978:158).

Key issues in socialist-feminist work on this task include: the relationship of women to the reserve army of labor; the problem of the family wage; and the origins of occupational sex segregation.

Marx discussed the reserve army of labor in the context of his analysis of capitalist accumulation. Socialist feminists at first took the reserve army to be among those Marxist concepts capable of direct application to the question of women's oppression. Women, it seemed, constitute a layer in reserve, alternately drawn into wage labor for capital and repelled back into the relative surplus population. Subordinate and economically dependent in the family, women find themselves disadvantaged at work as well; hence they constitute an exceptionally flexible and vulnerable sector of the population, to the general advantage of employers and/or male family members. The concept of the reserve army of labor was extremely attractive to socialist feminists, for it promised a way to link women's oppression to the demands of capitalist accumulation. As it turned out, however, the concept is relatively undeveloped in Marx, and its role in analyzing the maintenance of women's oppression and the changing character of female wage labor in capitalism has become a topic of some debate; see Dobbins (1977), Beechey (1977, 1978), Simeral (1978), Bruegel (1979), Anthias (1980), Power (1983), and Yanz and Smith (1983).

At the intersection of their studies of work and family in capitalist society, socialist feminists encountered the ideology of the family wage—the notion that an adult man should be able to earn enough to support a dependent wife and children. In reality, throughout the history of capitalism, most working-class households have required the wage labor of more than one family member in order to survive. The family wage norm retains its grip today, and the problem of its significance is therefore of importance to socialist feminists. Many maintain that it benefits primarily employers and male workers, thereby reflecting the ongoing complicity of patriarchy with capitalism (for example, Hartmann, 1976, 1981). Others argue that the struggle for the family wage embodies a measure of resistance and genuine anticapitalist content on the part of the working class (for example, Humphries, 1977a, 1977b, 1982). The controversy cannot be settled in the abstract, however, for the issue is largely historical. To what extent was the family wage a reality—that is, for which groups of men, in which industries and localities, during what periods of time? Where it existed, and how and why was the family wage achieved and what consequences did it have for families and communities? What is the history of the changing ideology of the family wage, and what specific part has it played in the evolution of class and gender relationships? Studies that address such questions can disentangle ideology from reality and thereby examine the role of the family wage historically; see, for example, Barrett and McIntosh (1980), and M. May (1982).

The malleability of family wage ideology has enabled it to coexist with steady labor force participation by certain sectors of the female population—for example, unmarried working-class daughters, wives in certain immigrant groups, or Afro-American women. From the start, the occupational structure has been divided along sex lines. Socialist-feminist research initially took the sex division of labor at the workplace as a given, supposedly derived from women's family roles. As with the family wage, a controversy emerged over the causal roles played by capitalism and patriarchy in the origins of an occupational sex segregation disadvantageous to women. Recent studies of specific industries suggest, however, that sex segregation in the labor market is a constantly evolving historical process that cannot be explained in monocausal terms; see, for example, Baron (1982), Blewett (1983), Milkman (1983), and Baron and Klepp (1984). As part of their investigation of this historical process, socialist-feminist scholars are also examining the role of organized labor and, more generally, the various factors involved in the collective mobilization of women workers; see, for example, Kessler-Harris (1975b), Tax (1980), Phillips and Taylor (1980), Milkman (1980, 1982, 1985), Tilly (1981), Kaplan (1982), Turbin (1984), and Gottfried and Fasenfest (1984).

SISTERHOOD

The contemporary women's movement has often used the notion of sisterhood to emphasize the commonalities and potential strengths arising from the experience of being female; we are all sisters, it suggests, and even more important, sisterhood is powerful. At the same time, modern feminists are acutely aware of the divisions along lines of class, race, and nationality that characterize contemporary societies. For socialist feminists, with their goal of an egalitarian society based on socialist principles, the problem of reconciling concepts of sisterhood with the very real existence of these divisions has been especially pressing. The most common approach in the United States has been to analyze sex, class, and race as oppressions of comparable nature that operate in tandem; strategically, this analysis has implied independent social movements, working together through alliances.

Despite a formal commitment to analyzing the three strands of oppression in today's world, socialist-feminist researchers tend at most to consider the relationship between sex and class. For example, the domestic labor literature attempted to situate women's oppression in the context of the reproduction of that labor-power borne by the working class; it said virtually nothing about the relation between these reproduction processes and the question of racial oppression.

Similarly, socialist-feminist studies of sex divisions of labor, families, and work ordinarily differentiate variations by social class, but relatively few examine race or nationality. In effect, the tripartite paralleling of sex, class, and race postulated by the socialist-feminist movement generally reduces in the practice of socialist-feminist scholarship to dualism—between sex and class, patriarchy and capitalism, or feminism and Marxism, as discussed in the previous sections.

A number of commentators, and most especially black feminists in the United States, have challenged the notion of a universal sisterhood transcending racial divisions. Instead, they emphasize the historical specificity of the social forces that have produced race subordination, and the particular ways this history is incorporated into the experience of minority women. In addition, they criticize the ethnocentrism underlying easy feminist analogies between sex and race oppression. Angela Davis (1971, 1981) was among the first to focus on these issues; see also D. Lewis (1977), Chafe (1977), Dill (1979), Joseph and Lewis (1981), Hooks (1981, 1984), Aptheker and White (1984). For critiques of feminist ethnocentrism in the analogy between women and blacks, see also Stimpson (1971), Simons (1979), and Palmer (1983).[5]

Some socialist feminists have begun to develop a critique of the tripartite analogy paralleling sex, class, and race oppression. This is no easy undertaking. Such a critique requires, first, an analysis that reveals the theoretical and historical specificity of each oppression as well as their interrelationships, and second, an adequate strategic orientation. As Bonnie Thornton Dill puts it:

> While analytically we must carefully examine the structures that differentiate us, politically we must fight the segmentation of oppression into categories such as "racial issues," "feminist issues," and "class issues." This is, of course, a task of almost overwhelming magnitude, and yet it seems to me the only viable way to avoid the errors of the past and to move forward to make sisterhood a meaningful feminist concept for all women, across the boundaries of race and class (Dill, 1983:148; see also Vogel, 1977, 1979; Joseph, 1981).

THE POLITICS OF WOMEN'S LIBERATION

In twentieth-century Western capitalist countries, the issue of women's liberation is closely linked to that of equality. Socialist feminists have been somewhat skeptical about the extent to which their goals can be encompassed within some notion of equality, for equality is a key component of liberal political theory. Zillah Eisenstein (1981, 1984) shows, however, that contemporary contradictions between liberal ideology, the realities of women's status, and feminist aspirations have a radical potential (see also Krouse, 1982, and Feldberg, 1984). A few researchers also note that implicit in political discourse are various concepts of equality, not just one (Mitchell, 1976; Nelson and Olesen, 1977; DuBois, 1978; Caulfield, 1981). Changes in both the ideology and the realities of women's equality may in fact have a material basis in the evolution of the capitalist mode of production over the past several centuries (Vogel, 1983:Chapter 11). It is necessary, then, to examine the historical development of equality with respect to women. For example, the concepts of human equality that today threaten to go beyond the limits of liberalism can be interpreted as counterparts to the challenges late capitalism faces, at the societal level, from socialism.

Equality is only one of many political issues that must be confronted in developing a strategy for women's liberation that is simultaneously feminist and socialist. Current controversies over the relation between sex subordination and other oppressions, or between feminism and socialism, are not unprecedented. Historians have begun to investigate, for example, how earlier feminist and socialist movements dealt with these issues. For the nineteenth- and early twentieth-century movements in Europe and North America, see, for example, Boxer and Quataert (1978), Quataert (1979), Honeycutt (1979), Hayden (1981), Buhle (1981), Sowerwine (1982), and Taylor (1983). For the post-1917 movements, see, for example, Shaffer (1979), De Grazia (1980), Pore (1981), Slaughter and Kern (1981), Schofield (1983), and Strom (1983). For research on women and the left in the United States since 1871, see also the thoroughly annotated guide to sources by Mari Jo Buhle (1983).

Women in the developing countries of the Third World confront conditions that are sharply distinct from those found in advanced capitalist societies. Their political goals have ranged from equality in the restricted sense of classical liberalism, to full participation in the processes of economic and social development, to socialist revolution. Socialist-feminist scholars who study women in Third World countries emphasize the dangers of projecting Western concepts of the politics of women's liberation onto societies with such distinct histories and realities. They explore the complex and specific ways women's experience and aspirations have been shaped through the intersection of particular traditional cultures with local, national, and international development strategies. While it can be argued that this complex interaction shapes women's lives in industrialized societies as well, the rapid-moving and wrenching character of development in the Third World makes it virtually impossible to isolate the study of women's experience from the international context. Socialist-feminist scholarship in this area is therefore often extremely sophisticated, for it is compelled to deal with economic, social, and political phenomena at a number of different levels, all embedded within an international system dominated by capitalism. For a sampling of this work, see the following collections: Etienne and Leacock (1980), "Development and the Sexual Division of Labor" (1981), Gailey and Etienne (1982), Benería (1982), Nash and Fernández Kelly (1983). Much of the research on women and development is policy oriented; in addition to the works already cited, see the critiques of conventional development strategies by Lourdes Benería and Gita Sen (1981, 1982). For studies of women actively involved in social movements in the Third World, see, for example, Chinchilla (1977, 1979, 1983), Omvedt (1978, 1979, 1980), Urdang (1979), and Lapchick and Urdang (1982).

The politics of women's liberation in socialist societies is a matter of great interest and debate among socialist feminists. Much of the socialist-feminist scholarship on the topic takes the form of studies on specific socialist countries. For the Soviet Union, see, for example, Stites (1978), Heinen (1978), Heitlinger (1979), Clements (1982), and Glickman (1984). The subject of women in China has been of particular concern to socialist feminists, many of whom came to political awareness in the 1960s' atmosphere of admiration for the Chinese Cultural Revolution. Socialist-feminist researchers have analyzed women's changing place within the framework of China's evolving socialist transformation, most recently examining the developments of the post-Mao period; see, for example, Andors (1983), Croll (1983), Johnson (1983), and Stacey (1983b). Some of the most interesting recent research on socialism and women's liberation looks at smaller countries, often in comparative context; see Croll (1981), Molyneux (1982, 1985), Nazzari (1983), and Seidman (1984).

Socialist societies provide an opportunity to examine the relationship between feminism and socialism as it develops in actual historical processes. In evaluating the accomplishments of this lived relationship, socialist-feminist researchers draw on socialist-feminist scholarship on the roots of women's oppression, on the relation of Marxism and feminism, and on the institutions of work, family, and sexuality. While they offer a variety of interpretations of both the obstacles to and the prospects for the liberation of women in socialist societies, they would probably agree on the following six points. First, numerous important positive changes in women's lives have been made in the course of socialist transformation. Second, women in socialist societies nevertheless continue to be in a subordinate position in important respects. This disadvantaged status cannot be explained purely in terms of cultural lag. Rather, it reflects the existence of a structural foundation for female subordination that is reproduced within the society.

Third, at least one element of this material foundation for women's disadvantaged status in socialist societies is constituted by particular family, kin, and sexual arrangements that require women to be disproportionately responsible for domestic labor and childrearing in kin-based households. It is not enough to involve women in public production if, like women in many capitalist societies, they endure the heavy burdens of a "double shift" of outside employment and domestic responsibilities. It may be necessary, furthermore, for a socialist society to focus critical attention on its existing institutions of marriage, kinship, and sexuality; in rural China, for example, traditional kinship patterns, especially the fact that a woman marries into her husband's family and moves to his village, place important structural limits on the possibilities for female equality. In the long run, women's liberation in socialist societies will require the redefinition of men's as well as women's roles in all areas of social life—including personal or "family" relations as well as work, culture, and politics.

Fourth, appropriate government action is critical, if socialist societies are to continue to establish more equitable conditions for female social participation. In particular, the state must pay careful attention to short- and long-term effects of policies in such areas as marriage and family reform, land redistribution, employment (for example, pay scales, occupational sex segregation, parenting leaves), social services (for example, child care), education, and popular political mobilization. It is necessary, however, to analyze state efforts to further women's liberation in a given socialist society in context, for socialist development ordinarily takes place within severe material and ideological constraints.

Fifth, the struggle for women's liberation in socialist societies requires special efforts. Liberation will not just automatically happen as a result of socialist development. To move toward it, women must mobilize on behalf of their own interests, and women's organizations with a degree of autonomy may be necessary. Sixth, socialist societies are hampered in their efforts to address the problem of women's liberation by the lack of a fully developed Marxist theoretical tradition on questions of women's oppression.

Taken together, these six points mark socialist-feminist analyses off from most traditional socialist approaches to the politics of women's liberation in the course of socialist transformation. Nearly a century ago, the socialist feminist Clara Zetkin (1896) noted that capitalism gives the so-called woman question its special character, and produces as well particular "woman questions" in different strata within capitalist society. Twentieth-century socialist feminists studying the experience of women in socialism are discovering that the question of women likewise takes a range of new forms in socialist societies. Their research constitutes an especially significant aspect of socialist-feminist scholarship, for it is developing an analysis that could suggest the basis for a more adequate socialist politics of women's liberation.

CONCLUSION

Modern feminism arose in response to irreversible trends in women's lives, and it is in turn producing a series of important effects on human experience and social institutions throughout the world. In the United States, the development of an organized women's movement has had a serious impact on the academy. Feminist perspectives have begun to transform the traditional disciplines, and have contributed as well to the development of more interdisciplinary modes of research. Although there is still a long way to go, it is fair to say that feminism has dramatically changed the character of scholarship in the United States. Socialist feminists in academia have been extremely active in the work necessary to bring about these advances, and have themselves made numerous pathbreaking contributions.

The impact of socialist feminism on contemporary Marxism has been much less profound, despite the Marxist tradition's long-standing commitment to resolving the so-called woman question, and its fairly respectable history of research on women and the family. In some cases, socialist-feminist work is ignored, with the implicit or explicit justification that it is, supposedly, insufficiently orthodox. Alternatively, socialist-feminist contributions are acknowledged as significant, but treated as a specialist literature on a subject that can legitimately be segregated. Either way, Marxism remains surprisingly untouched by socialist-feminist research. Judith Stacey and Barrie Thorne (in press) sketch the origins of this paradoxical situation:

> Socialist feminists who participated in the development of an autonomous women's movement sought to develop a relatively autonomous body of theory as a guide to political practice. Somewhat ironically, however, this has allowed the ghettoization of the "Woman Question" tradition to continue, now in the form of "hyphen" literature. Marxist-feminists have succeeded in developing entirely autonomous and almost exclusively female institutions, conferences, and publications. Resistance by many male Marxists to engaging with this increasingly sophisticated body of literature has left the rest of contemporary Marxist thought remarkably untransformed.

An important task for the future, then, is to reduce the distance between socialist feminism and Marxism. In the sphere of scholarship, this review of the literature has demonstrated that a number of socialist feminists have long been involved in empirical and theoretical research that effectively renders the gap smaller. It is up to those who define themselves as Marxists *tout court* to commit themselves to the task as well.[6]

FOOTNOTES

1. The contemporary women's movement embraces a broad diversity of views, not easily categorized, often overlapping, and still evolving. Most analysts identify three main trends: liberal feminism, radical feminism, and socialist feminism. In this categorization, liberal feminists would be those who identify women's liberation more or less as the extension of classical liberal principles to women, mainly in what is known as the public sphere. Radical feminists would be those who view women's oppression as deeply rooted in universal obstacles constituted by such phenomena as biological sex differences and the system of patriarchy; for radical feminists, women's liberation requires a radical restructuring of all aspects of social organization and culture—and especially of relations in what is known as the private sphere. See Jaggar (1983:Chapter 1) for a persuasive discussion of this categorization. H. Eisenstein (1983:xix-xx) and Flammang (1983) offer somewhat different analyses of the trends within the women's movement. It should be noted that some of the authors discussed here as socialist feminists might prefer the designation "Marxist-feminist" or even "Marxist" for their contributions.

2. The following publications review the literature in several disciplines either from a socialist-feminist perspective or with explicit discussion of socialist-feminist contributions. History: "Politics and Culture in Women's History: A Symposium" (1980), Fox-Genovese (1982), E. T. May (1982), McGaw (1982), Ryan (1982). Anthropology: Lamphere (1977), Rapp (1979), Rosaldo (1980), Atkinson (1982), Leacock (1982). Sociology: Acker (1980), Gould (1980), Stacey and Thorne (in press). Political Science: Carroll (1980), See (1982). Philosophy: English (1978), Wartofsky (1982). Economics: Amsden (1980), Gintis (1982), Harkess (1985). Natural Science: Keller (1982), Lowe and Hubbard,

(1983), Rose (1983). Literature: Marcus (1982), Williamson (1984), Showalter, (1985). Classics: Arthur and Konstan (1984). For overviews of the women's studies movement, see Boxer (1982), DuBois (1985), and Zinn (1986).

3. For socialist-feminist critiques of radical feminism's tendency to biological determinism, see Sayers (1982) and H. Eisenstein (1983).

4. A somewhat similar discussion took place within the U.S. Communist Party in the 1940s. See Inman (1940, 1942) and Landy (1941, 1943); and for summaries, see the annotated entries in Buhle (1983:162-65).

5. Surprisingly, such issues have only recently come to the attention of white English feminists. See Carby (1982), Parmar (1982), and Bourne (1983).

6. To be effective, this commitment on the part of Marxists *tout court* requires that they take several steps. First, they must recognize that the questions posed by socialist feminists are central to any social theory, and may result in alterations to conventional interpretations of Marxism. Second, they must thoroughly study and assimilate the relevant literature produced by socialist feminists over the past two decades. Third, if possible, they should contribute to this body of research. Regrettably, some male Marxists who are working on socialist-feminist questions tend to skip over the crucial second step; as a result, their efforts have to some extent recapitulated arguments long since debated, refined, and reformulated in the socialist-feminist literature (for example, critiques of the capitalist-patriarchy model, or analyses of a proposed domestic mode of production). Rather than reinvent the wheel in this individualistic manner, male Marxists have a political as well as a scholarly obligation to join as participants in what has become an ongoing socialist-feminist project. Not to do so suggests a residue, however unintended, of contempt for the accomplishments of socialist-feminist scholars and the socialist-feminist movement.

BIBLIOGRAPHY

Acker, Joan. "Women and Stratification: A Review of Recent Literature." *Contemporary Sociology* 9:1 (January 1980).

Amsden, Alice. "Introduction." In Amsden, Alice (ed.). *The Economics of Women and Work*. New York: St. Martin's Press, 1980.

Andors, Phyllis. *The Unfinished Liberation of Chinese Women, 1949-1980*. Bloomington: University of Indiana Press, 1983.

Anthias, Floya. "Women and the Reserve Army of Labour: A Critique of Veronica Beechey." *Capital and Class*, No. 10 (Spring 1980).

Aptheker, Bettina. *Woman's Legacy: Essays on Race, Sex, and Class in American History*. Amherst: University of Massachusetts Press, 1982.

Armstrong, Pat, and Armstrong, Hugh. "Beyond Sexless Class and Classless Sex: Towards Feminist Marxism." *Studies in Political Economy: A Socialist Review*, No. 10 (Winter 1983).

———. "More on Marxism and Feminism: A Response to Patricia Connelly." *Studies in Political Economy: A Socialist Review*, No. 15 (Fall 1984).

Arthur, Marylin B., and Konstan, David. "Marxism and the Study of Classical Antiquity." In Ollman, Bertell, and Vernoff, Edward (eds.). *The Left Academy: Marxist Scholarship on American Campuses*. Vol. II. New York: Praeger Publishers, 1984.

Atkinson, Jane. "Review Essay: Anthropology." *Signs* 8:2 (Winter 1982).

Baron, Ava. "Women and the Making of the American Working Class: A Study of the Proletarianization of Printers." *Review of Radical Political Economics* 14:3 (Fall 1982).

Baron, Ava, and Klepp, Susan. " 'If I Didn't Have My Sewing Machine': Women and Sewing Machine Technology." In Jensen, Joan, and Davidson, Sue (eds.). *A Needle, A Bobbin, A Strike: Women Needleworkers in America*. Philadelphia: Temple University Press, 1984.

Barrett, Michèle. *Women's Oppression Today: Problems in Marxist Feminist Analysis*. London: New Left Books, 1980.

________. "Rethinking Women's Oppression: A Reply to Brenner and Ramas." *New Left Review*, No. 146 (July-August 1984).

Barrett, Michèle, and McIntosh, Mary. "The 'Family Wage': Some Problems for Socialists and Feminists." *Capital and Class*, No. 11 (Summer 1980).

________. *The Anti-Social Family*. London: New Left Books, 1982.

Beechey, Veronica. "Some Notes on Female Wage Labour in Capitalist Production." *Capital and Class*, No. 3 (Autumn 1977).

________. "Women and Production: A Critical Analysis of Some Sociological Theories of Women's Work." In Kuhn, Annette, and Wolpe, Annemarie (eds.). *Feminism and Materialism: Women and Modes of Production*. Boston: Routledge and Kegan Paul, 1978.

________. "On Patriarchy." *Feminist Review*, No 3 (1979).

Benería, Lourdes. "Reproduction, Production, and the Sexual Division of Labour." *Cambridge Journal of Economics*, 3 (1979).

________ (ed.). *Women and Development: The Sexual Division of Labor in Rural Societies*. New York: Praeger Publishers, 1982.

Benería, Lourdes, and Sen, Gita. "Accumulation, Reproduction, and Women's Role in Economic Development: Boserup Revisited." *Signs* 7:2 (Winter 1981).

________. "Class and Gender Inequalities and Women's Role in Economic Development: Theoretical and Practical Implications." *Feminist Studies* 8:1 (Spring 1982).

Blewett, Mary. "Work, Gender and the Artisan Tradition in New England Shoemaking, 1780-1860." *Journal of Social History* 17:2 (December 1983).

Bourne, Jenny. "Towards an Anti-Racist Feminism." *Race and Class* 25:1 (Summer 1983).

Boxer, Marilyn. "Review Essay: For and About Women: The Theory and Practice of Women's Studies in the United States." *Signs* 7:3 (Spring 1982).

Boxer, Marilyn, and Quataert, Jean (eds.). *Socialist Women: European Socialist Feminism in the Nineteenth and Early Twentieth Centuries*. New York: Elsevier, 1978.

Breines, Wini, Cerullo, Margaret, and Stacey, Judith. "Social Biology, Family Studies, and Antifeminist Backlash." *Feminist Studies* 4:1 (February 1978).

Brenner, Johanna, and Ramas, María. "Rethinking Women's Oppression." *New Left Review*, No. 144 (March-April 1984).

Bridenthal, Renate. "The Dialectics of Production and Reproduction in History." *Radical America* 10:2 (March-April 1976).

Bruegel, Irene. "Women as a Reserve Army of Labour: A Note on Recent British Experience." *Feminist Review*, No. 3 (1979).

Buhle, Mari Jo. *Women and American Socialism, 1870-1920*. Champaign: University of Illinois Press, 1981.

________. *Women and the American Left: A Guide to Sources*. Boston: G. K. Hall, 1983.

Burris, Val. "The Dialectics of Women's Oppression: Notes on the Relation Between Capitalism and Patriarchy." *Berkeley Journal of Sociology* 27 (1982).

Carroll, Berenice. "Review Essay: Political Science, Part II: International Politics, Comparative Politics, and Feminist Radicals." *Signs* 5:3 (Spring 1980).

Caulfield, Mina Davis. "Imperialism, the Family, and Cultures of Resistance." *Socialist Revolution*, No. 20 (October 1974).

________. "Equality, Sex and Mode of Production." In Berreman, Gerald (ed.). *Social Inequality: Comparative and Developmental Approaches*. New York: Academic Press, 1981.

________. "Sexuality in Human Evolution: What is 'Natural' in Sex?" *Feminist Studies* 11:2 (Summer 1985).

Carby, Hazel. "White Woman Listen! Black Feminism and the Boundaries of Sisterhood." In Centre for Contemporary Cultural Studies (ed.). *The Empire Strikes Back: Race and Racism in 70s Britain*. London: Hutchinson, 1982.

Chafe, William. *Women and Equality: Changing Patterns in American Culture*. New York: Oxford University Press, 1977.

Chinchilla, Norma Stoltz. "Mobilizing Women: Revolution in the Revolution." *Latin American Perspectives* 4:4 (Fall 1977).

________. "Working-Class Feminism: Domitila and the Housewives Committee." *Latin American Perspectives* 6:3 (Summer 1979).

———. "Women in Revolutionary Movements: The Case of Nicaragua." In Stanford Central America Action Network (ed.). *Revolution in Central America*. Boulder, Colo: Westview Press, 1983.

Clements, Barbara Evans. "Working-Class and Peasant Women in the Russian Revolution, 1917-1923." *Signs* 8:2 (Winter 1982).

Connelly, Patricia. "On Marxism and Feminism." *Studies in Political Economy: A Socialist Review*, No. 12 (Fall 1983).

Cott, Nancy, and Pleck, Elizabeth (eds.). *A Heritage of Her Own: Toward a New Social History of American Women*. New York: Simon and Schuster, 1979.

Croll, Elisabeth. "Women in Rural Production and Reproduction in the Soviet Union, China, Cuba, and Tanzania." *Signs* 7:2 (Winter 1981).

———. *Chinese Women Since Mao*. Armonk, N.Y.: M. E. Sharpe, 1983.

Davis, Angela. "Reflections on the Black Woman's Role in the Community of Slaves." *Black Scholar* 3:4 (December 1971).

———. *Women, Race and Class*. New York: Random House, 1981.

Deere, Carmen Diana, and León de Leal, Magdalena. "Peasant Production, Pro-Periphery." *Review of Radical Political Economics* 8:1 (Spring 1976).

Deere, Carmen Diana, and León de Leal, Magdalena. "Peasant Production, Proletarianization, and the Sexual Division of Labor in the Andes." *Signs* 7:2 (Winter 1981).

De Grazia, Victoria. "Women and Communism in Advanced Capitalist Societies: Readings and Resources." *Radical History Review*, No. 23 (Spring 1980).

"Development and the Sexual Division of Labor." Special issue of *Signs* 7:2 (Winter 1981).

Dill, Bonnie Thornton. "The Dialectics of Black Womanhood." *Signs* 4:3 (Spring 1979).

———. "Race, Class, and Gender: Prospects for an All-inclusive Sisterhood." *Feminist Studies* 9:1 (Spring 1983).

Dobbins, Peggy. "Towards a Theory of the Women's Liberation Movement and Women's Wage-Labor." *Insurgent Sociologist* 7:3 (Summer 1977).

DuBois, Ellen Carol. *Feminism and Suffrage: The Emergence of an Independent Women's Movement in America 1848-1869*. Ithaca, N.Y.: Cornell University Press, 1978.

DuBois, Ellen Carol et al. *Feminist Scholarship: Kindling in the Groves of Academe*. Champaign: University of Illinois Press, 1985.

Dunayevskaya, Raya. *Rosa Luxemburg, Women's Liberation, and Marx's Philosophy of Revolution*. Atlantic Highlands, N.J.: Humanities Press, 1982.

Edholm, Felicity, Harris, Olivia, and Young, Kate. "Conceptualising Women." *Critique of Anthropology*, Nos. 9-10 (1977).

Eisenstein, Hester. *Contemporary Feminist Thought*. Boston: G. K. Hall, 1983.

Eisenstein, Sarah. *Give Us Bread But Give Us Roses: Working Women's Consciousness in the United States, 1890 to the First World War*. London: Routledge and Kegan Paul, 1983.

Eisenstein, Zillah. "Constructing a Theory of Capitalist Patriarchy and Socialist Feminism." *Insurgent Sociologist* 7:3 (Summer 1977).

_______. *The Radical Future of Liberal Feminism*. New York: Longman, 1981.

_______. *Feminism and Sexual Equality: Crisis in Liberal America*. New York: Monthly Review Press, 1984.

Eisenstein, Zillah (ed.). *Capitalist Patriarchy and the Case for Socialist Feminism*. New York: Monthly Review Press, 1979.

English, Jane. "Review Essay: Philosophy." *Signs* 3:4 (Summer 1978).

Etienne, Mona, and Leacock, Eleanor (eds.). *Women and Colonization: Anthropological Perspectives*. New York: Praeger Publishers, 1980.

Feldberg, Roslyn. "Comparable Worth: Toward Theory and Practice in the United States." *Signs* 10:2 (Winter 1984).

Flammang, Janet. "Feminist Theory: The Question of Power." *Current Perspectives in Social Theory* 4 (1983).

Flax, Jane. "The Family in Contemporary Feminist Thought: A Critical Review." In Elshtain, Jean Bethke (ed.). *The Family in Political Thought*. Amherst: University of Massachusetts Press, 1982.

Fox, Bonnie (ed.). *Hidden in the Household: Women's Domestic Labour under Capitalism*. Toronto: Women's Press, 1980.

Fox-Genovese, Elizabeth. "Placing Women's History in History." *New Left Review*, No. 133 (May-June 1982).

Gailey, Christine Ward, and Etienne, Mona (eds.). *Women and the State in Pre-Industrial Societies*. New York: J. F. Bergin, 1982.

Gintis, Herbert. "The Reemergence of Marxian Economics in America." In Ollman, Bertell, and Vernoff, Edward (eds.). *The Left Academy: Marxist Scholarship on American Campuses*. [Vol. I.] New York: McGraw-Hill, 1982.

Glickman, Rose. *Russian Factory Women: Workplace and Society, 1880-1914*. Berkeley: University of California Press, 1984.

Gottfried, Heidi, and Fasenfest, David. "Gender and Class Formation: Female Clerical Workers." *Review of Radical Political Economics* 16:1 (Spring 1984).

Gould, Meredith. "Review Essay: The New Sociology." *Signs* 5:3 (Spring 1980).

Guettel, Charnie. *Marxism and Feminism*. Toronto: Women's Press, 1974.

Harding, Sandra, and Hintikka, Merrill (eds.). *Discovering Reality: Feminist Perspectives on Epistemology, Metaphysics, Methodology, and Philosophy of Science*. Boston: Reidel, 1983.

Harkess, Shirley. "Review Essay: Women's Occupational Experiences in the 1970s: Sociology and Economics." *Signs* 10:3 (Spring 1985).

Harrison, John. "The Political Economy of Housework." *Bulletin of the Conference of Socialist Economists*, No. 7 (Winter 1973).

Hartmann, Heidi. "Capitalism, Patriarchy, and Job Segregation by Sex." *Signs* 1:3, pt. 2 (Spring 1976).

———. "The Unhappy Marriage of Marxism and Feminism: Towards a More Progressive Union." *Capital and Class*, No. 8 (Summer 1979).

———. "The Family as the Locus of Gender, Class, and Political Struggle: The Example of Housework." *Signs* 6:3 (Spring 1981).

Hartmann, Heidi, and Bridges, Amy. "The Unhappy Marriage of Marxism and Feminism." Unpublished working draft, July 1975.

Hartsock, Nancy. *Money, Sex, and Power: Toward a Feminist Historical Materialism*. New York: Longman, 1983a.

———. "The Feminist Standpoint: Developing the Ground for a Specifically Feminist Historical Materialism." In Harding, Sandra, and Hintikka, Merrill (eds.). *Discovering Reality: Feminist Perspectives on Epistemology, Metaphysics, Methodology, and Philosophy of Science*. Boston: Reidel, 1983b.

Hayden, Dolores. *The Grand Domestic Revolution: A History of Feminist Designs for American Homes, Neighborhoods, and Cities*. Cambridge, Mass.: M.I.T. Press, 1981.

Heinen, Jacqueline. "Kollontai and the History of Women's Oppression." *New Left Review*, No. 110 (July-August 1978).

Heitlinger, Alena. *Women and State Socialism: Sex Inequality in the Soviet Union and Czechoslovakia*. London: Macmillan, 1979.

Himmelweit, Susan. "The Real Dualism of Sex and Class." *Review of Radical Political Economics* 16:1 (Spring 1984).

Himmelweit, Susan, and Mohun, Simon. "Domestic Labour and Capital." *Cambridge Journal of Economics* 1 (1977).

Hirsch, Marianne. "Review Essay: Mothers and Daughters." *Signs* 7:1 (Autumn 1981).

Holmstrom, Nancy. " 'Women's Work,' The Family, and Capitalism." *Science and Society* 45:2 (Summer 1981).

Honeycutt, Karen. "Socialism and Feminism in Imperial Germany." *Signs* 5:1 (Autumn 1979).

Hooks, Bell. *Ain't I a Woman: Black Women and Feminism*. Boston: South End Press, 1981.

_______. *Feminist Theory: From Margin to Center*. Boston: South End Press, 1984.

Humphries, Jane. "Class Struggle and the Persistence of the Working-Class Family." *Cambridge Journal of Economics* 1 (1977a).

_______. "The Working Class Family, Women's Liberation, and Class Struggle: The Case of Nineteenth Century British History." *Review of Radical Political Economics* 9:3 (Fall 1977b).

_______. "The Working-Class Family: A Marxist Perspective." In Elshtain, Jean Bethke (ed.). *The Family in Political Thought*. Amherst: University of Massachusetts Press, 1982.

Inman, Mary. *In Women's Defense*. Los Angeles: The Committee to Organize the Advancement of Women, 1940.

_______. *Woman-Power*. Los Angeles: The Committee to Organize the Advancement of Women, 1942.

Jaggar, Alison. *Feminist Politics and Human Nature*. New York: Rowman and Allanheld, 1983.

Johnson, Kay Ann. *Women, the Family, and Peasant Revolution in China*. Chicago: University of Chicago Press, 1983.

Jones, Jacqueline. *Labor of Love, Labor of Sorrow: Black Women, Work, and the Family from Slavery to the Present*. New York: Basic Books, 1985.

Joseph, Gloria. "The Incompatible Ménage à Trois: Marxism, Feminism, and Racism." In Sargent, Lydia (ed.). *Women and Revolution: A Discussion of the Unhappy Marriage of Marxism and Feminism*. Boston: South End Press, 1981.

Joseph, Gloria, and Lewis, Jill. *Common Differences: Conflicts in Black and White Feminist Perspectives*. Garden City, N.Y.: Anchor Books, 1981.

Kaplan, Temma. "Female Consciousness and Collective Action: The Case of Barcelona, 1910-1918." *Signs* 7:3 (Spring 1982).

Keller, Evelyn Fox. "Feminism and Science." *Signs* 7:3 (Spring 1982).

Kelly, Joan. "The Doubled Vision of Feminist Theory." *Feminist Studies* 5:1 (Spring 1979).

Kelly-Gadol, Joan. "The Social Relation of the Sexes: Methodological Implications of Women's History." *Signs* 1:4 (Summer 1976).

Kessler-Harris, Alice. "Stratifying by Sex: Understanding the History of Working Women." In Edwards, Richard, Reich, Michael, and Gordon, David (eds.). *Labor Market Segmentation*. Lexington, Mass.: D.C. Heath 1975a.

———. "Where Are the Organized Women Workers?" *Feminist Studies* 3:1/2 (Fall 1975b).

———. *Out to Work: A History of Wage-Earning Women in the United States*. London: Oxford University Press, 1982.

Krouse, Richard. "Patriarchal Liberalism and Beyond: From John Stuart Mill to Harriet Taylor." In Elshtain, Jean Bethke (ed.). *The Family in Political Thought*. Amherst: University of Massachusetts Press, 1982.

Kuhn, Annette, and Wolpe, Annemarie (eds.). *Feminism and Materialism: Women and Modes of Production*. Boston: Routledge and Kegan Paul, 1978.

Lamphere, Louise. "Review Essay: Anthropology." *Signs* 2:3 (Spring 1977).

Landes, Joan. "Women, Labor and Family Life: A Theoretical Perspective." *Science and Society* 41:4 (Winter 1977-78).

Landy, Al. "Two Questions on the Status of Women under Capitalism." *The Communist* 20 (September 1941).

———. *Marxism and the Woman Question*. New York: Workers' Library Publishers, 1943.

Lapchick, Richard, and Urdang, Stephanie. *Oppression and Resistance: The Struggle of Women in Southern Africa*. Westport, Conn.: Greenwood Press, 1982.

Larguia, Isabel. "The Economic Basis of the Status of Women." In Rohrlich-Leavitt, Ruby (ed.). *Women Cross-Culturally: Change and Challenge*. The Hague: Mouton, 1975.

Leacock, Eleanor. "Marxism and Anthropology." In Ollman, Bertell, and Vernoff, Edward (eds.). *The Left Academy: Marxist Scholarship on American Campuses*. [Vol. I.] New York: McGraw-Hill, 1982.

———. "Interpreting the Origins of Gender Inequality: Conceptual and Historical Problems." *Dialectical Anthropology* 7:4 (February 1983).

Leibowitz, Lila. "Origins of the Sexual Division of Labor." In Lowe, Marian, and Hubbard, Ruth (eds.). *Woman's Nature: Rationalizations of Inequality*. New York: Pergamon Press, 1983.

Lewis, Diane. "A Response to Inequality: Black Women, Racism, and Sexism." *Signs* 3:2 (Winter 1977).

Lewis, Jane. "The Debate on Sex and Class." *New Left Review*, No. 149 (January-February 1985).

Lowe, Marian, and Hubbard, Ruth (eds.). *Woman's Nature: Rationalizations of Inequality*. New York: Pergamon Press, 1983.

McGaw, Judith. "Women and the History of American Technology." *Signs* 7:4 (Summer 1982).

Mackintosh, Maureen. "Reproduction and Patriarchy: A critique of Claude Meillassoux, 'Femmes, greniers, et capitaux.' " *Capital and Class*, No. 2 (Summer 1977).

Malos, Ellen (ed.). *The Politics of Housework*. London: Allison and Busby, 1980.

Marcus, Jane. "Storming the Toolshed." *Signs* 7:3 (Spring 1982).

May, Elaine Tyler. "Expanding the Past: Recent Scholarship on Women in Politics and Work." *Reviews in American History* 10:4 (December 1982).

May, Martha. "The Historical Problem of the Family Wage: The Ford Motor Company and the Five Dollar Day." *Feminist Studies* 8:2 (Summer 1982).

Meillassoux, Claude. *Femmes, greniers et capitaux*. Paris: François Maspero, 1975.

Middleton, Christopher. "The Sexual Division of Labour in Feudal England." *New Left Review*, Nos. 113-114 (January-April 1979).

Miles, Angela. "Economism and Feminism: Hidden in the Household: A Comment On the Domestic Labour Debate." *Studies in Political Economy: A Socialist Review*, No. 11 (Summer 1983).

Milkman, Ruth. "Organizing the Sexual Division of Labor: Historical Perspectives on 'Women's Work' and the American Labor Movement." *Socialist Review*, No. 49 (January-February 1980).

_______. "Redefining 'Women's Work': The Sexual Division of Labor in the Auto Industry During World War II." *Feminist Studies* 8:2 (Summer 1982).

_______. "Female Factory Labor and Industrial Structure: Control and Conflict Over 'Woman's Place' in Auto and Electrical Manufacturing." *Politics and Society* 12:2 (1983).

_______. (ed.). *Women, Work and Protest: A Century of Women's Labor History*. Boston: Routledge and Kegan Paul, 1985.

Mitchell, Juliet. "Women: The Longest Revolution." *New Left Review*, No. 40 (November-December 1966).

_______. *Woman's Estate*. Baltimore: Penguin Books, 1971.

_______. "Women and Equality." In Mitchell, Juliet, and Oakley, Ann (eds.). *The Rights and Wrongs of Women*. New York: Penguin Books, 1976.

Molyneux, Maxine. "Beyond the Domestic Labour Debate." *New Left Review*, No. 116 (July-August 1979).

_______. "Socialist Societies Old and New: Progress Towards Women's Emancipation?" *Monthly Review* 34:3 (July-August 1982).

_______. "Mobilization without Emancipation? Women's Interests, the State, and Revolution in Nicaragua." *Feminist Studies* 11:2 (Summer 1985).

Nash, June, and Fernández Kelly, María Patricia (eds.). *Women, Men, and the International Division of Labor*. Albany, N.Y.: SUNY Press, 1983.

Nazzari, Muriel. "The 'Woman Question' in Cuba: An Analysis of Material Constraints on Its Solution." *Signs* 9:2 (Winter 1983).

Nelson, Cynthia, and Olesen, Virginia. "Veil of Illusion: A Critique of the Concept of Equality in Western Thought." *Catalyst*, Nos. 10-11 (Summer 1977).

O'Laughlin, Bridget. "Marxist Approaches in Anthropology." *Annual Review of Anthropology* 4 (1975).

———. "Production and Reproduction: Meillassoux's *Femmes, greniers et capitaux*." *Critique of Anthropology*, No. 8 (Spring 1977).

Omvedt, Gail. "Women and Rural Revolt in India." *Journal of Peasant Studies* 5 (1978).

———. "On the Participant Study of Women's Movements." In Huizer, Gerrit (ed.). *The Politics of Anthropology*. The Hague: Mouton, 1979.

———. *We Will Smash This Prison! Indian Women in Struggle*. London: Zed Press, 1980.

Palmer, Phyllis Marynick. "White Women/Black Women: The Dualism of Female Identity and Experience in the United States." *Feminist Studies* 9:1 (Spring 1983).

Parmar, Pratibha. "Gender, Race and Class: Asian Women in Resistance." In Centre for Contemporary Cultural Studies (ed.). *The Empire Strikes Back: Race and Racism in 70s Britain*. London: Hutchinson, 1982.

Petchesky, Rosalind Pollack. *Abortion and Woman's Choice: The State, Sexuality, and Reproductive Freedom*. New York: Longman, 1984.

Phillips, Anne, and Taylor, Barbara. "Sex and Skill: Notes Towards a Feminist Economics." *Feminist Review*, No. 6 (October 1980).

"Politics and Culture in Women's History: A Symposium." *Feminist Studies* 6:1 (Spring 1980).

Pore, Renate. *A Conflict of Interest: Women in German Social Democracy, 1919-1933*. Westport, Conn.: Greenwood Press, 1981.

Power, Marilyn. "From Home Production to Wage Labor: Women as a Reserve Army of Labor." *Review of Radical Political Economics* 15:1 (Spring 1983).

Quataert, Jean. *Reluctant Feminists in German Social Democracy, 1885-1917*. Princeton, N.J.: Princeton University Press, 1979.

Quick, Paddy. "The Class Nature of Women's Oppression." *Review of Radical Political Economics* 9:3 (Fall 1977).

Rapp, Rayna. "Review of Claude Meillassoux, *Femmes, greniers et capitaux*." *Dialectical Anthropology* 2:4 (November 1977).

———. "Family and Class in Contemporary America: Notes Toward an Understanding of Ideology." *Science and Society* 42:3 (Fall 1978).

———. "Review Essay: Anthropology." *Signs* 4:3 (Spring 1979).

Rapp, Rayna, Ross, Ellen, and Bridenthal, Renate. "Examining Family History." *Feminist Studies* 5:1 (Spring 1979).

Reiter, Rayna Rapp. "The Search for Origins: Unraveling the Threads of Gender Hierarchy." *Critique of Anthropology*, Nos. 9-10 (1977).

Rosaldo, M. Z. "The Use and Abuse of Anthropology: Reflections on Feminism and Cross-cultural Understanding." *Signs* 5:3 (Spring 1980).

Rose, Hilary. "Hand, Brain, and Heart: A Feminist Epistemology for the Natural Sciences." *Signs* 9:1 (Autumn 1983).

Rubin, Gayle. "The Traffic in Women: Notes on the 'Political Economy' of Sex." In Reiter, Rayna (ed.). *Towards an Anthropology of Women*. New York: Monthly Review Press, 1975.

Ryan, Mary. "The Explosion of Family History." *Reviews in American History* 10:4 (December 1982).

Sacks, Karen Brodkin, and Remy, Dorothy (eds.). *My Troubles Are Going to Have Trouble with Me: Everyday Trials and Triumphs of Women Workers*. New Brunswick, N.J.: Rutgers University Press, 1984.

Sargent, Lydia (ed.). *Women and Revolution: A Discussion of the Unhappy Marriage of Marxism and Feminism*. Boston: South End Press, 1981.

Sayers, Janet. *Biological Politics: Feminist and Anti-Feminist Perspectives*. London: Tavistock Publications, 1982.

Schofield, Ann. "Rebel Girls and Union Maids: The Woman Question in the Journals of the AFL and IWW, 1905-1920." *Feminist Studies* 9:2 (Summer 1983).

See, Katherine O'Sullivan. "Feminism and Political Philosophy." *Feminist Studies* 8:1 (Spring 1982).

Seidman, Gay. "Women in Zimbabwe: Postindependence Struggles." *Feminist Studies* 10:3 (Fall 1984).

Sen, Gita. "The Sexual Division of Labor and the Working-Class Family: Towards a Conceptual Synthesis of Class Relations and the Subordination of Women." *Review of Radical Political Economics* 12:2 (Summer 1980).

Shaffer, Robert. "Women and the Communist Party, USA, 1930-1940." *Socialist Review*, No. 45 (May-June 1979).

Showalter, Elaine (ed.). *The New Feminist Criticism: Essays on Women, Literature, and Theory*. New York: Pantheon Books, 1985.

Simeral, Margaret. "Women and the Reserve Army of Labor." *Insurgent Sociologist* 8:2-3 (Fall 1978).

Simons, Margaret. "Racism and Feminism: A Schism in the Sisterhood." *Feminist Studies* 5:2 (Summer 1979).

Slaughter, Jane, and Kern, Robert (eds.). *European Women on the Left: Socialism, Feminism, and the Problems Faced by Political Women, 1880 to the Present*. Westport, Conn.: Greenwood Press, 1981.

Smith, Dorothy E. "Women, Class and Family." In Miliband, Ralph, and Saville, John (eds.). *The Socialist Register 1983*. London: Merlin Press, 1983.

Smith, Joan. "Feminism and Analytic Method: The Case of Unwaged Domestic Labor." *Current Perspectives in Social Theory* 4 (1983).

Snitow, Ann, Stansell, Christine, and Thompson, Sharon (eds.). *Powers of Desire: The Politics of Sexuality*. New York: Monthly Review Press, 1983.

Sokoloff, Natalie. *Between Money and Love: The Dialectics of Women's Home and Market Work*. New York: Praeger Publishers, 1980.

_______. "Theories of Women's Labor Force Status: A Review and Critique." *Current Perspectives in Social Theory* 2 (1981).

Sowerwine, Charles. *Sisters or Citizens? Women and Socialism in France since 1876*. Cambridge: Cambridge University Press, 1982.

Stacey, Judith. "The New Conservative Feminism." *Feminist Studies* 9:3 (Fall 1983a).

_______. *Patriarchy and Socialist Revolution in China*. Berkeley: University of California Press, 1983b.

Stacey, Judith, and Thorne, Barrie. "The Missing Feminist Revolution in Sociology." *Social Problems*, in press.

Stimpson, Catharine. " 'Thy Neighbor's Wife, Thy Neighbor's Servants': Women's Liberation and Black Civil Rights." In Gornick, Vivian, and Moran, Barbara (eds.). *Women in Sexist Society: Studies in Power and Powerlessness*. New York: Basic Books, 1971.

Stites, Richard. *The Women's Liberation Movement in Russia: Feminism, Nihilism, and Bolshevism, 1860-1930*. Princeton, N.J.: Princeton University Press, 1978.

Strasser, Susan. *Never Done: A History of American Housework*. New York: Pantheon Books, 1982.

Strom, Sharon Hartman. "Challenging 'Woman's Place': Feminism, the Left, and Industrial Unionism in the 1930s." *Feminist Studies* 9:2 (Summer 1983).

Tax, Meredith. *The Rising of the Women: Feminist Solidarity and Class Conflict, 1880-1917*. New York: Monthly Review Press, 1980.

Taylor, Barbara. *Eve and the New Jerusalem: Socialism and Feminism in the Nineteenth Century*. New York: Pantheon Books, 1983.

Thorne, Barrie, and Yalom, Marilyn (eds.). *Rethinking the Family: Some Feminist Questions*. New York, Longman, 1982.

Tilly, Louise. "Paths of Proletarianization: Organization of Production, Sexual Division of Labor, and Women's Collective Action." *Signs* 7:2 (Winter 1981).

Tilly, Louise, and Scott, Joan. *Women, Work, and Family*. New York: Holt, Rinehart and Winston, 1978.

Turbin, Carole. "Reconceptualizing Family, Work, and Labor Organizing: Working Women in Troy, 1860-1890." *Review of Radical Political Economics* 16:1 (Spring 1984).

Urdang, Stephanie. *Fighting Two Colonialisms: Women in Guinea-Bissau*. New York: Monthly Review Press, 1979.

Vance, Carole (ed.). *Pleasure and Danger: Exploring Female Sexuality*. Boston: Routledge and Kegan Paul, 1984.

Vicinus, Martha. "Sexuality and Power: A Review of Current Work in the History of Sexuality." *Feminist Studies* 8:1 (Spring 1982).

Vogel, Lise. "On: 'Class Roots of Feminism.' " *Monthly Review* 28:9 (February 1977).

_______. "Questions on the Woman Question." *Monthly Review* 31:2 (June 1979).

_______. *Marxism and the Oppression of Women: Toward a Unitary Theory*. New Brunswick, N.J.: Rutgers University Press, 1983.

Wartofsky, Marx. "Marx Among the Philosophers." In Ollman, Bertell, and Vernoff, Edward (eds.). *The Left Academy: Marxist Scholarship on American Campuses*. [Vol. I.] New York: McGraw-Hill, 1982.

White, E. Frances. "Listening to the Voices of Black Feminism." *Radical America* 18:2-3 (March-June 1984).

Williamson, Marilyn. "Toward a Feminist Literary History." *Signs* 10:1 (Autumn 1984).

Yanz, Lynda, and Smith, David. "Women as a Reserve Army of Labour: A Critique." *Review of Radical Political Economics* 15:1 (Spring 1983).

Young, Iris. "Socialist Feminism and the Limits of Dual Systems Theory." *Socialist Review*, Nos. 50-51 (March-June 1980).

_______. "Beyond the Unhappy Marriage: A Critique of the Dual Systems Theory." In Sargent, Lydia (ed.). *Women and Revolution: A Discussion of the Unhappy Marriage of Marxism and Feminism*. Boston: South End Press, 1981.

Zaretsky, Eli. *Capitalism, The Family, and Personal Life*. New York: Harper and Row, 1976.

Zinn, Maxine Baca, et al. "The Costs of Exclusionary Practices in Women's Studies." *Signs* 11:2 (Winter 1986).

2

BLACK STUDIES: MARXISM AND THE BLACK INTELLECTUAL TRADITION

Manning Marable

The relationship between Marxism and the various academic disciplines is fundamentally different from its relationship with Black Studies. One simple reason is that neither Marxism nor the black intellectual tradition, most recently embodied in the term "Black Studies," have readily been invited to the centers of white, bourgeois academia. The vast majority of white scholars did not recognize the existence of the black community prior to the 1960s, and the works of black intellectuals were extremely rare within white institutions. At best, for liberal paternalists, the Negro was an object to be studied, a litmus test on the viability of American democracy. At worst, the Negro was genetically inferior. In either case, Afro-Americans were not viewed as active creators of culture or political and social thought.

Second, there are certain parallels between Marxism as an intellectual tradition and Black Studies. The vast majority of black people in America are overwhelmingly represented within the working class or the poor. The barriers of institutional racism and the hegemonic ideology of white supremacy have been important factors that have created linkages between black intellectuals and cultural workers with the black masses. At least in theory, Marxist intellectuals also should exhibit some organic relationship with oppressed sectors of capitalist social formations. A proper definition of Black Studies is not genetic or racial: All black intellectuals do not produce Black Studies (for example, Thomas Sowell). Rather, the foundations of Black Studies are rooted in a critique of a particular cultural, political, and economic condition. Whether Marxists or not, many Afro-Americans intellectuals have tried to grapple with certain contradictions: the nexus between race and class, the role of culture and ethnicity within a hierarchical society, the conflict between human needs and private property.

EARLY SCHOLARS

Since the middle of the nineteenth century, black scholarship in the United States, Africa, and the Caribbean has tended to serve three functions, according to Alan Colon (1984:269):

> corrective—the distortions and fallacies surrounding and projected against blacks for elitist and racial and cultural supremacist purposes are countered with factual, knowledge and critical historical interpretation; descriptive—the past and present events that constitute the black experience are accurately documented; and prescriptive—concepts, theories, programs, and movements toward the alleviation or resolution of group problems faced by blacks are generated and promoted.

Black intellectuals have often labored in relative isolation, denied adequate research facilities and academic posts, yet driven by a commitment to the integrity of their people. Black scholarship has developed within a particular problematic that assumes the unity of academic work with practical concerns of the masses of working people; it takes for granted that the distinct division of traditional disciplines that parochialize inquiry within the bourgeois academy is more often than not a barrier to full human understanding. Black education is almost always a holistic enterprise, which seeks to create a praxis between daily life, work, and thought within the framework of the black sociopolitical condition.

By contrast, Marxists have not always applied a "Marxian analysis" of the black experience, and have frequently played, at best, a peripheral role in the development of black social thought. Part of the reason for this rests with the ambiguous legacy of Karl Marx. No one can deny that Marx was a passionate opponent of slavery: The famous statement from *Capital*, "labor with a white skin cannot emancipate itself where labor with a black skin is branded," revealed the symbiotic relationship between racism and capitalism. Yet the primary subjects of his intellectual inquiries were the nature of capitalism as a mode of production, and the rise and ultimate emancipation of the European working class. Consequently, when Marx did write about the United States, he frequently underestimated the racial bigotry of the white working class, and seriously misjudged the motivations of northern politicians vis-a-vis the status of black people. Not even Frederick Douglass, the stalwart of Black Republicanism, would have described Abraham Lincoln as "the single-minded son of the working class" who had "led his country through the matchless struggle for the rescue of an enchained race and the reconstruction of a social world."[1] On matters relating to non-Western civilizations, despite brilliant insights, Marx again displayed similar contradictions. In the *Communist Manifesto*, nonwhites were rudely categorized as "semi-barbarians," "barbarians," or simply "nations of peasants." Marx's writings on black societies, whether in the Caribbean, the Americas, or on the continent of Africa, are at best fragmentary. His sense of comparative political anthropology suffered from the omnipresent racist ideology of mid-nineteenth-century European societies. Hence his 1853 remark that "Indian society has no history at all, at least no known history," by implication included the evolution of African societies and cultures.[2]

Black intellectuals who were the contemporaries of Marx labored under no illusions about their people or their heritage. In Afro-American history, the earliest monographs written that accurately depicted blacks were those of Joseph T. Wilson, which included *Emancipation: Its Course and Progress from 1481 B.C. to A.D. 1875* (1882), and *The Black Phalanx* (1888), a study of blacks during the Civil War. The first truly great historian of black America was George Washington Williams, author of *History of the Negro Race in America from 1619 to 1880* (1883) and *History of the Negro Troops in the Rebellion* (1888). In literature, Frances Ellen Watkins Harper's *Pleasures and Other Miscellaneous Poems* had appeared as early as 1854. A generation later, her work was followed by that of novelist Charles W. Chesnutt and celebrated poet Paul Laurence Dunbar. The initial contributions to the field of black political economy were made by radical journalist Timothy Thomas Fortune. His major texts, *Black and White: Land, Labor and Politics in the South* (1884) and *The Negro in Politics* (1885), displayed an acute awareness of the nexus between race and class struggles that was missing within American socialist circles (Franklin, 1969:232, 409-411). Black political and social theory was from the beginning interdisciplinary in scope and militantly antiracist. The seminal black nationalist tract of the pre-Civil War period was Martin Delany's *The Condition, Elevation, Emigration and Destiny of the Colored People in the United States* (1852). Later works by

West Indian intellectuals Edward Blyden and Jacob J. Thomas, author of *Froudacity* (1888), projected the ideals of Pan-Africanism, anti-colonialism, and racial solidarity.

Perhaps the first true Black Studies scholar, in a contemporary sense, was W. E. B. Du Bois who was trained as a historian at Fisk University and Harvard University. His 1895 doctoral dissertation, *The Suppression of the African Slave Trade, 1638-1870*, was the first monograph published in the Harvard Historical Studies. Du Bois's concern about the immediate socioeconomic conditions of his people led his research into the new discipline of sociology. While working as an assistant instructor at the University of Pennsylvania from 1896 to 1898, he conducted interviews with over 5,000 black Philadelphia households. His *Philadelphia Negro* (1899) was the first sociological survey of black Americans. For the next sixty years, Du Bois produced a series of studies on the African diaspora. His annual reports on sociological topics considering Negro life in America (the Atlanta University publications between 1897 and 1913) established the links between the academy and the black community. Du Bois continued to write social and political histories: *John Brown* (1909), *The Negro* (1915), *The Gift of Black Folk: Negroes in the Making of America* (1924). But he also drew the cultural and political connections between Afro-Americans and Africa in mature political works such as *Color and Democracy: Colonies and Peace* (1945) and *The World and Africa* (1947). He wrote poetry, novels, literary criticism, and was a patron of the explosion of black artistic creativity after World War I, known as the Harlem Renaissance. His most famous collection of essays, *The Souls of Black Folk* (1903), combined critiques of black music, folk culture, history, and politics. Du Bois still found time to help establish the first black intellectual association, the American Negro Academy, in 1897; sponsor a series of international conferences between 1900 and 1945, which propelled the concept of Pan-Africanism into a major anti-colonialist movement; and co-found the National Association for the Advancement of Colored People (NAACP) and edit its publication, the *Crisis*, from 1910 until 1934. No scholar of historical materialism, with the notable exceptions of Marx, Lenin, Gramsci, and perhaps Bukharin, represents such a rich legacy of theoretical work and practical political engagement. As James B. Stewart (1984:299, 309) observes, Du Bois was "engaged in structuring an interdisciplinary policy-oriented enterprise" for over half a century. Du Bois viewed black education "in an Afro-centric perspective," and based on the synthesis of theory and practice.

Black intellectuals in following generations built upon the Du Boisian tradition. Historian Carter G. Woodson established the Association for the Study of Negro Life and History in 1916, which produced two publications, the *Journal of Negro History*, started also in 1916, and the *Negro History Bulletin* in 1926. Charles H. Thompson initiated the *Journal of Negro Education* at Howard University in 1932; eight years later, Du Bois published the first volume of *Phylon*, a social science review at Atlanta University. During the 1950s, three additional publications appeared: the *Negro Educational Review* (1950), edited by J. Irving Scott; the *Howard Law Journal* (1955), sponsored by the Howard University Law School; and the *CLA Journal* (1957) published by the College Language Association (Chicago Center for Afro-American Studies and Research, 1981:16, 26, 38). During the era of rigid racial segregation, the few institutions in the United States that made efforts to develop programs in Black Studies were the historically black colleges. During the early 1940s, the only American university that had a formal program in African Studies was Fisk University, under the direction of black scholar Lorenzo Turner. Fisk also initiated an institute of race relations in 1944, supervised by black sociologist Charles S. Johnson, which conducted extensive field research throughout the Deep South. Lincoln University of Pennsylvania and Howard University both organized African Studies programs in 1950 and 1953, respectively (Martin and Young, 1984:262-64). In the arts, Afro-Americans generated an impressive corpus of literature, rich in diversity and scope. In the 1920s, the greatest single novel was *Cane* (1923) by Jean Toomer. But other influential works on Afro-American culture were produced by Countee Cullen: *Ballad of the Brown Girl* (1927) and *Copper Sun* (1927); Claude McKay: *Harlem Shadow* (1922) and *Home to Harlem* (1928); Jessie Redmond Fauset: *There Is Confusion* (1924), *Plum Bun* (1929), and *The Chinaberry Tree* (1931); and Nella Larsen: *Quicksand* (1928) and *Passing* (1929). The most popular black poet and creative artist, Langston Hughes, had Du Bois's deep appreciation of racial pride and a firm commitment to progressive politics. Hughes's *Weary Blues* (1926), *Not Without Laughter* (1930), and *The Ways of White Folks* (1934) were widely acclaimed within black America (Franklin, 1969: 502-06).

THE EMERGENCE OF MARXISM

Marxism began to surface in black political circles several decades before it found its way into educational institutions. African Methodist Episcopal Bishop Reverdy Ransom had espoused the cause of socialism during the mid-1890s, and the Reverend George Washington Woodbey became a major leader of the Socialist Party in California in the early 1900s. This form of Christian socialism gave way to a more radical variety of black left-wing politics during World War I. Harlem became the focal point for the revolutionary nationalism of Hubert H. Harrison, an articulate but little-studied forerunner of Malcolm X and Stokely Carmichael.[3] Aligned with the Socialist Party were young militants A. Philip Randolph and Chandler Owen, editors of the *Messenger*. Randolph later founder the Brotherhood of Sleeping Car Porters in 1925 and the National Negro Congress during the Great Depression. More radical than Randolph and Owen were the "Black Bolsheviks" clustered in the vanguard formation, the African Blood Brotherhood, led by Cyril V. Briggs. These groups introduced Marxist and socialist works to black working-class communities, and thousands of black laborers and intellectuals were either members or on the periphery of the Communist Party by the 1930s.

Only at this point did historical materialism interact with Black Studies on black college campuses. Once again, the critical figure was Du Bois. The first course on "Marxism and the Negro" given at *any* American college was taught by Du Bois at Atlanta University in 1933. His major historical study, *Black Reconstruction* (1935), was an attempt to create a Marxian analysis of the Afro-American experience. Although the book is now considered a classic, its publication merited silence from the white historical profession of that period. The *American Historical Review* did not even publish a book review of *Black Reconstruction* (see Du Bois, 1935; Guzman, 1961:377-85; Walden, 1963:159-60, 164; and H. Aptheker, 1971:249-73). The only comparable historical studies produced by a black Marxist were the works of C. L. R. James. A Trinidadian journalist, cricket player, and sometime Trotskyist, James authored the seminal study of the Haitian Revolution, *The Black Jacobins*, which appeared in 1938. James's later historical and philosophical studies, including *Negro Revolt* (1939), *Notes on Dialectics* (1948), *Beyond a Boundary* (1963), and *Nkrumah and the Ghana Revolution* (1977), were ignored for decades by bourgeois academics and many Marxists, but found their way into radical and black political groupings across the Caribbean, Africa, and the United States. James's legacy to the radical tendency of Black Studies includes three great insights. Well before most Marxists, James argued that the Afro-American working class had its own vitality, deep cultural roots, and a unique organizational history. The basic thrust of the black movement would be for the expansion of bourgeois democratic rights; but the black movement was potentially the most radical of an American social protest current. Second, James emphasized the centrality of popular culture—values, aesthetics, literature, and, most of all, sports—to the dynamics of political struggle. The development of a national consciousness prefigures political transformation. And last, James's Marxism was profoundly democratic. No state and no party should "put barriers in the way of knowledge." James's thought has its weaknesses; black Marxists a generation later found his extreme anti-Sovietism hard to accept. Most disagreed with his theory of spontaneity, which relied too heavily upon Rosa Luxemburg and not sufficiently upon Lenin. But for his critics and followers, James was the central black Marxist intellectual of the mid-twentieth century (see James, 1963, 1969, 1977, 1980).

The major black literary figures first influenced by Marxism were Claude McKay and Langston Hughes. In 1921 McKay was serving as an associate editor of the radical left publication, the *Liberator*; the following year he attended the fourth Congress of the Communist International in Moscow (see Cruse, 1967:44, 54-57). Hughes's involvement on the left was less formal, and during the Cold War he made tactical compromises with anticommunists on several occasions. The main proponents of left politics in Afro-American culture after the Depression were novelist Richard Wright and actor-vocalist Paul Robeson. Wright joined the Communist Party during the 1930s but broke from the left bitterly in 1944. Robeson's commitment to socialism never wavered, despite widespread political ostracism and the near destruction of his artistic career. In the social sciences, several intellectuals employed a class analysis to describe the conditions of black workers. Under a grant from Columbia University, Sterling D. Spero and Abram L. Harris produced *The Black Worker: The Negro and the Labor Movement* (1931). Harris subsequently authored a major study of the Afro-American petit bourgeoisie, *The Negro as Capitalist* in 1936. Oliver Cromwell Cox was probably the first American sociologist to develop a Marxian analysis of comparative race relations. Cox's major work, *Caste, Class and Race*, first published in 1949, was important in several respects. Throughout the 1930s and 1940s, the dominant theorists of race relations employed a "caste" model to interpret American society. Cox illustrated that the caste theory was not simply static, but ahistorical. It lacked comprehension of the significance of social class stratification inside the black community that Du Bois's *Philadelphia Negro* and Atlanta University publications had illustrated. Cox argued that sociologists such as Gunnar Myrdal denied the possibility of class struggle and obscured the economic utility of racism in generating profits to the capitalist ruling class. There were some limitations to Cox's analysis, when compared to James or Du Bois: his underestimation of the role of culture and nationalism within the working class, in particular. But he prepared the field for later works by black social scientists who employed a Marxist method (Cox, 1972).

It is crucial to note that at no time did Marxism become a dominant current within American Negro social thought, despite these and other intellectuals who were influenced by the left. The primary political concern of the majority of black researchers, teachers, artists, and cultural workers, Marxist and non-Marxist alike, was the ultimate abolition of racial segregation within civil society and the expansion of bourgeois democracy to the Negro. Given the prevalence of racism among white workers, the concept of class struggle seemed distinctly abstract to most black scholars of the period.

CONTEMPORARY BLACK STUDIES

Contemporary Black Studies was produced by the conjuncture of four events between 1945 and 1970. The first was the rise of national liberation movements throughout the Third World periphery, and especially the independence movements in Africa and the Caribbean; the second factor was the Cold War between the United States and the Soviet Union. The continued existence of Jim Crow segregation greatly embarrassed the U.S. government, both in its relations with new African states and at the United Nations. As St. Clair Drake (1984: 227) comments,

> How could Africa and Asia be expected to trust the United States when, by custom generally and by law in some states, Black people were discriminated against on the basis of color? How could the U.S. propaganda agencies deal with Soviet ridicule of a "Free World" that included South Africa as well as European powers holding colonies?

In the effort to "keep Africa from going Communist" during the 1950s and early 1960s, the State Department appointed a number of Afro-American ambassadors, and greatly increased its personnel in African affairs. The federal government and philanthropic agencies funneled resources to organizations established by the black petit bourgeoisie, such as the American Negro Leadership Conference on Africa and the American Society for African Culture (Drake, 1984:

229). The African Studies Association, created in March 1957 by a small elite of American social scientists connected with African issues, was also the indirect product of governmental activity. The Central Intelligence Agency, the Ford Foundation, the Rockefeller Foundation, the Agency for International Development, and the State Department distributed grants to initiate African Studies Centers at major universities. Most of the "research" produced by such institutions assumed a "developmentalist paradigm," note Guy Martin and Carlene Young. The unspoken assumption of these programs is that "industrialized societies" are the "quintessential models which must absolutely be emulated by other, non-industrialized societies if they wish one day to taste the coveted fruits of economic growth and development, and technological and scientific progress" (Martin and Young, 1984:259-60). Politically and educationally, the emergence of such academic centers represented not simply a radical departure from the previous history of research in African Studies, but the attempt to manipulate scholarship for the calculating ends of U.S. hegemony over Africa.

The third factor in the rise of modern Black Studies is frequently ignored, but in many respects was crucial: the mass migration of Afro-Americans from the rural South to the urban North and West, and the creation of the black industrial working class. In the thirty-year period 1940-70, the percentage of blacks living in urban areas increased from barely 50 percent to above 80 percent. In Chicago alone, the Afro-American community soared in size, from 278,000 in 1940 to 1.1 million in 1970. Throughout the 1950s and 1960s, black Americans acquired greater influence within the dominant culture, especially in athletics, popular music, literature, and the arts. Large black populations existed in close proximity to many of the major white universities, and the numbers of black students enrolled in colleges and professional schools increased by over 1,000 percent during this thirty-year period. Finally, the emergence of the black social movement for democratic rights and desegregation had a tremendous impact upon American higher education. During the first phase of this movement, the period of integration and nonviolent direct action campaigns, the response of most institutions was simply to increase the numbers of black students admitted into programs. Few curriculum changes were made; the tacit belief that the American Negro should acquire "higher education" did not involve a concomitant commitment to introduce Afro-American Studies into the classroom. It was, in effect, a liberal version of the "white man's burden," updated to the tune of "We Shall Overcome."

Black Power changed all this fundamentally. Influenced by Malcolm X, Frantz Fanon, Stokely Carmichael, and other theoreticians of black liberation, Afro-American students brought the spirit of urban rebelliousness into the heart of bourgeois academia. Administration buildings, student unions, and computer centers were seized; black student associations and Afro-American cultural centers were established. In retrospect, the central demand of black radicalism on white university campuses during the late 1960s was the merger of two heretofore alien pedagogies: the black intellectual tradition as embodied by programs at black institutions such as Howard, Fisk, and Atlanta University with the implicitly racist, bourgeois structure of white education. Black studies represented a perspective that was holistic, interdisciplinary, and avowedly political; "white" studies, or the normative curriculum, symbolized the race/class inequality of the larger society and culture. "Students in the sixties did not have to be recruited for Black Studies programs," observe Veron E. McClean and Lois Lyles (1985:96). "On most campuses, black and white students, inspired by and caught up in the liberation struggle, *demanded* that such programs be established. They pressured college administrators to hire black faculty members to teach courses in Afro-American and African history, politics, sociology, literature, art, and music." Estimates of the number of programs established during these turbulent years vary widely, from a low figure of 300 to as many as 500 (see D. Smith, 1971:259-71, and Brossard, 1984:280). As these new programs began, black scholars began to carry the assault into professional associations. At the 1969 meeting of the African Studies Association in Montreal, African and Afro-American intellectuals "questioned the whole concept and function of African Studies," and charged that the organization was "designed to perpetuate the multidimensional exploitation of African and Afro-American peoples" (Martin and Young, 1984:260). New formations were developed by this latest generation of Black intellectuals: the African Heritage Studies Association, the Association of Concerned African Scholars, the National Council for Black Studies, the Association of Black Psychologists, the Association of Black Sociologists, as well as others.

The growth of Black Studies at white universities also sparked the development of many new academic journals. The two most prestigious publications of the late 1960s-1970s were *Black World*, edited by the late Hoyt Fuller, a fine cultural critic, and the *Black Scholar*, initiated in 1969 by Robert Chrisman and Nathan Hare. Some of the new publications were in the humanities: *Black Art* (founded in

1976), *Black American Literature Forum* (1967), *Black Perspectives in Music* (1973), and *Calahoo: A Black South Journal of Arts and Letters* (1976). Social science journals published articles within specific disciplines, such as the *Black Sociologist* (1975) and the *Journal of Black Psychology* (1974). But the majority of new journals were deliberately interdisciplinary, covering issues from the black nationalist-Marxist debates of the mid-1970s to black literary criticism: *Western Journal of Black Studies* (1977), *Review of Afro-American Issues and Culture* (1978), *Studia Africana* (1979), *Umoja: A Scholarly Journal of Black Studies* (1977), *Contributions to Black Studies* (1977), *Black Books Bulletin* (1972), *First World* (1977), and the *Journal of Black Studies* (1970) (Chicago Center for Afro-American Studies and Research, 1981:2-57).

A comprehensive history of the emergence and institutionalization of Black Studies since 1967 remains to be written. Nevertheless it is possible to highlight some major problems in the field. Most departments at white universities "refused to extend manpower and built-up intellectual resources, forcing protesting black students to insist on alternative structures for handling Black Studies," Carlos Brossard observes. Black Studies faculty "stood alone in resolving intellectual integration and discovering organizational building without shared support or prior role modeling of professional peers." Most of the faculty hired into Black Studies programs were graduate students or young doctorates. "Organizationally inexperienced and short on institutionally transferred resources for building new intellectual enterprises," Black Studies professors had to "build viable departments" in a hostile environment (Brossard, 1984:280-81). Complicating matters were the social and ideological tensions between faculty. Some professors tended to support black nationalist versions of the Afro-American experience, while others were inclined toward Marxism. Tenure and promotion decisions were sometimes made on the questionable basis of one's politics. The question of the selection of introductory texts was also a debatable issue. The two most widely used books represented two ideological poles: cultural nationalist Maulana Karenga's *Introduction to Black Studies* (1982a) and the Marxist-oriented *Introduction to Afro-American Studies* (1977), produced by Ronald Bailey, Gerald McWorter (Abdul Alkalimat), and other researchers at Chicago's Peoples College (see Peoples College, 1977; Karenga, 1982a; and Steward, 1983:113-117).

The growth of Black Studies departments has accelerated the integration of Marxism as a method of social analysis into Afro-American thought. As a rule, however, black Marxism cannot easily be categorized as a subset of social democracy, democratic socialism, or communism. Most black intellectuals acquired the tools of historical materialism after they had been involved in their research or political activities. The prism of race, and the shadow of colonialism, could never be reduced to a secondary function of the dynamics of capitalist exploitation. Marxism helped to provide many answers to the problems confronting people of color, but Marxism as a Western intellectual tradition did not embrace the full problematic developed by the early mentors of Black Studies, such as Du Bois. Thus black radicalism treads its own path toward human liberation and equality, conscious of its debt to Marx, but keenly aware of its great ties to the works of C. L. R. James, St. Clair Drake, Oliver C. Cox, and a host of others. This is not to suggest that white Marxists assumed no role in the development of Black Studies. Theoreticians in the Communist Party since the 1930s, as well as white intellectuals radicalized by the Civil Rights, Black Power, and antiwar movements of the 1960s, contributed greatly to the body of social science and humanities literature on Afro-Americans. Although excluded from the scope of this study, the research of Marxist intellectuals such as Herbert Aptheker, Philip S. Foner, Victor Perlo, Eugene D. Genovese, and others helped to shape the curriculum of many Black Studies departments and programs.[4]

Black Theology

One of the most important manifestations of radical thought since the late 1960s was in the area of black theology. With the publication of James Cone's *Black Theology and Black Power* (1969) and Albert Cleage's *The Black Messiah* (1969), a militant, prophetic tendency in black religion began to mature. These works, followed by the studies of William Jones (1973), Joseph R. Washington (1972), Major J. Jones (1971, 1974), Gayraud S. Wilmore (1973), J. Deotis Roberts (1971, 1974), and Cecil Cone (1975), were grounded in an appreciation of the historical role of the black church in the struggles for human rights and racial self-determination. The bulk of the writings in radical black theology tended toward a black nationalist position that devalued social class questions and eschewed the relevancy of socialism. Yet there were important exceptions. James Cone's search to develop a black theology that related directly to the pressing material conditions of Afro-Americans has sharpened his understanding of the role of social class exploitation within contemporary society (see J. Cone, 1970 and 1975). Further to his left is black Marxist theologian Cornel West. Unlike most proponents of black theology, West divides the Afro-American response to institutional racism into four types of "traditions": an "exceptional tradition," which "lauds the uniqueness" of black culture; an "assimilationist tradition," which views black "culture and personality to be pathological"; a "marginalist tradition," which emphasizes "the suppression of individuality, eccentricity and nonconformity with Afro-American culture"; and a "humanistic" response to racism, which "makes no ontological or sociological claims about Afro-American superiority or inferiority," and "accents the universal human content of Afro-American cultural forms." Each current is fully represented within the black church and among the black intelligentsia. But drawing upon the work of Antonio Gramsci and more fundamentally upon the literature of Jean Toomer, Du Bois, and Robeson, West illustrates that only the humanistic tradition creates an "honest encounter" with the black experience, and points to "the expansion of democratic control over the major institutions that regulate lives in America and abroad." In *Prophesy Deliverance! An Afro-American Revolutionary Christianity* (1982), West writes from this humanistic tradition, arguing that "the alliance of prophetic Christianity and progressive Marxism provides a last human hope for humankind." Implicitly, the prophetic tendency of black faith has spoken a language of social justice that has parallels with Marxism. The challenge of revolutionary black Christians, West concludes, must be to "eschew the paralyzing liberal outlook," to promote the values of humanism and democracy, and to avoid the contradictions inherent in "right-wing Marxism."

Cultural and Literary Criticism

The literature of contemporary Black Studies is an extension of the deeper trends within black aesthetics and culture throughout the entire twentieth century. Writers such as Andrew Salkey (1980) and Rex Nettleford (1980) in the Caribbean have addressed the roots of modern black culture by examining the folklore, music, and rituals of black people. Black literary criticism, initiated with the work of Alain Locke and Du Bois in the 1920s, continues to explore the patterns of black literature as it relates to political and social conditions. One notable text in this vein is George Kent's *Blackness and the Adventure of Western Culture* (1972). The greatest contributions to

Afro-American literature in recent years have been made by black women writers. The poetry and novels of Toni Morrison (1976), Alice Walker (1972, 1974, 1976, 1982), and Toni Cade Bambara (1980) represent rare instances where popularity has not been achieved at the price of technical and artistic achievement. Both Walker and Bambara have extensive histories in progressive and left politics, much like Hughes and Robeson in previous decades.

In the field of cultural criticism, the writings of Harold Cruse are especially important. Cruse was a member of the Communist Party in the late 1940s, and, like Richard Wright before him, he turned sharply against Leninism. Cruse's major work, *The Crisis of the Negro Intellectual* (1967), became something of a "bible" to thousands of young militants during the Black Power era. Although Cruse was frequently classified as a cultural nationalist, his thesis did not lapse into a romantic interpretation of black civil society. Cruse argued that American society was stratified primarily along ethnic lines, and that white Anglo-Saxon Protestants had seized control over the major apparatuses of economic, political, and cultural power. Drawing directly from sociologist C. Wright Mills—and to an extent from Du Bois's older "Talented Tenth" thesis of social change—Cruse suggested that intellectuals would be the vanguard in transforming the established order. The critical arena of struggle was the cultural sphere. The black intellectual had to

> assail the stultifying blight of the commercially depraved white middle-class who has poisoned the structural roots of the American ethos and transformed the American people into a nation of intellectual dolts. . . . He should tell black America how and why Negroes are trapped in this cultural degeneracy, and how it has dehumanized their essential identity, squeezed the lifeblood of their inherited cultural ingredients out of them, and then relegated them to the cultural slums (Cruse, 1967: 455-456)

In *Rebellion or Revolution*? (1968), Cruse perceptively argued that Black Power was largely "neo-Booker T. Washingtonism," a demand for black capitalism, racial separatism, and community-controlled educational institutions. In more recent writings, Cruse has analyzed the limitations of black nationalist political movements (1971:19-41, 66-71; 1974:10-17, 82-88; 1975:4-20), and has provided a critique of Karenga's Black Studies text (Cruse, 1984:41-47). Cruse's anti-Marxist yet provocative critiques ironically prepared younger black radicals for the work of Amilcar Cabral and Antonio

Gramsci, by pointing to the importance of cultural and ideological struggle within class movements.

One difficulty inherent in Cruse's analysis was the notion that ethnic blocs, rather than social classes, compete for state power and ideological hegemony. Two major figures in social and cultural criticism who posit the primacy of class over race and ethnicity are Ernest Kaiser and Robert Chrisman. Kaiser is best known as an editor of *Freedomways,* a journal of Black Studies that evolved from Paul Robeson's *Freedom* newspaper in the early 1950s. Kaiser was also an advisor to the Arno Press for the 141 volume series, "The American Negro: His History and Literature." His familiarity with Afro-American issues spans from slavery historiography (1968:45-49) to radical political movements. Perhaps Kaiser's most important single contribution to Black Studies was his edited volume, *A Freedomways Reader* (1976), which is one of the best sources on black literature, politics, mass media, and history written by black leftists in the 1970s. Chrisman's major role as editor and publisher of the *Black Scholar* is only one aspect of his central position in Black Studies. Chrisman's intimate connection with Cuban intellectuals has helped to introduce Marxism to numerous Afro-American scholars (1980:59-71). He has written primarily on cultural issues, but has expanded this to include analyses of the mass media and even the relationship between nuclear policy and social justice (1983a:13-17; 1983b:26-43). Like DuBois's *Crisis* and Charles S. Johnson's *Opportunity* magazines in the 1920s, the *Black Scholar* has also brought many young black scholars to a national audience. Chrisman's identity as a leftist has, to a great extent, helped to push the boundaries of black intellectual discourse and especially cultural inquiry toward Marxism.

Social Science

Much of the black social science literature in the late 1960s employed a class analysis, but the basic theoretical orientation was black nationalism. Black left scholars attempted to define theoretical models that placed roughly equal weight on the factors of race and social class. The best representative of this trend was Robert Allen's *Black Awakening in Capitalist America* (1970) and *Reluctant Reformers* (1975). Allen was extremely critical of the liberal reformist wing of the black movement, typified by the NAACP and Martin Luther King, Jr., and the conservative black nationalists who denied the importance of class within the black community. *Black Awakening* was based on a "domestic colonialism" model, which linked blacks' social movements with struggles for national liberation across the Third World. For Allen and other "left nationalists," it did not take many years to recognize the limitations of this theory. Some black radical political scientists came to a variant of historical materialism via the unorthodox work of Frantz Fanon (see Wright, 1975:19-29; R. Smith, 1973; 23-33). Others reached back into Afro-American social history to rediscover organic examples of black radicalism. One example of this is evident in the work of Earl Ofari. His *Myth of Black Capitalism* (1970) was an influential examination of class stratification within black society since the early nineteenth century. The immediate political objective was to illustrate the futility of the "Black Power-as-Black Capitalism" strategy. In the process, however, Ofari found representatives of black radicalism thoughout history who had rejected the black petit bourgeoisie's reformist, capitalist politics (1972a: 1974: 19-25; 1984:19-22). Ofari was one of the first Black Power-era social theorists who clearly identified with Marxism-Leninism (see Ofari, 1972b:35-46). Black political scientists who retained close relationships with militant working-class formations, such as the League of Revolutionary Black Workers and the Black Workers Congress, gravitated more rapidly to the left than other intellectuals (see Ofari, 1973: 42-47; Forman, 1972; and Mkalimoto, 1979:71-109).

The great debate over "race or class" accelerated in the mid-1970s, as some left nationalists adopted a "version" of Marxism. A veteran of the Student Nonviolent Coordinating Committee and the Black Workers Congress, M. Frank Wright, provided a critique of both the "petit bourgeois" nationalist and Communist Party positions on the Afro-American "nationalist question" in a widely discussed essay (1974:43-53). Mark Smith's "A Response to Haki Madhubuti" (1975: 44-53) illustrated both the strengths and flaws within the new black Marxist analysis. Smith correctly criticized the naive idealism and elitism of black cultural nationalism of the 1960s-early 1970s; and he located the source of racism as the social product of capitalist exploitation. But Smith's acquisition of Marxism also included the baggage of "Maoism," which imposed an inapplicable social theory upon Afro-American social conditions. In retrospect, the debate clarified relatively few issues at that time.

It was only in the late 1970s and early 1980s that a serious integration of Marxism occurred within a substantial sector of Black Studies social science research. The steady deterioration of black working-class conditions combined with the emergence of Reaganism was largely responsible for this. My own works, both *From The Grassroots* (1980) and *Blackwater* (1981a), reflect essentially a left nationalist theoretical position, which relegated equal value to racial and social class variables. My theoretical bridge from radical black nationalism to Marxism was made in 1981-82 (see Marable, 1981b:6-17; 1982a:130-161; 1982b:2-15). *How Capitalism Underdeveloped Black America* (1983) was in some respects an updated version of Allen's *Black Awakening* (1970), minus the domestic colonialism thesis. A symbolic analogy was drawn between the core-periphery Marxist models with the class conflicts between the Afro-American working class versus the black elite. Despite its many limitations, *How Capitalism* presented a fairly detailed anatomy of black society, and located the central cause of racism, gender equality, and poverty in the structures generated by American capitalism. The deepening economic crisis of black America also tended to sharpen the recognition of class conflict among black non-Marxists. The most prolific cultural nationalistic writer, Maulana Karenga, criticized the racial "mystification" of some nationalists a decade ago (1975:23-30; 1978:7-12). More recently he has written essays on the black middle class and the 1984 campaign of Jesse Jackson, which indicate a critical perception of class divisions inside the black community (1982b:16-31; 1984:57-71).

Two of the most important recent texts by black Marxists in political science and political economy are Cedric Robinson's *Black Marxism* (1983) and Lloyd Hogan's *Principles of Black Political Economy* (1984). Robinson explains the historical evolution of various modes of black resistance, from slave rebellions to working-class radicalism. He argues that Marxism expressed a specifically European experience, which was in many respects inapplicable to the African diaspora. Robinson's thoughtful critiques of DuBois, James, and Richard Wright locate their work within the tradition of black radicalism. Hogan's equally ambitious and complex study is an attempt to develop a fundamental theoretical framework for the entire discipline of Afro-American political economy. Hogan charts the historical periods in which blacks have been located within specific sectors of the capitalist economy, and explains the factors leading to their dislocation and reintegration into new sectors. To an extent, both books are efforts to create dynamic theoretical models of the black experience at a national and international level, which draw upon classical Marxism yet recognize the decisive and crucial role of racism in the whole evolution of capitalist societies and cultures. This is also true for my recent two-volume study of comparative political movements throughout the black world (see Marable, 1985). Volume I, *Race, Politics and Power*, is an attempt to chart a general theory of black class struggles for political reform and, in the periphery, for state power during the twentieth century. It explores the major political protests of Afro-Americans during the 1980s, including the Jesse Jackson campaign. Volume II, in progress, explores parallels between Kwame Nkrumah's Convention Peoples Party of Ghana, the New Jewel Movement of Grenada, and Black socialist movements in Guyana, Tanzania, Zimbabwe, and Senegal. Two main themes developed in both texts are the domination of the black petit bourgeoisie within reformist and radical movements, and the tendency for "democratic socialist" movements (for example, Forbes Burnham) and "African socialist" states (for example, Julius Nyerere, Leopold Sedar Senghor, Nkrumah) to degenerate into authoritarian regimes.

Caribbean and African scholars in the field of political economy have relatively few difficulties applying a Marxist analysis to their respective societies. One of the most prolific Marxist intellectuals is Clive Thomas, director of the Institute of Development Studies at the University of Guyana. In his early essays, Thomas criticized the popular notion of a "noncapitalist" strategy toward decolonization and economic development in the Third World. His recent text, *The Rise of the Authoritarian State in Peripheral Societies* may become a modern classic on the dynamics of how the Third World petit bourgeoisie consolidates itself as local ruling class (1974; 1977:10-18; 1978:59-71; 1979:1-20; 1984). Another promising scholar from Jamaica, Fitzroy Ambursley, is beginning to produce works of a similarly high standard (see Ambursely and Cohen, 1983).

The left is well represented in the disciplines of anthropology and sociology. St. Clair Drake remains a productive scholar, and he provides a vital link between the older tradition of black sociologists such as Cox, Horace Cayton, Allison Davis, and E. Franklin Frazier with the post-Black Power scholars (see Drake, 1980:2-31). The best recent studies available on the social structure of apartheid in South Africa are those of Marxist anthropologist Bernard Magubane (1980; 1981:13-30). Marxist anthropology professor Johnnetta Cole has written important essays on Afro-American women and on the evolution of race and gender contradictions in Cuban society (1977:73-80; 1978:38-44). Probably the most widely read black sociologist since the 1960s, Robert Staples, did much of his early research on the Afro-American family. During the 1980s Staples has clearly moved to the left, and has focused more directly on political movements and race/

class struggles within American universities (1982:37-45; 1984:2-17). A prominent Marxist political sociologist, Gerald McWorter (Abdul Alkalimat), has written on black electoral movements and on Black Studies curriculum development (1984a:53-179; 1984b:18-31). Some of the best work written on urban black political movements in the 1980s is that of James Jennings (1983-84:35-40; 1984:199-313). And among the works of younger black Marxist sociologists, the recent essays of Rose Brewer on plant closings and the systematic relationship between racism and monopoly capitalism are noteworthy (1982:1-11; 1983:9-13). What is particularly instructive about these left intellectuals is that, in most instances, their "Marxism" does not remain in the classroom. Many are actively involved in mass social movements; the concept of praxis is not reified as among many white left professionals. McWorter was a participant in the Harold Washington mayoral campaign of 1983 in Chicago; Brewer is heavily involved in progressive politics in Texas; Jennings was a major theorist in Mel King's mayoral campaign of 1983 in Boston; and virtually all of us took part, to a greater or lesser extent, in the Jesse Jackson campaign of 1984 and the more recent antiapartheid campaign.

Afro-American history has lagged behind the other social sciences in the integration of Marxism into the discipline. There are relatively few black historians whose writings could be classified in any way as Marxist; however, there are a few notable black historians who are clearly socialists, or who examine black social movements with an understanding of the importance of class. Three productive scholars in this group are Clayborne Carson, Vincent Harding, and Robert Hill. Carson's *In Struggle* (1981) is a detailed political history of the Student Nonviolent Coordinating Committee. Harding was the founder of the Institute of the Black World, based in Atlanta, which was the major center of progressive Black Studies research in the late 1960s-1970s. He wrote a series of influential historical and political commentaries on the black movement during the high point of the nationalist upsurge (1970:75-100; 1975a:14-21; 1975b:28-46). More recently he authored a powerful social history of black activism in the nineteenth century, *There Is a River: The Black Struggle for Freedom in America* (1981), and a narrative survey of Afro-American history from slavery to the present, *The Other American Revolution* (1980). Jamaican Marxist Robert Hill began to research the life and organizational activities of black nationalist leader Marcus Garvey fifteen years ago. Hill is currently the director of the Marcus Garvey and Universal Negro Improvement Association Papers, and is editing a projected ten-volume work based on over 30,000 archival documents and papers (1983). To date, the only Marxist social history of the entire Civil Rights and Black Power movement since 1945 is my book, *Race, Reform and Rebellion* (1984).

The black Marxist historian who best personified the tradition of Du Bois was Guyanese scholar Walter Rodney. His doctoral dissertation was a study of the slave trade and social conflicts in West Africa (1982). His initial collection of essays, *The Groundings with My Brothers* (1969), was an effort to adopt the "Black Power" concept to the complex racial and class structure of neocolonialist Caribbean societies. But Rodney first won international notice with his influential study, *How Europe Underdeveloped Africa* (1972). Rodney's writings included monographs on Tanzanian political economy, Pan-Africanism, black education, and black labor history (1976; 1981a:5-13; 1981b; 1981c:64-78; 1982). His role in the creation of the Working People's Alliance in Guyana and his 1980 assassination at the hands of the dictatorship of Forbes Burnham, cut short his brilliant career.

There are few examples of black Marxist scholarship in the field of legal studies. Probably the major reason for this is the evolution of the Afro-American desegregation movement throughout the twentieth century. Given the legal and de facto segregation of black Americans, their central political demand was the extension of civil rights, affirmative action, and equal opportunity—an agenda that did not require a Marxist perspective. Some of the more important legal studies on racism were authored by black liberals, including the work of U.S. Civil Rights Commission member Mary Berry (1971; 1977), Leon A. Higginbotham (1978), and Derrick A. Bell (1973). One of the better edited volumes in the field is Daniel Georges-Abeyie's *The Criminal Justice System and Blacks* (1984). A more radical interpretation of the relationship between racism and criminal justice is Lennox S. Hinds's *Illusions of Justice: Human Rights Violations in the United States* (1978).

Feminist Studies

Feminist Studies was introduced into universities shortly after Black Studies, and despite the theoretical parallels between racism and gender inequality, few viable links exist between most departments or programs. The vast majority of Black Studies directors and faculty members were males; many male professors, especially those who identified with black nationalism, were extremely chauvinistic in their relations with female colleagues and students. Courses on Afro-American women were almost nonexistent before 1970, and were still extremely rare in 1975. In the past decade, however, black feminist studies have found a major place within any credible Afro-American Studies curriculum. The most widely used anthologies and survey texts include Sharon Harley and Rosalyn T. Penn, eds., *The Afro-American Woman* (1978); Filomena Chioma Steady, ed., *The Black Woman Cross Culturally* (1981); Roseann P. Bell, Bettye J. Parker, and Beverly Guy-Sheftall, eds., *Sturdy Black Bridges: Visions of Black Women in Literature* (1979); and LaFrances Rodgers-Rose, ed., *The Black Woman* (1980). Two sources that provide extensive overviews of recent literature are Marilyn Richardson, *Black Women and Religion: A Bibliography* (1980) and Ora Williams, *American Black Women in the Arts and Social Sciences* (1978).

Two outstanding but very different representatives of black radical feminism are Barbara Smith and Angela Y. Davis. In many respects, Smith is part of a tradition of Black women writers and militants that embraces Frances Ellen Watkins Harper, Ida B. Wells, Alice Dunbar-Nelson, and Zora Neale Hurston. Smith was a founding member of the black feminist Combahee River Collective in 1974, which became well known for its political orientation against all forms of oppression—racial, sexual, heterosexual, and class. In *Home Girls: A Black Feminist Anthology* (1983), Smith observes that the Collective "saw no reason to rank oppressions, or, as many forces in the black community would have us do, to pretend that sexism, among all the 'isms', was not happening to us" (p. xxxii). Smith's research and activism focuses on issues of concern to women of color, including reproductive rights, sterilization abuse, violence against women, lesbian and gay rights, and police brutality. But she is primarily a perceptive cultural critic, who has challenged the homophobia and sexism of the black community as well as the racism of many white feminists. In a recent essay she also presents a thoughtful examination of the roots and manifestations of anti-Semitism among blacks (see Bulkin, Pratt, and Smith, 1984).

Angela Davis is undoubtedly the best-known communist in the United States. Trained by Herbert Marcuse in political philosophy, Davis first came to national attention as a political prisoner during the early 1970s. Davis's first major writings focused on the plight of black victims of governmental and class oppression (1971; 1974). Her collection of essays, *Women, Race, and Class* (1981), was one of the most important Black Studies texts of the 1980s. Davis's chief strength as a social theorist is her fine grasp of history. Her book includes an overview of the black woman's experience in slavery, and the racism inherent within the woman's suffrage movement. Like Smith, Davis's analysis examines reproductive rights and forced sterilization issues, and the economic subordination of black women workers. The critical points of departure between the two theorists are Davis's silence on questions relating to homophobia within the black community, and her emphasis on social class oppression as the fundamental contradiction that shapes and propels racism and gender inequality. For Davis, feminism and the struggle for black's human rights must "question the validity of monopoly capitalism and must ultimately point in the direction of socialism." As a major leader of the U.S. Communist Party, Davis symbolizes one element of the Du Bois heritage (see Parker, 1973; B. Aptheker, 1975; and Major, 1976).

The Role of Le Roi Jones (Imamu Baraka)

If one had to select the most influential Black Studies intellectual over the past quarter of a century, the choice would be Le Roi Jones (Imamu Amiri Baraka). His sojourn to Marxism involved numerous detours, as did that of Du Bois. Beginning his career as a bohemian poet, playwright, and music critic, he became a major figure in New York cultural circles before reaching the age of thirty (Jones 1961; 1963; 1964; 1965). With the rise of Black Power, Jones seemed to experience a metamorphosis. He became the central idological leader of black artists and writers who were attempting to define a "Black Aesthetic" in light of urban rebellions and new nationalist political movements (Jones, 1966; 1967; 1968; 1969a).

In the early 1970s Jones—now Imamu Baraka—assumed a national role as prime catalyst for two nationalist formations, the Congress of Afrikan People, and the National Black Political Assembly (Jones, 1969b:54-60; 1970; 1971; 1972a; 1972b:54-78; 1973). During the heated debates between black Marxists and cultural nationalists in the mid-1970s, Baraka astonished his long-time disciples by moving rapidly to the left. Effectively isolated and purged from the Black Assembly in late 1975, he now advocated a Maoist theory of revolutionary social change (Jones, 1975a:2-15; 1975b:22-27; 1975c:30-42; 1984). The studies of Baraka's literary and political activities are already quite extensive, although the final chapters in his theoretical evolution remain to be written (see K. Jackson, 1969:232-247; E. Jackson, 1973:33-56; Benson, 1976; Hudson, 1976; Sollors, 1978; Brown, 1980).

CONCLUSION

Black Studies reveals the historical evolution and social reality of American capitalist society from the perspective of "the bottom up." It embraces the totality of the social sciences and the humanities, and seeks to restructure the method and content of American education from the vantage point of the oppressed. Black Marxists, black feminists, and other radicals do not comprise a majority of Black Studies scholars, yet in many ways they are the most productive and creative trend of the black intellectual tradition. The common ground between radical Black Studies and Marxism is the recognition that American institutional racism cannot be ended unless the capitalist political economy is dismantled, and the insight that the various modes of colonialism and neocolonial hegemony are appendages of a larger system of world capitalism. As the domestic and international class struggles of people of color intensify in the coming decades, radical Black Studies should become a more prominent current in Marxist thought.

FOOTNOTES

1. Eugene D. Genovese, *In Red and Black: Marxian Explorations in Southern and Afro-American History* (New York: Vintage, 1971), p. 334. Also see Gerald Runkle, "Karl Marx and the American Civil War," *Comparative Studies in Society and History*, Vol. 6 (1963-64), pp. 117-41.

2. Shlomo Avineri, ed., *Karl Marx on Colonialism and Modernization* (Garden City, N.Y.: Anchor Books, 1969), pp. 4, 10.

3. On Harrison, see Wilfred D. Samuels, "Hubert H. Harrison and 'the New Negro Manhood Movement,'" *Afro-Americans in New York Life and History*, 5 (January 1981): 29-41.

4. White Marxists of radically different ideological orientations have long been involved in research on the Afro-American community. In black political economy, the work of Victor Perlo is noteworthy [See Perlo, *The Negro in Southern Agriculture* (New York: International Publishers, 1953); and *Economics of Racism U.S.A.: Roots of Black Inequality* (New York: International Publishers, 1975)]. Studies by left labor historians and sociologists include James A. Geschwender, *Class, Race, and Workers Insurgency: The League of Revolutionary Black Workers* (New York: Cambridge University Press, 1977); Philip S. Foner, *Organized Labor and the Black Worker, 1619-1981* (New York: International Publishers, 1981); and Robert S. Starobin, ed., *Blacks in Bondage: Letters of American Slaves* (New York: New Viewpoints, 1974). The most important work has been produced by white left historians in the area of Afro-American slavery. Jay R. Mandle's *The Roots of Black Poverty: The Southern Plantation Economy After the Civil War* (Durham, N.C.: Duke University Press, 1978) presents a brief but careful examination of the transition from slave labor to sharecropping and debt peonage. Herbert G. Gutman's *The Black Family in Slavery and Freedom, 1750-1925* (New York: Pantheon, 1975) is a definitive account of the evolution of

black kinship patterns and culture both within slavery and during the postbellum periods. One of the most influential, if at times controversial, left historians is Eugene D. Genovese. His reading of Antonio Gramsci has given form to his theory of paternalism in the Deep South, which is rather similar to the interpretations of Brazilian scholar Gilberto Freyre. Some of Genovese's works include: *The World the Slaveholders Made* (New York: Vintage, 1971); *In Red and Black: Marxian Explorations in Southern and Afro-American History* (New York: Vintage, 1971); *Roll, Jordan, Roll: The World the Slaves Made* (New York: Vintage, 1974); Elinor Miller and Eugene D. Genovese, eds., *Plantation, Town and Country: Essays on the Local History of American Slave Society* (Urbana: University of Illinois Press, 1974); and Elizabeth Fox-Genovese and Eugene D. Genovese, *Fruits of Merchant Capital: Slavery and Bourgeois Property in the Rise and Expansion of Capitalism* (New York: Oxford University Press, 1983). The white Marxist who has had the greatest impact upon Black Studies is Herbert Aptheker. His *American Negro Slave Revolts* (New York: Columbia University Press, 1943), ranks with Du Bois's *Black Reconstruction* and James's *Black Jacobins* as a pivotal source in Black historiography. Other volumes by Aptheker include: (ed.) *A Documentary History of the Negro People in the United States* (Secaucus, N.J.: Citadel Press, 1951); *Nat Turner's Slave Rebellion* (New York: Grove Press, 1966); (ed.), *The Correspondence of W.E.B. Du Bois, Volumes I, II and III* (Amherst: University of Massachusetts Press, 1973, 1976, 1978); (ed.), *The Education of Black People: Ten Critiques, 1906-1960 by W.E.B. Du Bois* (New York: Monthly Review, 1973); and (ed.), *Against Racism: Unpublished Essays, Papers, Addresses, 1887-1961, by W.E.B. Du Bois* (Amherst: University of Massachusetts Press, 1985).

BIBLIOGRAPHY

Allen, Robert L. *Black Awakening in Capitalist America: An Analytic History*. Garden City, N.Y.: Doubleday, 1970.

________. *Reluctant Reformers: Racism and Social Reform Movements in the United States*. Garden City, N.Y.: Doubleday, 1975.

Ambursley, Fitzroy, and Cohen, Robin (eds.). *Crisis in the Caribbean*. New York: Monthly Review Press, 1983.

Aptheker, Bettina (ed.). *The Morning Breaks: The Trial of Angela Davis*. New York: International Publishers, 1975.

Aptheker, Herbert. "The Historian." In Logan, Rayford W. (ed.). *W.E.B. Du Bois: A Profile*. New York: Hill and Wang, 1971.

Bambara, Toni Cade. *The Salt Eaters*. New York: Random House, 1980.

Bell, Derrick A., *Race, Racism and American Law*. Boston: Little, Brown, 1973.

Bell, Roseann P., Parker, Bettye J., and Guy-Sheftall, Beverly (eds.). *Sturdy Black Bridges: Visions of Black Women in Literature*. New York: Doubleday, 1979.

Benson, Kimberly W. *Baraka: The Renegade and the Mask*. New Haven, Conn.: Yale University Press, 1976.

Berry, Mary. *Black Resistance, White Law: A History of Constitutional Racism in America*. Englewood Cliffs, N.J.: Prentice-Hall, 1971.

________. *Military Necessity and Civil Rights Policy: Black Citizenship and the Constitution, 1861-1868*. Port Washington, N.Y.: Kennikat Press, 1977.

Brewer, Rose. "Capitalist State Crises and Black Inequality in the United States." In McWorter, Gerald A. (ed.). *Race/Class*. Urbana, Ill.: Afro-American Studies and Research Program, 1982.

________. "Black Workers and Corporate Flight." *Third World Socialists* 1 (1983).

Brossard, Carlos A. "Classifying Black Studies Programs." *Journal of Negro Education* 53 (1984).

Brown, Lloyd. *Amiri Baraka*. Boston: Twayne, 1980.

Bulkin, Elly, Pratt, Minnie Bruce, and Smith, Barbara. *Yours in Struggle: Three Perspectives on Anti-Semitism and Racism*. Brooklyn: Long Haul Press, 1984.

Carson, Clayborne. *In Struggle: SNCC and the Black Awakening of the 1960s*. Cambridge, Mass.: Harvard University Press, 1981.

Chicago Center for Afro-American Studies and Research. *Guide to Scholarly Journals in Black Studies*. Chicago: Peoples College Press, 1981.

Chrisman, Robert. "Cuba: Forge of the Revolution." *Black Scholar* 11 (1980).

________. "The Role of Mass Media in U.S. Imperialism." *Black Scholar* 14 (1983a).

________. "Nuclear Policy, Social Justice, and the Third World." *Black Scholar* 14 (1983b).

Cleage, Albert. *The Black Messiah*. New York: Sheed and Ward, 1969.

Cole, Johnnetta. "Afro-American Solidarity with Cuba." *Black Scholar* 8 (1977).

________. "Militant Black Women in Early U.S. History." *Black Scholar* 9 (1978).

Colon, Alan K., "Critical Issues in Black Studies: A Selective Analysis." *Journal of Negro Education* 53 (1984).

Cone, Cecil. *The Identity Crisis in Black Theology*. Nashville: African Methodist Episcopal Church, 1975.

Cone, James. *Black Theology and Black Power*. New York: Seabury Press, 1969.

________. *A Black Theology of Liberation*. Philadelphia: J.B. Lippincott, 1970.

________. *God of the Oppressed*. New York: Seabury Press, 1975.

Cox, Oliver Cromwell. *Caste, Class and Race*. New York: Monthly Review Press, 1972.

Cruse, Harold. *The Crisis of the Negro Intellectual*. New York: William Morrow, 1967.

________. *Rebellion or Revolution*? New York: William Morrow, 1968.

________. "Black and White: Outlines of the Next Stage." *Black World* 20 (1971).

________. "The Little Rock National Black Convention." *Black World* 23 (1974).

________. "The Methodology of Pan-Africanism." *Black World* 24 (1975).

________. "Contemporary Challenges to Black Studies." *Black Scholar* 15 (1984).

Davis, Angela (ed.). *If They Come in the Morning*. New York: Third Press, 1971.

________. *Angela Davis–An Autobiography*. New York: Random House, 1974.

________. *Women, Race, and Class*. New York: Random House, 1981.

Drake, St. Clair. "Anthropology and the Black Experience." *Black Scholar* 11 (1980).

________. "Black Studies and Global Perspectives: An Essay." *Journal of Negro Education* 53 (1984).

Du Bois, W. E. B., *Black Reconstruction in America: An Essay Toward a History of the Part Which Black Folk Played in the Attempt to Reconstruct Democracy in America, 1860-1880*. New York: Harcourt, Brace, 1935.

Forman, James. *The Making of Black Revolutionaries*. New York: Macmillan, 1972.

Franklin, John Hope. *From Slavery to Freedom: A History of Negro Americans*. New York: Vintage, 1969.

Georges-Abeyie, Daniel (ed.). *The Criminal Justice System and Blacks*. New York: Clark Boardman, 1984.

Guzman, Jessie P. "W.E.B. Du Bois–the Historian." *Journal of Negro Education* 30 (1961).

Harding, Vincent. "Black Students and the Impossible Revolution." *Journal of Black Studies* 1 (1970).

________. "Black Struggle and the International Crisis: Where Do We Go From Here?" *Black Books Bulletin* 2 (1975a).

________. "The Black Wedge in America: Struggle, Crisis and Hope, 1955-1975," *Black Scholar* 7 (1975b).

________. *The Other American Revolution*. Los Angeles: Center for Afro-American Studies, University of California-Los Angeles, 1980.

________. *There Is a River: The Black Struggle for Freedom in America*. New York: Harcourt, Brace, Jovenovich, 1981.

Harley, Sharon, and Penn, Rosalyn T. *The Afro-American Woman: Struggles and Images*. Port Washington, N.Y.: Kennikat, 1978.

Higginbotham, A. Leon. *In the Matter of Color: Race and the American Legal Process*. New York: Oxford University Press, 1978.

Hill, Robert (ed.). *The Marcus Garvey and Universal Negro Improvement Association Papers, Volume I*. Berkeley: University of California Press, 1983.

Hinds, Lennox S. *Illusions of Justice: Human Rights Violations in the United States*. Ames: Iowa State University Press, 1978.

Hogan, Lloyd. *Principles of Black Political Economy*. Boston: Routledge and Kegan Paul, 1984.

Hudson, Theodore. *From LeRoi Jones to Amiri Baraka: The Literary Works*. Durham, N.C.: Duke University Press, 1976.

Jackson, Esther M. "LeRoi Jones (Imamu Amiri Baraka): Form and Progression of Consciousness." *CLA Journal* 17 (1973).

Jackson, Kathryn. "LeRoi Jones and the New Black Writers of the Sixties." *Freedomways* 9 (1969).

James, C. L. R. *The Black Jacobins: Toussaint L'Ouverture and the San Domingo Revolution*. New York: Vintage, 1963.

———. *A History of Pan-African Revolt*. Washington, D.C.: Drum and Spear Press, 1969.

———. *Nkrumah and the Ghana Revolution*. Westport, Conn.: Lawrence Hill, 1977.

———. *Notes on Dialectics: Hegel, Marx, Lenin*. Westport, Conn.: Lawrence Hill, 1980.

Jennings, James. "America's New Urban Politics: Black Electorialism, Black Activism." *Radical America* 17-18 (1983-1984).

———. "Blacks and Progressive Politics." In Bush, Rod (ed.). *The New Black Vote: Politics and Power in Four American Cities*. San Francisco: Synthesis Publications, 1984.

Jones, LeRoi [Baraka, Imamu Amiri]. *Preface to a Twenty Volume Suicide Note*. New York: Totem Press, 1961.

———. *Blues People*. New York: William Morrow, 1963.

———. *Dutchman and the Slave: Two Plays*. New York: William Morrow, 1964.

———. *The System of Dante's Hell*. New York: Grove Press, 1965.

———. *Home: Social Essays*. New York: William Morrow, 1966.

———. *Tales*. New York: Grove Press, 1967.

———. *Black Fire*. New York: William Morrow, 1968.

———. *Black Magic: Sabotage, Target Study, Black Art*. Indianapolis: Bobbs-Merrill, 1969a.

———. "A Black Value System." *Black Scholar* 1 (1969b).

———. *It's Nation Time*. Chicago: Third World Press, 1970.

———. *Raise Race Rays Raze: Essays Since 1965.* New York: Random House, 1971.

———. (ed.). *African Congress.* New York: William Morrow, 1972a.

———. "Toward the Creation of Political Institutions for all African Peoples." *Black World* 21 (1972b).

———. *Afrikan Revolution.* Newark: Jihad Publishers, 1973.

———. "The Congress of Afrikan People: A Position Paper." *Black Scholar* 6 (1975a).

———. "The National Black Assembly and the Black Liberation Movement." *Black World* 24 (1975b).

———. "Why I Changed My Ideology: Black Nationalism and Socialist Revolution." *Black World* 24 (1975c).

———. *The Autobiography of LeRoi Jones/Amiri Baraka.* New York: Freundlich, 1984.

Jones, Major. *Black Awareness: A Theology of Hope.* Nashville: Abingdon Press, 1971.

———. *Christian Ethics for Black Theology.* Nashville: Abingdon Press, 1974.

Jones, William. *Is God a White Racist?* Garden City, N.Y.: Doubleday, 1973.

Kaiser, Ernest. "The Failure of William Styron." In Clarke, John Henrik (ed.). *Nat Turner: Ten Black Writers Respond.* Boston: Beacon Press, 1968.

———. (ed.). *A Freedomways Reader: Afro-America in the Seventies.* New York: International Publishers, 1976.

Karenga, Maulana. "Ideology and Struggle: Some Preliminary Notes." *Black Scholar* 6 (1975).

———. "Afro-American Nationalism: Beyond Mystification and Misconception." *Black Books Bulletin* 6 (1978).

———. *Introduction to Black Studies.* Inglewood, Calif.: Kawaida Publications, 1982a.

———. "The Crisis of Black Middle Class Leadership: A Critical Analysis." *Black Scholar* 13 (1982b).

———. "Jesse Jackson and the Presidential Campaign: The Invitation and the Oppositions to History." *Black Scholar* 15 (1984).

Kent, George. *Blackness and the Adventure of Western Culture.* Chicago: Third World Press, 1972.

Magubane, Bernard. *The Political Economy of Race and Class in South Africa.* New York: Monthly Review Press, 1980.

———. "The Political Economy of Racism and Imperialism in South Africa." *Journal of African Marxists* 1 (1981).

Major, Reginald. *Justice in the Round: The Trial of Angela Davis*. New York: Third Press, 1976.

Marable, Manning. *From The Grassroots: Social and Political Essays Towards Afro-American Liberation*. Boston: South End, 1980.

________. *Blackwater: Historical Studies in Race, Class Consciousness and Revolution*. Dayton, Ohio: Black Praxis, 1981a.

________. "The Military, Black People, and the Racist State: A History of Coercion." *Black Scholar* 12 (1981b).

________. "The Crisis of the Black Working Class: An Economic and Historical Analysis." *Science and Society* 46 (1982a).

________. "Reaganism, Racism and Reaction: Black Political Realignment in the 1980s." *Black Scholar* 13 (1982b).

________. *How Capitalism Underdeveloped Black America: Problems in Race, Political Economy and Society*. Boston: South End, 1983.

________. *Race, Reform and Rebellion: The Second Reconstruction in Black America; 1945-1982*. Jackson: University Press of Mississippi, 1984.

________. *Black American Politics: Volume I, Race, Politics and Power*. London: Verso, 1985.

Martin, Guy, and Young, Carlene. "The Paradox of Separate and Unequal: African Studies and Afro-American Studies." *Journal of Negro Education* 53 (1984).

McClean, Vernon, and Lyles, Lois. "The Survival of Afro-American Studies." *Chronicle of Higher Education* 30 (1985).

Mkalimoto, Ernie. "Dying from the Inside: The Decline of the League of Revolutionary Black Workers." In Cluster, Dick (ed.). *They Should Have Served That Cup of Coffee: Seven Radicals Remember the Sixties*. Boston: South End Press, 1979.

Morrison, Toni. *Sula*. New York: Alfred A. Knopf, 1976.

Nadelson, Regina. *Who is Angela Davis?* New York: Peter H. Wyden, 1972.

Nettleford, Rex. *Caribbean Cultural Identity: The Case of Jamaica*. Los Angeles: Center for Afro-American Studies, University of California-Los Angeles, 1980.

Ofari, Earl. *The Myth of Black Capitalism*. New York: Monthly Review Press, 1970.

________. *Let Your Motto Be Resistance: The Life and Thought of Henry Highland Garnet*. Boston: Beacon Press, 1972a.

________. "Marxism-Leninism-The Key to Black Liberation." *Black Scholar* 4 (1972b).

________. "Black Labor: Powerful Force for Liberation." *Black World* 22 (1973).

_______. "Black Activists and Nineteenth Century Radicalism." *Black Scholar* 5 (1974).

_______. "Independent Black Politics: An Old Idea." *Black Scholar* 15 (1984).

Parker, J. A. *Angela Davis: The Making of a Revolutionary*. New York: Arlington House, 1973.

Peoples College. *Introduction to Afro-American Studies*. Chicago: Peoples College Press, 1977.

Richardson, Marilyn. *Black Women and Religion: A Bibliography*. Boston: G. K. Hall, 1980.

Roberts, J. Deotis. *Liberation and Reconciliation: A Black Theology*. Philadelphia: Westminster Press, 1971.

_______. *A Black Political Theology*. Philadelphia: Westminster Press, 1974.

Robinson, Cedric J. *Black Marxism: The Making of the Black Radical Tradition*. London: Zed Press, 1983.

Rodgers-Rose, La Frances (ed.). *The Black Woman*. Beverly Hills, Calif.: Sage Publications, 1980.

Rodney, Walter. *The Groundings with My Brothers*. London: Bogle-L'Ouverture, 1969.

_______. *How Europe Underdeveloped Africa*. London: Bogle-L'Ouverture, 1972.

_______. *World War II and the Tanzanian Economy*. Ithaca, N.Y.: Africana Studies and Research Center, Cornell University, 1976.

_______. "The African Revolution." *Urgent Tasks* 12 (1981a).

_______. *A History of the Guyanese Working People*. Baltimore: Johns Hopkins University Press, 1981b.

_______. "People's Power, No Dictator." *Latin American Perspectives* 8 (1981c).

_______. *A History of the Upper Guinea Coast, 1545-1800*. New York: Monthly Review Press, 1982.

Salkey, Andrew (ed.). *Caribbean Folktales and Legends*. London: Bogle-L'Ouverture, 1980.

Smith, Barbara (ed.). *Home Girls: A Black Feminist Anthology*. New York: Kitchen Table: Women of Color Press, 1983.

Smith, David W. "Black Studies: A Survey of Models and Curricula." *Journal of Black Studies* 1 (1971).

Smith, Robert C. "Fanon and the Concept of Colonial Violence." *Black World* 22 (1973).

Smith, Mark. "A Response to Haki Madhubuti." *Black Scholar* 6 (1975).

Sollors, Werner. *Amiri Baraka/LeRoi Jones: The Quest for a "Populist Modernism"*. New York: Columbia University Press, 1978.

Spero, Sterling D., and Harris, Abram. *The Black Worker: The Negro and the Labor Movement*. New York: Columbia University Press, 1931.

Staples, Robert. "Tom Bradley's Defeat: The Impact of Racial Symbols on Political Campaigns." *Black Scholar* 13 (1982).

———. "Racial Ideology and Intellectual Racism: Blacks in Academia." *Black Scholar* 15 (1984).

Steady, Filomina Chioma (ed.). *The Black Woman Cross Culturally*. Cambridge, Mass.: Schenkman, 1981.

Stewart, James. "Book Review of Maulana Karenga's *An Introduction to Black Studies*." *Western Journal of Black Studies* 7 (1983).

———. "The Legacy of W.E.B. Du Bois for Contemporary Black Studies." *Journal of Negro Education* 53 (1984).

Thomas, Clive Y. *Dependency and Transformation*. New York: Monthly Review Press, 1974.

———. "The Non-Capitalist Path as Theory and Practice of Decolonization and Socialist Transformation." *Latin-American Perspectives* 5 (1977).

———. "On Formulating a Marxist Theory of Regional Integration." *Transition* 1 (1978).

———. "Socialist-Capitalist Economic Relations and the Struggle for a New International Economic Order." *Transition* 1 (1979).

———. *The Rise of the Authoritarian State in Peripheral Societies*. New York: Monthly Review Press, 1984.

Walden, Daniel. "Du Bois: Pioneer Reconstruction Historian." *Negro History Bulletin* 26 (1963).

Walker, Alice. *Revolutionary Petunias*. New York: Harcourt, Brace, Jovanovich, 1972.

———. *In Love and Trouble*. New York: Harcourt, Brace, Jovanovich, 1974.

———. *Meridian*. New York: Pocket Books, 1976.

———. *The Color Purple*. New York: Harcourt, Brace, Jovanovich, 1982.

Washington, Joseph. *Black Sects and Cults*. Garden City, N.Y.: Doubleday, 1972.

West, Cornel. *Prophesy Deliverance! An Afro-American Revolutionary Christianity*. Philadelphia: Westminster Press, 1982.

Williams, Ora. *American Black Women in the Arts and Social Sciences*. Metuchen, N.J.: Scarecrow Press, 1978.

Wilmore, Gayraud S. *Black Religion and Black Radicalism*. Garden City, N.Y.: Doubleday, 1973.

Wright, M. Frank. "The National Question: A Marxist Critique." *Black Scholar* 5 (1974).

________. "Frantz Fanon: His Work in Historical Perspective." *Black Scholar* 6 (1975).

3

PUERTO RICAN STUDIES: PROMPTINGS FOR THE ACADEMY AND THE LEFT

Frank Bonilla
Ricardo Campos
Juan Flores

> They want us to come into the colleges, learn a skill, learn to take orders, forget that we're Puerto Ricans and become instead carbon copies of white middle class "Americans." Our purpose in schools must be: 1. to learn a skill that will help us better understand the mechanical, economic and social workings of the system. 2. to learn about ourselves, our history both here and in Puerto Rico, our culture, our identity as a people. 3. to bring the services of the university to the community which is denied the knowledge behind those "ivy walls" because of jive requirements that are made to keep the majority of the people ignorant and make a minority of the people think they are together and can rule over others because they know more.
>
> Puerto Rican Student Union, 1969*

Couched as they were in the cadences of young people who had come on English and politics in the working class neighborhoods of New York City in the strident 1960s, early calls for Puerto Rican Studies such as this understandably met with indifference or amused tolerance if not with derision from within the academy. These were, after all, the voices of newcomers, street people, perhaps even interlopers on college campuses, most of them subway commuters or walk-ins straight from the ghettos and barrios, gradually encircling once-sheltered academic enclaves. The outrage and containing maneuvers

*Somos Puertorriqueños y Estamos Despertando, Unión Estudiantil Boricua (PRSU), from a proposed policy statement at the founding convention, December 1969.

would come later, as the seriousness and reach of these claims on the university and the broad-based community support that the students had mustered behind this project became clearer.

The barbarians stood well within the gates, clamoring for fundamental rearrangement in key institutions in whose making they had played no role and whose history and inner workings they only dimly comprehended. Ironically, students had on short acquaintance intuitively fastened on essential anomalies in the operation of higher schooling and the organization of university-based knowledge production. Since then, the patient articulation of these primary insights, through a many-sided effort extending into the present, has kept Puerto Rican Studies close to the center of much of the ferment generated by recent innovative left scholarship in the university.

A full account of those formative struggles and the subsequent diverse experiences in mounting Puerto Rican Studies, chiefly at the City University of New York, but also within a growing range of institutions scattered about the Northeast and Midwestern United States, cannot be undertaken here. Some minimal facts about the birth of those programs need to be mentioned and something of the context in which this occurred must be evoked. However, this chapter will focus on the substantial body of research that has been an integral accompaniment to the constitution of those programs, especially that part of the research effort that has adopted a critical stance toward the Puerto Rican experience and has drawn directly on Marxian concepts and methods.

Three points bear further emphasis as we get into that central theme. First, it is important to keep in mind that this teaching and research enterprise has been informed and driven at every stage by political contention in which the consciousness and participation of student and community leaders has provided the steadiest beacon. This is a strong assertion about a matter that is as often treated in a mechanical way on the left as it is trivialized in standard research handbooks. In the present instance these linkages have been far from problem-free, remain unevenly developed, and in the best of times have fallen well short of being fully realized. Because they remain fundamental anchorages and reference points for the whole Puerto Rican Studies endeavor, and Marxist social analysis generally, we feel it is indispensable to weave some comments on these relations into the review of research that follows.

Second, the particular ethnonational and class origins as well as the transdisciplinary nature of this enterprise have made the positioning of Puerto Rican Studies in some ways as problematic vis-à-vis what is being called here the "left academy" as within the academy at large. Carving out a space in the university for a new field or "interdiscipline" is simply not the same as working an alternative paradigm on the margin of fully institutionalized disciplinary domains. More to the point, working from within established fields leads left scholars along with others to continue to look to the most "advanced" social formations, institutions, and classes as embodiments of the most significant forces and processes now meriting scholarly attention. In particular, the experiences of small nations and "minorities" are generally taken as second or lesser order "contradictions" or as residual sidelights of earlier stages superseded by today's historical front-runners.

Finally, the very same class and ethnonational forces that bind Puerto Rican Studies to related quests for self-knowledge—Black, Chicano, Native American, Women's, and so-called Third World Studies—also act as a block to effective unity with them. Puerto Ricans, of course, have been as much at odds among themselves as have all such groups with respect to intellectual and political priorities and strategies. Beyond the more or less bureaucratic concerns of placement in the academy (Should we answer to the Dean of Humanities or to the Dean of Social Studies? Were we more akin to international area studies or to U.S. urban studies?) has lain the permanent concern with the unification and political projection of scholarship intended to stimulate emancipating thought and action.

TOWARD A NEW INSTITUTIONAL PRACTICE

In 1969 New York City's Board of Higher Education voted to give special priority to the development and funding of Black and Puerto Rican Studies. This decision coincided with the institution of an open admissions policy. The courageous move to open admissions, coupled with a tradition of free tuition, placed the City University of New York (CUNY) in the forefront of universities seeking to deal generously with new demands for access. During the six years that the new admissions initiative survived, Puerto Rican enrollments rose from 5,425 to 18,750. By 1973 seventeen CUNY colleges had Puerto Rican Studies programs or departments offering some 155 courses and enrolling well over 6,000 students (J. Nieves, 1978; Puerto Rican Studies Group, 1982:6). In that year CUNY established the Centro de Estudios Puertorriqueños, a research unit serving the entire university and operating initially from the Office of the Chancellor.

In almost every instance the initiation of these programs required concerted action by the newly arriving students, a relatively unseasoned Puerto Rican faculty also new to CUNY, and community supporters concerned with opening up opportunities for Puerto Rican youth and training committed leadership to staff a growing array of organizations. Where these supports were absent or feeble, Board of Higher Education directives had slight effect.

The contention at CUNY spilled over into other higher education institutions in the metropolitan area and beyond, to places as diverse as Columbia, Yale, and Princeton universities, as well as to units of both the New York and New Jersey state university systems. Events in Puerto Rico, where campus clashes between police and students led to fatalities in both 1970 and 1971, also cast their shadow over these distant confrontations. While more directly focused there on draft resistance and objections to ROTC programs on campus, it was the denial of rights in decisions to legally constituted student and faculty organisms by university administrators that exacerbated conflicts at the University of Puerto Rico. At issue at CUNY as well were not only the organization and placement of Puerto Rican programs along with their content and staffing, but more generically their governance. Students and ad hoc community organizations advanced claims over decisions in academic policy and administration that for the United States were unprecedented. The sweeping critique of the university that emerged from these often stormy negotiations came to center, as regards research, on two clusters of related practices. These were labeled by protesters as entrenched forms of academic free enterprise and "scientism" (Bonilla and Gonzalez, 1973).

Coming to the colleges fresh from the streets and ongoing community struggles, notably for the control of schools, students and community leaders at first looked to the university as a potential ally, as a sheltered site where learning and intellectual work vital to individual and community needs might be accomplished. At CUNY the announced commitments to a more generous admissions policy and Puerto Rican Studies fed these illusions. However, even there, the university's self-portrayal as an institution with critical and privileged functions in the creation and sharing of valued knowledge proved to be totally at odds with the bureaucratism, ritualism, secrecy, and arbitrariness shrouding almost all key decisions.

Emergent rationales in the drive for Puerto Rican Studies—which accented collective work and interests, consensus and broad sharing in decisions, and the broad inclusion of talents at many levels of development—clashed at once with the prevailing patterns of individualistic competition for positions and resources. Unperturbed by acknowledged ignorance of Puerto Rican realities and a record of past inaction and failure, administrators and established faculty fiercely resisted encroachments on their exclusive powers to define the parameters of all new undertakings. Nevertheless, a variety of sheltered spaces were won, where creative experiments with new modalities of academic management, instruction, group study, and the organization of research and its dissemination have taken place.

The aims of the Puerto Ricans in the forefront of this contention in the 1960s and 1970s were more modest though perhaps more fundamental than the simultaneous campaign by the left to deny the untrammeled use of the university to state and corporate power. The drive for ethnic studies generally was, in fact, overshadowed. Weightier contenders on the left and right saw assertions of ethnic interests as minor skirmishes in a more far-reaching struggle to bring the university's external transactions back into line with liberal traditions of intellectual independence, public accountability, and the free flow of academically produced knowledge.

In the mid-1980s—in the aftermath of a decade of fiscal crisis, government cutbacks, declining enrollments, and rampant conservatism—it will seem to many quixotic to imagine that any such lines of institutional demarcation can be redrawn. Universities, private and public, broadcast their readiness to shoulder the burden of creating made-to-order business environments wherever needed. Academic chairs, research centers, and entire departments of instruction are commodities marketed with the same verve and fanfare with which courses and programs are tailored to the tastes and convenience of prospective student clients. Thousands of academics find external bases for research and career advancement at centers unabashedly committed to the promotion of business perspectives and political interests. Corporate entities now maintain, often at public expense, a large array of higher education programs and institutions for the technical and political preparation and recharging of their own cadres. The reach of corporate and secret government monies and ideologies into the academy and their control over the activities they finance have probably attained a new peak (Saloma, 1984; Varrin and Kukich, 1985; Eurich, 1985; Norman, 1985).

The Marxist "cultural revolution" in the universities (Ollman and Vernoff, 1982:1) and the partial consolidation of ethnic studies over the last decade or so must be seen against this sobering backdrop. The small victories of Puerto Rican Studies have had little impact on the university as a whole, even in the unique circumstances at CUNY. But thousands of students and hundreds of young faculty and others in training for professions and related fields have had a glimpse of alternatives to the individualistic, competitive, and hierarchical habits and structures so deeply embedded in universities and the institutions with which they interlock. For a substantial core in a new generation of trained leadership, this has been a sustained and principled struggle now stretching over a good part of their lives. In contrast to the academic surge of Marxism, which has admittedly occurred in disconnection from any popular base, these efforts to prefigure and test new relations in producing and sharing knowledge have included the cultivation of working lifelines from the university to other sites where Puerto Ricans resist the pressures of class and national subordination. The importance of these experiences increases rather than diminishes as the conditions that originally ignited this movement reassert themselves and become more generalized (Puerto Rican Studies Group, 1982).

FRAMING A RESEARCH AGENDA

Throwing off passivity as learners also meant a rejection of the defeatist visions of Puerto Rican reality promulgated in academic research. The Puerto Rican Studies movement set out to contest any vision of the world that assumed or took for granted the inevitability or indefinite duration of the class and colonial relations so prominent in the Island's history and so visibly reproduced in the U.S. settings to which Puerto Ricans had gravitated. No longer, it was asserted, would Puerto Rican communities serve willy-nilly as passive objects of study. The motives of researchers and the desires and needs of the people themselves had to be considered. No matter how it was coupled to pragmatic or universalistic objectives, education or learning that did not see the attainment of full freedom and equality for Puerto Ricans as a vital and realistic goal was plainly wanting.

Yet not only the university as a whole but all the disciplines on which Puerto Rican Studies necessarily would draw—history, economics, sociology, anthropology, literature, psychology, pedagogy—were deeply implicated in the construction of that unacceptable vision of Puerto Ricans as an inferior, submissive people, trapped on the underside of relations from which there is no foreseeable exit. The problems were more grave than mere omission or neglect; they could not be remedied by simply turning attention to overlooked subject matters, by opening the way to training and research opportunities for a few Puerto Ricans, or by taking more seriously the needs of this new clientele. Facile formulas or slogans, however radical, would only add to the muddle. What did we in fact know about why the existing system of knowledge production had served us so poorly?

Over a period of many months of individual and group study and discussion, a broadly shared perspective on this complex of issues gradually took shape. This view was succinctly stated in the summary review of a three-day conference on Puerto Rican historiography at CUNY's Graduate Center in early 1974. It is important to note again that students and community activists, both Island and U.S. residents, joined academics in these deliberations.

> We have addressed two vital areas of Puerto Rican life—Puerto Rican culture and migration. The presentations dispute commonly held assumptions about Puerto Ricans and about the causes or significance of historical events; they also challenge the interpretations and at times the basis on which current social theories were established. . . . We hope to expose distortions of Puerto Rican reality that are so pervasive in the most common interpretations of social phenomena given by social scientists and to uncover the reasons for those distortions. We do not attribute these distortions to conscious malice or the personal inadequacies of individual investigators, but rather to a generalized ideological perspective that necessarily flows from the socio-economic base of this society, including the institutional biases that impair objective analysis.
>
> The importance of exposing those distortions relates to much more than an academic interest in objective facts. . . . It relates to the need for knowledge as an essential base on which to realize any transformation of society. . . . The confusing and fragmented pieces of information or false analysis so often passed along in educational institutions . . . serve to incapacitate movements for change by obfuscating goals and dissipating energies into strategies of accommodation and reforms (Centro, 1975:iv).

This was a quintessentially Marxian formulation, even though few who contributed to its articulation claimed sure knowledge of Marxist theory or method. The substantive focus on migration and culture, with a close fix on language, took initial inquiries on a path that has lastingly shaped research on the Puerto Rican condition. For Marxists who had a share in the enterprise, the challenge was clearly to demonstrate that the situational perspective of oppressed peoples in fact provides energies and effective leverage for the advancement of a scientific understanding of social processes and the raising of dialectical materialism to a genuinely liberating analytical resource.

TOWARD A POLITICAL ECONOMY OF MIGRATION

The major item on the new research agenda, explaining the presence of Puerto Ricans in the United States, sparked critical debate over matters of theory and daily living. The reigning theory of migration as a direct resultant of "push-pull" factors was manifestly inadequate for an analysis that needed to encompass the complex forms of repeated dislocations—emigration, periodic returns, explosive dispersal within the United States and sustained circulation—now commonly the experience of ever larger numbers of Puerto Rican workers. Indeed, the anchoring premise of this theory, which took as a given a chronic surplus population on the Island, was being brought seriously into question by the recent arrival of large numbers of immigrants to Puerto Rico, principally from Cuba and the Dominican Republic but ranging to other Latin American countries and the Middle East. These new realities posed a troubling conceptual dilemma that also baffled or angered other Puerto Ricans caught up in this relentless movement. What was to be made of the fact that eager homecomers, longing to pick up the threads of a cherished way of life, found themselves strangers and intruders in their own land? How in these circumstances were others, new to Island life, finding the economic accommodation that eluded the native born and their offspring? (History Task Force, 1979:8).

Along with this apparent anomaly in migration flows came another, still more puzzling intellectual challenge. The rapid modernization and industrialization of the Island via a massive influx of U.S. capital seemed to have successfully overcome the generalized problem of mass immiseration and devastation of national resources commonly associated with colonial exploitation. What could be more controversial and at odds with accepted understandings of imperialism than the image of a small tropical dependency saturated with industrial capital and the complacent recipient of federal outlays well exceeding total profits on external capitals? How could a tiny territory with a population of only 3 million and sheltering a full third of all direct U.S. investment in Latin America continue to generate growing masses of unemployed and persons dependent for their subsistence on welfare outlays from the metropolis? Had Puerto Ricans slyly managed to turn the tables on the colonizer, shifting the net flow of values toward the Island?

These untoward turns of events ran counter to all conventional lines of analysis, even those most imaginatively addressed to grasping new features in the contemporary workings of imperialism. What kind of colony is Puerto Rico? Economists in Puerto Rico (Gutiérrez, 1980; Villamil, 1976) have generally considered the fact of "dependency" on external capitals as the principal cause of the colony's economic malaise. The main problem, in this view, is that dependency has stunted or disarticulated the development of an export-oriented, industrialized society. Others have argued persuasively that activating domestic capital and anchoring industry in the local market would not alter the general tendency of capital to exert downward pressures on wages and to exclude growing numbers from unemployment (Pantojas, 1982). They point to the common elements in the contemporary crisis of capitalism manifest in advanced as well as highly dependent social formations as evidence of the underlying unity of the economic relations at work.

However, authors seeking to apply Marxian concepts and methods have also fallen short of an adequate account of the full range of socioeconomic forces and relations at work. Richard Weisskopf, for example, starts with the notion of the "extraction of surplus value" in identifying the particularities of imperialism in the colony. Yet, despite this theoretical point of departure, his analysis actually focuses on unequal exchange. His dominant concern with markets and exchange balances rather than relations of production brings him to denounce "economic leakages" (for example, profits repatriated to the United States) arising in the course of the introduction of an export-oriented industrialization process in a "small, open and densely populated economy" (Weisskopf, 1978:1).

Weisskopf clearly condemns the manifest failure of the Puerto Rican model of industrialization and sounds a warning alert to other Caribbean countries concerning this path of development. He fails to explain, however, a matter of crucial interest. How did the Island *come to be* a "surplus labor economy"? If historical origins are not kept clearly in view, labor surpluses tend to be treated as natural and permanent. As a result, projections of a viable path of economic development come to depend once again on the inclination and ability of local entrepreneurs and bureaucrats to diversify the economy, promote import substitution, and achieve more favorable terms of trade with the United States. The paradox inherent in all such prognoses is that they presuppose a continuation of the same relations of production that gave rise to the anomalies in the first place. Moreover, they fly in the face of powerful forces propelling a further internationalization of the Island and world economy and that decidedly constrain fresh assertions of national controls over capital.

The present condition of capitalism in the colony has also been approached on the basis of more directly articulated dualist understandings of the laws governing the movement of capital. James Dietz, for example, defines dependency as a "result of imperialist domination" of capital and its monopoly stage. "The monopoly capitalist system is not just capitalism as Marx analyzed it . . . it affects the 'laws' of motion and functioning of monopoly capitalist formations." In Puerto Rico, he argues, "capitalist social relations have become predominant, but the forces of production have developed to only a limited extent" (Dietz, 1979:19, 29). Evidence to the contrary is abundant. Puerto Rico today is saturated with capital of the highest organic composition; the Island's infrastructure (transportation, services, and communication) and labor force skills are unmatched in Latin America. The Island has passed rapidly through all phases of modern industrial development and presently manifests the basic configuration of an advanced service economy.

By the 1970s the development of the productive forces in the colony already made abundantly clear that the case of Puerto Rico runs directly counter to dependency theory, with its dualistic view of advanced centers as against underdeveloped peripheries. Precisely because Puerto Rico exhibits features of both worlds, and because Island economic activity is an integral part of the U.S. economy, it has become necessary to develop an analysis of modern imperialism that addresses these processes of economic convergence all along the capitalist chain.

Theoretical gaps in interpretations based on unequal exchange and dependency have been pointed up for more than a decade by other writers on the Puerto Rican economy. Rather than introducing new levels of analysis, however, these studies have tended to rest on claims to some degree of historical exceptionalism (Rúa, 1978; Owen and Sutcliffe, 1972). A variety of designations—the "privileged" colony, the "external-metropolitanized" colony, the "sui generis" colony—have been coined to express this singularity. These approaches not only give slight attention to migration as an integral dimension of the colonial relation but actually discard the possibility of establishing a common anchorage in theory for the Puerto Rican and other instances.

Exchanging People for Capitals

Study of the Puerto Rican case, coupling historical reconstruction with political economy, thus accentuates the need to analyze simultaneously the movement of capital and of labor power. A collective effort spanning more than a decade has brought home the need to treat capitalist development and working class migration as an inseparable totality, the two poles of capital as a single, integral social relation. Research at the Center for the Study of Puerto Rican Reality (CEREP) has made a valuable contribution in this connection. CEREP studies have not only brought to light events and processes neglected by earlier historians but have also set forth basic guidelines for a materialist approach to the reconstruction of the past, firmly grounded in the careful selection and use of primary sources. This group of researchers has substantially enlarged our understanding of the complex of forces that moved a small colony of Spain toward integration into world commodity markets and capitalist production (Quintero, 1974; García, 1974; Ramos Mattei, 1975).

The life of work, sacrifice, and resistance of slaves and agricultural day laborers during the critical period of the closing decades of the nineteenth century has been closely chronicled by other CEREP associates (Picó, 1979; Baralt, 1982). Other authors have put the role of immigration in the formation of the Island's social classes in proper perspective (Scarano, 1981). Recent studies have also called attention to the tradition of struggle and labor organization of Island women since the turn of the century (Azize, 1979). The participation of women in the heavily exploitative needle trades both in Puerto Rico and the United States has been of particular interest (Silvestrini, 1980; González, 1984; Vázquez et al., 1985). Though this remains a modest body of work, it now constitutes an indispensable point of departure for all those interested in tracing the historical processes that have shaped the emergence of capitalism in this Island variant.

The economic evolution of Puerto Rico and the migratory experience of the workers make up a common history that has passed through successive phases down to the present forms of multidirectional movement of capital and labor. The spatial relocation of workers in Puerto Rico must therefore be grasped in its historical progression through distinctive stages, rather than presupposing some natural or ahistorical condition of overpopulation. Puerto Rican history is characterized by successive and simultaneous situations of labor excess and shortage, depending in each case on the employment needs of the type of capital in operation. For migration patterns correspond not to the abundance or scarcity of workers but to the relative price of labor.

The work of the Centro de Estudios Puertorriqueños, beginning around 1975, has countered both dualistic and particularistic formulations, arguing that the basic concepts of Marxist political economy remain adequate to the task of explaining contemporary imperialism, including the apparent paradoxes of colonialism in Puerto Rico, as well as evolving patterns of migration to the United States. A return to Marx's original insights would focus attention once again on the class content rather than the more visible national contours of these relations. The main point in tracing the unequal circulation of values between nations, as Marx suggested, is to make note of the social classes that benefit from the process at any given stage. "The favoured country recovers more labour in exchange for less labour, although this difference, this excess, is pocketed, as in any exchange between labour and capital, by a certain class" (Marx, 1967:238). By examining the value circuits that connect classes with their counterparts in different nations, it becomes possible to explain how U.S. industrial capital can maintain its intensive exploitation of a diminishing active labor force while the metropolitan state allocates huge sums, extracted from its own working class, to sustain a growing proportion of the Island's population, thus preventing the total collapse of the system of value circulation.

From this standpoint it no longer appears paradoxical that at certain historical moments the flow of values channeled by the state to the colony exceeds profits on industrial capital. The contradiction, rather, is integral to the class dimensions of the imperialist relation itself. The same is true of the intensive capitalization of the Island accompanied by high worker unemployment. Once again it has to do with the common consequences of capitalist development at a moment when the advanced "center" is experiencing the very economic dislocations that had formerly appeared to pertain only to the periphery. The analysis of value circuits and cross-national class interests allows for a recognition of the convergence of economic relations and their social repercussions wherever capital defines the predominant social arrangement.

As basic as it might seem, it is this point—the basic unity of the movement of capital and labor—that has been consistently underplayed even by progressive authors who have turned to Marxism for theoretical and methodological bearings. The work of Manuel Maldonado Denis provides a notable example of this lapse. His *The Emigration Dialectic* goes a long way toward setting forth a coherent account of the Puerto Rican migration under U.S. imperialism. Maldonado Denis clearly approaches the migratory experience in its connection to the capitalist mode of production and the demands for labor emanating from the metropolitan center. While stressing the need for more refined study of the formation of an industrial reserve army and of relative overpopulation in the colony, Maldonado Denis repeatedly insists on identifying emigration as "one of the modalities of exile," that is, as a process forced by imperialism (Maldonado, Denis, 1980:19).

Fallen from view is the need to see migration as the necessary counterpart of the movement of capital. That is to say, as a social relation extended, broken, and renewed through redeployment of both workers and capitals. Contemporary Puerto Rico is not simply a country that expels exiles. Capitalist development has transformed the colony into a hub of multinational labor export and import, similar in this way to many of the world's capitalist centers. What is more, the ongoing circulation of Puerto Rican workers between the Island and a growing range of urban settings in the United States controverts the very notion of unilinear emigration and demonstrates clearly that Puerto Ricans are today caught up in a complex movement within a single labor market controlled by U.S.-based capitals. Rather than "forced exile" on a massive scale, Puerto Rican migration thus issues directly from the transnational fusion of capital markets. Just like formally sovereign nations and their regions (for example, Canada and Mexican border states), Puerto Rico now functions as a regional extension of U.S. capitalism.

The Migrant in the Metropolis

It is clear, therefore, that the 2 million Puerto Ricans living in different parts of the United States are here not simply because of the calculations of political decisionmakers or bureaucratic planners. Rather, like some groups of U.S. citizens or recently arrived immigrants, they form an integral part of a particular dynamic of labor incorporation and exclusion that forces them to subsist among the most impoverished sectors of the working class, with diminishing prospects of collective social advancement. It is important to recognize the regional diversity and class differentiation within and among those populations that are too simplistically referred to as the Puerto Rican, or Black, Chicano, Asian, or Native American "communities." The social cleavages evident in these communities indicate that any effort at collective regeneration and economic self-help needs to take into account the full range of differing and even conflicting interests at work in what is represented as a unified or homogeneous field of social relations. For it is clear that the bearers of these interests and the principal actors in such social relations share more economic ties and aspirations with their counterparts in other "communities" than with some members of their own national or ethnic groups. These cross-cutting lines of class and ethnic affiliation are key referents in explaining the complex pattern of labor absorption and expulsion experienced by Puerto Ricans, a national contingent comprised overwhelmingly of active and inactive wage-earners.

A decade ago, a government report entitled *Puerto Ricans in the United States: An Uncertain Future* (U.S. Commission on Civil Rights, 1976) documented convincingly the precarious economic situation facing Puerto Ricans a full generation after their massive arrival in the late 1940s and during the 1950s. Of still greater interest, it went on to predict in despairing tones an indefinite continuation of the tendencies observed. Among other bleak findings, the study stressed the discouraging fact that regardless of their knowledge of English, educational level, or length of residence, Puerto Ricans as a group had not only come no closer to the standard of living of white workers, but had seen a continuing erosion of their relative social position over the preceding decade.

What had befallen these U.S. citizens to prevent them from attaining the levels of social mobility achieved by other immigrant groups? Puerto Ricans have remained on the bottom rung of the social ladder in spite of the upward mobility of others. Instead of helping to propel Puerto Ricans higher in the social order, more recent arrivals seemed only to threaten them with further setbacks. These realities served to refute decisively the explanations of social ascension or "ethnic queue" leading to full participation in the American dream (Rodríguez, 1973).

Similar evidence militates against approaches based on the thesis of a "dual" labor market. The idea in this case is that two or more labor markets are operative in the United States, marked off from one another by factors of productivity, stability, and remuneration, and that the various ethnic groups ascend or stagnate along with their corresponding markets. It is clear that this position, like the notion of the ethnic queue, rests on the presumption of a constant and virtually limitless social mobility impelled by the force of entrepreneurial energy and by each collectivity's drive and investment in "human capital" (D. Gordon, 1972; Piore and Doeringer, 1971). The fact that the unemployment rate for a full generation of young Puerto Ricans is the same whether or not they have attained a high school diploma or mastered English points up the limitations of this line of analysis (Fabricant, 1975; Bonilla and Campos, 1985; Colón Warren 1984).

The main weakness here, even when account is taken of the structural and institutional dimensions of the problem, is the attempt to explain the social mechanisms governing unequal labor compensation largely on the basis of individual characteristics. Approaches to labor market segmentation that rely more directly on differences in productivity have also run into difficulties as new evidence is gathered. As some recent studies indicate, groups facing chronic social disadvantage seem to remain excluded from the better paying jobs independently of human capital and productivity attributes (Swinton, 1983; Harris, 1983; Galle et al., 1985).

Once again, basic Marxian concepts of labor segmentation remain pertinent to the present discussion. Clearly, employment levels in a capitalist society are determined by the supply of and demand for workers. But this very law of labor supply and demand is nothing other than the manifestation of capital as a social relation in which one component—personified in the owners of capital—regulates the demand for workers and, therefore, the level of employment or unemployment, according to the needs and resources of capital. Marx anticipated that as capitalism advanced, the imperatives of profit and accumulation and not the educational levels, skills, or entrepreneurial spirit of this or that racial, ethnic, or national group would basically define at any time the magnitude of labor reserves and differential wage rates (Marx, 1973:608-16). It is worth recalling that the world's first proletariat, engendered by British capital, was segmented according to nationality (*vide* notably the Irish), age, and sex, and that these differences corresponded to a scale of unequal occupations and wages. The history of capitalism has seen the systematic reproduction of such class segmentation with variations, of course, as to which groups occupy the various positions in the hierarchy.

Social inequality within the labor force may eventually be better understood as an integral feature of the interplay among diverse capitals operating in more or less lucrative processes of accumulation. What an adequate typification of distinctive forms of capitals and their particular trajectories and modes of transformation might look like has been sketched in a preliminary way (Bonilla and Campos, 1982). Such a theoretical perspective places in question the widespread perception of Puerto Ricans as permanent victims of prejudice and discrimination on the part of the bosses. Without denying the role of racial and national bias in employment practices, we would stress that such discrimination occurs within the social limits defined by the structure of the capital market and not independently, as a kind of autonomous force of its own. Even imagining a society free of prejudice, who would create all the additional, well-paying jobs so needed by Puerto Rican workers? Where would they come from?

The Research Mandate

The existence of a large array of social scientists calling for state intervention in the mechanisms of exchange between capital and labor indicates the blatant insufficiency of market relations for providing employment for all who wish to work. Proposals like those advanced by Lester Thurow aimed at generating "socialized sectors" overlook the many failed initiatives at previous stages, all of which signaled the limits of the state as an ultimate job provider (Thurow, 1981). But what is most important about these proposals is that they expose the inherent inability of capitalism to employ all available and willing workers, irrespective of race or ethnic origin. Only by recognizing this systemic incapacity are we able to develop an alternative sense of the labor market as it bears on Puerto Ricans in the United States.

This perspective guides us in studying the successive cyclical movement of capital and the corresponding demand for labor. Without implying that workers thereby become passive objects of an abstract historical process, we nevertheless would suggest that racial characteristics alone offer little by way of clues as to why groups like the Puerto Ricans occupy the least rewarding position in the labor force or are excluded altogether from the labor market. In our view, this social position and economic exclusion are to be seen as an integral part of the labor market itself, and not as temporary dislocations or distortions. Present-day research needs to probe how the particular historical circumstances of their incorporation into U.S. society has mired certain groups in conditions of underemployment or exclusion from labor.

This line of inquiry takes on importance as the ongoing "recomposition" of the U.S. economy clearly brings home the need for a serious stocktaking of the expectations and claims that groups like the Puerto Ricans may now make on the United States. An indispensable point of reference is a recognition of the tragic failure, as far as workers were concerned, of the development design that brought them to world attention. Puerto Rico stands today as an emblematic yet deeply troubled exemplar of what capitalism can accomplish within a colonial relation. The Island's rich yield for native and foreign investors contrasts with the fragility and limited scope of social gains for most of its people. Local experience seems to foreshadow the limits of capitalist expansion under present conditions rather than merely to lag behind the leading sectors in other regions of the U.S. and world economy. Proposals intended to overcome the very same social dislocations within the United States have already revealed their impotence to many in the colony or on the margin of stateside society who are consigned to repeated uprootings and restless circulation within an ever more restrictive and selective labor market. This particular historical placement confers on Puerto Rican workers an objective potential to grasp the underlying economic processes that condemn them along with most Native Americans, Chicanos, Asians, blacks, recent immigrants, women, and now even formerly privileged white males to poorly rewarded work, chronic exclusion from employment, dependency, and destitution.

No less instructive for Puerto Ricans and other similarly situated groups may be the understanding of ongoing change that stems from more advantaged perspectives. In contrast to Thurow, this vision of the future depicts the traumatizing adaptations now imposed on countless worker families as simply more promising vistas for social ascent in the U.S. tradition. What lies ahead, according to J. Fallows (1985:63), is a new chance to recapitulate the celebrated feats of our migrant forebears: "Something either about migration or about migrants promotes occupational success."

This is the encouraging word that Fallows extends to those now trapped on the underside of U.S. society. Ironically, it is once again Puerto Ricans, prototypical migrants, who are in the best position to demonstrate how far an unquestioning acceptance of migration may advance the fortunes of a disadvantaged collectivity. Constant repositioning has undoubtedly brought opportunities within reach of some and has created a community with a clearly demarcated and complex class configuration. For the mass of workers, however, migration has meant only a transfer or reconstitution of the system of relations that migration was to undo, while adding political and cultural complexities as problematic and disorienting as they were unforeseen.

MIGRATION AND CULTURE CHANGE

The constant repositioning of Puerto Ricans in relation to workers of other nationalities and ethnic backgrounds poses the issue of Puerto

Rican culture in ever more complex terms. "What does it mean to be a Puerto Rican?" This was a question raised frequently and pointedly in the early 1970s. What was to be made of the dramatic changes in Puerto Rican cultural experience as it mingled and merged with that of Dominicans and Cubans, Blacks and Italians, Chinese and Chicanos, in far-flung and highly diverse working-class settings? Why is is that, despite the disintegrating effects of demographic dispersal, wholesale cultural saturation, and the energetic leveling of native lifeways under the compelling sway of U.S. mass culture, Puerto Ricans still maintain and breathe new life and meaning into identifiable national legacies? What part do those enduring and reinvigorated traditions play in everyday efforts to unify with conjoining cultures, and to what extent does the deliberate or instinctive recourse to distinctive historical origins signal resistance to the forces of assimilation?

In response to these divergent and often conflicting tendencies, contemporary Puerto Rican culture stands as an example of both durability and resilience, steadfast continuity and momentous transformation, with both participants and interested onlookers left groping for lines of plausible explanation. The overall context remains one of colonial and class inequality, and the main cultural pressures, whether exclusion or incorporation, stem directly from that system of domination. But ongoing circulation between Puerto Rico and the United States, with increasingly diversified poles of origin and return, has made for an intricate cultural configuration defiant of any facile analysis or political strategy.

Marxist theory contributes crucially to our understanding of Puerto Rican culture, particularly as a framework for countering the multiple versions of cultural nationalism and ethnic pluralism that continue to color most discourse, both in the academy and on the left, both in Puerto Rico and in the United States. Accounting for the changes and continuities in Puerto Rican culture also represents a vital challenge to and within Marxism in the sense that it resists any pat resolution by way of internationalist or even antiimperialist formulas. For what is really at stake, underlying the pressing concerns of political tactics and the historical particularities of the Puerto Rican instance, is the need for a more embracing and dynamic concept of culture and cultural change. These broader implications of the debate over Puerto Rican culture thus project cogently into contemporary Marxist cultural theory at its most sensitive and suggestive points and at its furthest line of critical advance.

With its direct, abiding reference to a reality of colonial and class oppression, Puerto Rican culture is emphatically charged with practical significance; theorization about culture converges with a struggle *for* culture, and for a conception of culture that corresponds to and serves a people whose very life experience involves a struggle for social survival and self-definition. This organic unity of cultural theory and practice was conveyed with appropriate dramatic urgency by a leading member of the Young Lords Party in the early 1970s, and his words serve to set forth, in sharp dialectical interplay, the guiding contours of thinking about Puerto Rican culture in the United States today:

> Many of our people see that our culture has been destroyed by this country, and they react in an extreme way, and become cultural nationalists—whose sole purpose in life is to revive the culture of the Puerto Rican nation and to keep it alive, to speak only Spanish, to relate only to our music, to dress the way we dressed when we lived on the island. Now, our feeling is that nationalism is important—that we have to be proud of our nation, our history and our culture—but that pride alone is not gonna free us, the ability to speak Spanish fluently is not gonna stop landlords, the ability to run down Puerto Rican history like it was right from the beginning is not gonna stop the exploitation of our people on their jobs and everywhere else. We know that just going back to our culture is not gonna make it in and of itself. We have to use our culture as a revolutionary weapon to make ourselves stronger, to understand who we are, to understand where we come from, and therefore to be able to analyze correctly what we have to do in order to survive in this country (Abramson, 1971:68).

It is clear that culture ranked high on the agenda of Puerto Rican studies. It was a central priority in the political movement sparked by the Young Lords and other revolutionary groups of the time. No merely antiquarian or historicist interest lay behind this vigorous need to know; intellectual questioning arose from a vital quest for connections previously severed by historical distance and ideological distortion. Had the indigenous cultural legacy really become archaic with the decimation of the Island s original inhabitants, or are we not in some vital ways heirs to the Taino Indians, reluctant as they were to conform to an imposed and estranging cultural pressure? The textbooks typically presented the national culture as a felicitous syncretism of three racial strains—Indian, African, and Spanish—or actually, in the official version, as the grafting of non-European roots and branches onto the Hispanic trunk. But being caught up directly in the "American dilemma," our inextricable insertion in the intense racial antagonisms and interactions of U.S. society impelled us to question and rethink this standing paradigm. "Before they called me spic they called me nigger," another Young Lord recalled, as particular interest turned to African and Afro-Caribbean groundings of the inherited culture (Abramson, 1971:73).

Reconnecting has thus actually meant reconstructing, disaggregating, and recombining the relevant projections from the past in new terms. The revered pantheon of our culture's elite conspicuously did not include workers in the countryside (*jíbaros*) and former slaves, the dockworkers, cigarworkers, seamstresses, and washerwomen who represented the huge majority of the Puerto Rican population, our own parents and grandparents included. Getting at that popular culture has been a formidable task, particularly as it remained so thoroughly submerged by elitist and colonialist prejudice, or romanticized as so many quaint, folkloric trappings. It is precisely those omissions and demeaning views of the common people and their culture that have been extended to the whole nationality, giving origin to the self-defeating image of Puerto Ricans as a docile people.

While figuring as the title of one of the most influential Puerto Rican essays in recent years, first published in 1960, "El puertorriqueño dócil" (Marqués, 1972)—the image of Puerto Ricans as essentially docile, submissive, weak-willed and confused in national character—has permeated the writings of North American anthropologists and leading Puerto Rican thinkers of all political persuasions. Countering this entrenched intellectual stigmatization clearly involves more than mounting an argument for a "positive vision" of *puertorriqueñismo*, although Juan Angel Silén's book, *We the Puerto Rican People* (1971; translation of *Hacia una vision positiva del puertorriqueño*, 1970) was an important contribution to the debate along those lines. The real corrective could be found only in political action itself, and in a transformed relation between theoretical construction and social practice.

Moreover, to complicate matters, this effort has to be carried out in Spanish and English. Could we really claim cultural authenticity as Puerto Ricans when the primary means of communication was for many of us precisely the language that served as a crucial vehicle in the negation of our culture? The pivotal issue in the cultural struggle was the language question. Here was where emotional contention reached its highest pitch, and where the myths of cultural determination abounded. On this issue, again, U.S. social scientists and Puerto Rican culturalists concurred in detecting incontestable patterns of deculturation and assimilation. Both sides diagnosed the case as one of extreme cultural interference leading to anomie and the steady loss of conceptual powers.

Where to turn for answers to these troubling questions and responses to these destructive characterizations has been a challenge, with Marxism offering broad theoretical bearings and partial insights but no cohesive and directly pertinent body of explanation. The elements of a more satisfactory approach have been primarily derived from more or less spontaneous discussions among those active in various aspects of cultural activity. Long-term research on Puerto Rican language use, and critical reflection on the meaning of bilinguality and the social forces sustaining bilingualism, have also yielded valuable insights (Attinasi et al , 1983; Poplack, 1982; Padilla, 1979). Crucial new perspectives have above all found expression in cultural and artistic production itself, in the music, poetry, and pictorial work by contemporary Puerto Rican artists grappling for voices and images appropriate to this complex shifting cultural terrain.

Culture and National Consciousness

The resurgence of political and cultural consciousness among Puerto Ricans in the United States begins, as has often been the case, as anticolonial resistance and affirmation. Cultural nationalism and an orientation toward Island-based cultural traditions make for the major ideological response to recognized imperial domination and imposition. Yet reaching back to cultural traditions is a first step: Working-class consciousness intersects critically with this sense of national pride and defense of the threatened national culture, endorsing it forcefully, but in conditional, ironic terms. The class dimension allows for, and necessitates, a selective, realistic relation to the national background; at the same time, attention to national continuities provides concrete, historically grounded bearings within the multinational class struggle. These three aspects of cultural identification —nationalism, class analysis, and the integral reciprocal conditioning of the two—comprise the main thrusts in Marxist discussions of Puerto Rican culture and may thus help to structure a brief assessment of that debate as it now stands.

Emphasis on the colonial contradiction and the cultural impact of national oppression has been foremost in the formulation of a revolutionary theory of Puerto Rican culture. The simultaneous drive to assimilate and marginalize Puerto Rico and Puerto Ricans within the sweep of North American mass culture has engendered a long-standing response from the independence and socialist movements, whose intellectual leadership has sounded the frequent alarm of "cultural genocide" and the need for cohesive national resistance. Historically, this position extends back to the nineteenth-century patriotic movement as represented by Hostos and Betances, and beyond that to the earliest stirrings of opposition to Spanish colonial rule. In the twentieth century this nationalist tradition was carried forward by the spokesmen of the independence movement, notably José de Diego and Pedro Albizu Campos, and has gone to inform the varied non-Marxist "defenses" of the national culture, from Vicente Géigel Polanco, Antonio S. Pedreira, and René Marqués in earlier decades to more recent commentators (Seda, 1972; Fernández Mendez, 1970; Nieves Falcon, 1975). It represents, in other words, the central strain of the Puerto Rican intellectual tradition in its resistance to colonial status; as the examples indicate, it is a lineage that ranges widely in political and ideological perspective.

Though generally complementary to its antiimperialist impetus, the relation of Marxism to Puerto Rican cultural nationalism has been long and problematic. Traceable back to the beginnings of the workers' movement at the turn of the century, the intellectual encounter between Marxism and nationalism came to a head within the Puerto Rican Communist Party in the 1930s and 1940s (Andreu, 1951; Corretjer, 1972; Quintero, 1976; Campos and Flores, 1979). Only in recent decades, since the 1960s, have academically affiliated Marxist intellectuals come to address directly the question of Puerto Rican national culture, their interest spurred in large measure by the impact of industrialization and migration and the cultural reality of Puerto Ricans in the United States. The most prominent of these writers, in fact, such as Manuel Maldonado Denis, Juan Angel Silén, José Luis González, and James Blaut, developed their analyses of Puerto Rican culture in relation to and even as participants in Puerto Rican studies programs, and their works have served as the major texts for radically inclined instructors and students of the Puerto Rican experience.

As Marxists, writers like Maldonado Denis and José Luis González propose to interpret Puerto Rican culture as expressive of political and economic realities, and each has contributed significantly to an understanding of the cultural and ideological workings of imperialism (Maldonado Denis, 1976; 1980; J. González, 1980). Though in differing ways, they would both present the formation of the national culture and "consciousness" in relation to social production and the political motives and alignments of classes and class fractions. Both have recognized the need to account for the migration and the cultural situation of Puerto Ricans in the United States as an integral part of that historical experience.

What characterizes both of these influential writers, in remarkably similar ways despite the many differences between them, is their tendency to shift from a class to a national and ethnic frame of analysis. In key works of cultural interpretation, each begins with a motto from Marxism—Maldonado Denis from *The German Ideology* and González from Lenin's "Critical Remarks on the National Question"—asserting the analytical and historical primacy of class relations, only to hinge their main line of argument on factors of national contention and racial syncretism. Despite their programmatic allegiance to Marxist theory, the overbearing fact of colonial conquest in the national history seems effectively to divert critical attention away from the material, class grounding of cultural and political struggle. In each case, Marxism veers off into a socialist-oriented version of cultural nationalism, with little sustained discussion of the Puerto Rican working class and its constitutive role in the national history.

These shortcomings are particularly evident in their treatment of Puerto Rican culture and identity in the United States. Maldonado Denis, basing his analysis on a sense of two monolithically opposed national cultures and *Weltanschauungen*, considers the emigrant Puerto Ricans to be undergoing a ruthless process of cultural deracination and assimilation to North American values and lifeways, most conspicuously in their increasing use of English. Though he frames his book on *The Emigration Dialectic* in Marxist and strongly antiimperialist terms, when it comes to the Nuyoricans he relies on lengthy quotes from *Requiem por una cultura* (Seda, 1972) to bemoan this tragic case of "cultural genocide" and the supposed "lumpenization" of Puerto Ricans in U.S. ghettos. It is ironic that Maldonado Denis is also associated with the "divided nation" theory, which maintains that Puerto Ricans in the United States are inextricably part of the Puerto Rican nation, for here he concludes that they are to be regarded as an ethnic group or, at most, an oppressed minority along with other "nonwhites." This time Marxism collapses into cultural pluralism, with the model of social analysis drawn explicitly from *Assimilation in American Life* (M. Gordon, 1964).

José Luis González is less schematic and more patently circumspect and sympathetic in his views, especially in his many memorable stories about Puerto Rican life in New York. He brings out the working-class qualities of that experience and is sensitive to the potent personal and collective force of the national culture among the emigrant population, however remote and symbolical. But here too the elegiac tone prevails, with little other sense of cultural transformation than that of loss and imposition. Puerto Ricans are viewed in virtual isolation from other groups in the U.S. working class, and are thus left suspended between a uniformly hostile social environment and an ingenuous nostalgia for the Island heritage. The dynamic of class struggle and of national divisions and alliances within the working class goes unheeded. In fact, in his widely discussed work on Puerto Rican cultural history, *El país de cuatro pisos* (1980), González makes no mention of the Puerto Rican community in the United States nor of the cultural impact of return migration. His strident, sometimes shrill, ideological critique of nationalism has not made him any more attentive to the traditions of popular and working-class culture, nor to a dialectical concept of cultural change. In the face of such theoretical lapses, Puerto Ricans are again confounded with a sense of irretrievable loss and exclusion precisely where they turn most eagerly for intimations of recovery, continuity, and renewal. González's mechanical construct of Puerto Rican history, however innovative and progressive in conception, fails to address those pressing existential questions posed by people intent on situating themselves within bewildering, contradictory and intellectually uncharted cultural circumstances (Flores, 1984).

More vigorously and consistently than Maldonado Denis or González, the North American Marxist James Blaut has sought to interpret Puerto Rican history, including the position of Puerto Ricans in the United States, by drawing heavily on Leninist theory of imperialism and national oppression. A spokesman of the Puerto Rican Socialist Party, Blaut has been a vocal proponent of the "divided nation" thesis, rejecting the idea that Puerto Ricans in the United States are to be classified as "merely a 'national minority'—an ethnic subdivision of a different nation, the United States" (Blaut, 1977:35). It is not possible to take up Blaut's position at length—which is that emigrant Puerto Ricans categorically "belong to the Puerto Rican nation"—but the choice of words cited, especially "merely" and "ethnic subdivision," is revealing in its own right. In his programmatic essay ("Are Puerto Ricans a National Minority?") just cited, Blaut opens his treatment of the Puerto Rican "national question" with an implicit value judgment: Puerto Ricans are somehow of lesser stature if they are "merely" a "national minority." In fact the very idea of "national minority" is associated by Blaut with "the old idea of the melting pot, or at least . . . its liberal variant." If a group is not seen as an integral part of its nation of origin it is automatically relegated to the status of "ethnic subdivision." In this view, such important mediating concepts as national minority and nationality described by Lenin are not Marxist but assimilationist. It is interesting, too, that for the geographer Blaut, territorial attachment and change play such an inessential role in the fixing of national identity.

The strength of Blaut's position is its staunch antiassimilationism and, beyond that, its outright rejection of cultural pluralist theory with its insistent theme of the desirability or inevitability of cultural integration. By highlighting the Puerto Rican case he meets liberal U.S. sociology head-on. When he is less caught up in doctrinal polemics, as in his essays in *Antipode*, Blaut moves much closer to a lively, dialectical approach to Puerto Rican culture in the United States. Going beyond Robert Blauner's *Racial Oppression in America* and the theory of "internal colonialism," Blaut, in his *Antipode* article "Assimilation Versus Ghettoization," gives full play to the multinational, class dynamic that is transforming, but not necessarily assimilating, Puerto Rican culture in the U.S. setting (Blauner, 1972; Blaut, 1983). Particular attention is paid to the strong cultural interaction between Puerto Ricans and other oppressed nationalities—what he calls "the partial growing-together of the cultures of ghettoized communities." Turning from the negative, pathological imagery of deculturation and forced Americanization, this process is seen as engendering a "healthy interfertilization of cultures, the effluorescence of new creative forms in painting, poetry, music, and the like, and the linking-up of struggles" (Blaut, 1983:39).

While roundly discarding the reigning paradigms of assimilation and pluralist theory, Blaut leaves us with the unsatisfactory notion of "ghettoization." His intention, of course, is to place full stress on the class and colonial dimensions of cultural subordination, and to controvert the relativistic, ultimately symbolical conceptualization of ethnic identity. Despite its progressive intent and radical ring, however, talk of "ghetto culture" smacks unmistakably of sociological theories of marginality and subculture, and even calls to mind Oscar Lewis's infamous "culture of poverty" (Lewis, 1966). With all his appeal to the Puerto Ricans' perennial "will to national existence," Blaut ends by effectively disengaging Puerto Rican culture in the United States from its national and international ties, and deriving its decisive characteristics from the immediate socioeconomic environment, the "ghetto." Gone are any solid class and anticolonial coordinates of cultural analysis and any coherent sense of revolutionary strategy.

Culture in the New World Order

Arriving at a more creative Marxist understanding of Puerto Rican culture will require a clean break with all traces of cultural nationalism and ethnic pluralism, both of which project Puerto Ricans into a defensive, if not defenseless, cultural syndrome. The national culture needs to be comprehended in its totality, not in the manner typical of liberal social science, which accedes to the ideological enthronement of the culture of particular segments as the highest expression of the culture as a whole (see Mintz, 1966). But totality does not imply seamless unity, much less harmony: The national culture in all stages of its formation is comprised of two constellations of essentially contradictory cultures, one dominant and the other subordinate. Against the "general" national culture of the elites arise the elements of an alternative culture among the popular classes. With this internal interaction clearly in view, and particularly with an active concept of popular culture, it becomes possible to recognize Puerto Rican cultural experience in the United States as at once a continuity and a break with the historically formed culture of the Puerto Rican nation.

Rather than theoretical dead ends like "cultural genocide," "internal colonialism," or "ghettoization," Marxism suggests a process of internationalization, understanding, of course, as Lenin insisted to his Bundist adversaries, that "international does not mean non-national. Nobody said that it was" (Lenin, 1968). The most pronounced movement of fusion and interaction between Puerto Rican and North American cultures in the U.S. setting is at the level of popular culture, with workers of other nationalities facing cognate forms of class and colonial oppression. The binding element in this case is not violence or inequality but the compelling force of historical circumstance under advanced capitalism. The manifest capacity of Puerto Ricans to resist assimilation and mold cultural change to surviving collective interests and identities draws its strength not only from national traditions but, as has been noted, from active engagement in the parallel struggles of similarly situated peoples. It is this kind of cultural convergence, often mistaken for assimilation or haphazard syncretism, that seems to prefigure the progressive cross-national solidarity and exchanges envisioned by Marx and Lenin.

In various writings on Puerto Rican culture, researchers from the Centro de Estudios Puertorriqueños have sought to articulate some of these perspectives. An initial compilation of working papers (Centro, 1976) constituted a first attempt to associate Marxist concepts with major lines of Puerto Rican cultural interpretation. An extended critique of *Insularismo* (Pedreira, 1973, first published in 1934) exposes the class and Eurocentric biases of that classic work of national self-definition and proposes an alternative reading of Puerto Rican cultural history in light of the new social contexts introduced by industrialization and mass migration (Flores, 1979). Similar attempts at historical reinterpretation are evident in a growing body of work by social scientists and cultural critics on the Island (Quintero, 1983; Lauria, 1964; 1980; Díaz Quinoñes, 1982; Picó, 1983; Ramírez, 1976).

Another Centro paper, "Migración y cultura nacional puertorriquena: perspectivas proletarias," attempts to dramatize the class division in the national culture with the emergence of proletarian consciousness in the early years of the century, and then to trace this "popular" sense of nationality to the cultural production of Puerto Ricans in the United States (Campos and Flores, 1979). Abundant reference is made here and in other works to Bernardo Vega and Jesús Colón, working-class "pioneers" of the Puerto Rican migration whose memoirs recounting decades of life in New York offer remarkably clear, Marxist assessments of that experience (Andreu, 1984; Colón, 1982). In a range of essays we have focused more closely on the linguistic, artistic, and ethnic-racial reality of the present "Nuyorican" generation (Cortés, Falcón, and Flores, 1976; Flores, Pedraza, and Attinasi, 1981), drawing on significant insights from a wide range of community informants and active poets, musicians, and painters whose expressive work embodies and enunciates these perspectives.

A guiding theoretical aim of this work has been to activate the national and class determinants of cultural life, not as contrasting pressures leading to collective confusion but as complementary constituents of emergent cultural possibilities. Multinational cultural convergence along class lines need not mean submission in an ethnic melting pot, nor does the upholding of national roots necessarily involve a separatist weakening of class bonds and the uncritical cultivation of waning cultural traditions. As our initial quote from the leader of the Young Lords Party indicates, there is a second horizon of national affirmation instrumental to a revolutionary Puerto Rican culture, a selective, critical affirmation based on the needs and dynamics of the class struggle. "We know that going back to our culture is not gonna make it in and of itself," he said. "We have to use our culture as a revolutionary weapon to make ourselves stronger. . . ." In much the same spirit Marx spoke of revolutionary cultural consciousness, and his words from the beginning of *The 18th Brumaire* (1963:15) seem strikingly apt in reference to the critical cultural situation of Puerto Ricans in the United States:

> Men make their own history, but they make it not just as they please; they do not make it under circumstances chosen by themselves, but under circumstances directly encountered, given and transmitted from the past. . . . And just when they seem engaged in revolutionising themselves and things, in creating something that has not yet existed, precisely in such periods of revolutionary crisis they anxiously conjure up the spirits of the past to their service and borrow from them names, battle cries and costumes in order to present the new scene of world history in this time honoured disguise and this borrowed language.

The Continuing Struggle

Faced with an uncertain future, or rather with a future of economic and political uncertainty, Puerto Ricans in the United States maintain strong, active bonds with the cultural past, constantly reactivating those national and popular traditions and pressing them into service under changing life conditions. This historical conjuring, this replenishing and reconstitution of inherited expressive possibilities, is directed not just against the impinging national standard of U.S. culture. The invoked disguises and rekindled spirits are also guards against the homogenization process itself, sources of resistance to the leveling, melding pressure of labor and mass culture in its contemporary transnational form. What is upheld is not only a particular national history, or the particularities of a given historical legacy, but the power of recall, the right to memory, the defiance of the logic of standardization.

Viewed in these terms, Puerto Rican culture exemplifies with special clarity the locus of cultural struggle identified in recent Marxist theory. The emphasis on historically rooted "particularism" as the base of popular cultural alternatives, long of central concern to artists and intellectuals in Third World contexts, is taking on increasing importance among Marxist thinkers in Europe and the United States. Raymond Williams repeatedly refers to the force of that opposition to the dominant culture of late capitalism which comes from "incompletely assimilated or still actively hostile minority groups who have been incorporated within the nation-state" (Williams, 1984: 183). Over against the socially atomizing and massifying pressures of the transnational culture of consumption, Williams (p. 196) points to the persistence of "solid and mutually loyal communities . . . lived and formed identities, whether of a settled kind, if available, or of a possible kind, where dislocation and relocation require new formation." Similar conclusions, though with reference to the United States, are advanced in *Accumulation Crisis* (O'Connor, 1984). Moving "beyond neo-individualism" involves a conscious recourse to those regionally, ethnically, and nationally defined communal movements, especially those assuming an antichauvinist and antisexist character. Again it is the particularism, the historically constituted rootedness of such collectivities that lend them greater cultural cogency than that of a generalized "class" or "left" perspective.

The centrality of language to Puerto Rican cultural experience also contributes to its pertinence to current revolutionary analysis. Which language is "borrowed," to return to Marx's phrase, by Puerto Ricans in the process of cultural affirmation, and which is authentic to their social circumstances? The complexities of this issue and its weighty policy implications are, of course, best probed on the basis of practical research, as in some of the work on the "logic of nonstandard English," bilingualism and code-switching (Labov, 1970; Sankoff and Poplack, 1980). The most promising line of Marxist thinking on this intricate problem of language contact in its political dimensions focuses on the historical struggle between imposed language standards and persisting vernaculars as the crystallization of cultural and political contention in Europe (Bourdieu, 1982). In formulating an "economy of linguistic exchanges," this work provides the kind of flexible and creative framework necessary for a dialectical understanding of the linguistic and cultural reality of groups like the Puerto Ricans in the United States.

Bourdieu's sensitive and thoughtful treatment of the "force of representation," that is, the leveling power of capitalist ideology as embodied in a multitude of cultural expressions, makes it clear how literacy and its attendant cultural norms may function as major obstacles to social advance for oppressed groups. The direct links of language and literacy to educational success and failure bring such matters centrally into the community's struggles for schooling that is more responsive to its conditions and aspirations (Bennett and Pedraza, 1984).

The need for intellectual rigor in probing for the meaning of economic and cultural transformations now under way points up the most significant challenge of Puerto Rican Studies to academic as well as "left" approaches to social experience. For new knowledge stems not only from taking account of countervailing tendencies but from those alternative tendencies themselves; the current human crisis of capitalist society can be understood only from the perspective of "those to whom in effect all this has been done" (Williams, 1984:187). The universalist claims to "objectivity" on the matter of ethnic subordination, both economic and cultural, still prevails in academic discourse, whether traditional or on the left. Only an "organic" analysis, which draws its dynamic from the movements of the oppressed groups themselves, can fully address the theoretical limitations of cultural pluralism in all its variants and guises, while pinpointing the roots of ethnic inequality and contention in the capitalist relation itself (Muga, 1984).

Some circumspection and a keen anticipatory sense are needed to recognize that a focused and partisan approach is not necessarily a partial one, and that the "marginal" or "peripheral" may harbor key intimations about the future of life under capitalism at its political and cultural "center." A totalizing intellectual project or political strategy must reckon with and never underestimate the ways in which the problematic of small nations and dispersed peoples can illuminate the contradictions of the whole system. What has been an "uncertain future" for Puerto Ricans is now becoming so for people at all points in the capitalist hierarchy.

Such are some of the theoretical insights to be gained from collective, interdisciplinary work carried on in close association with the people. For it is the community itself, its political activists and cultural workers, its institutions and course of everyday life, that give most vibrant expression to new social possibilities. With their history of unrelenting colonial oppression, and in the face of a uniformly disadvantageous present, Puerto Ricans are indeed in the process of "revolutionizing themselves and things, in creating something that has not yet existed." One of the young Nuyorican poets (Laviera, 1985:94) voices his awareness of this radical, innovative direction of his people's life and culture when he writes:

we gave birth to a new generation
AmeRícan, broader than lost gold
never touched, hidden inside the
puerto rican mountains.

AmeRícan, across forth and across back
back across and forth back
forth across and back and forth
our trips are walking bridges!

it all dissolved into itself, the attempt
was truly made, the attempt was truly
absorbed, digested, we spit out
the poison, we spit out the malice,
we stand, affirmative in action,
to reproduce a broader answer to the
marginality that gobbled us up abruptly!

BIBLIOGRAPHY

Abramson, Michael. *Palante: The Young Lords Party*. New York: McGraw-Hill, 1971.

Andreu Iglesias, César. *Independencia y socialismo*. San Juan: Librería Estrella Roja, 1951.

———. *Memoirs of Bernardo Vega*. New York: Monthly Review Press, 1984.

Attinasi, John, Pedraza, Pedro, Jr., Poplack, Shana, and Pousada, Alicia. "Intergenerational Perspectives on Bilingualism: From Community to Classroom." NIE Report No. NIE G-780091, 1983.

Azize, Yamila. *Luchas de la mujer en Puerto Rico 1898-1919*. Santurce: Graficor, 1979.

Baralt, Guillermo. *Esclavos rebeldes: conspiraciones y sublevaciones de esclavos en Puerto Rico, 1795-1873*. Río Piedras: Huracán, 1982.

Bennett, Adrian, and Pedraza, Pedro, Jr. "Discourse, Consciousness and Literacy in a Puerto Rican Neighborhood." In Kramarae, C., Schulz, N., and O'Barr, M. (eds.). *Language and Power*. Beverly Hills, Calif.: Sage, 1984.

Blauner, Robert. *Racial Oppression in America*. New York: Harper and Row, 1972.

Blaut, James. "Are Puerto Ricans a National Minority?" *Monthly Review* 29:1 (1977).

———. "Assimilation Versus Ghettoization." *Antipode* 15 (1983).

Bonilla, Frank. "Remarks Presented on Behalf of the Centro Collective." First Minority Planning Conference on the Theme, "The New Imperative: Coalition of the Dispossessed." Indiana University Northwest, 1974.

———. "Puerto Rican Studies and the Interdisciplinary Approach." Presentation at a Conference, "Renaissance of Puerto Rican Studies: An Agenda for the Eighties." New York: Brooklyn College, CUNY, 1981.

Bonilla, Frank, and Campos, Ricardo. "Imperialist Initiatives and the Puerto Rican Workers: From Foraker to Reagan." *Contemporary Marxism* 5 (1982).

———. "Evolving Patterns of Puerto Rican Migration." In Sanderson, S. (ed.). *The Americas in the New International Division of Labor*. New York: Holmes and Meier, 1985.

Bonilla, Frank, and González, Emilio. "New Knowing, New Practice: Puerto Rican Studies." In Bonilla, F., and Girling, R. (eds.). *Structures of Dependency*. Stanford, Calif.: Institute of Political Studies, Stanford University, 1973.

Bourdieu, Pierre. *Ce que parler veut dire*. Paris: Fayard, 1982.

Campos, Ricardo, and Flores, Juan. "Migración y cultura nacional puertorriqueña: Perspectivas proletarias." In *Puerto Rico: Identidad nacional y clases sociales*. Río Piedras: Huracán, 1979.

Centro de Estudios Puertorriqueños, CUNY. *Taller de migración. Conferencia de Historiografía, abril, 1974*. New York: 1975.

———. *Los Puertorriqueños y la Cultura. Conferencia de Historiografía, abril, 1974*. New York: 1976.

Colón, Jesús. *A Puerto Rican in New York*. New York: International Publishers, 1982.

Colón Warren, Alicia. "Competition, Segregation, and Succession of Minority and White Women in the Middle Atlantic Region's Central Cities Labor Markets, 1960-1970." Unpublished Ph.D. dissertation, Department of Sociology and Anthropology, Fordham University, 1984.

Corretjer, Juan Antonio. *Albizu Campos: El líder de la desesperación*. Guaynabo, 1972.

Cortés, Félix, Falcón, Angel, and Flores, Juan. "The Cultural Expression of Puerto Ricans in New York." *Latin American Perspectives* 3:3 (1976).

Díaz Quiñones, Arcadio. *El almuerzo en la hierba*. Río Piedras: Huracán, 1982.

Dietz, James. "Imperialism and Underdevelopment: A Theoretical Perspective and a Case Study of Puerto Rico." *The Review of Radical Political Economics* 2:4 (1979).

Eurich, Nell. *Corporate Classrooms: The Learning Business*. Princeton, N.J.: Princeton University Press, 1985.

Fabricant, Ruth Lowell. *The Labor Market in New York City. A Study of Jobs and Low Income Area Workers in 1970*. New York: Department of Social Services, 1975.

Fallows, James. "The Changing Economic Landscape." *The Atlantic* 255:3 (1985).

Fernández Méndez, Eugenio. *La identidad y la cultura*. San Juan: Instituto de Cultura Puertorriqueña, 1970.

Flores, Juan. *Insularismo e ideología burguesa*. Río Piedras: Huracán, 1979.

———. "The Puerto Rico that José Luis González Built: Comments on Cultural History." *Latin American Perspectives* 11:3 (1984).

Flores, Juan, Pedraza, Pedro, Jr., and Attinasi, John. "La Carreta Made a U-turn: Puerto Rican Language and Culture in the United States." *Daedalus* 110:2 (1981).

Galle, D. K., Wiswell, C. H., and Bun, J. A. "Racial Mix and Industrial Productivity." *American Sociological Review* 50 (1985).

García, Gervasio. *La economía natural colonial de Puerto Rico en el siglo XIX*. Río Piedras: CEREP, 1974.

González, José Luis. *El país de cuatro pisos y otros ensayos*. Río Piedras: Huracan, 1980.

González, Lydia Milagros. "La olvidada historia de la industria de la aguja en Puerto Rico." New York: Centro de Estudios Puertorriqueños, Hunter College, CUNY, 1984.

Gordon, David. *Theories of Poverty and Underdevelopment*. Lexington, Mass.: D. C. Heath, 1972.

Gordon, Milton. *Assimilation in American Life*. New York: Oxford University Press, 1964.

Gutiérrez, Elías. *The Transfer Economy of Puerto Rico: Toward an Urban Ghetto?* University of Puerto Rico, Graduate Planning School, 1980.

Harris, Donald. "Economic Growth, Structural Change, and the Relative Income States of Blacks in the U.S. Economy, 1947-78." *The Review of Black Political Economy* 12:3 (1983).

History Task Force, Centro de Estudios Puertorriqueños. *Labor Migration Under Capitalism: The Puerto Rican Experience*. New York: Monthly Review Press, 1979.

Institute of Puerto Rican Studies. *A New Look at the Puerto Ricans and Their Society*. New York, Brooklyn College, CUNY, 1971.

Labov, William. "The Logic of Non-Standard English." In Kampf, Louis, and Lauter, Paul (eds.). *The Politics of Literature*. New York: Pantheon, 1970.

Lauria, Antonio. "'Respeto,' 'Relajo,' and Interpersonal Relations in Puerto Rico." *Anthropological Quarterly* 37:2 (1964).

———. "Reflexiones sobre la cuestión cultural en Puerto Rico." In Ramírez, R., and Serra, Wenceslao (eds.). *Crisis y crítica de las ciencias sociales en Puerto Rico*. Río Piedras: Centro de Investigaciones Sociales, 1980.

Laviera, Tato. *AmeRícan*. Houston: *Arte Público Press*, 1985.

Lenin, V. I. *National Liberation, Socialism and Imperialism*. New York: International Publishers, 1968.

Lewis, Oscar. *La Vida: A Puerto Rican Family in the Culture of Poverty*. New York: Random House, 1966.

Maldonado Denis, Manuel. *Puerto Rico y Estados Unidos: Emigración y colonialismo*. Mexico City: Siglo XXI, 1976.

________. *The Emigration Dialectic*. New York: International Publishers, 1980.

Marqués, René. *Ensayos (1953-1971)*. Barcelona: Editorial Antillana, 1972.

________. *The Docile Puerto Rican*. Philadelphia: Temple University Press, 1976.

Marx, Karl. *The 18th Brumaire of Luis Bonaparte*. New York: International Press, 1963.

________. *Capital* Vol. III. New York: International Publishers, 1967.

________. *Grundrisse*. New York: Vintage Books, 1973.

Mintz, Sydney. *Puerto Rico: An Essay in the Definition of a National Culture*. Washington, D.C.: Commission on the Status of Puerto Rico, 1966.

Muga, David. "Academic Sub-Cultural Theory and the Problematic of Ethnicity: a Tentative Critique." *Journal of Ethnic Studies* 1 (1984).

Nieves Falcón, Luis. *El emigrante puertorriqueño*. Río Piedras: Editorial Edil, 1975.

Nieves, Josephine. *Puerto Ricans in Higher Education*. New York: Centro de Estudios Puertorriqueños, CUNY, 1978.

Norman, Colin. "Pentagon Seeks to Build Bridges to Academe." *Science* 228 (1985).

O'Connor, James. *Accumulation Crisis*. New York: Basil Blackwell, 1984.

Ollman, Bertell, and Vernoff, Edward. *The Left Academy: Marxist Scholarship on American Campuses*. [Vol. I.] New York: McGraw-Hill, 1982.

Owen, R., and Sutcliffe, B. *Studies in the Theory of Imperialism*. London: Longman, 1972.

Padilla, Raymond V. *Ethnoperspectives in Bilingual Education Research: Bilingual Education and Public Policy in the United States*. Ypsilanti: Eastern Michigan University, 1979.

Pantojas, Emilio. "Reflexiones críticas en torno al uso del concepto de dependencia como categoría explicativa en el análisis del proceso de desarrollo en Puerto Rico." *Homines* 6:2 (1982).

Pedreira, Antonio S. *Insularismo*. Río Piedras: Editorial Edil, 1973.

Picó, Fernando. *Libertad y servidumbre en el Puerto Rico del siglo XIX*. Río Piedras: Huracán, 1979.

_______. *Los gallos peleados*. Río Piedras: Huracán, 1983.

Piore, M., and Doeringer, P. *Internal Labor Markets and Manpower Analysis*. Lexington, Mass.: D. C. Heath, 1971.

Poplack, Shana. "Bilingualism and the Vernacular." In Hartford, B., Valdman, A., and Foster, C. (eds.). *Issues in International Bilingual Education: The Role of the Vernacular*. New York: Plenum Press, 1982.

Puerto Rican Studies Group. "Puerto Rican Studies: Notes for the 1980s." Authors include Jessie Vázquez, Camille Rodríquez, Arsenio González, Hildamar Ortiz, María Canino, Sherry Gorelick, and Josephine Nieves. Editor, Carol Ascher. 1982.

Quintero Rivera, Angel. *De campesino y agregado a proletario: la economía de plantación*. Río Piedras: CEREP, 1974.

_______. *Workers Struggle in Puerto Rico: A Documentary History*. New York: Monthly Review Press, 1976.

_______. *Historia de unas clases sin historia: Comentarios críticos al pais de cuatro pisos*. Río Piedras: Cuadernos CEREP, 1983.

Ramírez, Rafael, L. "National Culture in Puerto Rico." *Latin American Perspectives* 3:3 (1976).

Ramos Mattei, Andrés. *Apuntes sobre la transición hacia el sistema de centrales en la industria azucarera*. San Juan: CEREP, 1975.

Rodríguez, Clara. *The Ethnic Queue in the U.S.: The Case of Puerto Ricans*. San Francisco: R & E Research Associates, 1973.

Rúa, Pedro Juan. *Bolívar ante Marx y ostros ensayos*. Río Piedras: Huracán, 1978.

Saloma, John S., III. *Ominous Politics: The New Conservative Labyrinth*. New York: Hill and Wang, 1984.

Sankoff, David, and Poplack, Shana. "A Formal Grammar for Code Switching." *Papers in Linguistics* 14:1 (1980).

Scarano, F. (ed.). *Inmigración y clases sociales en el Puerto Rico del siglo XIX*. Río Piedras: Huracán, 1981.

Seda Bonilla, Eduardo. *Requiem Por Una Cultura*. Río Piedras: Bayoán, 1972.

Silén, Juan Angel. *Hacia una visión positiva del puertorriqueño*. Rió Piedras: Edil, 1970. Translated as *We, the Puerto Rican People*. New York: Monthly Review Press, 1971.

Silvestrini Pacheco, Blanca. "The Needlework Industry in Puerto Rico, 1915-1940: Women's Transition from Home to Factory." Trinidad: 12th Conference of Caribbean Historians, April 1980.

Swinton, David. "Orthodox and Systemic Explanations for Unemployment and Racial Inequality: Implications for Policy." *The Review of Black Political Economy* 12:3 (1983).

Thurow, Lester. *The Zero-Sum Society*. New York: Basic Books, 1981.

United States Commission on Civil Rights. *Puerto Ricans in the United States: An Uncertain Future*. Washington, D.C., 1976.

Varrin, Robert D., and Kukich, Diane S. "Guidelines for Industry Sponsored Research." *Science* 227 (1985).

Vázquez, Blanca, Benmayor, Rina, Alvarez, Celia, Juarbe, Ana, and Tirado, Amílcar. "Nosotras trabajamos en la costura" (slide show). New York: Centro de Estudios Puertorriqueños, Hunter College, CUNY, 1985.

Villamil, J. J. "El modelo puertorriqueño: los límites del crecimiento dependiente." *Revista Puertorriqueña de Investigaciones Sociales* 1 (1976).

Weisskopf, Richard. *Puerto Rico and the Caribbean Economies: Model and Patterns*. Des Moines: Department of Economics, Iowa State University, 1978.

Williams, Raymond. *The Year 2000*. New York: Pantheon, 1984.

4

THE MEXICAN-ORIGIN PEOPLE IN THE UNITED STATES AND MARXIST THOUGHT IN CHICANO STUDIES

Estevan T. Flores

HISTORICAL OVERVIEW

Much of what is now the southwestern United States was once a part of Mexico. It is no accident that cities such as Los Angeles (The Angels), Santa Fe (Holy Faith) and San Antonio (Saint Anthony), bear Spanish names. These cities were founded in the seventeenth and eighteenth centuries by Spanish explorers who claimed the land for Spain.[1] Later, in 1821, when Mexico gained its independence from Spain, these cities and their territory formed the northern frontier of Mexico (see Nava, 1973).

The threat of war over this northern territory grew with the western expansion of the United States in the 1800s. The Mexican-Texas War, which began in 1836, ended with Mexico's loss of over one-half its land mass. The Treaty of Guadalupe Hidalgo, signed in 1848, provided citizenship rights for Mexicans who chose to remain north of the newly formed border–the Rio Grande (called the Rio Bravo by Mexicans). Thousands upon thousands of Mexicans chose to continue living in what they considered their homeland, even if that choice meant giving up Mexican citizenship.

The author expresses sincere gratitude to Dr. Marta Lopez-Garza (Southern Methodist University) for her many valuable suggestions. Also thanked are Dr. Manuel Avalos (University of Houston) for his comments and Mrs. Olivia Holguin for her steadfast assistance. This article is dedicated to my father, Tim G. Flores, whose decades of struggle have been an inspiration

This brief historical note provides some of the basic facts for understanding the contemporary Mexican American, or "Chicano": first, the new political border was set as a result of military conquest; second, the original settlers, the Mexicans living in Texas, for example, became "strangers in their own land" and were treated as second-class citizens; third, a legacy of mistrust, if not hatred, was sown; and fourth, the new territorial citizens were forced to accept a foreign language along with a new government and culture. In the eyes of many analysts, the war with Mexico was as much economic (over land) as it was political and cultural, coming shortly after the declaration of the Monroe Doctrine with its creed of "Manifest Destiny" (see Acuña, 1981 and Gomez-Quiñonez, 1982a).

The Mexican American people are a product of the Spanish and Indian historical legacies. Racially, they are "mestizos," that is, the biological product of the miscegenation of Spaniard and Indian. From 1848 on, the Mexican-origin people in the United States increased in population as a result of waves of migration from Mexico. Not much is known about the immigration of Mexicans during the last half of the nineteenth century, although Meier and Rivera (1972) and Cardoso (1980) provide some information. We do know that, beginning in 1917, a head tax and a literacy test were imposed on new immigrants, and a law setting up a border patrol was passed in 1924 (see Samora, 1971; and Romo, 1975).

Many Mexicans came to the United States during and after the 1910 Mexican revolution. Some feared for their lives or those of their families during this social upheaval. Others chose to leave Mexico rather than participate in the revolution. Another wave of immigrants came to the United States as a result of the Bracero Program (1942-64). This binational agreement between the United States and Mexico provided the United States with much-needed labor as World War II created a severe labor shortage in many sectors of the economy. "Braceros" (*brazo* refers to arm) received certain guarantees and were to return to Mexico upon the expiration of their contract. Many braceros simply stayed in the United States, while other Mexicans who could not make the bracero quota crossed the border to the states where jobs were plentiful (see Craig, 1971; and Garcia y Griego, 1983).

Throughout the twentieth century—except for the revolutionary period—Mexicans came to the United States in search of work or for reasons of family unification. The main demand for workers came from agriculturalists, mining and railroad interests (see Gomez-Quiñones, 1984; and Sierra, 1984, on this point), and, more recently, from service and light industries (R. Morales, 1983).

The typical Mexican American was a migrant farmworker until approximately the mid-1960s when the migrant flow turned toward urban areas. The 1982 Census estimates placed the Mexican-origin population at 8,829,000 persons, or almost 63 percent of the Spanish-origin population in the United States. The median age for the Mexican-origin population was 22.2 years of age compared to 31.0 for the non-Spanish-origin population. In terms of economic indicators, the Mexican-origin median family income in March 1982 was estimated at $16,900, or 74 percent of the non-Spanish-origin median of $22,800. Twenty-five percent (25 percent) of the Mexican-origin families earned below $10,000 in 1981 while only 16.7 percent of the non-Spanish-origin families earned less than this amount. Over 22 percent of Mexican-origin families were below the poverty level in 1981, while 10.5 percent of the non-Spanish-origin population fell below that level (Fernandez and DeNavas, 1982:7-10).[2]

In terms of occupational indicators, 60 percent of the male Mexican-origin population were blue-collar workers, while the male non-Spanish-origin rate was 42 percent. Almost 48 percent of Mexican-origin females were employed in blue-collar, service, or farm worker occupations (24, 22.2, and 1.6 percent respectively), while slightly over 33 percent of non-Spanish-origin females were so employed (12.5, 19.9, and 0.9 percent respectively). Over 13 percent of the Mexican-origin population was unemployed during the March 1982 enumeration period, while 8.7 percent of the non-Spanish-origin population was unemployed during the same period (Fernandez and DeNavas, 1982:9-10).

This brief overview of the labor, migration, and demographic status of the Mexican-origin people provides background for understanding the inception of Chicano Studies. However, before discussing Chicano Studies, it is important to review the scholars who first researched and wrote about the Mexican American people.

PIONEER SCHOLARS

Very few scholars studied the Mexican American prior to 1960. The early writers or pioneers in the field included Paul Taylor, Carey McWilliams, George I. Sanchez, Americo Paredes, Julian Samora, and Ernesto Galarza. One of the earliest and more sensitive accounts of the Mexican American work experience was offered by labor economist Paul S. Taylor. His *Mexican Labor in the United States* (1928-34), was published in ten volumes and covered a variety of issues and geographic areas where Mexicans worked. In *Factories in the Field*

(1939) and in other subsequent works, Carey McWilliams also displayed the exploitative conditions under which the migrant worked (see also McWilliams, 1942).

Yet, prior to the 1940s, no academic treatise on the Mexican American people as a whole was available. McWilliams published the first influential and popular (although somewhat journalistic) study of the Mexican Americans, *North From Mexico*, in 1948. This book stood as the standard text and chronicle of the Mexican American people for nearly two decades.

George I. Sanchez's contributions to the field of education are generally recognized as significant landmarks in the area of Mexican American Studies. One of his earliest works assessed the cultural adaptations of the Hispanos of New Mexico. *Forgotten People* (1940) was followed by many other works. His 1951 text, *Concerning Segregation of Spanish-Speaking Children in the Public Schools*, examined the illegality of segregation in the public schools. Sanchez was a tireless activist as well as an educator who served the community in a variety of ways.

Americo Paredes, an anthropologist at the University of Texas at Austin, is also recognized as a pioneer in the field of Mexican American Studies as well as an esteemed scholar in the field of folklore. His widely acclaimed "*With His Pistol in His Hand*": *A Border Ballad and Its Hero* (1958) is a social and folkloric account of the legend of Gregorio Cortez (this classic work, because of its humanistic appeal and social significance, was recently made into the motion picture "The Ballad of Gregorio Cortez"). Paredes's work is especially noteworthy for its depiction of cultural conflict, its interpretation of the alleged Mexican "thief" as a social bandit, à la E. J. Hobsbawm, and its account of the development of mutual stereotypes of Mexicans and Anglos (see also Simmons, 1961; and Dworkin, 1965).

The first Mexican American to earn a doctorate in sociology was Julian Samora in 1953. His edited work, *La Raza: Forgotten Americans* (1966), and his book *Mexican Americans in the Southwest* (1969), written with Ernesto Galarza and Herman Gallegos, provided scholarly overviews of the current plight of the nation's second largest minority group and largest language minority group. These books dealt with both private and governmental agencies. Data were also provided on the persistence of specific problems (for example, low education levels, high incidence of poverty, poor health care, and so on) of the Mexican American population.

No one documented social issues of concern to Mexican Americans, especially the plight of the California farmworkers, as thoroughly as the late Ernesto Galarza. His testimony in Congress about the damaging effects of the Bracero Program contributed to its termination (Galarza, 1964 and 1977). Galarza was also a political activist. As a learned man, he could have remained in the academy, but, as he remarked, "If I stay here much longer than three quarters, I'll feel that I am sinking roots into a cemetery" (quoted in Chabran, 1985, from Morris and Beard, 1982:34). The problem of choosing the academy *or* organizing in the community became a major issue of debate during the late 1960s and remains so to this day.

THE ORIGINS OF CHICANO STUDIES AND MEXICAN AMERICAN STUDIES

Chicano Studies and Mexican American Studies were forged out of student and community struggles for access to institutions of higher education. These struggles occurred during the middle and late 1960s when the status quo was being challenged on all sides by protest movements against the Vietnam War, the Black Power Movement, the war against poverty, and the Native American Indian Movement. Against this backdrop, the Mexican-origin students attending state universities in the Southwest actively engaged university administrations in order to establish "programs of study" that would focus academic attention on the history and culture of the Mexican people in the United States and on the struggle against racism (see Frisbie, 1973; Barrera, 1974; Gomez-Quiñones, 1974; A. Sanchez, 1974; Chicano Students Committee for Justice, 1974; Risco, 1974; Marin, 1980; and Muñoz, 1984, among others).

In the first section I omitted the explanation for the term "Chicano." I did so because it gained popularity only during the late 1960s and 1970s. The term "Chicano" essentially meant "a radicalization of politics. 'Chicano politics' emerged as a challenge to the dominant institutions, assumptions, politics, principles, political leaders and organizations within or without the community" (Gomez-Quiñonez, 1978:13). The term "Chicano" was at once political (social), individual, and philosophical. As regards the individual, "Chicanismo . . . was a response to the issue of national identity. It emphasized dignity, self-worth, pride, uniqueness, feeling of cultural rebirth, and equal economic opportunity" (Gomez-Quiñonez, 1978:13). The term also signified the willingness on the part of those so self-identified to use the methods of confrontation and radical politics for community improvement and gain. Rendon's (1971) *Chicano Manifesto* states clearly the political perspective and goals of that era.

The Chicano student movement was part of a larger social movement that included the "Alianza" of Reies Lopez Tijerina, which worked to recover lost New Mexican land; Rudolfo Corky Gonzalez's "Crusade for Justice" in Denver, which sought cultural and educational autonomy; the junior high and high school "blowouts" (walkouts or student strikes), which occurred throughout the Southwest; the struggle for educational access and bilingual education; and the farmworker movement, especially the United Farmworker's (UFW) led by Cesar Chavez.[3]

The Chicano student movement was part of each of these struggles. At their own colleges, students began to organize.

> At any campus with a half-dozen Chicano students they pressed for a Mexican-American studies (MAS) program and the admission of more Chicano students. . . . [T]hrough raw energy by the fall of 1969 some fifty Mexican American studies programs functioned in California alone —ranging from institutes and centers to departments (Acuña, 1981:356).

Much planning, organizing and confrontation eventually led to the semiinstitutionalization of studies programs for the Mexican-origin population during the late 1960s and early 1970s. Through courses taken in Chicano Studies (CS) or Mexican American Studies, students learned of "early Mexican-American *resistance* to domination in the form of political organizations, militant trade unionism, critical journalism, and folk heroes . . ." (Limon, 1982:143).

At the same time that they were organizing themselves around academic issues, student groups made a conscious effort to support and link up with the struggles taking place throughout the Southwest and Mexico. "From 1968 to 1971 the campuses provided a network which furnished information and provided the shock troops for the protests and marches of those years" (Acuña, 1981:358).

Chicano Studies programs were begun throughout the Southwest in the late 1960s and early 1970s. The struggles across campuses varied as did the types of programs eventually established. The first program established was the Mexican American Studies program at Cal State Los Angeles in 1968. Some universities or colleges, due to excellent organization and political lobbying, were able to establish independent departments (for example, Cal State at Northridge), others established full-blown research units (for example, UCLA's Chicano Studies Research Center), while other programs combined faculty from departments in a curriculum emphasizing undergraduate education and research (for example, University of Texas, Austin; see Rochin, 1973 for one of the first status reports). Rodolfo Acuña's *Occupied America: A History of Chicanos* provides the best overview of programs operating to 1981 (see Acuna, 1981:391-94).

What is paramount in the discussion of Chicano Studies is the focus and mission of the programs. Although the academic mission was primary, secondary goals were seen as vital, if not essential. In its first newsletter published in 1973, the National Caucus of Chicano Social Scientists listed the themes of its founding conference and what they called "a new direction for social science" for Chicano social scientists:

> (1) Social science research by Chicanos must be much more problem-oriented than traditional social science has been. . . . (2) Social science research projects should be interdisciplinary in nature. . . . [T]he traditional disciplinary orientation . . . obscures the interconnections among variables that operate to maintain the oppression of our people. (3) . . . Research and action should exist in a dialectical relationship. . . . [I]n order to bridge the gap between theory and action, Chicano social scientists must develop close ties with community action groups. (4) Chicano social science must be highly critical, in the double sense of rigorous analysis and a trenchant critique of American institutions. . . . [T]hese institutions have perpetuated the unfavorable condition of the Chicano. (5) Our levels of investigation must include the local, the regional, and the national, as well as the international dimension. . . . One pressing item requiring intensive research has to do with the relationship between class, race, and culture . . . (in Macias, 1977:215-16 and Muñoz, 1984:15).

Chicano Studies and Mexican American Studies were largely *products* of the contentious struggles waged by graduate and undergraduate students and a few nontenured faculty (there were very few Mexican-origin faculty at that time; see Rochin, 1973:890), whose careers were jeopardized by their participation. Students could expect suspension or expulsion while the contracts of professors could be terminated. At Fresno State, for example, the entire Chicano faculty was fired and their program was temporarily shut down (Muñoz, 1983:14).

Despite the sanctions and harassment, faculty and student groups succeeded in getting funds for many of their programs and began to develop an intellectual body of thought on the Mexican-origin population in the United States. The type of scholarship produced, of course, varies considerably from conservative mainstream research and writing to Marxist scholarship. It is to the latter topic that I now turn.

SCHOLARSHIP IN CHICANO STUDIES: CRITICISM, INTERNAL COLONIALISM, AND MARXISM

As Chicano students and faculty established their programs, they also developed the academic side of Chicano Studies. The *first* academic concern was to respond to the negative stereotyping and to the dehumanizing and inaccurate social science literature that dealt with the Mexican-origin people. *Second*, the young scholars sought an explanation for the decades of oppression and exploitation that the Mexican-origin people have suffered in our capitalist system. This scholarship was radical in approach and methodology. It went to the root of the problem.

At the time, the criticisms of biased (racist) literature were needed and were in sync with the militancy of the community. Yet as this line of scholarship developed, many people saw that critiques of racism, without class perspective, were ultimately reformist.

Chicano Studies also developed an interdisciplinary approach. Works in such diverse fields as anthropology, sociology, history, and political science, not to mention psychology, social work, and psychiatry, all had something useful to say about *La Raza*.[4] Earlier work on the Mexican American population was full of stereotypical images and interpretations, misunderstanding of their culture, and ahistorical biases. These and other problems led to social science that was misleading and inaccurate at best and politically damaging at worst. The responses to this social science, even if, in retrospect, reformist, were essential.

Beginning with the work of Octavio Romano in the Berkeley journal *El Grito* (see Romano, 1968, 1969), incisive critiques of the early anthropological and sociological literature were made. Criticisms of the psychological biases found in testing were made by Moreno (1970), while Tomas Martinez (1969) criticized the stereotyping found in advertising (remember the "Frito bandito"?); Montiel (1970) focused on the Mexican American family in social science literature in his critical review.

Upon reading material on Mexican Americans, written prior to the late 1960s primarily by Anglo social scientists, one would conclude that the Mexican American population was fatalistic, apolitical, criminalistic, childish, and so on, ad nauseum. In addition, Mexican Americans were considered by these authors as the source of their own problems. The "blame the victim" syndrome (Ryan, 1971), so popular in those days, was uncritically and mechanically applied to the population by mainstream social scientists.

In 1970 the first large-scale empirical assessment of the Mexican American people was published. Grebler, Moore, and Guzman's tome generated much debate and criticism because of its ahistorical and sometimes insensitive depiction of the Mexican-origin people (see D. Hernandez, 1970). The strongest and most astute academic critique summarizing the earliest responses and providing additional anthropological, folkloric, and linguistic evidence was made by Americo Paredes (1977). In this work, Paredes nailed the coffin shut on a body of literature long recognized as authoritative on the Mexican-origin people. In a similar vein, Mario Barrera's *Race and Class in the Southwest* systematically refuted a variety of racial inequality theories based on biology, culture, and social structure (Barrera, 1979:174-88).

Criticisms of the literature by Romano, Paredes, Barrera, and others usually appeared in nonmainstream journals. In all likelihood, the mainstream journals would not have published these strident articles. For this reason and others, journals such as *El Grito* (UC-Berkeley) and *Aztlan*: *Chicano Journal of the Social Sciences and the Arts* (UCLA) were established.

The second line of scholarship sought an historical explanation for the oppression and exploitation of the Chicano. With a primary focus on labor, the labor process, and the labor-capital relationship, Chicano historians retold, in a scholarly fashion, the story of the Mexican people in the United States. They did so without the biases of Anglo "apologist" historians who relied on the doctrine of "Manifest Destiny" or who failed to recognize issues of racism and class interest (see Gomez-Quiñones 1971 and 1972). Chicano Marxist historians described labor from the viewpoint of Chicano workers and not capital (see Luis Arroyo's excellent overview in 1975a; Gomez-Quiñones and Arroyo, 1976; as well as Arroyo's short update in 1983).

In the development of Chicano history, the authors cited above focused on and stressed the class nature of oppression and the rule of Mexican workers in the struggle against exploitation. Not all Chicano historians accepted this type of interpretation. Some historians, especially those doing community studies, broke new ground in their research, yet failed to write about the class dynamics of their subjects (see Camarillo, 1979; and Griswold del Castillo, 1979). Other writers used the concept of racism as *the* explanation for the group's exploitation (see O. Martinez, 1975; and M. Garcia, 1975, 1981). Barrera's (1983) review of the literature helps frame much of the work in this area as does Almaguer and Camarillo's (1983) review essay (also see Camarillo's 1983 short historiographical essay).

For issues of race *and* class, the importance of the journal *Aztlan*, which was started in 1970, cannot be overstated. Particularly noteworthy was the 1975 special edition, "Labor History of the Chicano," edited by Luis Arroyo and Victor Nelson Cisneros, which contained seminal articles by a number of scholars who utilized a class analysis focusing on the character of Chicanos as workers in their opposition to capital (see, in particular, Mazon, Nelson Cisneros, Zamora, Rosales and Simon, all 1975; and Luis Arroyo, 1975a).

This scholarship provided important information and divergent theoretical orientations on a variety of topics. For example, Victor Nelson Cisneros's work on farmworkers in Crystal City, Texas, during the 1930s opened a hidden chapter of Texas history on the struggles of U.S. Mexican workers against growers. (See also R. Lopez, 1970; Nelson Cisneros, 1978; and Devra Weber, 1972 for similar California examples.) Likewise, Emilio Zamora's (1975) study of socialist labor activity in the south Texas area of Laredo in the 1920s provided exciting history and complemented Gomez-Quiñones's (1973) monograph on Ricardo Flores Magon and the *Partido Liberal Mexicano* (PLM). The latter examined the PLM's communist and anarchist organizing in both Mexico and the United States. Gomez-Quiñones also shows the government (state) repression used to squelch the movement on both sides of the border during the early 1900s and 1910s.

The message to the Chicano Studies students was clear: there exists a rich historical legacy of conflict with the oppressors, and these struggles could be continued through the student's own actions. These lessons were not lost upon students, at least not until the late 1970s, by which time the Chicano student movement had lost most of its activist orientation.

Another radical theoretical approach adopted in this period was that of internal colonialism. The main ideas involved here were developed by a number of scholars who were well-schooled in the independence and nationalist literatures of Cuba, other countries of Latin America, and Africa (see especially Guevara, 1968; Memmi, 1965; Fanon, 1967; Freire, 1972; Amin, 1974; Gunder Frank, 1969; Cardosa and Reyna, 1968, among others). The attraction of this work was twofold. First, the analysis promoted independence from white

European colonialists; and second, the successes of some of these movements were encouraging and served as models. In his influential text, *Racial Oppression in America* (1972), Blauner used this approach in describing the lot of Native Americans, Blacks, and Chicanos.

The internal colonial framework was applied to Chicanos in particular by Moore (1970) and Tomas Almaguer (1971), who was then a sociology graduate student. Other articles in the same vein soon followed. The political scientists Mario Barrera, Carlos Muñoz, and Charles Ornelas published "The Barrio as Internal Colony" (1972) and Guillermo Flores published his influential piece in 1973 (see also Bailey and Flores, 1973).

Rodolfo Acuna's *Occupied America* (1972 edition), possibly the first book in Chicano studies, also relied on the internal colonial model. Acuna's book, which was widely read and very controversial, captured the fervor, anger, and militancy of the times:

> As I was researching and writing, I constantly had to fight the resentment I felt—a resentment generated by the tale of cruel and brutal exploitation that I saw unfolding. But my hope is that even those who disagree with me will consider the "other side" and perhaps increase their own awareness that this country's ideals of justice and equality are still not reality (Acuña, 1972:iv).

In these works, the authors argued that Chicanos were subjected to economic, governmental, social, and linguistic oppression and that they were second-class citizens. Viewed in this perspective, the logical as well as practical solution was to be found in "liberation" strategies; and the struggle for liberation passed through cultural nationalism.

> Nationalism provided an operative norm for politicalization and community development and provided the rationale and psychological substance for a collective Mexicano identity through the vehicle of symbols and sub-concepts which had the possibilities for wide acceptability. Nationalism was a mystique that offered the potentiality for binding a heterogeneous and fragmented community, providing the basis for operational unity, and the concomitant results (Gomez-Quiñonez, 1978: 28).

The Chicano student movement, as a microcosm of the Chicano movement, also used nationalism as a tool for organization. The academic side of Chicano Studies was less nationalistic, although, as individuals, Chicano Studies faculty, staff, and students were deeply imbued with this sentiment.

Along with the internal colony approach, a distinctive Chicano Marxism began to develop, and there was a clear tension between the two bodies of thought. While the internal colonial model focused on oppression and liberation, those who used the Marxist model dealt more with "exploitation" and the political economy of the Southwest's growth.

Almaguer, in "The Dialectics of Racial and Class Domination" (1974:47), concluded that "racial and class oppression in North America have become inextricably intertwined and the racial struggle in the U.S. must become a class struggle as well." Almaguer documented the growth of monopoly capitalism in the Southwest and the extraction of surplus value from Mexican-origin workers in a variety of occupations and industries. Mindiola discussed nascent Chicano Marxism and reviewed the political alternatives open to the Chicano population attempting to develop socialism in the United States. In his estimation, since Marxism had failed to incorporate race in its theoretical and practical formulations, it could not provide a convincing explanation of the Chicano reality (see Mindiola, 1977:185). On the other hand, Fred Cervantes (1977:132) argued: "We should be ready to close off the dead-ends of the model of internal colonialism but nevertheless extend the main marxist track on which this theoretical perspective has taken Chicano social scientists." As a research agenda, Cervantes proposed that we study the present as a postcolonial period while concentrating on patterns of Chicano resistance and struggle. Some Chicano scholars have followed his proposal and developed Marxist theory out of the study of and participation in class struggle. The concepts of political composition, decomposition, and recomposition have been particularly useful to a number of Chicano writers and researchers working with this orientation.

CHICANO STUDIES, POLITICAL ACTIVISM, AND MARXIST THOUGHT

In my estimation, Marxist thought in Chicano Studies has grown primarily out of activism. The labor historians developed a class perspective from their praxis on and off campus as well as from their more academic studies. Likewise, writing on immigration arose as much from participation in class struggle as from an understanding of the international division of labor. Educational, health, language, and cultural issues were also simultaneously political and research issues. Activists, and academics who were activists, developed theoretical critiques and practical alternatives to immigration legislation and policy at the same time.[5]

As Chicano Studies gained legitimacy, Mario Barrera (1974) argued that Chicano social scientists must utilize methodological strategies in the community to produce data for "grounded theory," focus on political and social control mechanisms and their relation to the Chicano community, and more clearly define the relationship between academia and the community, funding agencies, and others (see Cuellar's summary and application of these points in his case study, 1981:1-19). At this point, many graduate students and untenured faculty in Chicano Studies faced the problem of choosing between activism outside of the academy, activism within the academy, pure scholarship on the Mexican-origin population, pure scholarship within their discipline, or any combination of these alternatives (see Barrera and Vialpando, 1974).[6]

Mexican immigration to the United States is one area in which activism and Marxist research were clearly joined. In 1968, long-time Chicano labor and community activist Bert Corona started CASA (Centro de Acción Social Autonoma–Center for Autonomous Social Action) in the Los Angeles area in order to organize and defend undocumented Mexican immigrants. The activism of CASA on behalf of the undocumented worker and the viewpoint captured in the slogan *Somos un pueblo sin fronteras* (We are one community without a border) were instrumental in helping to build the Chicano student movement (Flores, 1982:150-58). More importantly, the idea of raising the issue of immigrants' rights forced both the Chicano community and the larger society to consider the question of a binational community. CASA argued that the undocumented Mexican population *and* the Chicano community were part of a larger Mexican-origin population residing on both sides of the border. The source of social, political, and economic exploitation of both communities was found in the class nature of racist multinational capitalism (see H. Corona, 1974:6; Rodriguez, 1977:10; and C. Vasquez, 1977:11, among others). On the basis of class and race (and later sex), CASA organized on campus, in the community, and at the workplace.

This activism was reflected in Marxist work by Cardenas and Bustamante (1971) who used a "proletarian" approach for studying immigrant workers. In his dissertation Bustamante (1974) explained the "use-value" functions of undocumented Mexican immigrant laborers, and in a later work (1978) referred to immigrants seeking employment as "commodities." Burawoy (1976) took the analysis further in examining the "functions and reproduction of migrant labor" in Southern California and South Africa (see Flores, 1982:99-102, for the detailed discussion of this topic). The Burawoy article was especially important in demonstrating the manner in which U.S.-based capitalist enterprises exploit foreign labor while not bearing any of the costs involved in its reproduction.

From about 1975 on, the issue of the exclusion of undocumented children from education, that is, the state's refusal to bear part of the reproduction costs of immigrant laborers, became a hotly contested topic in many parts of the country. This issue was finally resolved by the U.S. Supreme Court in 1982 when the justices ruled in favor of the children and against the state of Texas (Alien Children Education Litigation, 1980; *Doe* v. *Plyler and State of Texas*, 1980; Flores, 1982; and Torres, 1980). Of course, the Court based its ruling on constitutional grounds—equal protection rights—and not on grounds of class. Yet, from a political economy perspective, viewed from the vantage point of the reproduction of labor costs, educational, health, and other access issues are expressions of class struggle (see Cardenas and Flores, 1978). Research established that undocumented parents contribute more to the U.S. economy than they receive from state and federal agencies (for example, in entitlement programs). Results of this study were presented to the Court in the 1980 Houston case (Cardenas and Flores, 1980).

Another issue related to immigration that caused much debate on the left was the "national question," which dealt with the status of Chicanos as a people within the United States. Antonio Rios-Bustamante's (1978) critique of six left groups (Communist Party, 1972; Socialist Worker's Party, 1972; Communist League, 1974; Revolutionary Union, 1975; October League, 1975; and August 29th Movement, 1976) expounded on the status of theory and the self-interest of the political groups that were in the forefront of the discussion:

> These polemics evidence a lack of conviction in regard to self-determination, with no clear application of proletariat internationalism and much less evidence of understanding it. . . . All assert either culture or nationhood or both. . . . none satisfactorily explains the rise of a new nationality when it is proclaimed by the pamphlet. . . . all by implication but never forthrightly accept continuing Anglo hegemony even under socialism . . . none . . . explains what tactics are to be for the building of the mass movement which will lead to socialism (Rios-Bustamante, 1978:22-23).

Rios-Bustamante's timely article helped put an end to the posturing by these left groups by cutting through their rhetoric and ragged scholarship (Flores interview of Gomez-Quiñones, 1985). Gomez-Quiñones (1982b) provides a serious Marxist overview of this same question.

CASA, in its national paper *Sin Fronteras*, regularly discussed such questions, but not in a systematic or rigorous fashion. CASA activists and some Chicano social scientists focused on labor concerns, including the issue of organizing the unorganized. Gilbert Cardenas was one of the first to analyze the impact of immigration on the Chicano community (Cardenas, 1977). Magdalena Mora (1978) interpreted the role of undocumented immigrants in terms of a "reserve army of labor." She also studied the Tolteca tortilla factory strikes using the method of participant-observation (Mora, 1981). Baird and McCaughan (1979) took a more transnational perspective in assessing the nexus between U.S. and Mexican capitalism.

Cognizant of the binational nature of migratory labor, the Arizona Farmworker's Union (AFW) began organizing their workforce of undocumented workers with amazing success in 1976 (see Crewdson, 1978). To this day, the AFW's binational organizing represents an exemplary model to the rural Mexican farmworker. By obtaining from each grower a 20-cent deposit for every hour worked per union worker, the AFW builds an escrow account that is then used at the worker's point-of-origin in Mexico to construct homes, schools, irrigation systems, and water storage tanks. Such a binational economic development program was hard-earned and much needed. Through years of struggle and many strikes in the Maricopa County area of Phoenix, the AFW continues to grow (Sanchez and Romo, 1981; and Flores interview with Sanchez, 1984).

Chicano Studies has been significantly changed through the issue of undocumented Mexican migration. The scope of Chicano Studies was augmented through the social activism of CASA and other groups, while scholarly production on the topic made significant advances for both Marxist thought and Chicano Studies. By demonstrating through struggle (practice), the validity of a transnational movement, the core-periphery notions associated with the world systems approach as well as other literature on the U.S.-Mexico relationship were found to be deficient. By placing emphasis on organization and struggle, a more sound theoretical perspective on the Mexican people as a racial and class entity was also developed. While the question of immigrant workers was getting so much public attention, another issue that was being hotly debated was the women's issue.

GENDER ISSUES: LA MUJER

In Chicano Studies, theoretical issues of race, class, and culture often predominated academic debates, especially in the early days. To the extent that race and class issues have remained paramount in both research and practice, issues of sex have been neglected. To be sure, sexism by Chicanos has been evident throughout the Movement at all levels and mirrors the sexism found in society at large. However, the struggle waged by Chicanas against sexism began with the Movement and from the start has been an important factor in helping to shape and inform Chicano Studies.

Few scholarly articles on the Chicana were available during the early 1970s; however, many articles on this subject appeared in popular journals or community newspapers. The main themes that captured the attention of active Chicanas concerned within-group members, namely macho, sexist Chicanos (see Cotera, 1972; and Nieto-Gomez, 1973, 1974 and 1976). A more scholarly treatment of this subject can be found in Elizabeth (Martinez) Sutherland's "Colonized Women: The Chicana" (1970); see, too, the articles by Sosa-Riddell (1974) and Valdes Fallis (1974). Common to the above was the indictment of capitalist society for producing (and reproducing) sexist social and economic relations. Articles on the Chicana also spoke of the difficulties they encountered in establishing their own liberation within the family and Chicano culture as well as within the larger society.

Systematic analysis on the family and on *la Chicana* became available with the edited text *Essays on La Mujer* (Sanchez and Martinez Cruz, 1977). In that publication, written and edited by women, four articles utilized a Marxist framework: Rosaura Sanchez (1977), Sonia Lopez (1977), Garcia-Bahne (1977), and Marquez and Ramirez (1977). The balance of the writers relied on either a race-discrimination model of society (Solis, 1977; and Arroyo, 1977), or a historical/psychological orientation (Del Castillo, 1977; and Lizarraga, 1977). The main focus of the Marxist articles was on the economic nature of the family and the reproduction of labor power. Garcia-Bahne argued:

> The family survives to reproduce a labor force and is valuable and necessary as a basic consumptive unit. A major ideological foundation of the economy, society and family is the notion of private property, both in the sense that family members are subject to objectification and that

> the family implements the more conservative aspects of accumulation and maintenance of property in the name of security for future generations. Lastly, within the family, children learn the hierarchy of relationships necessary for low paid labor (Garcia-Bahne, 1977:40).

Garcia-Bahne expertly summarized much of the then current Marxist views on the family and applied her analysis to the Chicano family, including its social-psychological as well as psychological dimensions.

A more direct critique of sexism in the Chicano Movement was made by Sonia Lopez (1977). She focused on the sexism evident in the assignment of sex-typed roles, and on the reaction of Chicanos to female leadership. Men simply failed to recognize the contributions of women. It was such sexism that spurred the women to initiate their own organization.

With the publication of *Mexican Women in the United States: Struggles Past and Present* by Magdalena Mora and Adelaida Del Castillo in 1980, the complexity of the struggle of Mexican women on both sides of the border was further elucidated. They documented the struggle of Mexican-origin women against sex, class, and national oppression (see, too, C. Vasquez, 1980:28). The costs—personal as well as academic and political—of carrying on these struggles inside the university were also treated (see P. Hernandez, 1980). The lessons in these works have proved very useful for community and workplace organizing (see Del Castillo, 1980; and Schlein, 1980).[7]

Margarita Melville's edited book, *Twice a Minority: Mexican American Women* (1980), analyzed a number of different issues, including family planning (Andrade, 1980), abortion (Urdaneta, 1980), childbirth (Kay, 1980), breast feeding (Acosta Johnson, 1980), strategies for change (Mason, 1980), and the forced sterilization of Mexican women (Velez-I., 1980). A few of the articles took a class or Marxist stance. However, the case studies found throughout the volume document attitudes, incidents, and events that are of particular importance for the struggle. These articles also show a developing sophistication. The same cannot be said of Mirande and Enriquez's *La Chicana* (1979). The main purpose of this work is to rationalize and glorify the most oppressive and negative aspects of our culture—namely, the traditional male chauvinism of husbands and fathers. For example, the authors state:

> Men have power and authority relative to outside institutions, and women are responsible for the daily affairs of the family. Just as the world was divided into masculine and feminine realms in Aztec society, so there is a complex division of labor between men and women in Chicano

> culture, with each granted power and authority within their respective spheres (Mirande and Enriquez, 1979:117).

Exciting Marxist scholarship, based on practice, continues to develop in still other areas. Devon Peña's (1980) work on *maquiladoras* (twin plants along the U.S.-Mexican border), and the struggles of Mexican women workers organizing in both the work site and the community, is especially instructive. In a later work, Peña (1983) tries to relate strategies of transnational capitalism to oppressive technological innovations and Mexican women worker's organizational and informal reactions to these developments. His reliance on the circulation-of-struggle approach was innovative and his treatment of the relationship of the community (social factory) to the factory is exemplary.

Other useful work helping to explain the race and culture of the Mexican-origin family has been done by Baca-Zinn (1975, 1979, 1980) and Ybarra (1977). As Ybarra (1983) recently pointed out, however, there remains a need for a more rigorous class analysis of this subject. In my view, Baca-Zinn (1983:141) moves in the right direction when she argues for the study of "capitalist patriarchy" in her critique of Saragoza (1983), and says we should understand the family, as does Flax (1982) "as a source of resistance" against capitalism.

CONCLUSION AND DIRECTION FOR THE FUTURE

The Chicano Movement, which came into existence in turbulent times, was primarily a reaction against police repression (A. Morales, 1972; and Trujillo, 1983), political domination (Navarro, 1974; and Gutierrez and Hirsch, 1973), and a racist educational system (Macias, 1974). One of its major achievements is that it opened the doors of higher education to the Mexican-origin community (Lopez et al., 1976). Young Chicanos streamed into universities, colleges, and junior colleges throughout the country. From this vantage point they began an assault on mainstream interpretations of our history and culture. It was at college that many individuals first engaged in the discussion of Marxist thought, always questioning how the issue of race fit into the framework. As with other political groups, splits developed within various factions of Marxist theory and strategy.

Mirroring the political currents and splits in the academic and political community, Chicano Studies has known turbulent times, and yet has survived. On the academic side, a series of changes in theoretical focus and approach has occurred (see Almaguer, 1981). From vague criticism to emphasis on internal colonialism to various Marxist interpretations, the area—discipline—of Chicano Studies has grown. To be sure, conservative research and reformist theory have also developed apace.

Despite the numerous and impressive achievements summarized above, some cultural myopia in Chicano studies still remains. In his most recent work, *The Chicano Experience* (1985), for example, Mirande writes as follows of Chicano Marxists:

> First there is an inordinate concern with political economy to the neglect of other significant aspects of the Chicano experience. The result is a unidimensional and somewhat limiting view of Chicanos. . . . [S]econd . . . Chicano Marxists in effect simply take existing perspectives and apply them to Chicanos rather than develop perspectives that spring from a Chicano world view. . . . [A] full understanding of Chicanos lies within rather than outside of our rich cultural heritage. Hence we must go beyond existing perspectives if we are to develop a Chicano paradigm (Mirande, 1985:205-07).

From my review and assessment of Chicano Marxist works, one can see that the multidimensional experiences of the Mexican-origin people (farm labor, immigration, the gender issue, community life, and so on) are topics for serious scholarship, but, more importantly, for informing struggle. Second, Chicano Marxist scholarship has grown through years of serious study into a global Marxist perspective. Chicano Marxists have studied not only Marx, Lenin, Luxemburg, Stalin, Goldman, Mao, Gonzales-Casanova, Guevara, Castro, Sandino, the FSLN, and Flores Magon, but also Althusser, Gramsci, and Negri. In other words, our Marxism is eclectic and grounded in a binational and, at the same time, international culture and economic reality.

Moreover, for Mirande to favor the development of a Chicano paradigm is to argue provincially and chauvinistically since the Mexican-origin people, although unique because of Mexico's border relation with the United States, still share many qualities with other peoples of color working in and against capitalism (see, too, Munoz, 1983).

Half way through the 1980s, three major new trends are discernible in Marxist Chicano studies: world systems approaches, the circulation of struggle perspective, and the gender-race viewpoint. The world systems approach to Chicano history was applied by Almaguer to California (1981), Jiminez to Arizona (1981), Chapa to silver mining in colonial Mexico (1981), Trujillo to Parlier, California (1981), and Montejano to Texas (1981). These works integrated the racial dynamics of oppression in the developing Southwest and northern Mexico into the global capitalist system. However, the amount of attention devoted to class conflict in this approach was minimal.

This particular criticism does not apply to the works of authors who emphasize the circulation-of-struggle neo-Marxist approach. Beginning with an analysis of the struggles themselves—of workers organized against capital—we see how the struggles circulate, how the working class "politically composes" itself against capital. Next we look at how capital attempts to "politically decompose" or counter the workers. The outcome of such struggle will be the new order or the next "political composition." To be sure, the analysis must also deal with investment, technological planning, and other more general social and economic phenomena. The point is that the working class, whether at the point of production or in the community, is at the fore of the analysis.

The works of Peña (1980, 1983) and Flores (1982, 1984) are contributions to Chicano Studies that use this framework. Their works remain consistent with the Marx (1967) of Volume I of *Capital*, who places workers *in struggle* at the core of his analysis.[8] For further elaboration of this method, see Cleaver (1979). The Marxist historians who contributed to the 1975 *Aztlan* special issue on labor history (for example, Nelson Cisneros and L. Arroyo) also wrote from this general perspective. With some modifications, the same approach is used in Bracamonte's (1983) analysis of immigration and union organizing and in Acuña's work, *A Community Under Siege* (1984), on community struggles and capital's ruthless methods of land use.

Another promising trend in Chicano Marxist scholarship concerns the work of feminists on the role of gender in community, factory, and university affairs. A recent political agenda in *Chicanas in the 80s: Unsettled Issues* (Mujeres en Marcha, 1983) sets the stage for work still to be done. Topics that are being dealt with range from the "feminization of poverty," to single-headed households, to unpaid work, to the economics of capitalism (Lopez-Garza, 1985: ch. 5; the forthcoming work by Del Castillo, and Teresa Cordova et al. 1986). Arguelles's (1983) research on Cuban, Puerto Rican, and Mexican immigrant women demonstrates women's resilience and modes of struggle in these closely related cultures. Issues of gender can no longer be ignored in Chicano scholarship just as race and class can no longer be ignored by white feminists. The theme of the 1984 National Association for Chicano Studies meetings was *Voces de la Mujer* (Voices of the Woman).

The issues of activism in the mid-1980s remains a pressing one for the Chicano/a scholar (see B. Corona, 1983). Some Chicano scholars are no longer active in the community, while others successfully combine their role as teacher/researcher/scholar within the academy with that of public advocate (Flores interview of Gomez-Quiñones, 1985; also see Flores, 1983a for a model of Chicano social action research within the Marxist tradition).

More than one Chicano Studies program has been abolished over the last seventeen years (University of California-Riverside in 1983 may be the most recent). Yet, at the same time, many programs have been expanded. Julian Samora, a non-Marxist, has optimistically summarized the present state of affairs as follows:

> Chicano Studies is well established as a sub-discipline in many universities. . . . Research and publication continue at a steady pace with many excellent works appearing frequently. . . . The foremost problem in my estimation, lies with university administrators in such fields as budgets, curriculum and hiring practices. . . [S] service to the community, while ill-defined, continues in many places. . . . I am optimistic that the next twenty years will be bountiful years for Chicanos in higher education (Samora, 1985:19-20).

No one doubts that the "bountiful years" that Samora predicts will come only through concerted effort and struggle. The struggle in Chicano Studies, especially for Chicana Marxists, is a struggle to create "open spaces" for research and activism. We can also not forget that many "left-Chicano" scholars have been denied tenure because of their participation in this struggle (see G. Flores, 1985).

Even though the current student body exhibits more self-interest than in previous years, it is also true that, in Chicano Studies, we have many professors who take class positions in their writing and lectures. It is with this latter group—who have maintained a continuity of thought and action, from the inception of Chicano Studies to their support of and involvement in *circulating struggles* over issues of gender, binationalism, Central America, apartheid, and nuclear build up—that the hopes and future of the Mexican-origin people and larger society, in part, rests.

FOOTNOTES

1. Of course, a complete review of this historical period would cover the French rule of the Mexican territory as well as the Spanish Conquest (see Meier and Rivera 1972:11-32; and D. Weber, 1973).

2. Controversy over the accuracy of both the 1970 and 1980 Censuses ensued. The former census undercounted the Hispanic-origin population by at least

9 percent, while the latter Census may be equally flawed despite attempts to correct previous undercounts (see Estrada, Hernandez, and Alvirez, 1977).

3. The literature on Cesar Chavez's United Farmworker's Union is large; for sympathetic sources see Matthiessen (1969) and Taylor (1975). For a critical review see Meister and Loftis (1977).

4. *La Raza* refers to "the Race" or, when used by an in-group member, to "our race" or "our people." The third-party La Raza Unida took this concept and the ideas of liberation and self-determination to the political arena and challenged the Democrats and Republicans to a reformist movement.

5. For research on undocumented immigrants and health see Chavez (1983) and Chavez, Cornelius, and Jones (1985). For immigration legislation alternatives see Schey (1977) and Civil Liberties Report (1982).

6. In terms of Marxist *praxis*, Rodolfo Acuña holds that it is not what the particular program researches, publishes, or teaches but how the individuals or programs act in struggle on their theory (Flores interview with Acuña, 1985). Issues of community and scholarship are, for Acuña, united in action.

7. Space limitations prevent a review of the legal dimension of these struggles and the contributions of Chicano law students and lawyers. Note that UCLA's *Chicano Law Review* began publishing in 1972. See Gerald Lopez's (1981) legal-class "normative" overview of undocumented Mexican immigration.

8. It is my estimation that much of Marxist Chicano scholarship, although versed in the early Marx or the Marx of the critical theorists, or other versions of Marxism (French or Maoist), has failed to incorporate the Marx of Volume I of *Capital*. This conclusion also suggests itself from a reading of the bibliographies found in these works. A different though related problem is the failure to acknowledge Marxist thought when it has been used.

BIBLIOGRAPHY

Acosta Johnson, C. "Breast Feeding and Social Class Mobility: The Case of the Migrant Mothers in Houston, Texas." In Melville, Margarita (ed.). *Twice a Minority: Mexican American Women*. St. Louis: C. V. Mosby, 1980.

Acuña, Rodolfo. *Occupied America: The Chicano's Struggle Toward Liberation*. San Francisco: Canfield Press, 1972.

________. *Occupied America: A History of Chicanos*. New York: Harper and Row, 1981.

________. *A Community Under Siege: A Chronicle of Chicanos East of the Los Angeles River 1945-1975*. Monograph No. 11. Los Angeles: Chicano Studies Research Center, UCLA, 1984.

Alien Children Education Litigation. MDL No. 398 (S. D. Tex.), July 21, 1980.

Almaguer, Tomas. "Toward the Study of Chicano Colonialism." *Aztlan* 2 (1971).

________. "Historical Notes on Chicano Oppression: The Dialectics of Racial and Class Domination in North America." *Aztlan* 5 (1974).

________. "Class, Race and Chicano Oppression." *Socialist Revolution* 5 (July-September 1975).

________. "Interpreting Chicano History: The World-System Approach to Nineteenth-Century California." *Review* 4:3 (Winter 1981).

Almaguer, Tomas, and Camarillo, Albert. "Urban Chicano Workers in Historical Perspective: A Review of the Literature." In Valdez, Armando et al. (eds.). *The State of Chicano Research in Family, Labor and Migration Studies*. Stanford, Calif.: Stanford Center for Chicano Research (1983).

Amin, Samir. *Accumulation on a World Scale: A Critique of the Theory of Underdevelopment*. New York: Monthly Review Press, 1974.

Andrade, Sally J. "Family Planning Practices of Mexican Americans." In Melville, Margarita (ed.). *Twice a Minority: Mexican American Women*. St. Louis: C. V. Mosby, 1980.

Arguelles, Lourdes. "Cuban, Mexican and Puerto Rican Immigrant Women: Their Struggles and Modes of Adaptation." Unpublished paper. Los Angeles: Chicano Studies Research Center, UCLA, 1983.

Arroyo, Laura E. "Industrial and Occupational Distribution of Chicano Workers." In Sanchez, Rosaura, and Rosa, Martinez Cruz (eds.). *Essays on La Mujer*, Anthology No. 1. Los Angeles: Chicano Studies Center Publications, UCLA, 1977.

Arroyo, Luis Leobardo. "Notes on Past, Present and Future Directions of Chicano Labor Studies." *Aztlan* 6:2 (1975a).

________. "Chicano Participation in Organized Labor: The CIO in Los Angeles, 1938-1950: An Extended Research Note." *Aztlan* 6:2 (1975b).

________. "The State of Chicano Labor History 1970-1980." In Ortiz, Isidro (ed.). *Chicanos and the Social Sciences: A Decade of Research and Development (1970-1980)*. Santa Barbara: Center for Chicano Studies, University of California, 1983.

August 29th Movement. *Fan the Flames: A Revolutionary Position on the Chicano National Question* (1976).

Baca-Zinn, Maxine. "Political Familism: Toward Sex Role Equality in Chicano Families." *Aztlan* 6 (Spring 1975).

________. "Field Research in Minority Communities: Ethical, Methodological and Political Observations by an Insider." *Social Problems* 27 (1979).

________. "Gender and Ethnic Identity Among Chicanos." *Frontiers: A Journal of Women Studies* 5 (Summer 1980).

________. "Ongoing Questions in the Study of Chicano Families." In Valdez, Armando et al. (eds.). *The State of Chicano Research in Family, Labor and Migration Studies*. Stanford, Calif.: Stanford Center for Chicano Research, 1983.

Bailey, Ronald, and Flores, Guillermo. "Internal Colonialism and Racial Minorities in the U. S.: An Overview." In Bonilla, Frank, and Gerling, Robert (eds.). *Structures of Dependency*. Palo Alto, Calif.: Stanford University Press, 1973.

Baird, Peter, and McCaughan, Ed. *Beyond the Border: Mexico and the U. S. Today*. New York: North American Congress on Latin America, 1979.

Barrera, Mario. "The Study of Politics and the Chicano." *Aztlan* 5:1&2 (Spring and Fall 1974).

________. *Race and Class in the Southwest: A Theory of Racial Inequality*. Notre Dame Press, 1979.

________. "Traditions of Research on the Chicano Worker." Valdez, Armando et al. (eds.). *The State of Chicano Research in Family, Labor and Migration Studies*. Stanford, Calif.: Stanford Center for Chicano Research, 1983.

Barrera, Mario, Muñoz, Carlos, and Ornelas, Charles. "The Barrio as Internal Colony." In Hahn, Harlan (ed.). *Urban Politics and People*, Urban Affairs Annual Review, Vol. 6. Beverly Hills, Calif.: Sage Publications, 1972.

Barrera, Mario, and Vialpando, Geralda. *Action Research: In Defense of the Barrio*. Los Angeles: Aztlan Publications, 1974.

Blauner, Robert. *Racial Oppression in America*. New York: Harper and Row, 1972.

Bracamonte, Jose. "The National Labor Relations Act and Undocumented Workers: The De-Alienation of American Labor." *San Diego Law Review* 21:1. University of San Diego School of Law, 1983.

Burawoy, Michael. "The Functions and Reproduction of Migrant Labor: Comparative Material from Southern Africa and the United States." *American Journal of Sociology* 81:5 (1976).

Bustamante, Jorge A. "A Theoretical Approach to the Sociology of Mexican Labor Migration." Doctoral Dissertation, University of Notre Dame, 1974.

________. "Commodity Migrants: Structural Analysis of Mexican Immigration to the United States." In Ross, Stanley (ed.). *Views Across the Border*. Albuquerque: Weatherhead Foundation and New Mexico University Press, 1978.

Camarillo, Albert. *Chicanos in a Changing Society: From Mexican Pueblos to American Barrios in Santa Barbara and Southern California, 1848-1930*. Cambridge, Mass.: Harvard University Press, 1979.

________. "The 'New' Chicano History: Historiography of Chicanos of the 1970s." In Ortiz, Isidro (ed.). *Chicanos and the Social Sciences: A Decade of Research and Development (1970-1980)*. Santa Barbara: Center for Chicano Studies, University of California, 1983.

Cardenas, Gilberto. "Mexican Labor: A View to Conceptualizing the Effects of Migration, Immigration and the Chicano Population in the United States." In Teller, Charles et al. (eds.). *Cuantos Somos: A Demographic Study of the Mexican American Population*. Austin: Center for Mexican American Studies, University of Texas, 1977.

Cardenas, Gilberto, and Bustamante, Jorge. "Research Memorandum and Commentary on Some Salient Issues Concerning United States Immigration Policy Towards Mexico, Mexican Migratory Movements and Mexican Labor in the United States, With a Special Emphasis on Illegal Immigration." Testimony for the Subcommittee of the Judiciary, Chicago Hearings on Illegal Aliens, October 23, 1971.

Cardenas, Gilberto, and Flores, Estevan. "Political Economy of International Labor Migration." In Rios-Bustamante, Antonio (ed.). *Immigration and Public Policy: Human Rights for Undocumented Workers and Their Families*. Los Angeles: Chicano Studies Research Center, UCLA, 1978.

________. "Social, Economic and Demographic Characteristics of Undocumented Mexicans in the Houston Labor Market: A Preliminary Report." Houston: Gulf Coast Legal Foundation, 1980.

Cardoso, Fernando H., and Reyna, Jose Luis. "Industrialization, Occupational Structures and Social Stratification in Latin America." In Blasier, C. (ed.). *Constructive Change in Latin America*. Pittsburgh: University of Pittsburgh Press, 1968.

Cardoso, Laurence. *Mexican Immigration to the United States, 1897-1931*. Tucson: University of Arizona Press, 1980.

Cervantes, Fred. "Chicanos as a Post-Colonial Minority: Some Questions Concerning the Adequacy of the Paradigm of Internal Colonialism." In Macias, Reynaldo Flores (ed.). *Perspectivas En Chicano Studies*. Los Angeles: Chicano Studies Center Publications, UCLA, 1977.

Chabran, Richard. "Ernesto Galarza: August 15, 1905-June 22, 1984." *Hispanic Journal of Behavioral Sciences* 7:2 (1985).

Chapa, Jorge. "Wage Labor in the Periphery: Silver Mining in Colonial Mexico." *Review* 4:3 (1981).

Chavez, Leo. "Undocumented Immigrants and Access to Health Services: A Game of Pass the Buck." *Migration Today* 11:15 (1983).

Chavez, Leo, Cornelius, Wayne, and Jones, O. W. "Mexican Immigrants and the Utilization of Health Services: The Case of San Diego." *Social Science and Medicine* 20:2 (1985).

Chicano Students Committee for Justice. "Chicano Demonstrations at New Mexico Highlands University." In *Parameters of Institutional Change: Chicano Experiences in Education*. Hayward, Calif.: Southwest Network, 1974.

Civil Liberties Report. "Immigration Proposals Unveiled." 5:7 (Washington, D.C., 1982).

Cleaver, Harry. *Reading Capital Politically*. Austin: University of Texas Press, 1979.

Communist League. "Report to the Communist Collective of the Chicano Nation." *Proletariat*, Spring 1974.

Communist Party. *Toward Chicano Liberation: The Communist Party Position*. New York: New Outlook Publishers, 1972.

Cordova, Teresa, Sierra, Christine, Cantu, Norma, and Garcia, John, eds. *Chicana Voices: Intersection of Class, Race, and Gender*. Austin: National Association for Chicano Studies, University of Texas, 1986.

Corona, Bert. "Chicano Scholars and Public Issues in the United States in the Eighties." In Garcia, Mario T. et al. (eds.). *History, Culture and Society: Chicano Studies in the 1980s*. Ypsilanti, Mich.: National Association of Chicano Studies, Bilingual Press, 1983.

Corona, Humberto. "Activities of the Brotherhood of Immigrant Workers, C.A.S.A. . . . " *Sin Fronteras* 1 & 2 (March 1974).

Cotera, Marta. "Chicana Caucus." *Magazin* 1:6 (1972).

Craig, Richard B. *The Bracero Program: Interest Group Politics and Foreign Policy*. Austin: University of Texas Press, 1971.

Crewdson, John. "The New Migrant Militancy: Whether They are Illegal Aliens or Not, They are Unionizing and Striking." *New York Times*, April 16, 1978.

Cuellar, Jose. "Social Science Research in the U. S. Mexican Community: A Case Study." Los Angeles: Aztlan International Journal of Chicano Studies Research, Chicano Studies Research Center, UCLA, 1981.

Del Castillo, Adelaida. "Malintzin Tenepal: A Preliminary Look Into a New Perspective." In Sanchez, Rosaura, and Martinez Cruz, Rosa (eds.). *Essays on La Mujer*. Anthology No. 1. Los Angeles: Chicano Studies Center Publications, UCLA, 1977.

_______. "Mexican Women in Organization." In Mora, Magdalena, and Del Castillo, Adelaida (eds.). *Mexican Women in the United States: Struggles Past and Present*. Los Angeles: Chicano Studies Research Center, UCLA, 1980.

_______. *Turbulent Memories: Essays on the History of Mexicana/Chicana Women*. Los Angeles: Chicano Studies Research Center, UCLA, forthcoming.

Del Castillo, Adelaida, and Mora, Magdalena. "Sex, Nationality and Class: La Obrera Mexicana." In Mora, Magdalena, and Del Castillo, Adelaida (eds.). *Mexican Women in the United States: Struggles Past and Present*. Los Angeles: Chicano Studies Research Center, UCLA, 1980.

Doe v. *Plyler and State of Texas*. 628 F. 2d 448 (5th Cir.), 1980.

Dunbar Ortiz, Roxanne. "Toward A Democratic Women's Movement in the United States." In Mora, Magdalena, and Del Castillo, Adelaida (eds.). *Mexican Women in the United States: Struggles Past and Present*. Los Angeles: Chicano Studies Research Center, UCLA, 1980.

Dworkin, Anthony Gary. "Stereotypes and Self Images Held by Native-Born and Foreign-Born Mexican Americans." *Sociology and Social Research* 49 (1965).

Estrada, Leo, Hernandez, Jose, and Alvirez, David. "Using Census Data to Study Spanish Heritage Population of the United States." In Teller, C. et al. (eds.). *Cuantos Somos: A Demographic Study of the Mexican American Population*, Monograph No. 2. Austin: Center for Mexican American Studies, University of Texas, 1977.

Fanon, Frantz. *Black Skin, White Masks*. New York: Grove Press, 1967.

Fernandez, Edward, and DeNavas, Carmen. *Persons of Spanish Origin in the United States: March 1982*. Current Population Reports, Population Characteristics, Series P-20, No. 396. Washington, D.C.: U. S. Department of Commerce, Bureau of the Census, 1982.

Flax, J. "The Family in Contemporary Feminist Thought: A Critical Review." In Elshtain, Jean (ed.). *The Family in Political Thought*. Amherst: University of Massachusetts Press, 1982.

Flores, Estevan. "La Circulacion Internacional del Trabajo y de la Lucha de Clases." *Historia y Sociedad*, No. 20 (Mexico City, 1978).

________. "Post-Bracero Undocumented Mexican Immigration to the United States and Political Recomposition." Doctoral Dissertation, University of Texas, Austin, 1982.

________. "Chicanos and Sociological Research, 1970-1980." In Ortiz, Isidro (ed.). *Chicanos and the Social Sciences: A Decade of Research and Development (1970-1980)*. Santa Barbara: Center for Chicano Studies, University of California, 1983a.

________. "The Impact of Undocumented Migration on the United States Labor Market." *Houston Journal of International Law* 5:2 (Spring 1983b).

________. "Research on Undocumented Immigrants and Public Policy: A Study of the Texas School Case." *International Migration Review* 18:3 (1984).

________. Interview with Guadalupe Sanchez, Executive Director of Sin Fronteras, S.C.L. (Sociedad Cooperativa Multiactiva/"Multiactive Cooperative Society"), in Mexico City, July 1984.

________. Interview with Dr. Juan Gomez-Quiñones, Professor of History and recent Director of Chicano Studies Research Center (1975-85), UCLA, Los Angeles, July 26, 1985.

________. Interview with Dr. Rodolfo Acuña, Professor of History and former Director of Chicano Studies, California State University at Northridge, July 31, 1985.

Flores, Guillermo. "Race and Culture in the Internal Colony: Keeping the Chicano in His Place." In Bonilla, F., and Girling, R. (eds.). *Structures of Dependency*. Palo Alto, Calif.: Stanford University Press, 1973.

_______. "Chicano Studies and the Chicano Intellectual." *Unity Newspaper* (Oakland, Calif.), March 15, 1985.

Frank, Andre Gunder. *Latin America: Underdevelopment or Revolution*. New York: Monthly Review Press, 1969.

Freire, Paulo. *Pedagogy of the Oppressed*. New York: Herder and Herder, 1972.

Frisbie, Parker. "Militancy Among Mexican American High School Students." *Social Science Quarterly* 53:4 (1973).

Galarza, Ernesto. *Merchants of Labor: The Mexican Bracero History*. Santa Barbara, Calif.: McNally and Loftin, 1964.

_______. *Spiders in the House and Workers in the Field*. Notre Dame, Ind.: University of Notre Dame Press, 1970.

_______. *Farm Workers and Agri-business in California, 1947-1960*. Notre Dame, Ind.: University of Notre Dame Press, 1977.

Garcia, Mario T. "Racial Dualism in the El Paso Labor Market, 1920-1980." *Aztlan* 6:2 (1975).

_______. *Desert Immigrants: The Mexicans of El Paso*. New Haven, Conn.: Yale University Press, 1981.

Garcia-Bahne, Betty. "La Chicana and the Chicano Family." In Sanchez, Rosaura, and Cruz, Rosa Martinez (eds.). *Essays on La Mujer*, Anthology No. 1. Los Angeles: Chicano Studies Center Publications, University of California, 1977.

Garcia y Griego, Manuel. 'The Importation of Mexican Contract Laborers to the United States, 1942-1964: Antecedents, Operation and Legacy." In Brown, Peter, and Shue, Henry (eds.). *The Border That Joins: Mexican Immigrants and U. S. Responsibility*. Totowa, N.J.: Rowman and Littlefield, 1983.

Gomez-Quiñones, Juan. "Toward a Perspective on Chicano History." *Aztlan* 2:2 (1971).

_______. "The First Steps: Chicano Labor Conflict and Organizing, 1900-1920." *Aztlan* 3:1 (1972).

_______. *Sembradores: Ricardo Flores Magon y el Partido Liberal Mexicano: A Eulogy and Critique*. Los Angeles: Chicano Studies Research Center, University of California, 1973.

_______. "To Leave To Hope or Chance: Propositions on Chicano Studies, 1974." In *Parameters of Institutional Change: Chicano Experiences in Education*. Hayward, Calif.: Southwest Network, 1974.

_______. *Mexican Students Por la Raza: The Chicano Student Movement in Southern California*. Santa Barbara: Editorial La Causa, 1978.

_______. "The Origins and Development of the Mexican Working Class in the United States: Laborers and Artisans North of the Rio Bravo, 1600-1900." In Frost, Elsa C. (ed.). *El trabajo y los trabajadores en la historia de Mexico*. Tucson: University of Arizona Press, 1979.

________. *Development of the Mexican Working Class North of the Rio Bravo*. Popular Series No. 2. Los Angeles: Chicano Studies Research Center, UCLA, 1982a.

________. "Critique of the National Question, Self Determination and Nationalism." *Latin American Perspectives* Issue 33, Vol. 9:2 (Spring 1982b).

________. "Mexican Immigration to the United States, 1948-1980: An Overview." In García, Eugene et al. (eds.). *Chicano Studies: A Multidisciplinary Approach*. New York: Teachers College Press, 1984.

Gomez-Quiñones, Juan, and Arroyo, Luis L. "On the State of Chicano History: Observations on its Development, Interpretations and Theory, 1970-1974." *Western Historical Quarterly* 7:2 (1976).

Grebler, Leo, Moore, Joan W., and Guzman, Ralph. *The Mexican American People: The Nation's Second Largest Minority*. New York: The Free Press, 1970.

Griswold del Castillo, Richard. *The Los Angeles Barrio 1850-1890: A Social History*. Los Angeles: University of California Press, 1979.

Guevara, Ernesto (Che). *Reminiscences of the Cuban Revolutionary War*. New York: Grove Press, 1968.

Gutierrez, Armando, and Hirsch, Herbert. "The Militant Challenge to the American Ethos: 'Chicanos' and 'Mexican Americans.'" *Social Science Quarterly* 53:4 (March 1973).

Hernandez, Deluvina. *Mexican American Challenge to a Sacred Cow*. Chicano Studies Center, Monograph No. 1. Los Angeles: University of California, 1970.

Hernandez, Patricia. "Lives of Chicana Activists: The Chicano Student Movement (A Case Study)." In Mora, Magdalena, and Del Castillo, Adelaida (eds.). *Mexican Women in the United States: Struggles Past and Present*. Los Angeles: Chicano Studies Research Center, UCLA, 1980.

Jimenez, Andres E. "The Political Formation of a Mexican Working Class in the Arizona Copper Industry, 1870-1917." *Review* 4:3 (Winter 1981).

Kay, M. A. "Mexican, Mexican American and Chicano Childbirth." In Melville, Margarita (ed.). *Twice a Minority: Mexican American Women*. St. Louis: C. V. Mosby, 1980.

Limon, José. "History, Chicano Joking, and the Varieties of Higher Education: Tradition and Performance as Critical Symbolic Action." *Journal of the Folklore Institute* 19:2-3 (1982).

________. "Western Marxism and Folklore: A Critical Introduction." *Journal of American Folklore Society* 96:379 (1983).

Lizarraga, Sylvia. "From a Woman to a Woman." In Sanchez, Rosaura, and Cruz, Rosa Martinez (eds.). *Essays on La Mujer*. Anthology No. 1. Los Angeles: Chicano Studies Center Publications, University of California, 1977.

Lopez, Gerald. "Undocumented Mexican Migration: In Search of a Just Immigration Policy." *UCLA Law Review* 28:4 (April 1981).

Lopez, Ronald W. "The El Monte Berry Strike of 1933." *Aztlan* 1:1 (1970).

Lopez, Ronald W., Madrid-Barela, Arturo, and Macias, Renaldo Flores. *Chicanos in Higher Education: Status and Issues*. Monograph No. 7. Los Angeles: Chicano Studies Center Publications, UCLA, 1976.

Lopez, Sonia. "The Role of the Chicana Within the Student Movement." In Sanchez, Rosaura, and Cruz, Rosa Martinez (eds.). *Essays on La Mujer*. Anthology No. 1. Los Angeles: Chicano Studies Center Publications, University of California, 1977.

Lopez-Garza, Marta. "Informal Labor in a Capitalist Economy: Urban Mexico." Doctoral Dissertation, University of California at Los Angeles, 1985.

Macias, Reynoldo Flores. "Schooling of Chicanos in a Bilingual, Culturally Relevant Context." In *Parameters of Institutional Change: Chicano Experiences in Education*. Hayward, Calif.: Southwest Network, 1974.

________, ed. *Perspectivas En Chicano Studies*. Los Angeles: Chicano Studies Center Publications, UCLA, 1977.

Marin, M. V. "Protest in an Urban Barrio: A Study of the Chicano Movement." Doctoral Dissertation, University of California, Santa Barbara, 1980.

Marquez, Evelina, and Ramirez, Margarita. "Women's Task is to Gain Liberation." In Sanchez, Rosaura, and Cruz, Rosa Martinez (eds.). *Essays on La Mujer*. Anthology No. 1. Los Angeles: Chicano Studies Center Publications, University of California, 1977.

Martinez, Oscar. *Border Boom Town: Ciudad Juarez, 1880-1970*. Austin: University of Texas Press, 1975.

Martinez, Tomas M. "Advertising and Racism: The Case of the Mexican American." *El Grito* II:4 (1969).

Marx, Karl. *Capital I: The Process of Capitalist Production*. New York: International Publishers, 1967.

Mason, Terry. "Symbolic Strategies for Change: A Discussion of the Chicana Women's Movement." In Melville, Margarita (ed.). *Twice a Minority: Mexican American Women*. St. Louis: C. V. Mosby, 1980.

Matthiessen, Peter. *Sal Si Puedes: Cesar Chavez and The New American Revolution*. New York: Random House, 1969.

Mazon, Mauricio. "Illegal Alien Surrogates: A Psychohistorical Interpretation of Group Stereotyping in Time of Economic Stress." *Aztlan* 6:2 (1975).

McWilliams, Carey. *Factories in the Field*. Santa Barbara, Calif.: Peregrine, 1971. Originally published in 1939.

________. *Ill Fares the Land*. Boston: Little, Brown, 1942.

———. *North From Mexico*. New York: Greenwood Press, 1968. Originally published in 1948.

Meier, Matt S., and Rivera, Feliciano. *The Chicanos: A History of Mexican Americans*. New York: Hill and Wang, 1972.

Meister, Dick, and Loftis, Anne. *A Long Time Coming: The Struggle to Unionize America's Farmworkers*. New York: Macmillan, 1977.

Melville, Margarita. "Mexican Women Adapt to Migration." *International Migration Review* 12:2 (1978).

Memmi, Albert. *The Colonizer and the Colonized*. Boston: Beacon Press, 1965.

Mindiola, Tatcho. "Marxism and the Chicano Movement: Preliminary Remarks." In Macias, Reynaldo Flores (ed.). *Perspectivas En Chicano Studies*. Los Angeles: Chicano Studies Center, UCLA, 1977.

———. *Occupied America: A Chicano History Symposium*. Mexican American Studies. Monograph Series No. 3, University of Houston, 1982.

Mirande, Alfredo. "Chicano Sociology: A New Paradigm for Social Science." *Pacific Sociological Review* 21 (1978).

———. *The Chicano Experience*. Notre Dame, Ind.: University of Notre Dame Press, 1985.

Mirande, Alfredo, and Enriquez, Evangelina. *La Chicana: The Mexican American Woman*. Chicago: University of Chicago Press, 1979.

Montejano, David. "Is Texas Bigger Than the World-System? A Critique from a Provincial Point of View." *Review* 4:3 (Winter 1981).

Montiel, Miguel. "The Social Science Myth of the Mexican American Family." *El Grito* 3:4 (1970).

Moore, Joan W. "Colonialism: The Case of the Mexican American." *Social Problems* 17:4 (1970).

Mora, Magdalena. "Mexican Labor in the Economic Development of the Southwest." In Rios-Bustamente, A. (ed.). *Immigration and Public Policy: Human Rights for Undocumented Workers and Their Families*. Rev. ed. Los Angeles: Chicano Studies Research Center, UCLA, 1978.

———. "The Tolteca Strike: Mexican Women and the Struggle for Union Representation." In Rios-Bustamante, A. (ed.). *Mexican Immigrant Workers in the U. S.*, Anthology 12. Los Angeles: Chicano Studies Research Center, UCLA, 1981.

Mora, Magdalena, and Del Castillo, Adelaida. *Mexican Women in the United States: Struggles Past and Present*. Los Angeles: Chicano Studies Research Center, UCLA, 1980.

Morales, Armando. *Ando Sangrando: A Study of Mexican American-Police Conflict*. La Puente, Calif.: Perspectiva Publications, 1972.

Morales, Rebecca. "Transitional Labor: Undocumented Workers in The Los Angeles Automobile Industry." *International Migration Review* 17:4 (1983).

Moreno, Steve. "Problems Related to Present Testing Instruments." *El Grito* 3:3 (1970).

Morris, Gabrielle, and Beard, Timothy. *The Burning Light: Action and Organizing in the Mexican Community in California*. Berkeley: Bancroft Library, University of California, 1982.

Mujeres En Marcha. *Chicanas in the 80s: Unsettled Issues*. Teresa Cordova and Gloria Cuadraz, eds. Berkeley: Chicano Studies Library Publications Unit, University of California, 1983.

Muñoz, Carlos. "The Quest for Paradigm: The Development of Chicano Studies and Intellectuals." In Garcia, Mario T. et al. (eds.). *History, Culture and Society: Chicano Studies in the 1980s*. Ypsilanti, Mich.: Bilingual Press, 1983.

________. "The Development of Chicano Studies, 1968-1981." In Garcia, Eugene E. et al. (eds.). *Chicano Studies: A Multidisciplinary Approach*. New York: Teachers College Press, 1984.

Murguia, Edward. *Assimilation, Colonialism, and the Mexican American People*. Austin: Center for Mexican American Studies, University of Texas, 1975.

Nava, Julian. *Viva La Raza*. New York: Litton Education Publication, 1973.

Navarro, Armando. "The Evolution of Chicano Politics." *Aztlan* 5:1 and 2 (1974).

Nelson Cisneros, Victor B. "La clase trabajodora en Tejas, 1920-1940." Los Angeles: Aztlan International Journal of Chicano Studies Research, Chicano Studies Center, UCLA, 1975.

________. "UCAPAWA Organizing Activities in Texas, 1935-1950." Los Angeles: Aztlan International Journal of Chicano Studies Research, Chicano Studies Center, UCLA, 1978.

Nieto-Gomez, Anna. "The Chicana–Perspectives for Education." *Encuentro Femenil.* 1:2 (1973).

________. "La Femenista." *Encuentro Femenil* 2:2 (1974).

________. "Sexism in the Movimiento." *La Gente* 6:4 (1976).

October League. "Chicano Liberation." In *Class Struggle*, Summer 1975.

Paredes, Americo. "*With His Pistol in His Hand*": *A Border Ballad and Its Hero*. Austin: University of Texas Press, 1958.

________. *A Texas-Mexican Cancionero*. Urbana: University of Illinois Press, 1976.

________. "On Ethnographic Work Among Minority Groups: A Folklorist's Perspective." *New Scholar* 6 (Fall and Spring 1977).

________. "The Folk Base of Chicano Literature." In Sommers, Joseph, and Ybarra-Frausto, Tomas (eds.). *Modern Chicano Writers: A Collection of Critical Essays*. Englewood Cliffs, N.J.: Prentice-Hall, 1979.

Passel, Jeffrey S., and Woodrow, Karen A. "Geographic Distribution of Undocumented Immigrants: Estimates of Undocumented Aliens Counted in the 1980 Census by State." *International Migration Review* 18:3 (1984).

Peña, Devon G. "Las Maquiladoras: Mexican Women and Class Struggle in the Border Industries." *Aztlan* 11 (1980).

———. "The Class Politics of Abstract Labor: Organizational Form and Industrial Relations in the Mexican Maquiladoras." Doctoral dissertation, University of Texas at Austin, 1983.

Prago, Albert. *Strangers in Their Own Land: A History of Mexican Americans*. New York: Four Winds Press, 1973.

Rendon, Armando. *Chicano Manifesto*. New York: Collier Books, 1971.

Revolutionary Union. *The Chicano Struggle and the Struggle for Socialism*. Chicago, 1975.

Rios-Bustamante, Antonio. *Mexicans in the United States and the National Question: Current Polemics and Organizational Positions*. Santa Barbara, Calif.: Editorial La Causa, 1978.

Risco, Eliezer. "Before Universidad de Aztlan: Ethnic Studies at Fresno State College." In *Parameters of Institutional Change: Chicano Experiences in Education*. Hayward, Calif.: Southwest Network, 1974.

Rochin, Refugio. "The Short and Turbulent Life of Chicano Studies: A Preliminary Study of Emerging Programs and Problems." *Social Science Quarterly* 53:4 (1973).

Rodriguez, Antonio. "El Informe y El Imperialismo." *Sin Fronteras* (Los Angeles) 4:2 (1977).

Romano, Octavio. "The Anthropology and Sociology of the Mexican-Americans: The Distortion of Mexican American History." *El Grito* 2:1 (1968).

———. "The Historical and Intellectual Presence of Mexican-Americans." *El Grito* 2:2 (1969).

Romo, Ricardo. "Responses to Mexican Immigration, 1910-1930." *Aztlan* 6:2 (1975).

Rosaldo, Renato. "Anthropological Perspectives on Chicanos 1970-1980." In Ortiz, Isidro (ed.). *Chicanos and the Social Sciences: A Decade of Research and Development (1970-1980)*. Santa Barbara: Center for Chicano Studies, University of California, 1983.

Rosales, Francisco A., and Simon, Daniel T. "Chicano Steel Workers and Unionism in the Midwest, 1919-1945." *Aztlan* 6:2 (1975).

Ryan, William. *Blaming the Victim*. New York: Vintage, 1971.

Samora, Julian. *La Raza: Forgotten Americans*. Notre Dame, Ind.: University of Notre Dame Press, 1966.

_______. *Los Mojados: The Wetback Story*. Notre Dame, Ind.: University of Notre Dame Press, 1971.

_______. "Chicano Studies Programs." Unpublished paper, Mexican American Studies, University of Notre Dame, Notre Dame, Ind., 1985.

Samora, Julian, Galarza, Ernesto, and Gallegos, Herman. *Mexican Americans in the Southwest*. Santa Barbara, Calif.: McNally and Loftin, 1969.

Sanchez, Alfredo. "Chicano Student Movement at San Jose." In *Parameters of Institutional Change: Chicano Experiences in Education*. Hayward, Calif.: Southwest Network, 1974.

Sanchez, George I. *Forgotten People*. Albuquerque: Calvin Horn, 1967. Originally published in 1940.

_______. *Concerning Segregation of Spanish-Speaking Children in the Public Schools*. Austin: University of Texas Press, 1951.

Sanchez, Guadalupe L., and Romo, Jesus. "Organizing Mexican Undocumented Farm Workers on Both Sides of the Border." *Working Paper in U.S.-Mexican Studies*, No. 27. Program in United States-Mexican Studies, University of California at San Diego, 1981.

Sanchez, Rosaura. "The Chicana Labor Force." In Sanchez, Rosaura, and Martinez Cruz, Rosa (eds.). *Essays on La Mujer*, Anthology No. 1. Los Angeles: Chicano Studies Research Center, UCLA, 1977.

Sanchez, Rosaura, and Cruz, Rosa Martinez. *Essays on La Mujer*, Anthology No. 1. Los Angeles: Chicano Studies Research Center, UCLA, 1977.

Saragoza, Alex M. "The Conceptualization of the History of the Chicano Family." In Valdez, Armando et al. (eds.). *State of Chicano Research on Family, Labor and Migration Studies*. Stanford, Calif.: Stanford Center for Chicano Research, 1983.

Schey, Peter. "Carter's Immigration Package." San Ysidro, Calif.: United California Mexican-American Association, October 1977.

Schlein, Lisa. "Los Angeles Garment District Sews a Cloak of Shame." In Mora, Magdalena, and Del Castillo, Adelaida (eds.). *Mexican Women in the United States: Struggles Past and Present*. Los Angeles: Chicano Studies Research Center, UCLA, 1980.

Sierra, Christine. "Chicano Political Development: Historical Considerations." In Garcia, Eugene F. et al. (eds.). *Chicano Studies: A Multidisciplinary Approach*. New York: Teachers College Press, 1984.

Simmons, Ozzie. "The Mutual Images and Expectations of Anglo-Americans and Mexican-Americans." *Daedalus* 90:2 (1961).

Socialist Worker's Party. *The Struggle for Chicano Liberation*. New York: Pathfinder Press, 1972.

Solis, Faustina. "Commentary on the Chicana and Health Service." In Sanchez, Rosaura, and Cruz, Rosa Martinez (eds.). *Essays on La Mujer*, Anthology No. 1. Los Angeles: Chicano Studies Research Center, UCLA, 1977.

Sosa-Riddell, Adaljiza. "Chicanas y el Movimiento." *Aztlan* 5:1 & 2 (1974).

Sutherland (Martinez), Elizabeth. "Colonized Women: The Chicana." In Morgan, Robin (ed.). *Sisterhood Is Powerful*. New York: Vintage Books, 1970.

Taylor, Paul S. *Mexican Labor in the United States: Imperial Valley*. Berkeley: University of California Publications in Economics, Vol. 6, No. 1, 1928.

________. *An American Frontier: Nueces County, Texas*. Chapel Hill: University of North Carolina Press, 1934.

Taylor, Ronald. *Chavez and The Farmworkers*. Boston: Beacon Press, 1975.

Torres, Isaias. "Civil Rights of Undocumented Immigrants in the United States." Paper presented at the National Association of Chicano Studies, Houston, Texas, April 1980.

Trujillo, Larry. "La Evolucion del 'Bandido' al 'Pachuco': A Re-examination of the Criminology Literature on Chicanos." *Issues of Criminology* 9 (1974).

________. "Race, Class, Labor and Community: A Local History of Capitalist Development." *Review* 4:3 (Winter 1981).

________. "Police Crimes in the Barrio." In Garcia, Mario T. et al. (eds.). *History, Culture and Society: Chicano Studies in the 1980s*. Ypsilanti, Mich.: National Association of Chicano Studies, Bilingual Press, 1983.

Urdaneta, M. L. "Chicana Use of Abortion: The Case of Alcala." In Melville, Margarita (ed.). *Twice a Minority: Mexican American Women*. St. Louis: C. V. Mosby, 1980.

Vaca, Nick C. "The Mexican American in the Social Sciences." *El Grito* 4 (1970).

Valdes, Dennis Nodin. "From Following the Crops to Chasing the Corporations: The Farm Labor Organizing Committee, 1967-1983." In Garcia, John A. et al. (eds.). *The Chicano Struggle: Analyses of Past and Present Efforts*. (A National Association for Chicano Studies publication.) Binghamton, N.Y.: Bilingual Press, 1984.

Valdez Fallis, Guadalupe. "The Liberated Chicana–A Struggle Against Tradition." *Women: A Journal of Liberation* 3:4 (1974).

Vasquez, Carlos. "El Movimiento Chicano-Un Paso." Part 9 of the series "Regeneracion." *Sin Fronteras* (Los Angeles) 1977.

________. "Women in the Chicano Movement." In Mora, Magdalena, and Del Castillo, Adelaida (eds.). *Mexican Women in the United States: Struggles Past and Present*. Los Angeles: Chicano Studies Research Center, UCLA, 1980.

Vasquez, Mario F. "The Election Day Immigration Raid at Lilli Diamond Originals and The Response of the ILGWU." In Mora, Magdelena, and Del Castillo,

Adelaida (eds.). *Mexican Women in the United States: Struggles Past and Present*. Los Angeles: Chicano Studies Research Center, UCLA, 1980.

Velez-I., Carlos. "The Non-Consenting Sterilization of Mexican Women in Los Angeles: Issues of Psychocultural Rupture and Legal Redress in Paternalistic Behavioral Environments." In Melville, Margarita (ed.). *Twice a Minority: Mexican American Women*. St. Louis: C. V. Mosby, 1980.

Warren, R., and Passel, J. "Estimates of Illegal Aliens from Mexico Counted in the 1980 United States Census." Paper presented at the Population Association Meetings, Pittsburgh, April 15, 1983.

Weber, David. *Foreigners in Their Native Land*. Albuquerque: University of New Mexico Press, 1973.

Weber, Devra Ann. "The Organization of Mexican American Agricultural Workers: The Imperial Valley and Los Angeles, 1928-1934, An Oral History Approach." *Aztlan* 3:2 (Fall 1972).

Ybarra, Lea. "Conjugal Relations in the Chicano Family." Doctoral Dissertation, University of California, Berkeley, 1977.

________. "Empirical and Theoretical Developments in Studies of the Chicano Family." In Valdez, Armando et al. (eds.). *The State of Chicano Research on Family, Labor and Migration Studies*. Stanford, Calif.: Center for Chicano Studies, 1983.

Zamora, Emilio. "Chicano Socialist Labor Activity in Texas, 1900-1920." Los Angeles: Aztlan International Journal of Chicano Studies Research, Chicano Studies Center, UCLA, 1975.

________. "Sara Estela Ramirez: Una Rosa Roja en el Movimiento." In Mora, Magdalena, and Del Castillo, Adelaida (eds.). *Mexican Women in the United States: Struggles Past and Present*. Los Angeles: Chicano Studies Research Center, UCLA, 1980.

5

A DIALOGUE ON RACE AND CLASS: ASIAN AMERICAN STUDIES AND MARXISM

John M. Liu
Lucie Cheng

The linkage between Asian American Studies and Marxism has been a tenuous one, due both to the historical activities of Marxist political parties in Asian American communities and to the current position that both fields occupy within the university. In order to understand the emergence of Asian American Studies and its relation to Marxism, it will be necessary to discuss briefly what the Marxian tradition has been within the Asian American communities prior to the 1960s. The chapter will then discuss the context in which Asian American Studies arose and the central questions the field has addressed. The focus of the discussion will be on issues that are also of relevance to Marxism. Broadly speaking, the two principal issues that Asian American Studies and Marxism have confronted during the 1970s and 1980s are the relationships between race and ethnicity and between race and class. Analysis of how Asian American Studies and Marxism have dealt with these issues will perhaps provide a basis for understanding how each field of inquiry has become increasingly relevant to the other.

ASIAN AMERICAN COMMUNITES AND MARXISM PRIOR TO 1960

Marxism has made its presence felt through various political organizations since the turn of the century and has been the dominant form

We are indebted to Edna Bonacich and Russell Leong for their helpful comments. We would also like to thank Kazue Shibata for her assistance in gathering material for this article.

of socialism in different Asian American communities since the late 1920s. Marxists within these communities created strong bonds between Asians in the United States and their countries of origin as they kept immigrants abreast of events unfolding in Asia and helped them to understand the meaning of these trends. Developments in Asia and in Asian American communities were thus interrelated through this linkage, an association that continues to exist. Marxists also played an important role in organizing both Asian urban and agricultural workers in the United States, especially during the 1930s. Yet despite this activity, there is little support for the notion that Marxists in this early period developed a perspective that adequately explained the situation of Asians in this country.

The activities of various socialist and communist parties both here and in Asia have exposed Asian American communities to Marxism since the early 1900s. Japanese and Chinese intellectuals, who were exposed to Marxism prior to their arrival in the United States, influenced much of this activity. As early as 1904, Japanese immigrants organized a branch of the Japanese Socialist Party in the San Francisco Bay Area after a visit by Sen Katayama (1860-1933) from Japan. The organization dissolved soon after its founding, however, and was followed by the formation of the Social Revolutionary Party in 1906. Unlike its predecessor, which organized around Marxist principles, the Social Revolutionary Party also incorporated a second strand of socialism: anarchosyndicalism (Ichioka, 1976:50-53). Both socialisms advocated the organization of workers in opposition to the state but only the anarchosyndicalists through the Industrial Workers of the World (IWW) recruited workers in the United States across racial lines during the early part of the century. In contrast, Marxists in the American Socialist Party mirrored the xenophobic activities of most American labor leaders of the period and called for the exclusion of Japanese and other Asians from the United States.

The exclusionist policy of the American Socialist Party also explains in part why the IWW was the first major socialist organization to successfully recruit immigrant workers in Chinese communities after the turn of the century. Syndicalist ideas were also prominent among early Chinese radicals because of the anarchist writings that originated from China after 1905 (Lai, 1976b:64-67). The IWW, however, declined between World War I and 1930. During the war, the federal government imprisoned many of the organization's leaders because of the its antimilitaristic stance. In 1924 the IWW split as dissident members challenged the organization's position on the decentralization of leadership and the refusal to enter into alliances with political parties.

Meanwhile, Marxism became the prominent strand of socialism in the various Asian American communities after the formation of the American Communist Party (CP) in 1919. Unlike the American Socialist Party, the CP recruited Asians into the organization. By the end of the 1920s it established itself as the dominant socialist organization in both the Chinese and Japanese communities (Hom, 1982:75-77; Lai, 1976b:66-71; Yoneda, 1983:13-107 *passim*). The CP's influence extended into the Filipino community during the 1930s as Communists organized Filipino cannery and agricultural workers who had begun migrating to the West Coast in the preceding decade (Bulosan, 1981:265-304; Daniel, 1981:105-40; De Witt, 1980:17-18; Yoneda, 1983:23-60).

From the late 1930s until the mid-1950s, Marxists both within the Asian American communities and the larger American communist movement focused more on international events than on local affairs. In 1935 the Communist International (Comintern) adopted the "Popular Front" strategy of forming coalitions with Social Democrats and other liberal parties in order to combat Fascism. In the United States, Marxist activity in both the Chinese and Japanese communities centered around developing a mass movement against Imperial Japan's aggression in Asia. With the outbreak of World War II, Marxists concentrated on aiding the war effort. This included the CP's support of the U.S. government's decision to incarcerate West Coast Japanese for the duration of the war and the party's suspension of all Japanese members (Yoneda, 1983:115-24; 213-15).

After the war, the American Communist Party prepared for what it believed was an inevitable war between the United States and the USSR (the "five minutes to midnight" line). The international situation similarly preoccupied the attention of community Marxists. In Chinatown, for instance, the success of the Chinese Revolution of 1949 inspired many Chinese as well as other Asian Americans. Chinese American students gave accounts of their trips back to China, Chinatown theaters showed films from the People's Republic of China, and groups formed to the study the thoughts of Mao Zedong. Moreover, the political struggle between the Chinese Communist Party and the Nationalist Chinese Party was repeated between supporters of each group in Chinatowns throughout the United States (Lai, 1976a:156-58).

However, even before Marxists became preoccupied with internatinal affairs they had not directed much attention toward the development of a position that interpreted the experience of Asians in the United States. In line with the dominant Marxist thinking of the time, Marxists emphasized the common position that Asian workers shared with all other proletariat under capitalism and tended to downplay the oppression that Asians encountered because of their race. There is no indication that Marxism gave any theoretical consideration to the question of race despite the special place occupied by black Americans in the international communist movement.

In 1928 the Comintern had adopted the position that black Americans possessed the characteristics of a nation and were therefore entitled to the right of self-determination, a position maintained by the American Communist Party until 1958 (Carr, 1981). The Comintern argued that because black Americans were "a stable community of people, formed on the basis of a common language, territory, economic life, and psychological make-up manifested in a common culture" (Stalin, as quoted in Carr, 1981:46), they constituted an oppressed nationality that should be allowed the right to form a nation in the American South. What is important to note is that Marxists gave black Americans special theoretical consideration for cultural or ethnic reasons rather than for racial ones. The American Communist Party apparently never extended the oppressed nationality thesis to include Asians in America. Consideration of Japanese as an oppressed national minority certainly was not manifest in the CP's support of the relocation during World War II.

Besides the theoretical void at the Comintern level, there is little indication that American Marxism gave much specific thought to the position of Asians in the United States. Although Asian Americans comprised a sizable segment of the West Coast labor force, they did not constitute a large enough number to merit separate attention by Marxists; nor were Asian workers generally located in occupations that required special organizing efforts by American communists. Marxists at the time were concerned mainly with organizing the industrial proletariat and agricultural wage earners. Discriminatory laws and labor union practices excluded the large majority of Asian workers from the basic industries that communists attempted to organize. Asians worked in service occupations and businesses located within their own communities or they operated small businesses (including farms). At this time, among Asians only Filipinos were predominantly employed in the fields and canneries.

During the 1950s, Marxist influence within the Asian American communities waned. The overt reason for this decline was the strong anti-Communist environment created by the onset of the Cold War and the activities of Senator Joseph McCarthy. China's entry into the Korean War against the United States had a particularly dampening effect among Chinese Americans. The U.S. government deprived the Chinese community of leftist leadership by deporting individuals who were Communist Party members or sympathizers. It also refused to readmit Chinese who had temporarily left the United States if they were alleged communists (Kwong, 1979:144-45). People ceased attending communist-sponsored social functions and membership in various Marxist organizations steeply declined as immigration authorities and FBI agents continuously harassed communist leaders (Lai, 1976b:71-72). Similar actions took place in the Japanese and Filipino communities as the U.S. government deported Communist Party members and prosecuted labor leaders suspected of being communists (Yoneda, 1983:173-74; Cordova, 1983:79).

Contributing to the decline of Marxist influence in the Asian American communities was the virtual collapse of the American Communist Party. At the beginning of 1956 there were between 17,000 and 20,000 party members. Twenty months later there were only about 3,000 members. Governmental harassment, the CP's "five minutes to midnight" line, and the lack of internal democracy within the CP, particularly following the USSR's invasion of Hungary in 1956, led to mass defections from the party (Isserman, 1982:73-87). As a result of the Communist Party's breakup, "for the first time in the twentieth century the United States had no significant nationally organized socialist movement" (Isserman, 1982:71).

The suppression and dismissal of Marxism in the academy accentuated the inability of American Marxism to deal with the Asian experience in the United States. The anticommunist repression of the 1950s and the absence of a strong socialist movement prevented Marxist thinkers from sustaining a creative dialogue and critique within the academic community. Many intellectuals in the United States saw the 1950s as the onset of the "American century" and extolled the virtues of American society. One aspect of this national aggrandizement involved the assertion that differences based on cultural and racial criteria would eventually vanish. People in American society would be judged on their individual merits rather than on traditional distinctions (Greeley, 1974:18-26). Marxists were unable to develop critical analyses that might have nourished new perspectives on the position of

Asians and other minorities in American society. By 1965, Talcott Parsons, one of the doyens of American sociology, confidently dismissed Marxist thought as irrelevant to contemporary events (Burawoy, 1982:S-3; Teodori, 1969:7-8).

Thus the political repression of the 1950s, the collapse of the American Communist Party, the lack of special attention by party organizers toward the position of Asians in the United States, and the suppression of Marxist thought in the academic community contributed to a situation in which Marxism had a tangential relevance to the various Asian American communities by the end of the 1950s. By the time Asian American Studies emerged around 1969, its appearance was not markedly influenced by the Marxist thought of the Old Left. However, the connection of Asian American communities to occurrences in Asia was never broken. On the one hand, Asian Americans closely followed events in the People's Republic of China, the defeat of French forces in Dienbienphu, Vietnam, and the Bandung Conference of 1955. On the other hand, Americans continued to transfer their attitudes and politics toward Asia to Asian Americans. Thus, after the People's Republic of China's entry into the Korean War, there was talk of interning all Chinese Americans just as the Japanese Americans had been during World War II (Kwong, 1979: 144; Bosworth, 1967).

THE EMERGENCE OF THE ASIAN AMERICAN MOVEMENT

The events of the late 1960s and early 1970s formed the immediate context in which Asian American Studies arose. The student, Civil Rights, Black Power, and anti-Vietnam War movements each contributed to the emergence and development of an Asian American movement, which led to the establishment of Asian American Studies. All these movements arose with the formation of a New Left that diverged from the Old Left in many areas, including its belief over which classes or strata would lead the revolution and which countries constituted models of socialist development (Flacks, 1971:23-24, 31-32; Gilbert, 1969:351; Omi and Winant, 1983:37-40). The Old Left saw the working class as the leading revolutionary stratum while the New Left sought to organize people across class lines. Where the Old Left esteemed the Soviet Union as the model of socialism, the New Left looked to the People's Republic of China and the Vietnamese National Liberation Front. These differences between the two Lefts in terms of philosophy and practice reflected the middle-class origins of the

New Left and it was the latter's version of socialism that would initially influence the thinking of Asian American activists.

At the beginning of the decade, students on college campuses throughout the country exhibited an activism that questioned America's involvement against various decolonization and nationalistic movements in Africa, Asia, and Latin America. They questioned the image of America as the richest and freest nation in the world in light of Michael Harrington's exposure in *The Other America* (1962), of the poverty that continued to exist in the land of affluence, while the struggles of blacks to gain the franchise raised doubts about America's commitment to democracy at home. They also questioned whether the universities properly educated students to deal with these basic discrepancies.

Student participation in the Civil Rights and antiwar movements of this period made race and ethnicity into issues of the highest priority. The central focus of the Civil Rights movement was integration into American society. To raise the very question of integration assumed that blacks and other racial groups would be able to assimilate into American society once people became aware of the barriers that prevented the upward mobility of minorities. The resistance of governmental and private bodies toward implementing changes led blacks, Latinos, Native Americans, and Asian Americans to doubt whether nonwhites would ever voluntarily be given the same opportunities to assimilate into American society that previous groups had received.

The antiwar movement had a similar polarizing effect. When the government expressed concerns about the costs of implementing various social reforms, students in general pointed to the vast resources expended in Vietnam. Nonwhite students had additional objections. Blacks and Latinos asked why the war casualties were disproportionately higher among their people than among white soldiers. Asian Americans protested the ferociousness of the Vietnam conflict in comparison to prior wars. Nonwhites also began to question the sincerity of their fellow white students in the antiwar movement when the latter denied the various racial minorities a forum in which to raise their specific concerns. In the 1971 antiwar march on Washington, D.C., the Asian American contingent refused to participate when the coordinating committee denied the contingent an opportunity to include an antiracist statement in the march's program (Wong, 1972:36).

These concerns and doubts led blacks to form their own movement based on a stance that confronted not only the Establishment but also blacks in the civil rights movement and white student activists.

Black movement advocates argued that white society would never peacefully and freely give blacks their share of the American pie because a racist thread ran through the entire American social fabric. Contrary to assertions of social scientists that blacks represented the newest ethnic group and would eventually assimilate as had previous ethnic groups (for example, see Glazer, 1972), black radicals maintained that America's institutional make-up denied certain racially defined groups economic and social mobility. Racism–that is, the belief in white superiority–was so pervasive that even white radicals unconsciously practiced it as evidenced by the lack of blacks and other nonwhites in positions of leadership in the student and antiwar movements and by the failure of white leadership to boldly raise racial issues before their constituents. Black radicals proclaimed that the only alternative they had left was to engage in revolutionary nationalism.

The black nationalist or liberation position struck a responsive chord among other racial groups, including Asian Americans. Paul Wong (1972:33-36) suggested several reasons for this. Prior to the late 1960s there existed distinct cultural differences and strong historical animosities among the different Asian groups in the United States. Yet on the college campuses distinct national origins tended to blur as the various Asian groups intermingled with one another. The fact that governmental agencies, school authorities, and the general student body could not distinguish among the various Asian groups also contributed to a tendency for them to identify themselves as Asian Americans. Finally, as Asian Americans involved themselves in the antiwar movement, they began to identify with the liberation struggles of the Asian peoples. While most participants in the antiwar movement used slogans such as "Give peace a chance," and "Bring the G.I.'s home," Asian Americans emphasized "the *racist* nature of war, using such slogans as 'Stop killing *our* Asian brothers and sisters,' and 'We don't want *your* racist war'" (Wong, 1972:35-36).

In the same period, Asian American students began fighting for academic recognition of their common interests and concerns. Beginning in 1969, Asian American Studies programs were established on major university campuses located on the West Coast, in Hawaii, and in New York City.[1]

ASIAN AMERICAN STUDIES–THE COMMUNITY INFLUENCE

Once established, Asian American Studies programs needed to determine how they could fulfill their obligations to the community that brought the programs into existence and still survive within an academic setting. In this struggle, Asian American Studies came into contact with Marxism through the activities of Asian American community activists and through the resurgence of Marxian thinking in the university.

One consequence of Asian American student activism was that many students, despite their predominantly middle-class origins (Wong, 1972:37), chose to work in poor urban Asian American communities such as Chinatown, Nihonmachi, and Manilatown. Two desires motivated these students: one to ameliorate the deplorable conditions in existing urban Asian American communities, the other to build revolutionary nationalism among the masses. This was evident in the activities of two major political organizations in the Chinatown community: The Red Guard and I Wor Kuen (IWK). The Red Guard, for instance, copied a program developed by the Black Panthers and instituted a free breakfast program for indigent Chinatown children (Lyman, 1970:106). As part of its organizing efforts, the IWK issued a twelve-point program and platform that included demands for self-determination for Asian Americans and Asians, community control of institutions and land, an end to racism, and the establishment of a socialist party (IWK, circa 1969/70).

Marxism was not the initial guiding philosophy of these and many other Asian American community groups despite their desires for revolutionary change and a socialist society.[2] This is evident in a statement issued by the IWK:

> First of all, we did not begin as a Marxist-Leninist organization. But we did begin as a consciously revolutionary organization. That is, we sought a revolutionary, total solution to the roots of the problems we face as Asian peoples.
>
> Our organization, like many others here in America, arose as a response to national oppression and racial discrimination, and as part of the growing anti-imperialist movement in the 1960's. We formed as an Asian organization because, in 1968-69, the national oppression and corresponding national struggles of Third World peoples was the sharpest in the nationwide progressive movement. Furthermore, the bankruptcy of the Communist Party, USA and Progressive Labor Party, among others, especially in relation to the national question, made joining their ranks out of the question (IWK, 1974:6-7).[3]

It was over the question of national oppression that Asian American community activists reacquainted themselves with Marxism, but it was a Marxism in which race rather than class tended to receive the prominent emphasis.[4] The inspiration for many activists came from the politics of the Vietnamese National Liberation Front and the People's Republic of China, which stressed the importance of achieving national liberation as a crucial step in the attainment of socialism. Community activists transposed this position by referring to Asian Americans as oppressed national minorities living in a colonial situation. Thus, in an ironic fashion, they adopted a position similar to the American Communist Party's "black nation thesis." There was, however, one critical difference. Community activists followed the lead of Marxist writers such as Frantz Fanon (1968:40) who observed that

> when you examine at close quarters the colonial context, it is evident that what parcels out the world is to begin with the fact of belonging to or not belonging to a given race, . . . you are rich because you are white, you are white because you are rich. That is why Marxist analysis should always be slightly stretched every time we have to do with the colonial problem.

In this perspective race tended to assume a greater importance than class in analyzing the situation of racial minorities in the United States. Community newspapers urged the mobilization of Asian Americans around their race irrespective of class background. *Gidra*, a Los Angeles-based newspaper that later adopted a Marxist stance, initially promoted the line that

> the Yellow Power movement has been motivated largely by the problem of self-identity in Asian Americans. The psychological focus of this movement is vital, for Asian Americans suffer the critical mental crises of having "integrated" into American society. . . . Yellow consciousness is the immediate goal of concerned Asian Americans (Uyematsu, 1969: 8).

The first research agendas of the various Asian American Studies programs reflected the emphasis on identity. They also explored the ambiguous ties among race, the national question, and Marxism.

ASIAN AMERICAN STUDIES AND THE ACADEMIC RESPONSE

The national oppression position advocated by community activists spawned two closely related lines of research in Asian American Studies: one focused around the question of identity and the significance of the Asian American experience, the other around the theoretical implications of the national question and race.[5] Two seminal texts, *Roots: An Asian American Reader* (Tachiki et al., 1971) and *Asian Women* (Asian Women's Journal, 1971), clearly indicated the concerns of Asian American Studies programs with the identity issue.

> Identity is a question to which we return time and time again. It is never neatly solved and incorporated into the computation of other variables. Identity is crucial to ideology and action—central to the problem of self-determination at any level. The Asian who "identifies" white (or *anything* other than he is) faces the insurmountable problem of his physical makeup (Tachiki et al., 1971:viii).

> We were not satisfied with the traditional roles, the white middle-class standards, nor the typical Asian women stereotypes in America. We wanted our own identity (Asian Women's Journal, 1971:4).

The importance of the identity question was also apparent in a series of articles by Sue and Sue (1971, 1972), Sue (1974), Tong (1971, 1972a,b; 1974), Abbot (1972), and Surh (1974), which debated the factors that shaped the personality of Asian Americans. Each of the participants agreed that racism was a central factor in the development of Asian American identity. Surh (1974:166-67) injected a Marxian analysis into the debate by examining racism as a subjective manifestation of capitalism's early development in the United States. His article, however, was a rare instance in its use of a specifically Marxian framework. These articles all appeared in the initial issues of *Amerasia Journal*, the oldest continuously published periodical in the field and the only national publication devoted exclusively to a scholarly examination of the Asian American experience.[6]

The question of identity and the central role of racism was also the subject matter of *Aiiieeeee! An Anthology of Asian-American Writers* (Chin et al., 1974), which disputed the idea that Asian Americans were an equal blend of Asia and America. The editors equally contested the notion that Asian Americans wholly preserved the cultural traditions of their societies of origin in Asian because racism had prevented them from becoming white Americans. Instead, they asserted that Asian Americans possessed *unique* "sensibilities and cultures that might be related to but are distinct from Asia and white America" (viii).[7]

If Asian Americans were to establish a new collective identity, then it was necessary to see themselves as active historical persons rather than as passive objects and to provide their own interpretations of the Asian experience in the United States. As Daniels (1966:375) noted in a review of previous research done on Asian Americans: "Other immigrant groups were celebrated for what they had accomplished; Orientals were important for what was done to them." Hence some of the early research in the field critically reassessed the existing research on Asian Americans. Ichioka et al. (1974) and Daniels (1974) offered perceptive critiques of the existing literature on Japanese Americans while noting the need to use Asian language resources.[8] Hirata (1976) offered a similar critical appraisal of past sociological research done on Chinese Americans. Victor G. and Brett de Bary Nee (1972) provided new insights on the social structure of San Francisco Chinatown. Their division of San Francisco into classes, which were actually status groups, demonstrated the necessity of examining the inner dynamics of Asian American communities and their connection to developments within the larger American society.

Establishing the significance of Asian American Studies rested on more than the development of a new collective identity. It was also necessary to establish that the significance of the Asian American experience was not limited to the West Coast and Hawaii. Lyman (1970) discussed how the Asian American experience shaped the development of institutional racism in American society, while Saxton (1971) examined the crucial role Chinese labor had in the emergence of labor unions in the West and in the revival of the Democratic Party after the Civil War. The vast literature on the incarceration of Japanese during World War II (for example, see Okamura [1976] for a survey of this literature, see also Weglyn, 1976; Commission on Wartime Relocation and Internment of Civilians, 1983; Irons, 1983; Daniels, 1962, 1972) further confirmed that events that had an impact upon Asian Americans also had national importance. Nakanishi (1975) proposed a theoretical model that analyzed Asians in the United States within both a national and international context because of the strong association that has existed between Asian American communities and Asia.

Race played a prominent conceptual role in these studies, yet it was not always clearly distinguished from the concept of ethnicity. This was understandable given the prevailing preference of social scientists at the time to "subsume groups racially distinguished within the broad category of 'ethnic'" (Yetman and Steele, 1971:10). However, one of the main premises underlying Asian American Studies as well as other ethnic studies programs was that racially and ethnically defined groups had differential access to the basic institutions of American society and that race and ethnicity therefore represented two separate social realities. The appearance of two new basic texts,

Letters in Exile: An Introductory Reader on the History of Pilipinos in America (Quinsaat, 1976) and *Counterpoint: Perspectives on Asian America* (Gee, 1976), reflected this fundamental distinction. The latter book moreover contained studies that suggested that research interests in the field were beginning to engage in an exchange with Marxism.

Although a distinctly progressive political position guided most of the above research, there was a noticeable lack of any Marxian analysis. During the mid-1970s this changed as research in Asian American Studies programs moved away from questions of identity toward examining the theoretical implications of the national question and race. Much of this new research explored the manner in which the American economic structure integrated Asian Americans. Consequently, researchers turned toward Marxism as a way of understanding the interaction between race and class. As noted earlier, one impetus for this increased interest originated out of the debates among Asian American community activists over the national question. A second catalyst came from within the academic community.

The very same forces that had led to the creation of Asian American Studies also brought about a renewal of interest in Marxism during the early 1970s. Strong anticommunist sentiment in segments of the working class and the weakness of the American Communist Party restricted the revival primarily to the academic community, which enjoyed the greater intellectual freedom created by student activism (Burawoy, 1982:S6-7). The renaissance provoked a reassessment of Marxian thought because of the prominence given to race in the analyses by minorities of the domestic and international situations. Traditionally, Marxists considered race to be an ideological or superstructural phenomenon, that is, determined by class relations, which would become irrelevant with the founding of a socialist society (for example, Cox, 1970). Moreover, there was a tendency to treat race as a form of ethnicity. (Although believing that traditional distinctions such as ethnicity would disappear, Cox was one of the few early Marxists to make a clear theoretical distinction between race and ethnicity.) The concern of Marxists with the problem of race and the interest of Asian American Studies in investigating economic integration led to an overlapping of interests.

The debate over the national question and the centrality of race in the Asian American experience among community activists generated two closely related lines of inquiry: One explored the implications of the national question while the other investigated the structural significance of race in the economic participation of Asian Americans. Researchers within Asian American Studies programs sought a perspective that adequately explained the oppressed national minority status held by Asians in the United States. They first gave serious attention to the internal colonial model advanced by Clark (1965), Carmichael and Hamilton (1967), and Tabb (1970).

The internal colonial model contended that though racial minorities were never colonized by the United States, they nevertheless occupied a position akin to that held by subjugated people in colonies. As in colonial situations, some form of coercion—for example, slavery, contract labor, or annexation—accompanied racial minority participation in American society. Whites, that is, the colonizers, kept racial minorities economically and politically subjugated in order to exploit their labor. Nonwhites were confined to occupations in competitive, low-paying industries, while whites were concentrated in the monopolistic, high-paying sector of the economy. Racism was essential to the preservation of this arrangement since it prevented the mobility of racially defined people. Unlike colonized people, however, internal colonized minorities in the United States formally had legal equality with white Americans (Blauner, 1972: 19-81).

The internal colonial model and its emphasis on race polarized opinion among Marxists whose research involved Asian Americans. Fujimoto (1971) found the model a valuable tool in interpreting the experience of Asians in the United States. Blauner (1972: 10) likewise contended that the internal colonial model was a necessary corrective to the "failure of Marxism to appreciate the significance of racial groups and racial conflict." This contrasted with the position taken by Peter Kwong (1979: 12-13) in his study of New York City's Chinatown, where he opposed

> the tendency to use "racial" factors to explain the condition of minorities in this country. . . . [I] t fails to explain the many subtle differences in the way the U.S. social system operates vis-a-vis each racial group, as well as to encompass within its framework class divisions within such groups.

Specific application of this model to Asian Americans posed more questions than answers. On the positive side, the dual labor market thesis coincided with the influential work done by Chiu (1963) on the distribution of Chinese labor in nineteenth-century California. However, in a comparison of classical and internal colonialism, Liu (1976) observed that the model raised questions about the negation of internal colonialism, that is, the nature of decolonization. When carried out to its logical conclusion, the model offered internal colonized people only two possible paths: nationhood or reconstruction of American society.

Community activists within the Asian American communities gave these two choices serious consideration. In 1972 a Marxist-oriented community group known as East Wind adopted the "Asian nation" line. The group declared that as racially oppressed national minorities Asian Americans were entitled to form their own nation. Two years later a study group in New York went so far as to claim that Chinatown could serve as a territorial base for a Chinese American nation. East Wind dropped the "Asian nation" line the following year in 1975 (Nakano, 1984:11). In hindsight, the belief that the Chinese or any other Asian group in the United States could create their own viable nation was never a tenable one. Yet consideration of this position and its rejection allowed researchers in Asian American Studies to concentrate their efforts on developing a more comprehensive knowledge of Asian participation in the U.S. economy as a prelude to any social reconstruction. As they did so, scholars relied to a greater extent on Marxian perspectives.

Work with the internal colonial model stimulated additional studies on community control and Asian labor participation. As part of a larger interest in understanding the political economy of Asian American communities, Hirata (1975) analyzed tax rolls covering the Los Angeles Chinatown area to determine who owned and controlled the land. Her study questioned the applicability of the model in its failure to differentiate among different classes within the Chinese community, but noted that any class analysis that failed to take race into account would be totally inadequate given the mixed-racial composition of Chinatown. Kagiwada (1982/83) reached a similar conclusion in his analysis of the model's relevance to the Japanese American experience. The model was more successful in describing the economic roles maintained by Asian Americans. Ng's (1977) study of Chinese distribution in the labor market lent some support to the existence of a dual labor market, particularly in the case of Chinese women. Ng's research also lent partial support to the middleman hypothesis, which was another line of investigation in Asian American Studies that spurred a greater use of Marxian perspectives.

Research on the middleman minority theory grew out of an interest in how Asian Americans fit into the American social structure. Work in this area has been done by Bonacich (1973), Bonacich and

Modell (1980), Kitano (1974), and Modell (1977), principally in regard to Japanese Americans. Each of these studies examined the interaction between race and economic participation. All three scholars tended to treat middleman minorities as status groups. In Kitano's work, however, the status group was undifferentiated, whereas both Bonacich and Modell suggested that class differences existed within the grouping but were suppressed. Moreover, both Bonacich and Modell in their work on middleman minorities implied that race was a superstructural phenomenon, as can be inferred from their conclusions about the rapid assimilation of Japanese Americans.

Marxian class perspectives were subsequently used in studies that examined the patterns of cooperation and conflict within each racial group. DeWitt (1978) and Ichioka (1979, 1980) revealed how racial labor contractors as a class within their communities could both exploit and represent the interests of workers. Mei (1984) similarly applied a Marxian perspective in her study of San Francisco's Chinatown class structure during the latter half of the nineteenth century. These later studies also indicated the structural importance of race by analyzing the emergence of class relations within the context formed by racial criteria rather than by treating racial factors as secondary to class formation.

NEW DIRECTIONS IN RESEARCH

Since the late 1970s, several additional areas of overlapping research have developed between Asian American Studies and Marxism. The most significant overlapping has occurred in the area of immigration. Although immigration has always been a main topic of investigation in Asian American Studies, it has become even more important because of the rapid growth of Asian populations in the United States. Since the early 1970s, the liberalization of U.S. immigration laws and the large influx of political refugees from southeast Asia have greatly expanded the size and number of Asian American communities as well as shown the continuing importance of international trends to the development of Asian American communities.

This recent immigration has likewise affected the composition and politics of Asian American communities. The increase in immigration has made immigrants the dominant strata among certain Asian American populations such as Chinese, Koreans, Filipinos, and Vietnamese. Present laws have also resulted in the admittance of refugees and politicos supported by the American government. Consequently, Asian

American communities have been wracked anew by conflicts between progressive and right-wing elements as seen in the clashes between supporters and foes of the present governments in Vietnam, Korea, China, and the Philippines. Existing class structures in various Asian American communities has been further complicated by the shift in world trade from Europe to the Pacific as Asian and American multinational corporations have shifted capital and personnel across national lines.

The implications of these trends are just now being explored, frequently from a Marxist perspective. Studies of these trends include Takagi (1983), who examined the consequences of recent immigration for the class structure of Asian American communities; Mazumdar (1982, 1984), whose studies of Punjabi immigrants and agribusiness development in California placed the immigration question within a larger historical context; and Kaiwar (1982) who explored the overall explication of the relationship between immigration and capitalist development in the United States.

The interest in the historical importance of immigration to the growth of American capitalism was the subject of the latest major text in Asian American Studies, *Labor Immigration under Capitalism: Asian Workers in the United States before World War II* by Cheng and Bonacich (1984). Impetus for this work came not only from a need to understand the relation of Asian immigration to U.S. capitalism but also from recent Marxist studies on the world capitalist economy. Stimulated by the work of Wallerstein (1974), Marxists (for example, Bergesen, 1982; Bonacich, 1980; Cheng and Bonacich, 1984; Chase-Dunn and Rubinson, 1977; Ekholm, 1980; Portes, 1978) have been working with the conception that the spread of capitalism has created a world economy characterized by a global extension of capitalist class relations, an international division of labor, and participation in a single market. International migration is seen to have a critical role in the expansion and reproduction of this world economy, hence the increased attention given by Marxists to immigration.

Asian American and Marxist research interests have converged in other areas as well. While the bulk of Asian American research influenced by Marxism has centered around economic questions, more recent studies have treated culture and gender as well. See, for example, Takaki (1983), who examined the evolution of a common culture among Asian sugar plantation workers in Hawaii, and Okihiro (1984), who studied religion and cultural resistance among Japanese Americans interned during World War II (see also Okihiro, 1973 and forthcoming). Work on women has been done by Glenn (1981, 1984), whose studies illuminated the contributions of Issei women, and by Hirata (1979), who delved into the lives of Chinese prostitutes during the late nineteenth century. The investigation of women will undoubtedly expand since current immigration laws, which favor family reunification, have resulted in a preponderance of women over men immigrants.

A recent collaborative effort by Omi and Winant (1983) suggests a further coincidence of interests between Asian American Studies and Marxism. As this chapter has shown, one of the primary concerns of Asian American Studies has been with the structural significance of race, whereas Marxism has been mainly concerned with class issues. Inspired by the thinking of Gramsci, Omi and Winant have developed a novel approach to the study of race and class in holding that race relations have shaped class relations in the United States. According to them, both race and class are evolving rather than static sets of social relationships, and are best understood as racial and class formations, respectively. They view racial formation as "the complex process, at once political, economic, and ideological, by which racial meanings are developed and applied, both to individual identities and to institutions. Racial formation is the counterpart of the *class-formation* process suggested in the Gramscian analysis of hegemony" (1983: 10). Omi and Winant assert therefore that racial and class formations have interpenetrated with one another in the United States. The possibilities offered by an *interactive* conception of the relationship between race and class have also been explored in recent studies of Asian sugar plantation workers in Hawaii (Liu, 1984, 1985).

As Asian American communities grow, the need to keep race and class in an international perspective will remain the heart of Asian American Studies. If Marxism continues to address these and other issues central to the lives of Asians in the United States, then the tenuous relationship that has existed between Asian American Studies and Marxism could transform itself into a firm partnership.

FOOTNOTES

1. Exploration of the Asian experience in the United States has not been confined to academia. Activists have also initiated programs centered around their specific communities, especially in regions where Asian American Studies programs were not firmly established in the university. Two such programs are the Asian American Research Institute, which runs the New York [City] Chinatown History Project, and the Asian American Resource Workshop in Boston.

2. For a contemporary account of Marxist groups within Asian American communities, particularly in the Los Angeles area, see Nakano (1984).

3. This same theme is repeated in the first issues of *Gidra* (Uyematsu, 1969), one of the first Asian American movement papers in the Los Angeles community, in its discussion of the Yellow Power position: "Yellow power is against capitalism as it exists in America, but it does not align itself with communist powers. Yellow power supports revolution against traditional values and institutions of the U.S. but this is too often misunderstood as an expression of communist aims."

4. The debate between IWK (1974) and Wei Min Shê (1974) provides an example of the disagreements that Asian American community Marxists had over the relationship of race, class, and national oppression. For a recent statement on the continuing importance of the race issue to Asian American Leftists, see Fa (1983).

5. In the following discussion, many of the works referred to are published through the Asian American Studies Center at UCLA. This reflects more than the authors' personal familiarity with Center publications but the fact that among all the Asian American Studies programs in the nation, the one at UCLA has had the strongest research program. For a recent review of the status of Asian American Studies, see Wang (1981). Some other programs offer a larger curricula than does the UCLA program. For a statement of philosophy as well as early course offerings, see the statement by the Asian Studies Division, University of California at Berkeley (1973).

6. Currently there are two other periodicals that deal exclusively with Asian American issues. One is *Bridge* Magazine, published in New York City. Although *Bridge* has been in existence since 1971, it unfortunately has been issued irregularly. The other publication is *East-Wind*, published in San Francisco beginning in 1982. The Ethnic Studies Union at the University of California at Berkeley started a new journal, *Critical Perspectives of Third World America*, in 1983 that has also included material on Asian Americans.

7. For a more detailed discussion of the relationship between Asian American writing and the social context from which it emerged, see Kim (1982). See also San Juan Jr. (1979), who analyzes Carlos Bulosan's writings specifically from a Marxian perspective.

8. H. Mark Lai has also actively advocated the need to use Chinese language sources in order to gain a fuller understanding of the Chinese American experience. The value of this material is evident in his articles that have been cited in this chapter and in his work, "A History Reclaimed: An Annotated Bibliography of Chinese Language Materials on the Chinese in America," by the Asian American Studies Center, UCLA, 1986.

BIBLIOGRAPHY

Abbot, Kenneth. "Chinese-American Society." *Amerasia Journal* 1 (February 1972).

Asian Studies Division, University of California at Berkeley. "Curriculum Philosophy for Asian American Studies." *Amerasia Journal* 2 (1973).

Asian Women's Journal. *Asian Women*. Berkeley: University of California, 1971.

Bergesen, Albert. "Is There a World Mode of Production? A Comment." *Contemporary Crises* 6 (January 1982).

Blauner, Robert. *Racial Oppression in America*. New York: Harper & Row, 1972.

Bonacich, Edna. "A Theory of Middleman Minorities." *American Sociological Review* 38 (October 1973).

_______. "Class Approaches to Ethnicity and Race." *Insurgent Sociologist* 10 (Fall 1980).

Bonacich, Edna, and Modell, John. *The Economic Basis of Ethnic Solidarity: A Study of Japanese Americans*. Berkeley: University of California Press, 1980.

Bosworth, Allan R. *America's Concentration Camps*. New York: W. W. Norton, 1967.

Bulletin of Concerned Asian Scholars. "Special Issue: Asian America." 4 (Fall 1972).

Bulosan, Carlos. *America Is in the Heart*. Seattle: University of Washington Press (5th printing), 1981.

Burawoy, Michael. "Introduction: The Resurgence of Marxism in American Sociology." In Burawoy, Michael, and Skocpol, Theda (eds.). *Marxist Inquiries: Studies of Labor, Class and States*. Chicago: The University of Chicago Press, 1982.

Carmichael, Stokely, and Hamilton, Charles V. *Black Power: The Politics of Liberation in America*. New York: Random House, 1967.

Carr, Leslie G. "The Origins of the Communists Party's Theory of Black Self-determination: Draper vs. Haywood." *Insurgent Sociologist* 10 (Winter 1981).

Chase-Dunn, Christopher, and Rubinson, Richard. "Toward a Structural Perspective on the World System." *Politics and Society* 7:4 (1977).

Cheng, Lucie, and Bonacich, Edna. *Labor Immigration under Capitalism: Asian Workers in the United States before World War II*. Berkeley: University of California Press, 1984.

Chin, Frank, Chan, Jeffery Paul, Inada, Lawson Fusao, and Wong, Shawn Hsu. *Aiiieeeee! An Anthology of Asian-American Writers*. Washington, D.C.: Howard University Press, 1974.

Chiu, Ping. *Chinese Labor in California, 1850-1880: An Economic Study*. Madison: State Historical Society of Wisconsin for the Department of History, University of Wisconsin, 1963.

Clark, Kenneth. *Dark Ghetto: Dilemmas of Social Power*. New York: Harper & Row, 1965.

Commission on Wartime Relocation and Internment of Civilians. *Personal Justice Denied: Report of the Commission on Wartime Relocation and Internment*. Washington, D.C.: U.S. Government Printing Office, 1983.

Cordova, Fred. *Filipinos: Forgotten Asian Americans, A Pictorial Essay/1763-circa-1963*. Iowa: Kendall/Hunt, 1983.

Cox, Oliver C. *Caste, Class and Race: A Study in Social Dynamics*. New York: Modern Reader, 1970. First published by Doubleday, 1948.

Daniel, Cletus E. *Bitter Harvest: A History of California Farmworkers, 1870-1941*. Ithaca, N.Y.: Cornell University Press, 1981.

Daniels, Roger. *The Politics of Prejudice: The Anti-Japanese Movement in California and the Struggle for Japanese Exclusion*. Berkeley: University of California Press, 1962.

———. "Westerners from the East: Oriental Immigrants Reappraised." *Pacific Historical Review* 35 (November 1966).

———. *Concentration Camps USA: Japanese Americans and World War II*. New York: Holt, Rinehart, and Winston, 1972.

———. "American Historians and East Asian Immigrants." *Pacific Historical Review* 43 (November 1974).

DeWitt, Howard A. "The Filipino Labor Union: The Salinas Lettuce Strike of 1934." *Amerasia Journal* 5 (Spring 1978).

———. *Violence in the Field: California Filipino Farm Labor Unionization During the Great Depression*. Saratoga, Calif.: Century Twenty One Publishing, 1980.

Ekholm, Kajsa. "On the Limitation of Civilizations: The Structure and Dynamics of Global Systems." *Dialectical Anthropology* 5 (July 1980).

Fa, Angie. "Community Issues: Asian Americans and the Left." *Critical Perspectives of Third World America* 1 (Fall 1983).

Fanon, Frantz. *The Wretched of the Earth: The Handbook for the Black Revolution that is Changing the Shape of the World*. New York: Grove Press, 1968.

Flacks, Richard. "The New Left and American Politics after Ten Years." *The Journal of Social Issues* 27:1 (1971).

Fujimoto, Isao. "Internal Colonialism: Its Impact on Asians in America." (mimeo) (1971).

Gee, Emma, ed. *Counterpoint: Perspectives on Asian America*. Los Angeles: Asian American Studies Center, University of California, 1976.

Gilbert, James. "Left Young and Old." *Partisan Review* 36:3 (1969).

Glazer, Nathan. "America's Race Paradox." In Rose, Peter I. (ed.). *Nation of Nations: the Ethnic Experience and the Racial Crisis*. New York: Random House, 1972.

Glenn, Evelyn Nakano. "Occupational Ghettoization: Japanese American Women and Domestic Service, 1905-1970." *Ethnicity* 8 (December 1981).

———. "The Dialectics of Wage Work: Japanese American Women and Domestic Service, 1905-1940." In Cheng, Lucie, and Bonacich, Edna (eds.). *Labor Immigration under Capitalism: Asian Workers in the United States before World War II*. Berkeley: University of California Press, 1984.

Greeley, Andrew M. *Ethnicity in the United States: A Preliminary Reconnaissance*. New York: John Wiley, 1974.

Harrington, Michael. *The Other America: Poverty in the United States*. New York: Macmillan, 1962.

Hirata (Cheng), Lucie. "Toward a Political Economy of Chinese America: A Study of Property Ownership in Los Angeles Chinatown." *Amerasia Journal* 3 (Summer 1975).

———. "The Chinese American in Sociology." In Gee, Emma (ed.). *Counterpoint: Perspectives on Asian America*. Los Angeles: Asian American Studies Center, University of California, 1976.

———. "Free, Indentured, Enslaved: Chinese Prostitutes in Nineteenth-Century America." *Signs* 5 (Autumn 1979).

Hom, Marlon K. "Chinatown Literature during the Last Ten Years (1939-1949) by Wenquan." *Amerasia Journal* 9 (Fall/Winter 1982).

Ichioka, Yuji. "Early Issei Socialists and the Japanese Community." In Gee, Emma (ed.). *Counterpoint: Perspectives on Asian America*. Los Angeles: Asian American Studies Center, University of California, 1976.

———. "Asian Immigrant Coal Miners and the United Mine Workers of America: Race and Class at Rock Springs, Wyoming, 1907." *Amerasia Journal* 6 (Fall 1979).

———. "Amerika Nadeshiko: Japanese Immigrant Women in the United States, 1900-1924." *Pacific Historical Review* 48 (May 1980).

Ichioka, Yuji, Sakata, Yasuo, Tsuchida, Nobuya, and Yasuhara, Eri. *A Buried Past: An Annotated Bibliography of the Japanese American Research Project Collection*. Berkeley: University of California, 1974.

Irons, Peter. *Justice at War*. New York: Oxford University Press, 1983.

Isserman, Maurice. "The Half-swept House: American Communism in 1956." *Socialist Review* 12 (January-February 1982).

I Wor Kuen. "12 Point Platform and Program" (mimeo). New York City, ca. 1969-70.

———. "The National Question & Asian Americans." IWK *Journal* 1 (August 1974).

Kagiwada, George. "Beyond Internal Colonialism: Reflections from the Japanese American Experience." *Humboldt Journal of Social Relations* 10 (Fall/Winter 1982-83).

Kaiwar, Vasant. "Some Reflections on Capitalism, Race and Class." *South Asian Bulletin* 2 (Spring 1982).

Kim, Elaine. *Asian American Literature: An Introduction to the Writings and Their Social Context*. Philadelphia: Temple University Press, 1982.

Kitano, Harry H. L. "Japanese Americans: The Development of a Middleman Minority." *Pacific Historical Review* 43 (November 1974).

Kwong, Peter. *Chinatown, New York: Labor and Politics, 1930-50*. New York: Monthly Review Press, 1979.

Lai, H. Mark. "China Politics and the U.S. Chinese Communities." In Gee, Emma (ed.). *Counterpoint: Perspectives on Asian America*. Los Angeles: Asian American Studies Center, University of California, 1976a.

________. "A Historical Survey of the Chinese Left in America." In Gee, Emma (ed.). *Counterpoint: Perspectives on Asian America*. Los Angeles: Asian American Studies Center, University of California, 1976b.

________. "A History Reclaimed: An Annotated Bibliography of Chinese Language Materials on the Chinese in America." Los Angeles: Asian American Studies Center, University of California, 1985.

Liu, John M. "Towards an Understanding of the Internal Colonial Model." In Gee, Emma (ed.). *Counterpoint: Perspectives on Asian America*. Los Angeles: Asian American Studies Center, University of California, 1976.

________. "Race, Ethnicity, and the Sugar Plantation System: Asian Labor in Hawaii, 1850-1900." In Cheng, Lucie, and Bonacich, Edna (eds.). *Labor Immigration under Capitalism: Asian Workers in the United States before World War II*. Berkeley: University of California Press, 1984.

________. "Cultivating Cane: Asian Labor and the Hawaiian Sugar Plantation System within the Capitalist World Economy, 1835-1920." Ph.D. dissertation, University of California, 1985.

Lyman, Stanford M. *The Asian in the West*. Reno, Nev.: Western Studies Center, Desert Research Institute, University of Nevada System, 1970.

Mazumdar, Sucheta. "Punjabi Immigration to California in the Context of Capitalist Development." *South Asian Bulletin* 2 (Spring 1982).

________. "Punjabi Agricultural Workers in California, 1905-1945." In Cheng, Lucie, and Bonacich, Edna (eds.). *Labor Immigration under Capitalism: Asian Workers in the United States before World War II*. Berkeley: University of California Press, 1984.

Mei, June. "Socioeconomic Developments among the Chinese in San Francisco, 1848-1906." In Cheng, Lucie, and Bonacich, Edna (eds.). *Labor Immigration under Capitalism: Asian Workers in the United States before World War II*. Berkeley: University of California Press, 1984.

Modell, John. *The Economics and Politics of Racial Accommodation: The Japanese of Los Angeles 1900-1942*. Chicago: University of Illinois Press, 1977.

Nakanishi, Don T. "In Search of a New Paradigm: Minorities in the Context of International Politics." *Studies in Race and Nations*, Monograph Series 6:2 (1975).

Nakano, Roy. "Marxist-Leninist Organizing in the Asian American Community: Los Angeles, 1969-79." Unpublished paper, 1984.

Nee, Victor G., and Nee, Brett de Bary. *Longtime Californ': A Documentary Study of an American Chinatown*. New York: Pantheon Books, 1972.

Ng, Wing-cheung. "An Evaluation of the Labor Market Status of Chinese Americans." *Amerasia Journal* 4 (Spring 1977).

Okihiro, Gary Y. "Japanese Resistance in America's Concentration Camps: A Reevaluation." *Amerasia Journal* 2 (Fall 1977).

———. "Religion and Resistance in America's Concentration Camps." *Phylon* 45 (1984).

———. *Japanese Legacy: Farming and Community Life in California's Santa Clara Valley*. Cupertino: California History Center (forthcoming).

Omi, Michael, and Winant, Howard. "By the Rivers of Babylon: Race in the United States." *Socialist Review* 13 (September-October 1983).

Okamura, Raymond. "The Concentration Camp Experience from a Japanese American Perspective: A Bibliography Essay and Review of Michi Weglyn's *Years of Infamy*." In Gee, Emma (ed.). *Counterpoint: Perspectives on Asian America*. Los Angeles: Asian American Studies Center, University of California, 1976.

Portes, Alejandro. "Migration and Underdevelopment." *Politics and Society* 8:1 (1978).

Quinsaat, Jesse. *Letters in Exile: An Introductory Reader on the History of Pilipinos in America*. Los Angeles: Asian American Studies Center, University of California, 1976.

San Juan, E., Jr. "Introduction" (Essay on Carlos Bulosan). *Amerasia Journal* 6 (1979).

Saxton, Alexander. *The Indispensable Enemy: Labor and the Anti-Chinese Movement in California*. Berkeley: University of California Press, 1971.

Sue, Stanley, and Sue, Derald. "Chinese-American Personality and Mental Health." *Amerasia Journal* 1 (July 1971).

———. "Chinese-American Personality and Mental Health: A Reply to Tong's Criticisms." *Amerasia Journal* 1 (February 1972).

Sue, Stanley. "Personality and Mental Health: A Clarification." *Amerasia Journal* 2 (Fall 1974).

Surh, Jerry. "Asian American Identity and Politics." *Amerasia Journal* 2 (Fall 1974).

Tabb, William. *The Political Economy of the Black Ghetto*. New York: W. W. Norton, 1970.

Tachiki, Amy, Wong, Eddie, Odo, Franklin, and Wong, Buck. *Roots: An Asian American Reader*. Los Angeles: Asian American Studies Center, University of California, 1976.

Takagi, Paul. "Asian Communities in the United States." *Our Socialism* 1 (May 1983).

Takaki, Ronald. *Iron Cages: Race and Culture in 19th Century America*. New York: Knopf, 1979.

________. *Pau Hana: Plantation Life and Labor in Hawaii, 1835-1920*. Honolulu: University of Hawaii Press, 1983.

Teodori, Massimo. *The New Left: A Documentary History*. New York: Bobbs-Merrill, 1969.

Tong, Ben. "The Ghetto of the Mind: Notes on the Historical Psychology of Chinese America." *Amerasia Journal* 1 (November 1971).

________. "Reply to Sues." *Amerasia Journal* 1 (February 1972a).

________. "Response to Abbot Article." *Amerasia Journal* 1 (February 1972b).

________. "A Living Death Defended as the Legacy of a Superior Culture." *Amerasia Journal* 2 (Fall 1974).

Uyematsu, Amy. "The Emergence of Yellow Power." *Gidra* 1 (October 1969).

Wallerstein, Immanuel. *The Modern World-System: Capitalist Agriculture and the Origins of the European World-Economy in the Sixteenth Century*. New York: Academic Press, 1974.

Wang, Ling-chi. "Asian American Studies." *American Quarterly* 33:3 (1981).

Weglyn, Michi. *Years of Infamy: The Untold Story of America's Concentration Camps*. New York: William Morrow, 1976.

Wei Min Shè. *I Wor Kuen's Reactionary Line on May Day and the Workers Movement; Wei Min Shè Reply to IWK Criticism of 1974 May Day Asian Contingent Statement*. San Francisco: Wei Min Shè, 1974.

Wong, Paul. "The Emergence of the Asian American Movement." *Bridge Magazine* 2 (September/October 1972).

Yetman, Norman R., and Steele, C. Hoy. *Majority and Minority: The Dynamics of Racial and Ethnic Relations*. Boston: Allyn and Bacon, 1971.

Yoneda, Karl G. *Ganbatte: Sixty-year Struggle of a Kibei Worker*. Los Angeles: Asian American Studies Center, University of California, 1983.

6

MARXIST CRIMINOLOGY

David F. Greenberg

The 1970s saw the rise of a new school of criminological thought, known variously as "radical," "critical," or Marxist. It challenged dominant criminological ideas and drew on the insights of New Left social criticism to develop a host of new and controversial ways of thinking about crime. Over the past decade, radicals have refined and developed these new ideas.

Current radical ideas about crime have earlier antecedents. Nineteenth-century utopian socialists, anarchists, and Marxists all discussed crime and punishment in terms that foreshadowed contemporary analyses. From the 1920s on, however, radical perspectives virtually disappeared from the criminological literature. The few pioneering works that did draw on Marxist theory (for example, Rusche and Kirchheimer, 1939) went almost unnoticed.

As it developed in the decades following World War I, mainstream criminology was heavily social-psychological: It drew on such concepts as subculture, anomie, and reaction formation to explain why some individuals but not others became delinquent or criminal.[1] Whatever their differences, many theorists viewed crime as fundamentally irrational. With the demise of eugenics in the 1930s, policy recommendations veered toward the liberal: Government was to prevent crime by rehabilitating criminals, and by improving opportunities for minorities. Crime was *not* considered to be inherent in capitalism

Major portions of this chapter are adapted from Greenberg (1981) and Humphries and Greenberg (1981, 1984).

itself. Either it was regarded as intrinsic to all societies, so that nothing could be done about it, or it was attributed to arrangements that a benign and enlightened government could eliminate without fundamental social change. In the 1970s this conception of crime came under sustained attack from the left.

ROOTS OF MARXIST CRIMINOLOGY

During the 1960s several developments in mainstream criminology helped prepare the way for new approaches by casting doubt on ideas long taken for granted. For example, to avoid using suspect official crime statistics, some criminologists carried out studies in which school children were asked to report on their own delinquent acts. Typically, these studies found a weak or vanishing relationship between involvement in crime or delinquency on the one hand, and race or socioeconomic status on the other. Crime seemed to be spread much more evenly through the class structure than official statistics suggested. These findings cast doubt on the belief, shared up to then by most criminologists, that most crimes were committed by the poor.

Taking the self-reporting studies at face value, many researchers interpreted the overrepresentation of blacks and poor people in crime statistics as stemming from the discriminatory practices of the enforcement agencies. It was not that the poor stole more, but rather that when they did, the police were more likely to arrest them, prosecutors to charge them, and judges to convict and sentence them. By inference, official crime statistics told us more about the practices of law enforcement agencies than about crime or criminals.

Following this line of reasoning, researchers turned away from the study of criminals to the study of law enforcement agencies. They treated agency claims skeptically, and made much of the discrepancy between what the agencies did and what they said they did. Drawing on symbolic interactionist social psychology,[2] sociologists known as "labeling theorists" argued that efforts to punish or treat those involved in crime tended to stigmatize offenders and transform their self-concepts in such a way as to increase rather than reduce their subsequent criminality (Schur, 1971). This view, along with research pointing to serious failings in treatment programs, did much to discredit the idea that the crime problem could be solved by rehabilitating individual criminals. The thrust of the message that labeling theorists directed to social workers, probation officers, and juvenile court judges was: "The less you do, the better off we will all be" (Schur, 1973).

This conclusion meshed perfectly with the rejection on the part of some sociologists of the notion that crime was pathological. Instead, it was to be considered no less meaningful or authentic than any other form of human activity. Thus it was to be understood not as a reflex conditioned by an unfavorable social or physical environment, but as conscious, purposeful action. Its meaning was to be learned through participant observation, not inferred on the basis of armchair theorizing or the analysis of computer output. Rather than something to be eradicated, it was to be "appreciated" as a manifestation of human diversity (Matza, 1969). This stance implied a repudiation of *both* positions in the long-standing debate about whether it was better to punish criminals because they were wicked, or to cure them because they were sick.

This radical cultural relativism had instant appeal for students and professors who were active in the civil rights and antiwar movements, or were sympathetic to a hedonistic counterculture that approved drug use and less restrictive sexual mores. They certainly did not consider themselves pathological. Harassed by college deans who meddled in students' private lives, and by police detectives trying to stop marijuana use, students found the labeling theorists' portrayal of deviants as the victims of moralistic busybodies or repressive bureaucracies especially congenial.

As cultural radicalism proceeded, students and their teachers began to reject conventional ways of earning a living. As they saw it, most jobs offered little opportunity for self-expression, and required the acceptance of institutionalized racism and militarism. The suburban nuclear family masked boredom, hypocrisy, intrafamilial hostility, and male domination. Disenchanted criminologists made cultural heroes of deviants who rejected the seductive material rewards of a morally corrupt society; defending them, and criticizing the theories earlier criminologists had developed to explain them, became a form of cultural criticism (Pearson, 1975).

Once crime comes to be considered a life-style no less legitimate than any other, its prohibition inevitably seems arbitrary and repressive. Those who took this view pointed to deep social disagreements about whether it was appropriate to treat some forms of behavior, especially those they considered victimless, as criminal. The processes by which these behaviors (sale and consumption of illegal drugs, including alcohol; consensual sexual expression; abortion) had become criminal became a subject for study.

These developments, both within criminology and in the larger society, were an important source of ideas for radical criminology. The other major source was the New Left. All the social sciences were invigorated by the ideas that came out of the Civil Rights, Black Power, antiwar, and feminist movements of the 1960s. In the case of criminology the stimulus was direct and powerful: The experience of being spied on, arrested, jailed, and sometimes brutalized forced many criminologists to reject the belief in a benevolent state that informed liberal criminology.

RADICAL CRIMINOLOGY OF THE EARLY 1970s

Radical criminologists of the early 1970s subjected the major theoretical perspectives of mainstream criminology to far-reaching criticism. Taylor, Walton, and Young (1973) dissected a number of the leading theories of crime causation. They demanded of theory that it provide a fully social account of action, respecting its purposefulness and avoiding value-laden concepts of individual pathology. In itself, this demand had limited political significance; but they went beyond this to demand that criminologists take account of the socially structured inequalities of wealth and power that shape human action. Finally, they called on theorists to show how society might be transformed so that it did not need to criminalize diversity. By these standards, the major criminological theories were seriously deficient: They could not explain the social origins of crime, and they were politically objectionable insofar as they denied the possibility of fundamentally egalitarian change.

Some writers went further by investing crime with political meaning. Instead of dismissing it as pathological, they characterized it as a protest against oppressive social conditions, a refusal to play the game by the established rules (rules that favored some and disadvantaged others), or even a rejection of the existing game in favor of another one altogether (Taylor, Walton, and Young, 1973). Prisoners' writings on crime and criminal justice were given prominence as points of view to be incorporated into the new developing perspective (Krisberg, 1975).

Focusing more directly on policy-related research and analysis, Platt (1974) criticized the cynicism, defeatism, and pragmatism that characterized liberal criminology, and argued that as an academic discipline, criminology has strengthened the state and supported the extension of welfare capitalism. With the weakening of liberalism and the rise of the New Right in the late 1970s, Platt and Takagi (1977) denounced the viciousness and antiworking-class bias of the "new realists" who called for more punitive crime control policies and the weakening of civil liberties.

Radical criminologists went beyond the criticism of specific theories of crime causation to call the legal definition of crime into question, thereby opening a debate about the very scope of the field of criminology. Herman and Julia Schwendinger (1970), for example, argued that to restrict research to violations of state-made law is to accept the definitions of harm and wrongfulness that the state asserts. Legal definitions of crime are based on the conceptions of harm held by those who have the power to make laws, and consequently to exclude from scrutiny harms caused by the actions of the capitalist class. The Schwendingers urged that crime be redefined as a violation of human rights, and they called on criminologists to join the struggle to put an end to such violations.

Prior to the advent of labeling theory, only a handful of criminologists gave the criminal law more than passing attention. Many implicitly portrayed it as socially neutral, standing above classes and interest groups, providing protection to all members of society, who in return give it their support. In opposition to this "consensus" perspective on law, radical criminologists substituted a "conflict" perspective, already present in rudimentary form in some of the labeling theory literature. It depicts society as a collection of diverse groups in conflict with one another about a multitude of issues. The more powerful groups are characterized as using the law to advance their own values and interests over those of the less powerful groups (Turk, 1969; Chambliss and Seidman, 1971; Chambliss, 1974, 1976; Quinney, 1970, 1979: 115-60).

It was differences in power, then, that explained why the police, courts, and prisons dealt almost entirely with victimless crimes and the relatively minor delicts of the poor, while systematically ignoring the loss of life and well-being for which the upper classes are responsible through imperialistic wars, genocide against indigenous peoples, systematic racism and sexism, maintenance of dangerous working conditions, manufacture of unsafe products, and environmental pollution. Because these priorities are established politically, and reflect the social distribution of power, the social category of crime is inherently and unavoidably political.

Although liberal criminologists had not entirely ignored racial and class discrimination in the administration of justice, the radicals gave it much greater attention, pointing to the ways the discretionary decisionmaking powers of prejudiced officials combined with institutionally structured disadvantage to yield disproportionately harsh treatment of blacks, the poor, and political and cultural minorities. Police discretion in making arrests, prosecutors' discretion in setting sentences, and parole boards' discretion in releasing prisoners from custody all operated to the advantage of the privileged. Moreover, the right to an attorney benefited those who could afford superior legal representation more than those who had to accept a legal defender or court-appointed counsel—or do without an attorney altogether (AFSC Working Party, 1971; Chambliss and Seidman, 1971; Krisberg, 1975; Reiman, 1979).

Radical research collectives and individuals, often bridging the academic and off-campus "movement" worlds, analyzed the origins and development of police forces, paying particular attention to their involvement in the suppression of black and working-class militancy and left-wing political opposition (NARMIC, 1971; Takagi, 1974; Center for Research on Criminal Justice, 1975). Others exposed the nightmarish conditions and brutal regimen of the prison system and revealed the brutal repression directed toward prisoners who challenged the system (AFSC Working Party, 1971; Greenberg and Stender, 1972; Wright, 1973; Mitford, 1973).

Radical criminologists developed a stinging critique of liberal reform. For example, Platt's (1969) study of the juvenile court movement argued that the Protestant, upper-class Republican women who led the movement sought to advance their own interests, not those of the Catholic and Jewish working-class immigrant children they claimed they wanted to help. The consequences of establishing the juvenile court, Platt maintained, were not beneficial to juveniles.[3] Before the court was created, much juvenile mischief was ignored or handled informally. By founding a court with jurisdiction over juveniles who had broken no criminal law, and who were not entitled to the procedural due process guaranteed adults in the criminal courts, reformers increased young people's vulnerability to deprivation of liberty through commitment to reformatories.

Another component of the critique of liberal reform was an attack on correctionalism. For a century, liberals had argued that more should be done to rehabilitate criminals. Yet if crime is not considered the result of personal pathology, it makes no sense to deal with it by trying to "cure" individuals. Indeed, the very notion of "corrections" implies that the authorities know what is correct, an assumption the radicals now challenged. The radical critics went on to argue that in practice, treatment programs had accomplished little by way of rehabilitation, but had led to longer sentences and greater administrative capacity to repress prisoner militancy (AFSC Working Party, 1971; Mitford, 1973; Smith and Fried, 1974).

Radical criminologists began to investigate the content and sources of popular beliefs about crime, law, and criminal justice. They argued that many of these beliefs, spread by criminologists, government spokesmen, and the mass media, were false and tended to reinforce capitalist domination. The notion that crimes are largely committed by the poor, for example, blinds people to the crimes of the wealthy. The identification of legal harm with social harm distracts attention from the injurious acts of capitalists and government officials that have never been prohibited by law (Quinney, 1970; Michalowski and Bohlander, 1976; Reiman, 1979:162-68). A panic about mugging distracts the population from potentially delegitimating crises in capitalist hegemony (Hall et al., 1977). When opinion surveys showed a consensus about crime, some criminologists argued that this proved the radicals wrong, but the radical criminologists countered that the consensus was manufactured.[4]

Some of the radical criminology of the early 1970s suffered from serious weaknesses. At times it naively portrayed criminals as protorevolutionaries, and compared the police to the Gestapo. Fear of crime and popular support for law enforcement was dismissed as "false consciousness," the product of government propaganda designed to distract people from the true source of their problems, capitalism. A few writers substituted the clichés, oversimplification, and insufficiently qualified generalizations of left romanticism for those of mainstream criminology (Young, 1975). Empirical research to verify claims being made about crime and criminal justice was sometimes neglected. When it was performed, it did not always confirm the radicals' claims.

Dissatisfaction with this state of affairs developed at around the same time that radical criminologists, like their counterparts in the other social sciences, turned in a more serious way to Marxism, which in the late 1960s and early 1970s had been only one of many influences. A search of the writings of Marx and Engels quickly disclosed that they never gave crime a systematic treatment. Although they wrote about it from time to time, their observations were too superficial to provide the basis for a major new thrust in criminology.

Quite a few late-nineteenth-century European criminologists did draw on Marxist thought; however, they were writing at a time when much of Marx's work had not been published. Consequently these authors derived their understanding of Marxism from a limited portion of his writings, and from secondhand sources that tended to vulgarize Marxism by depicting it as a form of economic or technological determinism. Though this is a misinterpretation, it made possible the synthesis of Marxism and positivist criminology. By comparison with non-Marxist criminological writings of the time, which gave great play to supposed biological causes, this literature, which highlights the role of poverty and capitalist-induced greed, is not bad; one can find in it insights that remain provocative and suggestive today. Yet its authors had little first-hand knowledge of crime, and consequently accepted many conventional stereotypes of criminals without question. It became clear that if a Marxist criminology were to be created, it had to be based more on Marx's general theoretical insights and methods than on the writings of Marx and Engels or their followers. This is what Marxist criminologists have been doing for the past decade: using Marxist theory to analyze the sources of criminal law, the reasons it is broken, and the way the government responds to those who break it. This new body is rich and varied; only a few of many noteworthy contributions can be highlighted here.

THE SOURCES OF CRIMINAL LAW

As the Marxist influence was assimilated into radical criminology, some scholars began to specify the conflict perspective on law by writing of the ruling class as a preeminent interest group, one that used the law to stifle working-class initiatives and to reinforce inequalities of wealth and power (Quinney, 1977:45). Thus Chambliss (1964) demonstrated that English vagrancy law arose in response to the needs of agricultural employers when wages rose in response to the shortage of labor caused by the Black Plague of 1348. As the growth of commerce reduced landowners' needs for coerced labor, the law fell into desuetude, but was then revived and amended under the Tudors to protect traveling merchants from highway robbery. Similarly, under pressure from the pharmaceutical industry, Nixon-era federal legislation failed to control amphetamines and tranquilizers when measures were taken to control other drugs, despite evidence of widespread abuse (Chambliss, 1976).

These studies, along with numerous others, showed law being made by members of a dominant class holding state office and possessing sufficient class consciousness to legislate on behalf of their class; or by members of other classes who were under the thumb of the dominant class and did its bidding. This perspective on law, called instrumentalism because it views law as a tool that the ruling class uses to advance its interests, quickly came in for criticism. Although many individual legislative acts do seem to reflect the interests of the capitalist class, the theory seems to exaggerate its unity and its ability to act cohesively (Chambliss, 1976). It cannot easily explain why capitalists sometimes fail to achieve their legislative goals. It seems to neglect the influence that "common people" sometimes have on the formulation of law, and it fails to indicate why the ruling class chooses to rule through law rather than naked and arbitrary terror (Greenberg and Anderson, 1981).

In particular instances, the thrust of these skeptical questions could be blunted by demonstrating that laws that seemed to benefit other classes, or everyone, were actually adopted because they helped capitalists. Thus it was argued that Progressive-era legislation regulating the railroad and meatpacking industries was adopted in response to pressure from the largest firms, who sought competitive advantages over small firms and wanted to expand their markets by reassuring customers about the safety of their products (Chambliss, 1974).

As persuasive as these arguments were in individual cases, it seemed doubtful that they could always be true. In a variety of ways, therefore, Marxists tried to formulate less simplistic conceptions of the state and law.[5] Influenced by French structuralist readings of Marx, they argued that the state–and therefore law–are "partly autonomous" from the ruling class, rather than directly under its control. This independence helps to legitimate law to subordinate classes, and thus contributes ideologically to the reproduction of a class society (Hepburn, 1977; Greenberg and Anderson, 1981; Tushnet, 1984).

If law is to achieve its ideological function by appearing to be fair, it must cometimes *be* fair (Beirne, 1979). The procedures that establish the possibility of fairness (for example, universal suffrage, party politics) allow subordinate classes or class fractions to influence the law. Criminal legislation is thus the product of shifting alliances of classes and class fractions (Chambliss, 1969:10; Humphries and Greenberg, 1981, 1984).

This position differs from liberal pluralism in two important ways. First, it notes that the superior financial and ideological resources of capitalists give them a considerable edge over other classes in conflicts over legislation; it is simply that in a democratic polity this advantage is not always decisive (Chambliss, 1976). Second, the positions of the parties to these conflicts, as well as their capacities for effective political action, are traced to their positions in capitalist production.

Building on the earlier work of Gusfield (1963) and Levine (1978, 1979), Humphries and Greenberg (1981) showed that Prohibition legislation could be understood in these terms. The American colonists, including the Puritans, had valued alcohol for the contributions it made to health and conviviality. It was widely consumed by all social classes. Work discipline for artisans and craftsmen in the petty commodity mode of production was not rigorous and included drinking rituals as part of a noncompetitive work culture.

As the capitalist mode of production became dominant, the middle class abandoned these rituals and tightened work discipline—though drinking remained an important feature of male working-class culture. This middle-class response developed as an adaptation to the structural position of small capitalists in a competitive economy. It was crucial for entrepreneurs who operated their businesses on thin margins to work hard for long hours, and to eliminate the distractions and costs associated with unnecessary personal consumption, including consumption of alcohol. With labor costs making up a large part of the cost of doing business, it was equally important for employers to minimize the wages paid to employees. Middle-class culture served these needs by encouraging the cultivation of abstemiousness, thrift, frugality, and industriousness. Temperance societies encouraged moderation in drinking and, later, abstinence; and heavy chronic drinking came to be explained as the consequence of a pathological loss of self-control. The hysterical tone of much midnineteenth-century temperance literature reflected the precariousness of middle-class status and the danger uncontrolled drinking posed to that status.

Following the Civil War, industrialization shifted the emphasis of the middle-class temperance movement away from an exclusive preoccupation with self-control. The expansion of capitalism gave the large corporation an increasingly prominent role in the economy; and the industrial proletariat grew rapidly, swelled by culturally alien immigrants attracted by high wages. Upwardly mobile fractions of the working class adopted the abstinence patterns of the middle class they aspired to join, and in some cases they became active prohibitionists.

By excluding middle-class women from the cash economy, capitalist industrialization left them financially dependent on men. Consequently, wives' class positions were jeopardized by male drinking as much as their husbands' were. In addition, prostitutes often solicited in saloons, posing a potential threat of venereal disease—to wives as well as to male clients. As an exclusively male preserve, the saloon symbolized male prerogative and privilege. For these reasons, middle-class women gave Prohibition strong support; many of the leaders of the movement were women. They were joined by evangelical clergy whose involvement was provoked by the decline in their occupational status being brought about by the growth of industry and the accompanying secularization of society, and who were able to draw on the organizational resources of their churches to mobilize support for the cause.

With the backbone of the movement remaining a petit bourgeoisie that was being squeezed economically and politically between labor and capital, antiliquor agitation began to embody nativist fears of immigrant workers—and of ruthless capitalists. The liquor trust, denounced for profiting by promoting human misery, became a symbol of capitalist greed. Middle-class prohibitionists also blamed alcohol for working-class crime, labor militancy, industrial inefficiency and accidents, the high level of wages (they hoped that if workers stopped drinking they could lower their employees' wages without resistance), and political corruption (the saloon played a major role in the urban ethnic political machines). Thus alcohol control became linked with class control.

Following a period of dormancy, the Prohibition movement revived in the years 1907-19. After attempts to gain support from the labor movement failed, leaders abandoned their antibusiness rhetoric and gained broad support from a middle class whose anxieties over immigration and class conflict grew with the intensification of industrial violence. Business funding of the movement was critical in making Prohibition effective nationally.

Normally, capitalists would strongly oppose an attempt to criminalize a major sector of industry. In this case they were willing to do so because they felt so threatened. To protect their own rights to earn profits, they were willing to sacrifice the right of other capitalists to do the same. Of course the liquor industry was opposed to Prohibition, but it was divided; wine, beer, and liquor firms were unable to agree on a common strategy (each tried to shape the legislation to prohibit only the other sectors of the industry). Many workers were also opposed, but they were divided along ethnic lines. Some thought that alcoholism was an obstacle to class struggle, and many immigrant workers could not vote because they were not citizens. In the face of a divided opposition, Prohibition was established throughout the nation through the efforts of a coalition of businessmen and the middle class. Gusfield (1963), who attributed the Prohibition movement to status politics, ignored the material concerns of the participants.

Analysis of the earliest legislation against smoking opium shows that it, too, grew out of the social conflicts engendered by competitive capitalism, but through a different process. During the nineteenth century, tens of thousands of Chinese immigrants had come to California to work in railroad construction, mining, and agriculture. So long as the economy remained prosperous, opium-smoking Chinese laborers attracted little attention. Then, as the labor market contracted during the depression of the 1870s, white workers organized to protect their jobs by excluding new Chinese immigrants. These white workers gained support from the white petit bourgeoisie, who also suffered from competition when unemployed Chinese workers opened small retail businesses.[6] A considerable body of anti-Chinese legislation was passed in response to this sentiment. In this atmosphere, statutes against the smoking of opium were also adopted. Ingestion of opium and its derivatives by other means remained lawful; only the usage associated with the Chinese was banned. Until early in the twentieth century, the only federal restrictions on opium consisted of tariffs on its importation (Helmer, 1975; Morgan, 1976; Embree, 1977).

We see here a process in which an economic crisis associated with the capitalist mode of production occurs at a time of weak class consciousness, engendering conflict within the working class along lines of race, national origin, language, and class experience before immigration. Social practices of groups regarded as different but not deviant before the crisis become more salient in the face of economic competition and, by association with the competitor fraction of the class, come to be viewed as reprehensible in themselves. It is this ideological process that leads to the criminal prohibition of practices associated with the politically weaker fractions of the class.

Subsequent legislation criminalizing the possession and nonmedical distribution of opiates (the 1914 Harrison Act) was adopted primarily in connection with imperialist rivalry. The State Department sought a treaty prohibiting international traffic in opium because it wanted to deprive England of the revenue it earned by exporting opium to China. As China had no interest in purchasing British manufactured goods, England depended on the opium trade to finance its foreign trade deficit with China. By supporting the Chinese government's attempt to protect its own population from opium, the State Department also hoped to promote the Open Door policy (opening Chinese doors to American products). In this way it was acting to promote the collective interests of commercial capitalists. The Harrison Act was adopted to fulfill America's treaty obligations under the International Opium Convention. The prohibition of domestic narcotics use was an outcome of this legislation, but not the main reason for its adoption (Embree, 1973, 1977; Musto, 1973:24-68).

Non-Marxist explanations of criminal law typically invoke the public good, morally driven entrepreneurs (Becker, 1963), or agencies pursuing organizational interests (Dickson, 1968), but have not considered the possibility examined by Marxists, namely that the state could seek legislation on behalf of the capitalist class or a fraction of that class. Analyses of the decriminalization of formerly prohibited activities have been undertaken within the same framework (for example, see Humphries, 1977, for the decriminalization of abortion, and Humphries, 1983, for the repeal of the Comstock Law forbidding the dissemination of birth control information).

Through these studies we are beginning to understand how the conflicts within and between classes associated with different stages of capitalism are expressed in the contents of the criminal law. Most of these studies make no assumptions about the objective effects of particular statutes, though they are very much concerned with the benefits that proponents of a statute hope to gain from it. These hopes may, of course, be based on mistaken beliefs about the consequences of passing a law. For example, leading Prohibitionists were surely mistaken in thinking that capitalism was seriously threatened by alcohol.

THE CRIMINAL JUSTICE SYSTEM

Many of the same theoretical issues that arise in the criminological analysis of the law also come up in studying the history and functioning of the criminal justice system. Marxists who began writing about law enforcement often did so within an instrumentalist framework, arguing that the police, courts, and prisons operated to the benefit of the ruling class alone. Soon it was realized that this was an oversimplification. As Engels (1959) suggested, just because capitalists benefit from a law does not mean that other classes are injured by it. No class gains from having its property appropriated without compensation, or from random bodily assaults. To the extent that law enforcement effectively prevents these crimes (how well it does this is very much an open question), it provides some benefit to all classes. While Marxists have often contended that in a society free from class contradictions the criminal law would not be needed to prevent these occurrences, it does not follow that it is detrimental to workers in a capitalist society to discourage them.

Much work has focused on the growth of the police, and on the development of new forms of punishment. A simpleminded view, endorsed in many non-Marxist textbooks, sees the establishment of police departments as a response to problems of increasing crime created by the weakening of informal social control in small rural villages under the impact of urbanization and industrialization. But problems do not automatically create their solutions (assuming for the sake of argument the debatable contention that police are a solution to the problems of crime). Eighteenth-century Englishmen worried about highway robbery and were frightened by riots. Even though they considered existing responses to these problems inadequate, they were slow to set up police forces to deal with them. Indeed, so long as rioters limited their aims to the enforcement of the "just price" of the vanishing moral economy, or the achievement of a higher wage, the riots were not treated as major threats. At times members of the upper classes even encouraged, manipulated, or led them.

When riots got out of hand and threatened landed estates or houses of industry, magistrates called out associations of gentry with their servants to put them down—a form of control based on personal authority. At times the militia and army were also used, but magistrates mistrusted the loyalty of the militia, whose members were socially similar to the mob. At the same time, large landowners feared that a standing army or bureaucratic police force would strengthen the centralized state, weakening their own political power (Silver, 1967; Shelton, 1973).

When it was first proposed in the late eighteenth century, the gentry found a permanent salaried civilian police force unacceptable because it would have tended to undermine their personal authority. Already weakened by the commercialization of rural society, their patrimonial authority was sustained by personal domination of law enforcement. By pardoning criminals and declining to prosecute, the gentry could win popular gratitude (Hay, 1975). Yet personal forms of enforcement had drawbacks as well as advantages. The hostilities generated in putting down riots continued to divide communities afterward, for the parties to the conflict all resided in the community. Calling out the army was too much an all-or-nothing affair; it risked exacerbating the conflict and escalating events unnecessarily.

As the expanded reproduction of capitalism drew more and more of the population into relations governed by the cash nexus, and exposed increasing numbers of the laboring classes to the vicissitudes of the marketplace, labor militancy and radicalism grew. Conspiracies sprang up. Fear of a revolution, intensified by the French example, ultimately led the landowners to accept a regular police force, for the army would have been incapable of coping with a domestic uprising had it had French support (Shelton, 1973; Stevenson, 1977).

Merchants and industrialists concerned about riot and theft also supported the establishment of a police force. As Spitzer and Scull (1977) note, riots were extremely disruptive to the marketplace. Farmers and middlemen traders tended to avoid rural markets disrupted by mob action. In addition, owners of factories threatened with destruction by displaced craftsmen wanted protection (Shelton, 1973).

Beyond the threat of riot, however, merchants wanted to reduce their losses to theft. As the geographical extent of trade grew, private protection on an individual basis became less feasible. Yet the "free rider" problem made collective private arrangements difficult. The existing system of enforcement, which relied heavily on private prosecution, rewards to informers, and recovery of stolen goods for a fee paid by the victim, had sprung up unplanned as the commercial revolution eroded traditional enforcement arrangements like the "hue and cry." But it didn't work well. Many victims could not afford to prosecute, and informers sometimes instigated crimes so that they could collect rewards. A tax-supported, salaried police patrol emerged as the only feasible solution to the problem of riot and theft in rural market and industrial towns, and in commercial cities in transition from a mercantile to a competitive capitalist economy (Spitzer and Scull, 1977; Sugarman, Palmer, and Rubin, 1982).

Despite the clear and widely discussed advantages that a public police had for capitalists, it took a long time to establish one: Not until 1829 was the Metropolitan Police Force introduced to London, three decades after Colquhoun's Thames River Police had demonstrated its feasibility. Opposition came not only from those who feared the restoration of absolutism, but also from elements of the nascent working class, and from London politicians who resisted the loss of patronage jobs in the watch-and-ward system. As prime minister, Sir Robert Peel, a Tory politician and landowner, *and* son of a large textile manufacturer, was perfectly positioned to weld the alliance of gentry, manufacturers, and fractions of the petit bourgeoisie that finally succeeded in establishing a bureaucratized police force in England (Donajgrodzki, 1977; Manning, 1977; Sugarman, Palmer, and Rubin, 1982).

The establishment of a salaried, preventive patrol was significant not merely as a more efficient way of carrying out social control; it represented two qualitatively new developments: rule through impersonal, bureaucratically administered general law, and a deeper, more finely tuned penetration of formal control into everyday social life (Spitzer, 1979).

Bureaucratic enforcement had become possible in a politically decentralized society because economic change had weakened patrimonial sources of authority in the countryside, while exacerbating class conflict to the point where the propertied classes realized that they needed a more depersonalized form of control.[7] The landowner who as magistrate dispersed the mob was too readily identified with the interests he defended, while the lower gentry who served as parish judges sympathized too much with rioters, and sometimes refused to act against them (Shelton, 1973). A salaried police, it was hoped, could more effectively claim to represent a law that embodied general interests rather than those of a particular class, as it would not be a direct party to the disputes that erupted into riots. The creation of the new police thus had an important ideological dimension having to do with the legitimation of control. Reformers argued that those who were punished would acknowledge the fairness of their punishment and feel guilty only if it were evident that the law was enforced impartially (Ignatieff, 1978:70-75).

The creation of a police force also permitted the state to adjust its response to the magnitude of a perceived threat with greater precision, and thus represented an attempt to bring the social control machinery itself under greater control. Furthermore, as a proactive force, the police were to prevent crime rather than merely respond to it after it had occurred. This was to be done by bringing a visible personification of the law into working-class communities on a regular basis. Middle-class leaders interpreted traditional working-class culture as a "generating milieu" of crime, and called on the police to eliminate it. The bureaucratization of enforcement made this possible, for the police could arrest and prosecute without regard to the wishes of complainants. Outside of the context of bureaucratized enforcement this assault on working-class culture would have been unthinkable.[8]

The circumstances surrounding the establishment of police departments along the Eastern seaboard in the United States were strikingly similar to those in England. Riots broke out frequently in preindustrial Boston, New York, Philadelphia, Baltimore, St. Louis, and Cincinnati (Lane, 1975; Richardson, 1970; Walker, 1977). As rioting took on social and political overtones in the decades preceding the Civil War, proposals for a police system something like London's were debated. Again it took years before reformers could overcome fears that the police would be used to establish a tyranny and the reluctance of local political leaders to lose patronage jobs.

Harring (1981, 1983) has pointed out that the mere establishment of a police force did not always mean much, since often little more was involved than a formal reorganization of existing watch systems under a single agency, without administrative change. Before the invention of the telegraph and telephone, administrative decentralization was a technological necessity. Moreover, budgetary constraints limited the growth of police departments.

Capitalist reluctance to pay for increased protection with higher taxes was eventually overcome by labor strife in the decades following the Civil War. Together with petit bourgeois shopkeepers and professionals, industrialists lobbied successfully for appropriations to hire more police, and helped to develop new deployment strategies in response to strikes. Better prepared, the police could be called on to intervene on behalf of owners.

The extent to which a police force actually carries out class control functions is always limited by organizational and political constraints (Marenin, 1982). In nineteenth-century American cities, bribes paid by saloon keepers, who were important figures in urban politics, substantially nullified the enforcement of laws against saloons and vice, though not necessarily drunkenness. The widening of suffrage limited the use of the police against the working class only to a small degree. On occasion (for example, in Boss Tweed's New York) big-city mayors did refuse to use the police to break strikes. The loyalty of the police, who mostly came from working-class backgrounds, could not always be guaranteed in actions against strikes, but in large cities the conservatism of the larger middle class, and the inability of new immigrants to vote, limited working-class ability to influence policing policy. The ethnic divisions that separated the police from the policed, along with a variety of organizational strategies designed to preserve the loyalty of the force, generally sufficed to ward off large-scale defection.

The situation was somewhat different in smaller industrial towns dominated by a single factory or mine, where the working class was proportionately larger, and often had support from small storekeepers. Under those circumstances the small local police forces could not be used to repress strikes. Consequently capitalists employed private forces to break strikes and to spy on union organizing efforts. Eventually the system declined: As the economy expanded, fewer towns were so exclusively dominated by a single company; and unions lobbied against private police because of their brutality. Still, they never disappeared. Today they largely perform functions public police cannot do well, such as guarding department stores from shoplifting and employee theft (Spitzer and Scull, 1977; Weiss, 1978).

Critics of the Marxist analysis of policing sometimes object that the police performed other functions besides suppressing strikes. Although true, this objection is not particularly damaging to Marxist claims. Harring (1983), for example, notes that the police did deal with interpersonal violence and the theft of personal property; yet differential allocation of resources left working-class communities underprotected from these crimes. The police accepted bribes from professional thieves, leaving workers (and members of other classes) unprotected. In the meantime, the burden of arrests and harassment of vagrants, drinkers, and prostitutes was borne almost entirely by working-class communities. Though the local cop on the beat was sometimes a popular figure, the police as a whole were not. Their priorities were not those of the working class and were often detrimental to it.

Until recently, textbooks portrayed the history of penal sanctions as one of ineluctable progress from barbarism to enlightenment. Under the impact of eighteenth-century rationality and of religiously inspired humanitarianism, punishments for crime became less brutal. Retribution fell by the wayside, replaced by efforts to rescue and restore the unfortunate to full social membership.

A close examination of penal trends suggests a more complex history, one that cannot be characterized by linear trends, and whose dynamic has little to do with the immanent march of progress. Rusche and Kirchheimer (1939), drawing on the theoretical resources of the Frankfurt Institute for Social Research, pointed to a more fruitful approach by examining punishment in the context of class society.

In primitive stateless societies and kingdoms, many "crimes" were treated as private injuries—the way the courts nowadays treat torts. The perpetrator compensated the victim or the victim's family, or risked private revenge, not public punishment. As the state began to centralize, it began to assert responsibility for maintaining order. In return for this "service," fines had to be paid to the crown instead of the victim. Penalties of mutilation and death were introduced, especially for peasants who could not pay heavy fines because they were becoming enserfed.[9]

Rusche and Kirchheimer went on to argue that when labor is scarce, penal sanctions are used to make cheap labor available to capitalists. Thus in the mercantile era the Dutch and English governments set up houses of correction in which inmates worked for private entrepreneurs to produce goods for the market. By reducing labor costs below the going wage at a time when displaced laborers resisted workshop production, the houses subsidized the accumulation of capital and gave a boost to early capitalism. In periods of labor surplus, on the other hand, it is difficult to use prison labor profitably. Then penal conditions deteriorate, and the emphasis shifts toward deterring the lower classes from crime by maintaining standards of living in prison that are worse than those of the lowest level of the working class.

At their best, Rusche and Kirchheimer were sensitive to the impact of a complex conjuncture of economic constraints, political agendas, and ideological influences on the character of punishment. At their worst, they were prone to economic reductionism and took casually to a crudely instrumentalist conception of the state by assuming that judges, prison reformers, and administrators could be counted on to serve the needs of the capitalist class. Despite these weaknesses their work has remained the touchstone for all subsequent Marxist analyses of penal institutions.

Movements to curtail capital punishment and replace it with penitentiary confinement have received particularly close attention. In eighteenth-century France and England, proposals to abolish the death penalty for most offenses and to establish a rough proportionality between the gravity of the offense and the severity of the penalty reflected concerns for both the legitimacy of the law and its effectiveness. The carnival-like atmosphere at executions, occasional riots, and defiance on the part of the condemned were eroding respect for the majesty of the law. In addition, English juries refused to convict petty thieves to avoid sending them to the gallows. Frequent pardons further reduced the certainty of punishment (Cooper, 1974; Linebaugh, 1975; Foucault, 1977; Ignatieff, 1978).

Insisting that these conditions jeopardized property by undermining the deterrent effect of the law, the petit bourgeoisie and capitalists from all over England flooded Parliament with petitions urging a reform of sentencing (Rustigan, 1981). In alliance with reforming Tory landlords, who were equally concerned with the legitimacy of the law, this middle class successfully pressured Parliament into abolishing the death penalty for most offenses. By the time parliamentary reform gave the middle class formal political representation in 1832, much of this reform had already been carried out, though business interests continued to press for further reductions in capital punishment in succeeding decades (Cooper, 1974: 41).

The argument for reducing the use of the death penalty was also posed on humanitarian grounds.[10] Rusche and Kirchheimer attributed this humanitarianism to the Industrial Revolution, which increased the demand for labor, and thus raised the social value of a human life. Consistent with this explanation, the American colonies, where labor was scarce, used the death penalty much less often than England did. But Rusche and Kirchheimer took too narrow a view of the matter. The reformers' humanitarianism was part of a shift in religious ideology associated with their upward mobility. The break from the Calvinist doctrine of predestination in favor of the belief that anyone could be saved, which underlay some of the anticapital-punishment campaigns, came as the petit bourgeois religious dissenters prospered and became well-to-do capitalists. Their humanitarianism was a response to the contradiction between their former ascetic, self-denying orientation to the world, adopted when they were part of the lower middle class, and the economic success that adherence to this doctrine helped to bring about. Campaigning for reform was their way of expressing a common humanity with the poor and outcast. At the same time, the new class position of the reformers lent a strong social control component to their paternalistic humanitarianism (Ignatieff, 1978: 58).

The Russian jurist Pashukanis (1978: 180-81), whose ideas have been influential among contemporary Marxist criminologists, has argued that there is a deep connection between the principle of proportionality in punishment advocated by criminal law reformers and the development of industrial capitalism:

> Deprivation of freedom, for a period stipulated in the court sentence, is the specific form in which modern, that is to say bourgeois capitalist, criminal law embodies the principle of equivalent recompense. This form is unconsciously yet deeply linked with the conception of man in the abstract, and abstract human labour measurable in time. Industrial capitalism, the declaration of human rights, the political economy of

> Ricardo, and the system of imprisonment for a stipulated term are phenomena peculiar to one and the same historical epoch.

Significantly, this is not an instrumentalist argument. Pashukanis did not assert that imprisonment for fixed periods was in the interest of capitalists, but rather that the reduction of human labor to abstract, interchangable "labor time" in the industrial phase of capitalism leads members of a capitalist society toward notions of appropriate sanctions based on the metaphor of commodity exchange. His argument explains why it was in the period when the capitalist mode of production became fully established that imprisonment for fixed periods of time proportional to the injury caused by the crime became a major form of punishment.

Yet, Humphries and Greenberg (1981) remind us, public sentiment regarding punishment was translated into new penal practices only insofar as that sentiment was manifested politically. In England, this took the form of acquittals of defendants (made possible by the jury, an institutional survival from precapitalist times), petitions to Parliament, and, after 1832, parliamentary representation. Before the new system could be established, the gentry, who had enacted a large volume of sanguinary legislation in the eighteenth century, and whose political authority was reinforced by obtaining pardons for their clients, had to be defeated politically.

By the middle of the nineteenth century the uniformity of sentences associated with competitive capitalism began to draw criticism, first in England, then in the United States, for failing to give prisoners an incentive to reform. As an alternative, reformers proposed that release from custody should occur in stages, with the duration of the sentence to depend on a prisoner's comportment. This arrangement was to permit prisoners to develop their powers of self-control under supervision, while the rewards of greater liberty and early release were to reinforce good behavior.

This proposed departure from formal legal equality reflected a growing awareness of a problem in the creation of an appropriately motivated labor force (Currie, 1973). The classical social contract theorists had supposed that everyone possesses the personal qualities required by capitalism (notably rationality). As industrialization began and encountered resistance from workers, it became clear that the production of appropriately motivated workers did not occur automatically, but had to be secured through institutions not directly involved in production, namely, the family, the school, and the church.

When these institutions failed, as nineteenth-century crime and pauperism seemed to show they sometimes did, the prison had to step in. Architecture alone could not do the job, as the Jacksonians had believed. A system of discipline was needed that would more closely resemble the capitalist economy outside the prison. Rewards for performance in prison fulfilled this need. This phase of sentencing reform, then, reflected the contradiction between the capitalist-derived notion of punishment as exchange for past injury (equal punishment for the same offense), and the individualization required by the social control function the prison was to serve in a capitalist society.

The "time off for good behavior" systems adopted in many states did not go far enough to suit the post-Civil War reformers. Comparing crime to a disease, these reformers wanted sentences that were open-ended, regardless of offense. Prisoners were to be held until reformed and supervised after release so that they could be reincarcerated at the first sign of relapse, without the necessity of waiting for a new crime to be committed. At the same time, the permanent incarceration of incurable "born criminals" would become possible.

The theorists who advocated this approach to sentencing tended to explain crime, along with many other social problems, in biological terms, as the consequence of hereditary degeneration or atavism.[11] As criminals were deemed to lack responsibility, the concepts of blame, retribution, and even deterrence were considered to be irrelevant to social control. Imprisonment was no longer to be considered a punishment at all, but a treatment bestowed on the prisoner by a benevolent state. The adversarial relationship between the criminal and the state that formed the basis for criminal procedure in the competitive stage of capitalism was now to be dissolved by the interest both were presumed to hold in the criminal's being cured. Consequently, limits on the state's power to coerce were no longer needed.

The reformers who campaigned for this innovation were mostly professionals (especially physicians) seeking the bureaucratization and professionalization of penal and social welfare agencies, which they hoped to administer on the basis of "scientific" principles. Their proposals won considerable support from middle-class and capitalist constituencies attracted by the possibility of dealing more effectively with crime, insanity, pauperism, and social unrest. But they were also favored by Populists and anarchists, who were attracted by what seemed to be a step away from moralistic, punitive responses to crime (Currie, 1973). With major sectors of the economy coming to be dominated by a small number of corporations and trusts, the limited, "nightwatchman" conception of the state that had appealed to classical liberals made less sense, and the idea that the state should play a more active role in society gained support across the political spectrum. It is no coincidence that state legislatures began to adopt indeterminate sentencing and parole during the Progressive Era, when regulation of the economy and interference with market outcomes also gained wider support.

The prison system devised by the English reformers reflected the same concerns that informed their campaign against the death penalty. To legitimate punishment, all prisoners had to be treated equally, regardless of social status. Prisons that operated privately under contract from the state had to be eliminated, for in these, a prisoner's standard of living was determined by payments to the jailkeeper, and these naturally depended on the prisoner's wealth (Sheehan, 1977). Unlike the old gaols, the new penitentiaries were to be administered impartially through a system of formal rules established by a bureaucratic government agency (Ignatieff, 1978:77-78).

Based on a vision of reconciliation between classes that economic and social change had driven apart, the prison was to reform miscreants, not demolish them (Ignatieff, 1978:210). Implicitly, this meant turning them into model proletarians. Since crime was attributed to indolence, avarice, the decline of authority, and irreligiosity—that is, to those vices of laborers that induced them to resist wage labor—the new prison discipline was to consist of a regimented daily routine, hard labor, an abstemious, alcohol-free diet, submission to orders, and religious exhortation. Because popular lower-class culture was believed to sustain crime, prisoners were to be cut off from the outside world and from one another: Visitors and correspondence were restricted, and the cell system and the rule of silence were imposed to prevent even the slightest communication among inmates.

Although the prison was established to cope with a crisis in preindustrial capitalism, the architectural form that the prison took (cellular confinement) and the disciplinary methods it adopted were not entirely determined by that crisis: They were also shaped by the theories of crime causation then prevalent, and by the organizational innovations being introduced in connection with the Industrial Revolution. Declining profits for the outwork masters who were given contracts for the use of inmate labor in the earlier houses of correction had, along with the continuing difficulty of supervising cottage industry, stimulated the introduction of the factory. Many of the new disciplinary techniques the English reformers introduced into the penitentiary (such as intense surveillance) had first been devised as solutions to administrative problems in "free" production, or in the schools, hospitals, and other institutions that the same group of reformers managed for the poor. For example, Jeremy Bentham's Panoptican design for penitentiaries was adapted from a plan his half-brother Samuel had devised to stop carpenters employed in a shipyard from pilfering materials (Hartwell, 1971:77; Geis, 1972; Ignatieff, 1978:32, 62; Hogg, 1979; Fine, 1980; Melossi, 1980; Linebaugh, 1985). The similar methods introduced by upper-class continental reformers were likewise borrowed from the army, the hospital, and the classroom (Foucault, 1977), where they were deployed as an expression and instrument of absolutist power in the mercantile state (Steinert, 1984).

Much work has examined the evolution of the American prison in relation to the capitalist economy and to political crises (Miller, 1974, 1980; Takagi, 1975; Shelden, 1981; Melossi and Pavarini, 1981; Petchesky, 1981; Adamson, 1983, 1984). Particular attention has been given to the prison as a productive enterprise. In a capitalist economy, production is normally organized privately, for profit; but the prison is a state agency. How it is to interface with the private economy becomes an issue.

The shift from corporal and capital punishment, and forced labor in public, to imprisonment was a product of the centralization of political power after Independence. The innovation was guided by European enlightenment thought as well as by religious currents, but humanitarianism (the usual non-Marxist explanation) is a misleading explanation for the change. Conservative professionals, religious leaders, and merchants were preoccupied with the vice, immorality, and disrespect for authority that seemed to be developing even before the War of Independence (Lewis, 1970). Their worries intensified when the end of the war brought economic stagnation and political crises. They hoped that the prison would deter crime more effectively than existing sanctions, and would restore traditional authority. The prison was to isolate offenders from their communities more effectively than the colonial gaol and force them to obey their superiors. Prisoners worked to offset the cost of keeping them, and to prepare them to become self-supporting when released.

Debates about systems of penitentiary discipline raged for several decades of the early nineteenth century, but economic factors decided the matter. To financially pressed legislatures, the disadvantage of the Philadelphia system was not that total solitary confinement drove inmates mad, but that craft labor was inefficient. The Auburn system, on the other hand, featuring factory-like collective production, promised profits that could pay for the administration of the prison. At the same time, it could accustom those outside the regular workforce to the discipline of the factory. Later, in the Western territories, it exemplified the industrial future that politicians were trying to promote (Conley, 1980, 1982).

Labor shortages developed in the North along with the expansion of industry; and as one would expect from reading Rusche and Kirchheimer, prisoners were turned into a resource to help supply the deficiency. Under the contract system, entrepreneurs paid a fee to the prison, which in turn provided a workshop, machinery, and cheap labor (prisoners were paid much less than prevailing wages) subject to prison discipline.

The system did not always work smoothly. When wage labor entered the prison, so did class conflict: Prisoners resisted speedups. Endemic corruption in the awarding of contracts led to revenue losses for the state. Manufacturers who did not use prison labor complained of unfair competition, and free workers protested that prison manufacturing undercut free labor. Over time, the expanded scale of industrial production made prison labor less useful; the growth of the labor force made it less essential; and the enlarged tax base made revenues from prison industries less critical. Eventually the contract system was replaced by production for state use. The prison was no longer to be used to subsidize capital accumulation, but to control crime.

Antebellum Southern prisons were much like those in the North, but held only small numbers of black prisoners. Masters usually punished their slaves with a whipping; imprisoning them would have resulted in the loss of the use of productive property. After the Civil War the prison population became predominantly black. Prisoners were leased to private corporations, which used them to build roads, lay railroad tracks, and mine coal—that is, to build the infrastructure needed to industrialize. The brutal, often lethal conditions of work reflected a major purpose of the system: to maintain white capitalist domination over a potentially dangerous population of emancipated slaves. Because the black population could be exploited only under conditions of extreme coercion, and was quite large, individual prisoners could be—in fact, had to be—treated as expendable. Opposition from labor eventually ended the lease system, but road gangs working under appalling conditions continued under state supervision well into the twentieth century, continuing to serve the twin needs of subsidizing capital and perpetuating white supremacy.

During periods of prosperity, discipline in the Northern prisons was strict but not harsh; in depressions, however, penal conditions deteriorated. Analysis of twentieth-century prison statistics shows that the size of the prison population is equally responsive to the state of the economy. Noting that, in several countries, per capita prison populations oscillate within narrow limits over long stretches of time, Blumstein, Cohen, and Nagin (1976) explain this pattern in Durkheimian terms as a response to the periodic strengthening and weakening of the collective conscience. Subsequent work by Greenberg (1977a), Jankovic (1977), Yeager (1979), Box and Hale (1982), and Melossi (1984) suggests that the oscillations are rather due to changing levels of unemployment, which transform the moral climate. Conservative politicians and government spokesmen scapegoat criminals by channeling frustration over the economy into "law and order" issues, and judges sentence more punitively (Ratner and McMullan, 1983).

Over the past fifteen years, the ideals of diversion and decarceration have dominated the correctional literature, but rising unemployment and a growing sense of social threat have caused prison populations to increase to unprecedented levels. Yet probation and parole have grown even more rapidly. Much as hard-liners would like to build more prisons, the fiscal crisis of the state makes it difficult to do so (Scull, 1977; Melossi, 1980).

THE CAUSES OF CRIME

Until recently, criminologists devoted most of their energies to studying the causes of crime. They looked for causes primarily in the personal attributes of offenders (their chromosomes, IQ scores, school grades, self-esteem) or their immediate social environment (broken homes, delinquent peers). Specific explanations often suffered from blatant class bias by assuming that serious criminality was restricted to the working class.

A few theorists did consider the larger social context of crime. Thus Merton (1938) attributed criminality to the discrepancy between culturally induced aspirations for material success and structural limitations on individuals' ability to fulfill their aspirations lawfully. But the existence of this discrepancy was never explained; thus the theoretical advance was limited.

In the 1960s, many symbolic interactionists and phenomenologists attacked explanations of crime for dehumanizing criminals by treating their consciousness as irrelevant to an explanation of their crimes.

Though now denounced as politically conservative, crudely deterministic explanations of crime had been offered in the past by scholars on the left as well as the right. Thus Engels (1950: 130) wrote:

> If the influences demoralizing the working man act more powerfully, more concentratedly than usual, he becomes an offender as certainly as water abandons the fluid for the vapourous state at 80 degrees Réaumur. Under the brutal and brutalising treatment of the bourgeoisie, the working man becomes precisely as such a thing without volition as water, and is subject to the laws of Nature with precisely the same necessity; at a certain point freedom ceases.

As the author could hardly have imaged himself as deprived of volition in quite the same way, this positivist logic implies a radical dichotomy between criminals and "honest" citizens.

This dichotomy was called into question during the 1970s by the previously mentioned studies of self-reported crime, which showed widespread involvement in delinquency for many youths who never came to the attention of law enforcement, and who were thus never officially labeled as delinquent. The determinism of many causal theories also drew criticism for its inability to explain why many of those predicted to be criminal were not, or why many delinquents eventually desisted.

Under the weight of these criticisms some criminologists stopped trying to explain crime and turned their attention to law enforcement instead. Yet for Marxists this was theoretically and politically unsatisfactory: It left the level of crime in society, and its distribution across the population, entirely unexplained. Radicals were thus ill-equipped to participate in the political debates that arose over the increase in common forms of crime that took place in the 1960s (Young, 1975).

As the radicals had no way to account for increased crime, they tended at first to deny that there had been any (referring glibly to the poor quality of crime statistics), and thus they had little to say to residents of neighborhoods being invaded by junkies and teenage thieves, or burned down by paid arsonists. Although radicals could engage in muckraking in connection with crimes committed by corporations or government officials, they could not explain these either, except as the doings of wicked people. Of necessity, Marxist criminologists returned to the task of explaining crime, drawing on Marxist theory to conceptualize the sociopolitical context within which crime occurs, while at the same time attempting to avoid the pitfalls of a simplistic positivism.

Much of this new work has focused on historically changing patterns of crime. The recent study of rape by Herman and Julia Schwendinger (1984) illustrates this development. Rape has traditionally been explained as the product of some type of psychopathology, though in some recent feminist writings it has been viewed as an historically unchanging technique by which psychologically normal men dominate women. The Schwendingers reject both explanations. While they concede that some rapists may be psychotic, this does not appear to be true of the great majority. Nor has rape been a historical universal: Anthropologists have found many "primitive" societies in which it is extremely rare.

Drawing on ideas developed in Engels' *Origins of the Family, Private Property, and the State* (1942), the Schwendingers argue that rape develops historically when the rise of commerce, class stratification, exploitative private property relations, and the state destroy a tribal social order characterized by relatively high social status and autonomy for women and harmonious, cooperative relations between the sexes. As the institutional basis of women's power in the economy, and their role in collective public decisionmaking, are eroded, male supremacy takes hold. One of its correlates is an ideology that legitimates male violence against women. The Schwendingers identify other factors that contribute to sexual violence as well, notably war (which has often been waged in connection with commercial rivalries), which places a premium on male violence and undermines informal social controls.

The Schwendingers contend that while female subordination and rape may have originated in precapitalist social formations, capitalism brings about conditions that perpetuate male sexual violence. The sharpening of the sexual division of labor in the course of capitalist industrialization, only now being eroded in modest ways, created or strengthened preexisting cultural stereotypes of violence as distinctively male, thereby encouraging males to "prove" their masculinity by attacking women. The cynical, exploitative outlook of young ghetto males, which permits guilt-free victimization of others, is an adaptation to the competition for survival required of those who have been marginalized from capitalist production. Extramarital rape is committed most often, though not exclusively, by young men of the lower classes. In special circumstances, like war, it may occur without respect to class.

Major episodes of marginalization have occurred in conjunction with each reconstitution of class relations and each of these episodes has made its mark in the annals of crime. The commercialization of English agriculture in the late fifteenth and sixteenth centuries led the great landlords to evict tenant farmers and enclose common lands where peasants had previously grazed livestock and raised poultry. The monastery lands, which had supported monks and paupers, were confiscated and turned over to followers of the crown for commercial exploitation, adding to the rural population deprived of traditional sustenance. Feudal retainers, discharged when the centralizing state forced aristocrats to disband their private armies, further swelled the ranks of the surplus population. This vast army of the dispossessed supported itself by begging and stealing on an unprecedented scale (Marx, 1967:717-49).

The reconstitution of class relations continued to fill the ranks of crime in the eighteenth century. Enclosures still drove yeoman farmers from the land, and advances in production and distribution marginalized laborers and sectors of the petit bourgeoisie. From time immemorial, English farmers drove their cattle to market, to be sold and butchered. However, to meet the growing demand for meat in London, whose population was rising rapidly, the slaughter of cattle was becoming centralized, with loss of income to local butchers and, of course, their apprentices. Still, some farmers did bring their cattle to market, receiving coin in return. The butchers' apprentices, knowing just what route the farmers would take to return home, and needing extra income, rode after them and robbed them on the road. A substantial fraction of the young men hanged for highway robbery in eighteenth-century London were butchers' apprentices. Branch banking was invented to prevent such thefts by enabling payments for commercial dealings to be handled as paper transactions. Simultaneously, new definitions of property connected with the capitalist mode of production were introduced into law, making criminal many traditional sources of income for farmers and workingmen, such as hunting small game, gathering fallen wood in forests, and appropriating raw materials spoiled during manufacture (Linebaugh, 1976, 1985; Sugarman, Palmer and Rubin, 1982).

Robinson (1977) has examined the implications of the displacement of Southern black farmers for American criminal history. The mechanization of Southern agriculture with federal subsidies in the years following World War II made small-scale farming economically unviable—an outcome that had been anticipated by farm policy administrators. Poor farmers, many of them black, were forced to relinquish their land and, in the absence of employment opportunities in the South, to migrate to Northern cities. Some were absorbed into the manufacturing and service sectors of the expanding postwar economy, but racial discrimination prevented many from entering the ranks of the working class except as irregularly employed unskilled laborers.

These blacks had made a quick transition from the "latent" fraction of the rural, relative surplus population to the urban "stagnant" fraction[12]—a fraction from which petty criminals and addicts are easily recruited. While this was happening, the white middle-class population of the Northern cities was moving from city to suburb, a population shift made possible by federal subsidies for home mortgages and highway construction. This middle-class exodus eroded the tax base that cities could have used in programs to help its new immigrants. In the absence of such programs, crime rates in urban ghettos rose to levels unknown in half a century.

Several theorists have argued that the historical exclusion of juveniles from the labor force has had major consequences for their involvement in delinquency (Schwendinger and Schwendinger, 1976, 1982, 1985; Greenberg, 1977b). In preindustrial societies children typically work alongside their parents or masters and thus have little opportunity to engage in crime, and little to gain from it. Even in the early years of industrialization, many youths were able to earn a meager income by working in factories and mines, or as vendors and household servants. Relative to adults, their crime rates were fairly low.

The spread of industrialization led to the exclusion of juveniles from full-time work. Periodic downswings in the economy threw heads of families out of work, and as labor organized and grew militant, it demanded that child labor laws be passed to preserve jobs for adults. Support from Progressive-era middle- and upper-class reformers gained passage for child labor laws, depriving young people of opportunities to earn spending money in an age when the mass-media-induced culture increased their subjective needs for monetary income. Many parents subsidize their children's social life, making crime unnecessary. However, when they are unable or unwilling to do so, their offspring are left with the options of curtailing their social life or stealing. Many opt for the latter, then desist when a job alleviates their financial needs.

The adoption of child labor laws went hand in hand with the passage of mandatory school attendance statutes, which were needed to keep children, no longer able to work, from congregating on street corners and causing trouble. Reformers were eager to subject working-class children, many of them progeny of immigrants, to the Americanizing and character-forming influence of public education. The turn of the century was a time of labor militancy, and schooling was seen as an important means of undermining the working-class cultures in which it was rooted.

Bowles and Gintis (1976) have pointed out the many ways in which features of contemporary education, such as regimentation, ranking, and suppression of sociality among peers, serve the imperatives of a capitalist economy, particularly in preparing youths to enter the working class. The restrictions these imperatives require are probably frustrating to all students, but for some, the immediate social rewards or the anticipated occupational payoff in adulthood lead to a tacit willingness to put up with the frustration. Other students, though, do not find schoolwork rewarding, and because of their class or race, they cannot expect much from an investment in education. These students have less reason to refrain from venting their resentment and may express their feelings through assaultive behavior. By beating up someone they can regain the sense of potency that the school denies them.

Non-Marxist criminologists have also explained delinquency as a response to school problems. What distinguishes the Marxist explanation is the insight that institutions like the school (or the family) do not function independently of the basic social relations of the mode of production. It is fully consistent with Marxism to maintain that these constraints produce alienated social relations between teachers and students, and among the students themselves; and that this alienation can lead to delinquency. Further Marxist theorizing about delinquency has examined such issues as its class and sex distribution, and the kinds of subcultures that surround it (Messerschmidt, 1981; Schwendinger and Schwendinger, 1982, 1985; Colvin and Pauly, 1983; Hagan et al., 1985).

The British Marxist historians E. P. Thompson (1971) and Eric Hobsbawm (1971) initiated a different way of thinking about crime by documenting episodes of collective resistance to capitalism. In the regulated economy of the mercantilist era, the price of foodstuffs was controlled to prevent profiteering and to ensure that no one would starve. These controls were later repealed in the name of "free trade," enabling large-scale farmers to raise prices or withhold produce from the market in times of scarcity. When this happened, villagers acting in the name of a traditional "moral economy" illegally took produce and distributed it to the crowd, sometimes collecting the "fair" price for the farmer.

English textile workers of the 1760s smashed the spinning jennies that threatened their livelihoods, and in the 1820s, when owners began replacing farm hands with threshing machines and hay ricks, "Luddites"—anonymous laborers acting under the mythical leadership of General Ludd—again banded together to destroy the machines covertly. Whiggish historians who see only progress in industrialization have described these movements as acting blindly and irrationally; some Marxists, too, have treated them with condescension, or deplored their attempts to stop the forward march of history. But resistance to capitalism remains class conflict even when it defends a way of life that is doomed. Today's Marxist historians point out that it is hardly irrational of workers to oppose innovations that were impoverishing them and resulting in the manufacture of defective goods. The smashers did not oppose the introduction of machinery; they simply wanted the cost of mechanization to be carried by those who were profiting from it, not by employees (Pearson, 1978).

Capitalists also commit crime. For them it is often "the pursuit of profits by other means" (Pearce, 1976:77-109; Quinney, 1979: 197-203; Barnett, 1979). More is at work than the utility-maximizing so beloved by microeconomists. Rational choices are certainly involved. In the case of arson-for-profit of urban residential buildings, however, these choices are structured by "such processes as redlining [on the part of banks and conventional insurance companies], gentrification, condominium conversion [small fires are a good way to get rid of existing tenants] and large-scale redevelopment" (Brady, 1984) —as well as by indifference on the part of law enforcement, city government policy decisions that housing renovation should be done privately,[13] and the existence of a large class of impoverished, marginalized tenants who cannot pay rents high enough to give owners a satisfactory return.

Auto dealers, whose crimes have also been studied, must buy cars from an industry dominated by three firms, whose market power is large enough to permit them to dictate franchise terms to dealers, despite warranties that ostensibly make the manufacturers responsible for defects in parts. Dealers respond to these market pressures through overcharges and fraudulent repairs (Leonard and Weber, 1970; Farberman, 1975). Here, too, enforcement efforts are usually weak, and customers have no easy way of ascertaining that they've been cheated.

The explanation of business crime as a product of the structures and incentives of a capitalist economy is quite different from the sorts of explanations offered by non-Marxists. Stone (1975), for example, contends that *all* instances of business crime stem from organizational defects that prevent information from reaching those within the company who could intervene to stop the crime. Yet sometimes those at or near the top want crime, and create internal communications barriers to protect themselves. At the same time, unwritten, informal messages indicating that legal constraints should be ignored in pursuit of profits can convey management intent quite adequately.

Most explanations of crime focus on factors that "push" or propel people toward crime, or make it attractive. Yet those pushed will engage in crime only if it is feasible to do so. McIntosh (1975) and McMullin (1984) have sketched the ways the advance of capitalism has changed opportunities to commit crime. Theft is rare in small self-contained peasant villages. Because everyone knows everyone else it is impossible for someone to steal on a continuing basis without being identified. The growth of commercial cities destroys this informal social control; its anonymity facilitates theft. At the same time, the concentration of monetary wealth and movable consumer goods in homes and shops creates abundant targets—enough to make it possible for full-time burglars, pickpockets, and confidence men to support themselves by stealing and worthwhile to acquire specialized training.

The political weakness of the absolutist states in which many of the early commercial cities developed was a further factor stimulating the growth of professional crime. Medieval church sanctuaries where the secular authorities could not enter still survived, giving many criminals a tacit immunity. Public offices were bought and sold, or were filled through political patronage, obstructing efforts to rationalize state administration. These political features were not simply antiquated survivals of feudalism; they reflected the particular character of the absolutist state, which was that of a class compromise between aristocracy and commercial bourgeoisie.

The rapid development of the forces of production in the course of the twentieth century and the establishment of a full-time salaried police force have simultaneously rendered some traditional forms of professional theft antiquated, while making new forms possible. As workers are now paid by check rather than by cash, it has become harder to make a living by pickpocketing, but credit card fraud has mushroomed. Sophisticated detection systems discourage commercial burglaries, but now we have computer theft. The technology to curb auto thefts already exists, but automakers, who profit when victims buy new cars, refuse to install it in their products (Karmen, 1981; Brill, 1982).

Increased consumption of illegal narcotic drugs in the 1960s reflected not only the growth of consumer demand but also the increased supply made possible by CIA support of right-wing cultivators or processors in Southern Europe, Southeast Asia, and Latin America in connection with anti-Communist foreign policy objectives (Chambliss, 1977).

POLITICAL PRACTICE

From the start, radical criminologists attempted to move criminology out of the ivory tower and the police department by wedding research to radical action. They worked in community campaigns to curb police brutality, raise bail for indigent defendants, end the death penalty, halt the repression of political militants, support prisoners, and stop arson for profit.

Some posited the goal of radical action to be the creation of a society that did not criminalize diversity, and that would utilize informal, community-controlled forms of social control such as arbitration and negotiation of conflict (Taylor, Walton, and Young, 1973; Mathiesen, 1974; Quinney, 1974; Pepinsky, 1976). Others expected such institutions as the prison to survive the transition to socialism, but with a restricted class of prisoners and more humane conditions (Wright, 1973; Smith and Fried, 1974).

Radical criminology journals (*Crime and Social Justice*, *Contemporary Crises*) continue to publish discussions of the positions socialist criminologists should take on policy issues; Taylor (1981a, 1983) and Lea and Young (1984) have given the subject extended treatment. One senses, though, that the ratio of talk to action is high. Given the salience of crime to the public, a socialist movement can hardly ignore the issue. It must combat the repressive use of the criminal justice system; and to gain credibility it must advance alternative methods of preventing or dealing with crime compatible with a socialist vision. Criminologists in the movement will have an important role in these tasks, but they cannot bring a movement into existence. Without it, what they can do is quite limited.

FOOTNOTES

1. The work of Merton (1938) is an exception, insofar as it introduces a rudimentary notion of social structure, albeit one that is terribly underdeveloped.

2. Symbolic interactionism has its roots in the writings of William James, John Dewey, William Thomas, Charles H. Cooley, and George Herbert Mead. Blumer (1969) is a modern exponent. In brief, it holds that (a) people act toward things on the basis of the meanings that the things have for them; these meanings are a product of social interaction, and are modified through interpretation; (b) behavior is consciously enacted by the self, rather than an unconscious response to internal or external stimuli; (c) the self originates in social interaction.

3. Some of these claims were later challenged; see Humphries and Greenberg (1981) for a review of the debates.

4. Later some of this work was justly criticized for an overly conspiratorial view of how crime is depicted in the mass media. Current work focuses on why crime is reported or depicted in particular ways, on how crime reporting can simultaneously be factually accurate and nonetheless ideological, and on how readers or viewers interpret representations of crime in the media (Pandiani, 1978; Humphries, 1981; Taylor, 1981).

5. For fuller accounts of Marxist work on law see Greenberg and Anderson (1981) and Tushnet (1984).

6. They also suffered from the completion of the transcontinental railroad, which opened the California market to factory-produced goods made in the East, but Eastern capitalists were too far away and too powerful to make a convenient target.

7. In France, where state administration was more centralized, a bureaucratic police force was begun as early as 1667, by Louis XIV (Steinert, 1984).

8. This assault, as well as police intervention in strikes and demonstrations, blocked attempts to win working-class support for the police for at least a century (Sugarman, Palmer, and Rubin, 1982).

9. As our discussion of the history of policing indicates, the transition was slow. Only with the Industrial Revolution were many forms of taking movable property transformed from civil wrongs to crimes (Sugarman, Palmer, and Rubin, 1982). To gain support for the creation of a public police force, reformers had to argue that highway robbery was a public harm, not simply an injury to the private party who was robbed (Palmer, 1976).

10. Reformers were not alone in claiming the mantle of humanitarianism. Defenders of capital punishment claimed that it was humane because its superior effectiveness as a deterrent spared more people from punishment (Palmer, 1976).

11. Nye (1984) presents a brilliant materialist analysis of late-nineteenth-century biological explanations of crime.

12. The "latent" form of the relative surplus population is so called because it is capable of moving (usually from the countryside to the city) only when alternative employment or income (for example, welfare payments) becomes available. The "stagnant" form consists of very low-paid and irregularly employed workers, often in decaying sectors of the economy.

13. One New York City prosecutor told the author that much arson for profit would be prevented were the city to condemn buildings for serious violations and carry out rehabilitation itself. This could not be done, he added, because political considerations made it impossible for the city to compete with the private real estate industry.

BIBLIOGRAPHY

Adamson, Christopher R. "Punishment After Slavery: Southern State Penal Systems, 1865-1890." *Social Problems* 30 (1983).

________. "Towards a Marxian Penology: Captive Criminal Populations as Economic Threats and Resources." *Social Problems* 31 (1984).

AFSC Working Party. *Struggle for Justice*. New York: Hill and Wang, 1971.

Balkan, Sheila, Berger, Ronald J., and Schmidt, Janet. *Crime and Deviance in America: A Critical Approach*. Belmont, Calif.: Wadsworth, 1980.

Barnett, Harold. "Wealth, Crime and Capital Accumulation." *Contemporary Crises* 3 (1979).

Becker, Howard S. *Outsiders: Studies in the Sociology of Deviance*. New York: The Free Press, 1963.

Beirne, Piers. "Empiricism and the Critique of Marxism on Law and Crime." *Social Problems* 26 (1979).

Blumer, Herbert. *Symbolic Interactionism*. Englewood Cliffs, N.J.: Prentice-Hall, 1969.

Blumstein, Alfred, Cohen, Jacqueline, and Nagin, Daniel. "The Dynamics of a Homeostatic Punishment Process." *Journal of Criminal Law and Criminology* 68 (1976).

Bowles, Samuel, and Gintis, Herbert. *Schooling in Capitalist America: Educational Reform and the Contradictions of Economic Life*. New York: Basic Books, 1976.

Box, Steven, and Hale, Chris. "Economic Crisis and the Rising Prisoner Population in England and Wales." *Crime and Social Justice* 17 (1982).

Brady, James. "The Social Economy of Arson: Vandals, Gangsters, Bankers and Officials in the Making of an Urban Problem." In Spitzer, Steven, and Scull, Andrew T. (eds.). *Research in Law, Deviance and Social Control*, Vol. 6. Greenwich, Conn.: JAI Press, 1984.

Brill, Harry. "Auto Theft and the Role of Big Business." *Crime and Social Justice* 18 (1982).

Center for Research on Criminal Justice. *The Iron Fist and Velvet Glove: An Analysis of the U.S. Police*. Berkeley Center for Research on Criminal Justice, 1975.

Chambliss, William J. "A Sociological Analysis of the Law of Vagrancy." *Social Problems* 11 (1964).

________. *Crime and the Legal Process*. New York: McGraw-Hill, 1969.

________. "The State, the Law, and the Definition of Behavior as Criminal or Delinquent." In Glaser, Daniel (ed.). *Handbook of Criminology*. Chicago: Rand McNally, 1974.

_______. "Functional and Conflict Theories of Crime." In Chambliss, William J., and Mankoff, Milton (eds.). *Whose Law, What Order? A Conflict Approach to Criminology*. New York: John Wiley, 1976.

_______. "Markets, Profits, Labor and Smack." *Contemporary Crises* 1 (1977).

_______. "Contradictions and Conflicts in Law Creation." In Spitzer, Steven (ed.). *Research in Law and Sociology 2*. Greenwich, Conn.: JAI Press, 1979.

_______, and Seidman, Robert B. *Law, Order and Power*. Reading, Mass.: Addison-Wesley, 1971.

Clarke, Dean. "Marxism, Justice and the Justice Model." *Contemporary Crises* 2 (1978).

Cohen, Stanley. "The Punitive City: Notes on the Dispersal of Social Control." *Contemporary Crises* 3 (1979).

_______. *Visions of Social Control*. New York: Basil Blackwell, 1985.

Colvin, Mark, and Pauly, John. "A Critique of Criminology: Toward an Integrated Structural-Marxist Theory of Delinquency Production." *American Journal of Sociology* 89 (1983).

Conley, John. "Prisons, Production and Profit: Reconsidering the Importance of Prison Industries." *Journal of Social History* 14 (1980).

_______. "Economics and the Social Reality of Prisons." *Journal of Criminal Justice* 10 (1982).

Cooper, David D. *The Lesson of the Scaffold: The Public Execution Controversy in Victorian England*. Athens: Ohio University Press, 1974.

Currie, Elliot Park. "Managing the Minds of Men: The Reformatory Movement, 1865-1920." Ph.D. Dissertation, University of California, Berkeley, 1973.

Dickson, Donald T. "Bureaucracy and Morality: An Organizational Perspective on a Moral Crusade." *Social Problems* 16 (1968).

Donajgrodzki, A. P. "'Social Police' and the Bureaucratic Elite: A Vision of Order in the Age of Reform." In Donajgrodzki, A. P. (ed.). *Social Control in Nineteenth Century Britain*. Totawa, N.J.: Rowman and Littlefield, 1977.

Embree, Scotty S. "The Politics of Expertise: A Profession and Jurisdiction." Ph.D. Dissertation, New York University, 1973.

_______. "The State Department as Moral Entrepreneur: Racism and Imperialism as Factors in the Passage of the Harrison Narcotics Act." In Greenberg, David F. (ed.). *Corrections and Punishment*. Beverly Hills, Calif.: Sage, 1977.

Engels, Friedrich. *The Origin of the Family, Private Property, and the State*. New York: International Publishers, 1942.

_______. *The Condition of the Working Class in England in 1844*. London: Allen and Unwin, 1950.

_______. "Herr Eugen Dühring's Revolution in Science." Chapter 9 in Feuer, Lewis S. (ed.). *Karl Marx and Friedrich Engels' Basic Writings on Politics and Philosophy*. Garden City, N.Y.: Anchor, 1959.

Farberman, Harvey A. "A Criminogenic Market Structure: The Automobile Industry." *Sociological Quarterly* 16 (1975).

Fine, Bob. "The Birth of Bourgeois Punishment." *Crime and Social Justice* 13 (1980).

_______, Kinsey, Richard, Lea, John, Picciotto, Sol, and Young, Jock. *Capitalism and the Rule of Law: From Deviancy Theory to Marxism*. London: Hutchinson, 1979.

Foucault, Michel. *Discipline and Punish: The Birth of the Prison*. New York: Pantheon, 1977.

Geis, Gilbert. "Jeremy Bentham." In Mannheim, Hermann (ed.). *Pioneers in Criminology*. Montclair, N.J.: Patterson Smith, 1972.

Greenberg, David F. "The Dynamics of Oscillatory Punishment Processes." *Journal of Criminal Law and Criminology* 68 (1977a).

_______. "Delinquency and the Age Structure of Society." *Contemporary Crises* 1 (1977b).

_______. (ed.). *Crime and Capitalism: Readings in Marxist Criminology*. Palo Alto, Calif.: Mayfield, 1981.

_______, and Anderson, Nancy. "Recent Marxisant Books on Law: A Review Essay." *Contemporary Crises* 5 (1981).

_______, and Stender, Fay. "The Prison as a Lawless Agency." *Buffalo Law Review* 21 (1972).

Gusfield, Joseph R. *Symbolic Crusade: Status Politics and the American Temperance Movement*. Urbana: University of Illinois Press, 1963.

Hagan, John, Simpson, John, and Gillis, A. R. "The Class Structure of Gender and Delinquency: Toward a Power-Control Theory of Common Delinquent Behavior." *American Journal of Sociology* 91 (1985).

Hall, Stuart, Critcher, Charles, Jefferson, Tony, Clarke, John, and Roberts, Brian. *Policing the Crisis: Mugging, the State and Law and Order*. New York: Holmes and Meier, 1977.

Harring, Sidney L. "Policing a Class Society: The Expansion of the Urban Police in the Late Nineteenth and Early Twentieth Centuries." In Greenberg, David F. (ed.). *Crime and Capitalism*. Palo Alto, Calif.: Mayfield, 1981.

_______. *Policing a Class Society: The Experience of American Cities, 1865-1915*. New Brunswick, N.J.: Rutgers University Press, 1983.

Hartwell, R. M. *The Industrial Revolution and Economic Growth*. London: Methuen, 1971.

Hay, Douglas. "Property, Authority and the Criminal Law." In Hay, Douglas, et al. (eds.). *Albion's Fatal Tree: Crime and Society in Eighteenth Century England*. New York: Pantheon, 1975.

Helmer, John. *Drugs and Minority Oppression*. New York: Seabury, 1975.

Hepburn, John R. "Social Control and the Legal Order: Legitimate Repression in a Capitalist State." *Contemporary Crises* 1 (1977).

Hobsbawm, Eric J. *Primitive Rebels*. Manchester: Manchester University Press, 1971.

Hogg, Russell. "Imprisonment and Society under Early British Capitalism." *Crime and Social Justice* 12 (1979).

Humphries, Drew. "The Movement to Legalize Abortion: An Historical Account." In Greenberg, David F. (ed.). *Corrections and Punishment*. Beverly Hills, Calif.: Sage, 1977.

_______. "Serious Crime, News Coverage, and Ideology." *Crime and Delinquency* 27 (1981).

_______. "Social Class and Legal Change: The Birth Control Controversy." *Contemporary Crises* 7 (1983).

_______, and David F. Greenberg. "The Dialectics of Crime Control." In Greenberg, David F. (ed.). *Crime and Capitalism*. Palo Alto, Calif.: Mayfield, 1981.

_______, and David F. Greenberg. "Social Control and Social Formation: A Marxian Analysis." In Black, Donald (ed.). *Toward a General Theory of Social Control*. Vol. 2. New York: Academic Press, 1984.

Ignatieff, Michael. *A Just Measure of Pain: The Penitentiary in the Industrial Revolution, 1750-1850*. New York: Pantheon, 1978.

Inciardi, James (ed.). *Radical Criminology: The Coming Crises*. Beverly Hills, Calif.: Sage, 1980.

Jankovic, Ivan. "Labor Market and Imprisonment." *Crime and Social Justice* 8 (1977).

Karmen, Andrew A. "Auto Theft and Corporate Irresponsibility." *Contemporary Crises* 5 (1981).

Krisberg, Barry. *Crime and Privilege: Toward a New Criminology*. Englewood Cliffs, N.J.: Prentice-Hall, 1975.

Lane, Roger. *Policing the City: Boston, 1822-1885*. New York: Atheneum, 1975.

Lea, John, and Young, Jock. *What is To Be Done About Law and Order*? Harmondsworth: Penguin, 1984.

Leonard, William N., and Weber, Marvin Glenn. "Automakers and Dealers: A Study of Criminogenic Market Forces." *Law and Society Review* 4 (1970).

Levine, Harry Gene. "The Discovery of Addiction: Changing Conceptions of Habitual Drunkenness in America." *Journal of Studies on Alcohol* 39 (1978).

———. "Temperance and Women in 19th Century United States." In *Research Advances in Alcohol and Drug Problems*, Vol. 5. New York: Plenum, 1979.

Lewis, W. David. "The Reformer as Conservative: Protestant Counter-subversion in the Early Republic." In Cohen, Stanley, and Ratner, Lorman (eds.). *The Development of an American Culture*. Englewood Cliffs, N.J.: Prentice-Hall, 1970.

Linebaugh, Peter. "The Tyburn Riots against the Surgeons." In Hay, Douglas, et al. (eds.). *Albion's Fatal Tree: Crime and Society in Eighteenth Century England*. New York: Pantheon, 1975.

———. "Karl Marx, the Theft of Wood, and Working Class Composition: A Contribution to the Current Debate." *Crime and Social Justice* 6 (1976).

———. *The London Hanged: Crime and Civil Society in the Eighteenth Century*. London: Allen Lane, 1985.

Manning, Peter. *Police Work: The Social Organization of Policing*. Cambridge, Mass.: MIT Press, 1977.

Marenin, Otwin. "Parking Tickets and Class Repression: The Concept of Policing in Critical Theories of Criminal Justice." *Contemporary Crises* 6 (1982).

Marx, Karl. *Capital*, Vol. 1. New York: International Press, 1967.

Mathiesen, Thomas. *The Politics of Abolition.* New York: Halsted, 1974.

Matza, David. *Becoming Deviant*. New York: John Wiley, 1969.

McIntosh, Mary. *The Organization of Crime*. London: Macmillan, 1975.

McMullin, John L. *The Canting Crew: London's Criminal Underworld, 1550-1700*. New Brunswick, N.J.: Rutgers University Press, 1984.

Melossi, Dario. "Strategies of Social Control in Capitalism: A Comment on Recent Work." *Contemporary Crises* 4 (1980).

———. "Punishment and Social Control: Toward a Theoretical Model of the Relationships between the Political Business Cycle and Imprisonment in Italy (1896-1965)." Paper presented to the American Society of Criminology, 1984.

———, and Pavarini, Massimo. *The Prison and the Factory: Origins of the Penitentiary System*. New York: Barnes and Noble, 1981.

Merton, Robert. "Social Structure and Anomie." *American Sociological Review* 3 (1938).

Messerschmidt, Jim. "Marginalization, Reproduction and Assaults against Teachers: Ideas on the Contradictions of Ideological Social Control." *Contemporary Crises* 5 (1981).

Michalowski, Raymond, and Bohlander, Edward W. "Repression and Criminal Justice in Capitalist America." *Sociological Inquiry* 46 (1976).

Miller, Martin B. "At Hard Labor: Rediscovering the 19th Century Prison." *Issues in Criminology* 9 (1974).

_______. "Sinking Gradually into the Proletariat: The Emergence of the Penitentiary in the United States." *Crime and Social Justice* 14 (1980).

Mitford, Jessica. *Kind and Usual Punishment: The Prison Business*. New York: Alfred A. Knopf, 1973.

Morgan, Patricia A. "The Legislation of Drug Law: Economic Crisis and Social Control." Paper presented to the Society for the Study of Social Problems, 1976.

Musto, David. *The American Disease*. New Haven, Conn.: Yale University Press, 1973.

NARMIC. *Police on the Homefront*. Philadelphia: AFSC, 1971.

Nye, Robert A. *Crime, Madness, and Politics in Modern France: The Medical Concept of National Decline*. Princeton, N.J.: Princeton University Press, 1984.

Palmer, Jeremy. "Evils Merely Prohibited." *British Journal of Law and Society* 3 (1976).

Pandiani, John A. "Crime Time TV: If All We Knew Is What We Saw." *Contemporary Crises* 2 (1978).

Pashukanis, Evgeny B. *Law and Marxism: A General Theory*. London: Ink Links, 1978.

Pearce, Frank. *Crimes of the Powerful: Marxism, Crime and Deviance*. New York: Pluto Press, 1976.

Pearson, Geoffrey. *The Deviant Imagination: Psychiatry, Social Work and Social Change*. New York: Holmes and Meier, 1975.

_______. "Goths and Vandals—Crime in History." *Contemporary Crises* 2 (1978).

Pepinsky, Harold E. *Crime and Conflict: A Study of Law and Society*. New York: Academic, 1976.

Petchesky, Rosalind P. "At Hard Labor: Penal Confinement and Production in Nineteenth-Century America." In Greenberg, David F. (ed.). *Crime and Capitalism*. Palo Alto, Calif.: Mayfield, 1981.

Platt, Anthony. *The Child Savers: The Invention of Delinquency*. Chicago: University of Chicago Press, 1969.

_______. "The Triumph of Benevolence: The Origins of the Juvenile Justice System in the United States." In Quinney, Richard (ed.). *Criminal Justice in America: A Critical Understanding*. Boston: Little, Brown, 1974.

_______, and Takagi, Paul. "Intellectuals for Law and Order: A Critique of the New 'Realists.' " *Crime and Social Justice* 7:1-16, 1977.

Quinney, Richard. *The Social Reality of Crime*. Boston: Little, Brown, 1970.

_______. *Critique of Legal Order: Crime Control in Capitalist Society*. Boston: Little, Brown, 1974.

———. *Class, State, and Crime*. New York: Longman, 1977.

———. *Criminology*. Boston: Little, Brown, 1979.

Ratner, R. S., and John L. McMullan. "Social Control and the Rise of the 'Exceptional State' in Britain, the United States, and Canada." *Crime and Social Justice* 19 (1983).

Reiman, Jeffrey H. *The Rich Get Richer and the Poor Get Prison*. New York: Wiley, 1979.

Richardson, James F. *The New York Police, Colonial Times to 1901*. New York: Oxford, 1970.

Robinson, Cyril. "Historical and Economic Underpinnings to Problems in Police-Community Relations." Paper presented to the Society for the Study of Social Problems, 1977.

Rusche, Georg, and Kirchheimer, Otto. *Punishment and Social Structure*. New York: Russell and Russell, 1939.

Rustigan, Michael. "A Reinterpretation of Criminal Law Reform in Nineteenth-Century England." In Greenberg, David F. (ed.). *Crime and Capitalism*. Palo Alto, Calif.: Mayfield, 1981.

Schur, Edwin M. *Labeling Deviant Behavior*. New York: Harper and Row, 1971.

———. *Radical Decarceration: Rethinking the Delinquency Problem*. Englewood Cliffs, N.J.: Prentice-Hall, 1973.

Schwendinger, Herman, and Schwendinger, Julia. "Defenders of Order or Guardians of Human Rights." *Issues in Criminology* 7 (1970).

———. "Delinquency and the Collective Varieties of Youth." *Crime and Social Justice* 5 (1976).

———. "The Paradigm Crisis in Delinquency Theory." *Crime and Social Justice* 18 (1982).

———. *Rape and Social Inequality*. Beverly Hills, Calif.: Sage, 1984.

———. *Adolescent Subcultures and Delinquency*. New York: Praeger, 1985.

Scull, Andrew. *Decarceration: Community Treatment and the Deviant—A Radical View*. Englewood Cliffs, N.J.: Prentice-Hall, 1977.

Sheehan, W. J. "Finding Solace in Eighteenth-Century Newgate." In Cockburn, J. S. (ed.). *Crime in England, 1550-1800*. Princeton, N.J.: Princeton University Press, 1977.

Shelden, Randall G. "Convict Leasing: An Application of the Rusche-Kirchheimer Thesis to Penal Changes in Tennessee, 1830-1915." In Greenberg, David F. (ed.). *Crime and Capitalism*. Palo Alto, Calif.: Mayfield, 1981.

Shelton, Walter J. *English Hunger and Industrial Disorders*. Toronto: University of Toronto Press, 1973.

Silver, Allan. "The Demand for Order in Civil Society: A Review of Some Themes in the History of Urban Crime, Police and Riot." In Bordua, David J. (ed.). *The Police: Six Sociological Essays*. New York: John Wiley, 1967.

Smith, Joan, and Fried, William. *The Uses of the American Prison: Political Theory and Penal Practice*. Lexington, Mass.: Lexington Books, 1974.

Spitzer, Steven. "The Rationalization of Crime Control in Capitalist Society." *Contemporary Crises* 3 (1979).

_______, and Scull, Andrew. "Privatization and Capitalist Development: The Case of the Private Police." *Social Problems* 25 (1977).

Steinert, Heinz. "The Development of 'Discipline' According to Michel Foucault: Discourse Analysis vs. Social History." *Crime and Social Justice* 20 (1984).

Stevenson, John. "Social Control and the Prevention of Riots in England, 1789-1829." In Donajgrodzki, A. P. (ed.). *Social Control in Nineteenth Century Britain*. Totawa, N.J.: Rowman and Littlefield, 1977.

Stone, Christopher. *Where the Law Ends: The Social Control of Corporative Behavior*. New York: Harper and Row, 1975.

Sugarman, David, Palmer, J. N. J., and Rubin, G. R. "Crime, Law and Authority in Nineteenth Century Britain." *Middlesex Polytechnic History Journal* 1 (1982).

Takagi, Paul. "A Garrison State in a 'Democratic' Society." *Crime and Social Justice* 1 (1974).

_______. "The Walnut Street Jail: A Penal Reform to Centralize the Powers of the State." *Federal Probation* 39 (1975).

Taylor, Ian. "Crime Waves in Post-War Britain." *Contemporary Crises* 5 (1981a).

_______. *Law and Order: Arguments for Socialism*. London: Macmillan, 1981b.

_______. *Crime, Capitalism and Community: Three Essays in Socialist Criminology*. Toronto: Butterworths, 1983.

_______, Walton, Paul, and Young, Jock. *The New Criminology*. New York: Harper and Row, 1973.

_______, Walton, Paul, and Young, Jock, eds., *Critical Criminology*. Boston: Routledge and Kegan Paul, 1975.

Thompson, E. P. "The Moral Economy of the English Crown in the Eighteenth Century." *Past and Present* 50 (1971).

Turk, Austin T. *Criminality and the Legal Order*. Chicago: Rand McNally, 1969.

Tushnet, Mark. "Marxism and Law." In Ollman, Bertell, and Vernoff, Edward (eds.). *The Left Academy: Volume 2*. New York: Praeger, 1984.

Walker, Samuel. *A Critical History of Police Reform*. Lexington, Mass.: Lexington Books, 1977.

Weiss, Robert. "The Emergence and Transformation of Private Detective Industrial Policing in the United States, 1850-1940." *Crime and Social Justice* 9 (1978).

Wright, Erik Olin. *The Politics of Punishment: A Critical Analysis of Prisons in America*. New York: Harper and Row, 1973.

Yeager, Matthew G. "Unemployment and Imprisonment." *Journal of Criminal Law and Criminology* 70 (1979).

Young, Jock. "Working-Class Criminology." In Taylor, Ian, Walton, Paul, and Young, Jock (eds.). *Critical Criminology*. Boston: Routledge and Kegan Paul, 1975.

7

U.S. MARXIST SCHOLARSHIP IN THE ANALYSIS OF HEALTH AND MEDICINE

Vicente Navarro

INTRODUCTION

An examination of Marxist theoretical production in the analysis of health and medicine in U.S. academia needs to be prefaced by two observations. The first is that this theoretical production (like any other production) cannot be understood unless it is analyzed within its historical context. The second is that any theoretical production carries with it a vision of reality that reproduces, consciously or unconsciously, the interests of a specific class, gender, race, and other power categories in society. Whether a theoretical position is dominant or not depends on its articulation with the dominant power relations in a given society.

Dominant theoretical positions explain, legitimize, rationalize, and reproduce the dominant/dominated relations in society, within a pattern of dominance that is reproduced not only through persuasion but primarily through repression of the alternative dominated positions. This situation explains the brutal repression in U.S. academia (a major set of intellectual agencies that reproduce, for the most part, dominant ideological positions) against Marxist positions, a repression that is reproduced not only by excluding, silencing, and ignoring Marxist positions, but also by their manipulation, stereotyping, and caricaturization. An example of the former is the chapter on "The State of the Art on Medical Sociology" prepared for the International Sociological Association by a leading U.S. sociologist (Twaddle, 1982). Not one Marxist reference is even mentioned in that compilation of social science studies in medicine. Similarly, Marxist analyses rarely appear in major social science journals covering the areas of health and medicine. Moreover, this silence occurs in spite of the enormous theoretical Marxist production that has taken place in this area, primarily in the last fifteen years, and that will be presented in this chapter. A major forum for that production has been the *International Journal of Health Services*, a journal open to all positions, with Marxist contributions well represented in its pages.

While repression is the most important form of reproduction of dominance, it is not the only one. Dominant theoretical production in the social sciences cannot completely ignore the continuous threat presented by the dominated forces, of which Marxist ones are perceived as the most threatening. Dominant positions must respond to these threats in a continuous process of adaptation and change. Thus, although Marxist positons may be silenced, they are not without influence. The dominant positions are frequently forced to respond directly or indirectly to this threat to their dominance.

This chapter will discuss the main theoretical production in the analyses of health and medicine that have emerged in the United States (with primary focus on the last fifteen years), locating them within the social context in which they are reproduced. As part of that context, this chapter will also analyze the interaction between dominant positions (referred to in daily parlance as mainstream and in Marxist discourse as bourgeoise) and the Marxist ones. In other words, this chapter will also analyze how Marxist theoretical production has interrelated with and challenged the dominant theoretical positions in the analysis of health and medicine put forward by the social sciences.

THE ROOTS OF THE MARXIST ANALYSIS OF HEALTH AND MEDICINE

From the very beginning, there have been two major conceptions of health, disease, and medicine under capitalism. Reflecting the opposing interests of the capitalist and working classes, these two conceptions have formed the bases for two major bodies of theory and practice: the social and the materialist, and the clinical and the individualist. The first approach, represented by Virchow and Engels, defined the social causes and origins of health and disease, relating them to the power relations in society. Virchow had studied the typhus epidemic and the famine of 1847-48 in Upper Silesia, an economically depressed Prussian province. His study took place within a social context of revolt. The Paris Commune had just occurred and the revolutionary wars and popular uprisings spread through Germany as well.

Virchow joined the barricades and for a short time was a member of the Democratic Congress. He founded *Medical Reform* and concluded his report with the effective slogan that "Medicine is a social science and politics nothing but medicine on a grand scale." Disease was the individual realization of a social problem. Virchow, considered one of the founders of social medicine and public health, was aware that social reform was needed to improve the health of the population and that those reforms threatened the dominant class relations in society. His report on the typhus problem in Silesia called for land reform, income redistribution, betterment of housing conditions, and other social programs (Taylor and Rieger, 1984).

Virchow was influenced by Engels, whose *The Conditions of the Working Class in England* was the first Marxist analysis of health and medicine (Engels, 1969). In that work, Engels presented a detailed analysis of the etiology and epidemiology of typhoid, tuberculosis, scrofula, and rickets, and insisted that medical intervention was insufficient to deal with such diseases. His analysis of the health conditions of the working class was part of an overall analysis of the working and living conditions of the working class under capitalism. He specifically related disease to the social relations of production and the class structure that they determined. Since the problem resided in capitalism, real solutions required transcending capitalism. With Marx, Engels later wrote *The Communist Manifesto*, which asserted the need for changing working-class conditions through revolutionary transformations. This position is the root of the Marxist analysis of health and medicine. This Marxist tradition was introduced in the United States in the 1930s by Henry Sigerist, an immigrant from Europe, who had an enormous influence on the development of social medicine and public health, not only in the United States but in other countries as well (Terris, 1975).

The dominant classes in Engels's and Virchow's time did not support these social (Virchow) and materialist (Engels) understandings of health. They viewed such interpretations as a threat to the social order in which they were dominant. Instead, they supported an alternative conception of disease in which social phenomena were redefined as natural phenomena, governed by natural, biological, and harmonious laws. Disease was explained as caused by an agent—the bacteria—always present in the diseased body. Within that theoretical construct, causality was defined as an association of the observable phenomena, with the subject for investigation being the microagent analyzed under the microscope. In focusing on the micro level, the macro social conditions were conveniently put aside. This is the root of Flexnerian, technological, individualistic medicine of which the hospital is its fullest realization. The dominance of this construct lies in its articulation with the dominant/dominated relations in society.

The dramatic insufficiency of Flexnerian medicine to resolve the disease problems confronting society explains why frequent calls are made, by spokespersons of the dominant position, for health policy to include other interventions besides medical care. In the middle 1970s, for example, the Canadian government published the well-known Lalonde report, named after that government's minister of health. In this report, medical care reforms were regarded as just one set of interventions among many other interventions that were also needed, including interventions in the environment, occupational health, living conditions, and social reforms (A New Perspective on the Health of Canadians, 1974). None of these proposed interventions has been implemented; only some of the medical reforms have been. Curative and individual clinical interventions frequently have been put forward as a way of avoiding more profound social reforms.

As a result of the historical roots of Flexnerian medicine and the articulation of the knowledge, practice, and institutions of medicine with the dominant power relations in society, medical institutions, including academic ones, are profoundly conservative. George Bernard Shaw once defined medicine, the military, and the clergy as the most conservative forces in society. This conservatism extends to the different disciplines in the social sciences that analyze health and medicine. The following sections explain these dominant positions and the alternative Marxist positions in selected areas of health and medicine.

DOMINANT AND MARXIST INTERPRETATIONS OF THE INSTITUTIONS OF MEDICINE

Pluralist Interpretations and Their Marxist Critiques

For the dominant interpretations of medicine in the last thirty years, class and class struggle in the United States did not exist. In the tranquil years of the 1950s and early 1960s, these realities did not penetrate the academic press. Terms such as capitalist class, capitalism, and class struggle were not mentioned, or they appeared in quotes as if to signal the reader that they were subject to suspicion, relevant for ideologues but not for serious scholars. As a result of welfare state policies, social mobility, and an enlargement of opportunities, the United States was recast after World War II in a mold of middle-class conditions and life-styles that obviated its characterization as a class society and falsified its designation as a capitalist one. In the words of one of the founders of contemporary American medical sociology, O. Anderson (1972:26):

> The middle class was and still is the source of entrepreneurial, technical, and managerial skills, which exploited natural resources, developed the economy, and thus . . . created a social surplus that spilled over into other endeavours such as the arts, education, health services and warring for national honor and expansion.

In this theoretical scenario there are no dominant classes, nor even dominant groups or elites. Rather, there exist competing blocs of interests, no one of which has control over the state, assumed to be an independent entity. Thus, "government became more or less another group or interest in cooperation, competition, and negotiation with the private individual or group" (Anderson, 1972:24-25).

These are the main tenets of the "pluralist" school that dominated the explanation and justification of power relations within all dimensions of our society, including medicine. Power was defined as diffuse, spread all over society, with different competing blocs balancing each other and themselves and with no particular group or interest able to weigh too heavily upon the state. The state was perceived in this explanation as the supervisor and arbiter of the competitive game, providing a guarantee against the concentration of power. Anderson (1972), in his major analysis of equity in the United States, Sweden, and Great Britain, does not even refer to class, much less to class struggle. The evolution of the health services in this study—considered to be a classic in Western medical sociology—is seen as the outcome of a competition of values in those societies within the context of the cultural peculiarities of each country. For example, the National Health Service in Great Britain is presented as primarily the outcome of the noblesse oblige of the British establishment, which benevolently supervised the competition of values and positions among the different power blocs in the health sector. Within the Marxist tradition, Navarro has explained why this pluralist position was dominant in Western capitalist societies. It legitimized the actual power relations in these societies. Navarro explains the evolution of the British medical institutions, including the establishment of the National Health Service, as the outcome of the class struggle in Great Britain, which appears and is reproduced in all sectors of society, including its medicine (Navarro, 1978a).

The pluralist interpretation of medicine was discredited in the late 1960s and 1970s when it became overwhelmingly clear that power was consistently skewed in favor of some groups against others, and that the state, far from being an arbiter, was very much a part of the problem, that is, it was supporting some groups more than others. It was clear, for example, that state health policies were more influenced by commercial health insurance than by patient associations. It is interesting to note that the pluralist interpretation remained in the background until recently, when a new version imported from France appeared in medical bibliography via Foucault (1973, 1975, 1977). This revision has given a new life to pluralist interpretations of reality, including medicine. According to this new version of pluralism, power is widely diffused in our society (minipowers) with no one power category being the organizer of how those minipowers are articulated and reproduced. Class power and state power are denied the centrality that they have in Marxist analysis. This latest version of pluralism has similar problems to the old version, however. To paraphrase Orwell, some powers are more equal than others. Indeed, the Marxist theoretical production in medicine (Navarro, 1976; Renaud, 1975; Stark, 1982; Waitzkin, 1983) has shown that (1) some powers are more important than others in reproducing the Western system of medicine, (2) all power (including professional power) has a class significance, and (3) the state, as a crystalizer of power relations, reproduces the matrix in which all forms of power are articulated inside and outside of medicine.

The political practice derived from the "old" pluralist interpretation is for each group or individual to act through current or newly existent competing blocs that operate through the parliamentarian system, in which a plurality of ideas and opportunities exist, openly exchanged in fair competition. The practice suggested by the new pluralist interpretation (the minipowers version) is for each group to develop its own space outside the state (for example, the holistic counterculture medicine). Neither of the two interpretations accepts the primacy of social agents for the transformation of capitalism or the importance of the state as part of the key relations that reproduce the whole system. The denial of these two realities makes these political strategies nonthreatening to the capitalist system. In fact, they rationalize that system.

Power Elite Interpretations and Their Marxist Critiques

The limited value of pluralist theories in explaining our realities accounts for the development in the late 1960s and 1970s of the "power elite" theories, which eclipsed much of the prominence of pluralist explanations. In this new paradigm (also referred to as power group theories), competition is reduced to a small group of elite groups that essentially dominate the different branches of the state. Eliot Friedson (1970) in sociology and Ted Marmor (1973) and R. Alford (1975) in political science became the main proponents of this approach in the mainstream analysis of medicine. Its radical version was formulated by Barbara and John Ehrenreich (1970). Considerable variation exists among these theorists, but all use a similar conceptualization and methodology. Their method of analysis includes, first, identification of the groups of elites that play a dominant role in the different sectors of medicine and of the state; second, analysis of how that power is exercised and through which mechanisms of state intervention; and third, description of the nature of the benefits those groups obtain as a result of their intervention. In these analyses, the actors (hospitals, universities, medical associations, insurance companies, and so on) are seen as power groups competing in their quest for dominance of or influence in the different agencies of the state. According to this analysis, the *campagne de bataille* is control over knowledge, licensure, instruments of care, funds, and so forth.

The contribution to the study of medicine made by these authors has not been small. They have provided valuable empirical information of use for the analysis of medicine. Yet the explanatory value of these works has been limited. By focusing their analytical lenses on medicine, these theorists fail to include in their analysis the nonactors and nondecisions that may be far more important than the visible and intervening actors and the studied actual decisions. Marxist authors such as Navarro (1976) and McKinlay (1977) have shown that competition among "power groups" takes place within the parameters defined by the struggle of larger power categories such as class (as well as race, gender, and other power categories) that define what can or cannot occur within that competition. Some alternatives (for example, the establishment of a national health service in the United States) are not even considered in these power interplays. Thus the final decision is not merely an outcome of the interplay of the visible actors. The nonvisible actors also count. Moreover, these power elite groups are segments of broader categories of power, such as classes, which explains why, in spite of tactical disagreements, they all have broader agreements based on the cohesiveness supplied by their class position in our society.

This power elite interpretation has recently reappeared in a more radical form in the work of Ivan Illich (1976) and the new writings of Barbara and John Ehrenreich (1974). The latter writings are particularly influenced by Friedson and Parsons, defined by the Ehrenreichs as "the most important contributors to the sociological description of medicine." These radical authors define the nature of our society and its medicine as a result of the ideological manipulation of our populations by the professional bureaucracies that have taken the place of the capitalist class as the main agents of oppression. According to these theorists of bureaucratic and professional control, the process of industrialization has reshaped the nature of our societies in such a way that power, assumed to be divorced from ownership of capital, has passed from the owners of capital—the capitalists—to the managers of that capital, and from there to the technocrats—those who have the skills and knowledge needed to operate the major social edifices of industrialism, the professional bureaucracies. The new elite are the professionals who have supplanted the capitalists. Illich and the Ehrenreichs assume that the nature of medicine and medical care is an outcome of the manipulation of medical knowledge, practice, and institutions by the medical profession that, in order to perpetuate its power, has created an addiction to medicine that legitimizes its control over the population. Class struggle disappears, to be replaced by the conflict between professional and patient.

Marxist scholarship (Navarro, 1975, and Stark, 1982) has challenged these interpretations, criticizing them on methodological, conceptual, and political grounds. By focusing on medicine, radicals have been unable to see medicine as the interplay of power conflicts that operate within a matrix of social power categories (class, race, gender, and others), of which class is the organizer of how those conflicts, including the professional-patient conflict, take place. Historical studies within the Marxist tradition have shown how the American medical profession was established with the support of the capitalist class (Berliner, 1975, 1977), how the evolution of the knowledge, practice, and institutions of medicine reproduced class power relations (Navarro, 1980c, and Smith, 1982), and how the patient-physician relationship is a bearer of power categories of which class is a critical one (Waitzkin and Waterman, 1974).

Marxists have further argued (Navarro, 1983b) that to view medicine primarily as an agency of control (as power elite theorists, including its radical versions tend to) is to take an instrumentalist view of power. Medicine appears merely as an instrument manipulated by power groups. Medicine, however, is a social relation in contradiction, in which different functions in contradiction are reproduced under a set of power relations in which class power traverses and utilizes other powers, assigning them specific political significance. Racism and sexism in medicine, for example, are functional to the reproduction of power of not only the white male professions but, far more important, of the dominant class. Racism and sexism appear in medicine through the knowledge, practice, and institutions of medicine, in which the dominant class is hegemonic. Racism and sexism do not appear independently of each other, but, rather, reinforce each other through class-dominated medicine. These different forms of oppression do not relate to one another in conditions of exteriority; rather, they are articulated within a set of relations in which class is the organizer of the power matrix in which these other forms of power exist. That is, medicine is not an instrument that exists first and is taken over by the power groups afterward.

The unawareness of this reality explains how another radical author, Linda Gordon (1978), can see the creation of Flexnerian medicine as an outcome of the male takeover of the institutions of medicine. As Marxist scholar Evan Stark (1982) has indicated, it was more than that. It was not so much a "takeover" as the creation of a medicine within a social formation in which a class (as well as a sex and a race) dominated the process of transformation. Gender, race, and class were not additive characteristics of that process of dominance. The appearance of male domination in medicine indeed had a clear class significance. Marxist feminist Elizabeth Fee (1982) has provided a socialist understanding of gender exploitation and its implications for health, science, and medicine.

This articulation of medicine with the social relations of production also explains the contradictory functions within medicine: one, the dominating and controlling function (which Marx, in referring to the foreman, termed the bourgeois function) and the other, the useful, curing, and caring function (which Marx, again using the case of the foreman, referred to as the coordinating and needed function). Again, these two functions do not relate to each other in conditions of exteriority (that is, the good and bad branches of medicine); rather, the controlling function is exerted through the useful function. To see medicine only as control—as radical authors do—is to fail to see the dialectical nature of medicine in which there is also a useful, needed function. To believe otherwise is to think that when the majority of

Americans demand a national health program, they are asking for more control. It is because of this erroneous interpretation that the radical position came remarkably close to embracing the reactionary position that the welfare state should be dismantled. The working class demands medical services because, in large degree, it gets benefits from the utilization of these services (for example, Medicare has contributed substantially to the decline of mortality among the elderly). However, as long as these services exist under capitalism, they will be under the influence of the dominant class, which will try to use these medical services and also to influence medical knowledge and practice to optimize its own interests. In the same degree that the capitalist and working classes are intrinsically in conflict (capital is expropriated labor), these two functions—the dominating and the useful in medicine—are also in contradiction.

Marxist critiques of the explanation of medicine as primarily an agent of social control have led to a further redefinition of the radical position. The best known among these redefinitions was developed by John Ehrenreich (1978), who called for carrying the struggle inside the medical institutions in order to change the values of medicine and eliminate its racism and sexism. According to this radical strategy, what is needed is to carry out a cultural revolution within those medical institutions to purify them and instill new values of service. The primary area of intervention in this strategy, which calls for "an unleashing of people's imagination," is in the realm of culture and values. How is this to occur? Ehrenreich remains silent on this point, aside from a vague call for social mobilization toward an undefined end. The absence of any analysis of how racist and sexist practices are reproduced and the material basis on which they rest makes his analysis and the strategy deriving from it insufficient. Culture has to be understood from a materialist perspective, within the context in which it is reproduced. Navarro (1983b) has criticized this interpretation's inadequate understanding of power and the voluntaristic practice that it generates.

THE CORPORATIZATION OF MEDICINE: DOMINANT AND MARXIST INTERPRETATIONS

A major methodological difference between non-Marxist and Marxist scholarship in the study of medicine has been that the former has focused its analysis on the behavior and motivation of power groups within medicine, while the latter has analyzed these groups as part of broader categories (such as class) whose conflicts are the organizing parameters of all other conflicts and their realization. Consequently, Marxists view the evolution of American medicine as part and parcel of the evolution of American capitalism. Because of this, they were able to describe and predict the corporatization of American medicine, that is, the heavy involvement of finance and corporate capital in the funding, administration, ownership, and possession of medical services. Kelman (1971), Navarro (1976), Salmon (1977, 1978), Himmelstein and Woolhandler (1984), and McKinlay (1978), among others, have written extensively on this. McKinlay (1985) has also analyzed the consequences of that corporatization of medicine for the medical profession, using the problematic concept of the proletarianization of physicians (with physicians working as employees of corporate America), briefly predicted earlier by Kelman and Navarro. Recently, and because of the overwhelming evidence of the corporatization of medicine, the dominant social sciences have started describing this phenomenon as well. However, in their description, those authors belonging to the "power elite" school (Relman, 1980, and Starr, 1983) define corporatization as the entry into medicine of a new "power group," that is, the corporations. Thus a powerful stratum of the capitalist class appears redefined as an aggregate of several interest groups, part of which is presented as the business community. One of the best known representatives of this school is Paul Starr, the Pulitzer Prize winner of 1984. Not unexpectedly, in Starr's analysis of the corporatization of medicine, no mention is made of previous work in this area done by Marxists. By ignoring these previous works, however, he remains stuck in the same trenches with other "interest group" analysts. Indeed, this new version of the "corporatization of medicine," by ignoring the social-economic-political context in which it takes place, and by seeing corporate America as one more interest group competing for government favors, is incapable of explaining why that corporatization is taking place now. It is not surprising that Starr finds corporatization an unexpected event. (Starr finds this corporatization of medicine to be, besides unexpected, a worrisome development. This position partially explains the book's favorable review among liberals and even some radical reviewers.) That event, however, is expected and predictable. As Marxist authors explained, this corporatization of medicine is the logical outcome of the dynamics of U.S. capitalism within a process of class struggle in which the dominant capitalist class continues to have an overwhelming influence over the organs of the state. This overwhelming dominance explains why, even when government responds to popular demands from working America, that response takes place within the parameters and conditions defined by the hegemonic elements within that capitalist or corporate class. The very limited power of the working class in the United States (a situation unparalleled among developed capitalist societies) explains not only the underdevelopment of the U.S. welfare state but also the corporatization of its medicine (Navarro, 1984b).

THE CURRENT CRISIS OF THE WESTERN SYSTEM OF MEDICINE

Another major area that has been the subject of great debate in the last fifteen years has been the crisis of medicine, conceptualized as the combination of rapid growth of expenditures without parallel improvements in the health of Western populations. Particularly in the late 1970s, there appeared in the medical and general press an extensive bibliography expressing concern about that crisis. There did not seem to be a correlation of health indexes with the level of medical expenditures. The dominant interpretation of that crisis saw the root of the problem in the industrialization of medicine. According to David Mechanic, a main proponent of this position, the evolution of medical technology determines not only the underlying assumptions of practitioners and patients but, most importantly, the organization of medicine and its uses. Why this organization, distribution, and crisis? According to Mechanic (1980), it is because of the logic and dynamics of technological development itself. According to others (Illich, 1976), it is because of the medical profession's manipulation of industrialization. To Illich, technological medicine, controlled by the medical bureaucracy and technocracy, has become a source of harm and oppression rather than a source of relief and liberation. The medical profession manipulated medicine, stimulating its growth. That growth, however, was not only not beneficial; it was actually harmful.

Navarro (1978b, 1982b) has criticized this theoretical position, indicating that it is not only medicine that is in crisis. It is the welfare state that is in crisis as part and parcel of the crisis of capitalism. In other words, the crisis in medicine is the crisis of capitalism reflected in the institutions of medicine. Without denying the existence of professional manipulation of medicine, it is erroneous to trace the growth of medicine to that manipulation (or to a technological determinism). Rather, that growth is based on a popular demand for health services that can alleviate the damage that the population suffers as a result of daily working, living, and other social conditions. On the other hand, medicine cannot resolve the major health problems (for example, cancer, cardiovascular conditions, stress-related conditions) that Western capitalist societies face. Those problems are, in large degree, rooted in conditions outside medicine; thus, medicine's limited effectiveness. Similar explanations can be applied to other sectors of the welfare state. P. Brown (1985), for example, has made a Marxist critique of the crisis of psychiatry and McBride (1984) has shown the impossibility of solving the heroin problem within the dynamics of U.S. capitalism.

The fact that medicine (and other social services) cannot resolve the major health problems does not mean that medicine is not useful. It can ameliorate the damage. This material reality explains the potency of its ideology. People want more of it. This popular demand explains the growth of medicine in the 1960s and 1970s. During this period, the working class and other popular forces, including the social movements, fought and obtained an expansion of the welfare state and, as part of this process, of medical services as well (for example, Medicare, Medicaid). New programs were established that not only responded to the power of the working class but empowered that class in its struggle with the capitalist class. A worker with health insurance is in a better position to resist the bosses than one without it. The Occupational Safety and Health Administration (OSHA), the National Institute for Occupational Safety and Health (NIOSH), and the Environmental Protection Agency (EPA) were other important victories for the working class. It is because of popular pressure and working-class demands that these medical and health interventions increased.

The late 1970s and early 1980s witnessed the successful attempts by the capitalist class to reduce social expenditures and health services in order to weaken the working class and recover the power that it had in society, a power that was never lost but was weakened by the growth of the welfare state. The dominant theoretical positions in medical social sciences explain cuts in health expenditures, and weakening of government interventions to protect the health of the workers, consumers, and of the environment, by reference to a popular mandate (Rogers et al., 1982), to the rebellion of people against government (Altman, 1984), and to the awareness that government intervention makes things worse rather than better (Mechanic, 1984). This position has been put forward in most academic journals, but very much in particular in *Health Affairs*, the organic ideological instrument of corporate America in the analysis of health and medicine. One of the most interesting phenomena in recent bibliography has been the quick adaptation of leading liberals to this new, profoundly conservative conventional wisdom. Navarro (1982c) has shown the lack of an empirical base to support such ideological interpretations of current events within and outside medicine.

The conservative response to the crisis has also included emphasis on individual life-style as the solution to the major health problems. In the words of Victor Fuchs (1972):

> It is becoming increasingly evident that many health problems are related to individual behavior. In the absence of dramatic breakthroughs in medical science the greatest potential for improving health is through changes in what people do and do not do to and for themselves.

Crawford (1977, 1984) has criticized this new form of victim blaming that implies that if people are sick, it is their own fault. Available evidence shows that most people have limited freedom to choose their work, place of residence, environmental exposure, and the type of relations they are part of. Other authors within the Marxist tradition (Guttmacher and Berliner, 1974; Stark, 1978; and others) have identified the position that an individual has in the power relations in society (including class, race, gender, and others) as the most important determinant of his or her health.

HEALTH, WORK, AND THE RELATION OF PRODUCTION

An important development in the analysis of health in Western society and in the United States in the last ten years has been the rediscovery of the relationship between work and health; and Marxist scholars have contributed significantly to this rediscovery. The theorization of that relationship has varied quite considerably, depending, to a large degree, on how work is conceptualized. In the largest number of references, work is conceived of as an environmental problem. It exposes individual workers to physical, chemical, and psychological agents that may make them sick or cause them to have accidents. The strategy of intervention derived from this understanding of work is to reduce the frequency of workers' exposures to pathological agents. While the enormous importance of this task should not be minimized, the theory and practice derived from that understanding of work reproduce the individual-environment dichotomy, which seriously hinders the understanding of the social relations that determine both the individual worker and the environment.

Another conceptualization of work has been that of regarding work as a source of resources—for example, income—that may enable the worker to meet his or her needs and expectations. This understanding of work has been the most prevalent one within the Weberian tradition, the dominant tradition within Anglo-Saxon sociology. In this tradition, the worker is seen primarily as a wage earner or consumer with specific attributes—for example, income, education, status—all defined in the spheres of exchange, distribution, and consumption rather than in the world of production. Work as an activity and as a social relation does not appear in this theoretical scenario. Citizens are primarily perceived and defined as consumers rather than workers.

Breaking with these two traditions are the very interesting works of Eyer (1975, 1984) and Karasek (1979; Karasek et al., 1981), both influenced by the Marxist tradition. Both authors see health and disease as determined by the social organization of society, which, through stress (Eyer) and the different degrees of control of the laborers over the labor process (Karasek), determines health and disease. The great merit of these contributions has been their break with past Weberian tradition and their focus on totalities, relating those totalities to the relations of production.

Other authors have considered work as an organizer of social life and as a concrete expression of social contradictions. Navarro (1982a) has theorized the relationship between the labor process and health, and Coye (1979) has criticized the mainstream explanations of the relationship between work and health. It is important to stress that in the Marxist tradition, production appears as the organizer of society, with the place that the individual has in the world of production (his or her class) determining his or her place in the world of consumption, exchange, distribution, and legitimization, *as well as his or her health*. Needless to say, what happens in other instances besides production—such as exchange and consumption—and what happens on other levels—ideological and political—has an autonomy of its own and has also great importance in explaining health and medicine. These movements and levels influence production and are influenced by it, but they are created and articulated within a whole—a social formation or society—where production is a determinant movement that characterizes the social formation.

Within this area of Marxist analysis, occupational health and safety has been an area of large Marxist theoretical production. Worthy of special mention are Berman (1978), the collection of articles edited by Navarro and Berman (1984), and by Chavkin (1984), and the contributions of Elling (1983), Goldsmith and Kerr (1984), Kotelchuck (1982), and Navarro (1984a), among others. By focusing on occupational health and safety, these studies have been able to link two major areas of Marxist scholarship in the United States: the study of the evolution of the labor process and the analysis of the state. How changes at the workplace impact on the health of the workers and how the state responds to that situation has been a focus of fruitful investigation. Occupational health and safety has also been an area of study that has enabled Marxists to establish a direct rapport with the working class.

IMPERIALISM, HEALTH, AND MEDICINE

In trying to understand poverty, death, and disease in the world of underdevelopment, one may go through the extensive bibliography existent in developed capitalist countries, including the United States, on health and medicine in what is usually referred to as the Third World, and rarely, if ever, find imperialism and capitalism presented as causes of that poverty, death, and disease. In most references on the underdevelopment of health, there is a deafening silence about these concepts and realities. In its stead, the literature reflects for the most part the positions of the Development Establishment,* which have been evolving in response to the challenge presented by Marxist and other antiimperialist forces. In the 1960s and early 1970s a great emphasis was placed by those establishments on population control. Population growth was considered to be either the cause or a major contributor to world poverty. The two sides of the coin of poverty were too many people on the one hand and too few resources on the other. The theoretical framework sustaining this position was remarkably simple. Looking at the gross national product (GNP) rate per capita, it seemed obvious that the fewer the "capitas," the more GNP for the existing ones. The poor countries were assumed to be poor because they did not have resources or, at least, not enough resources. Thus the answer was to control the size of their populations. Population control programs were the solution to the problem.

The "oil and other raw materials crisis" of the developed countries in the early 1970s showed, however, that if those less developed countries (LDCs) were poor, it was not because they lacked resources. Ac-

---

*Development Establishment is the body of internationally minded individuals who are active in major Western health and food aid agencies.

tually, a great deal of the key materials used in the rich countries came from the poor ones. Thus it could no longer be said that poor countries were poor because they did not have resources. They did have them, and in large quantities; however, the resources were consumed by the rich and not by the poor countries.

The new position that the Development Establishment took (not necessarily in substitution for but usually complementing the "population control" position) was that although the poor countries have material resources, they do not have the intellectual resources (the know-how or technology) to exploit them. Technological transfer from the developed to the less developed countries became the name of the game. Scientific, medical, and technological assistance became important instruments of intervention to resolve world poverty. Variants of this position soon appeared. One, represented by Schumacher (1975), among others, included a concern about the type of technological transfer. "Appropriate technology" was a term frequently used to voice the claim that not all technological transfer was positive; only the appropriate form was helpful. The meaning of "appropriate," however, varied quite considerably. For some, appropriate meant small (of the "small is beautiful" variety). For others, it meant "labor intensive." And so on.

Still another variant was the antitechnology position represented by Illich. (This position appeared side by side with the antiinstitutional positions, for example, antimedicine and antipsychiatry, voiced in the developed countries.) Its proponents opposed technological transfer, since they perceived such transfer as a process whereby a dependency on that technology would be created, thereby hindering the possibility for individual and collective development. The alternative offered was the development of autonomous spaces outside formal institutions, placing great emphasis on self-care and self-reliance–terms that were used almost interchangeably. Self-reliance was supposed to be for the community what self-care was for the individual.

All these ideological and political positions–population control, technological transfer, self-care, and self-reliance–were elaborated by the Development Establishment not independently of but, rather, in response to events occurring in the underdeveloped countries during that period and to antiimperialist critiques of their work. It was during those years that there appeared within the political and intellectual centers of the underdeveloped capitalist countries an increased awareness that their poverty was an outcome not of too many people, nor of the use of the right (or wrong) type of technology but, rather, of a pattern of worldwide relations in which the few control quite a lot and the many control very little. The problem was perceived in those centers to be structural, not conjunctural. It required changes, not in the variables and factors of the developmental equation, but in the equation itself. It required and demanded a New Economic Order with a redistribution of worldwide resources. Moreover, an increased number of LDC's were breaking with that old order through confrontation and revolutionary transformation.

The Development Establishment's response to this new situation was to agree that some changes needed to be made in the worldwide distribution of resources, but to insist that change should be based on cooperation rather than confrontation. This cooperation would be triggered by moral calls to the worldwide community, appealing to its humanitarianism and sense of social justice, side by side with calls for the capitalist developed countries to be more aware of their self-interest. Indeed, it is assumed in this new position that it is in the developed countries' interests that poverty and disease in the less developed countries be eradicated. Thus it is proposed that developed countries share some of their riches with the less developed ones. Otherwise, the world order will collapse or explode. Moreover, less poverty in LDC's will mean more capacity to consume and thus more markets for the products of the developed countries.

A typical example of these positions appears in the Willy Brandt Commission Report (*North and South: A Program for Survival, 1980*), the brainchild of Robert McNamara, the past president of the World Bank, and prepared by representatives of the development establishments of developed (referred to in the commission as "Northern") and underdeveloped (referred to as "Southern") countries. These positions are also evident in the Alma Ata Report (International Conference on Primary Health Care, 1978), a major WHO (World Health Organization) document, which aims at guiding the important worldwide policies on health and medicine. Navarro (1984c) has shown how the Development Establishment's positions are conveyed through these supposedly technological documents (see also Navarro, 1983a). In these reports, the world is divided, not into capitalist and socialist systems and subsystems, but rather into the North (the "haves") and the South (the "have nots"); and categories such as exploitation and conflict do not appear. Rather, they intend to provide a framework for conciliation and dialogue. Change does not need to be conflictive. The "haves" and powerful do not need to give up anything. To the contrary, they may see change as an opportunity to expand their powers. In medicine, clinical establishments, for example, can expand their responsibilities and the pharmaceutical industries can further increase their profits in those changes. Navarro has shown the ideological nature of this position, challenging on conceptual and empirical grounds the assumptions that sustain them. Also, the collection of articles in the volume edited by Navarro (1983a), and the works of Brown (1979), Taussig (1983), Young (1983), and Campbell (1984), among others, have shown that the underdevelopment of health and disease in the world of underdevelopment is rooted in imperialist and capitalist relations.

SOCIALISM, HEALTH, AND MEDICINE

The functions of dominant theoretical positions include not only the rationalization and reproduction of current power relations within capitalism, but also the dismissal of its alternatives. Thus, most dominant interpretations of socialist experiences have been motivated by a Cold War spirit in which socialist or postcapitalist countries are viewed as the enemy. Most empirical information in these studies is based on interviews with exiles whose answers corroborate the researchers' hypotheses. Mainstream analyses of Soviet medicine, for example, are no exception. In that act of Cold War soldiering, analysis frequently deteriorated into a vulgar but rewarding anti-Sovietism, which received much applause and support in the Cold War's centers of power. In that atmosphere, the undeniable achievements made in the medical sector of the Soviet Union are quickly dismissed as largely the result of the fantasies and delusions considered typical of what Mark Field (1967), a major representative of that position, calls the world of Leniniana. Field's position, for example, is well represented in his interpretation of the Bolshevik Revolution and the repression by the Bolsheviks of the medical profession because of the latter's sabotage of reforms pushed forward by the former. Field believes that this sabotage was a Bolshevik invention. According to him, there was none. He comes to this conclusion through the remarkable statement that no such sabotage could have existed since it would have gone against "the traditional sense of social duty and professional ethics, which makes the alleged refusal to help wounded men difficult to believe." This idealist interpretation of the medical profession defies all historical experience—from the October Revolution to Chile's Allende—that shows the majority of medical professionals have opposed by all means reforms that have affected their material interests.

On the other side of the "intellectual barricades" are authors within the socialist tradition who perceived the Soviet Union as the "model" for the construction of socialism. Sigerist's (1947) study of Soviet medicine represented in its period the most informative, detailed, and uncritical reporting of that experience. For many years it was the standard reference for progressive scholars. The reappraisal of the Soviet experience within Western Marxism has also appeared in medicine. Navarro's *Social Security and Medicine in the USSR: A Marxist Critique* (1977) analyzes the historical evolution of Soviet medicine within the context of the class conflict that exists under socialism. Other socialist experiences analyzed within the Marxist tradition or influenced by it include the People's Republic of China (R. and V. Sidel, 1982, and Coye and Livingston, 1975); Cuba (Navarro 1972a, 1972b, 1980b; Danielson, 1979; Guttmacher and Danielson, 1977); Chile (Navarro, 1974, and Waitzkin and Modell, 1974); and more recently Nicaragua (Strelnick, 1984).

It is important to notice that the debates about socialism and socialist medicine have occurred not only between non-Marxists and Marxists, but also among Marxists. Indeed, there have been two different understandings of socialist medicine within the Marxist tradition, each determining different political practices. One, widely reflected in large sectors of the labor movement in the Western world, has considered medicine and science as part of the forces of production, which are perceived as intrinsically positive. They are considered to be separate from the relations of production. Well stated in Stalin's famous booklet, *Dialectical and Historical Materialism*, this position views the growth of the forces of production as the main motor of history and states that that growth requires a change in the relations of production (from capitalism to socialism) to allow a full flourishing of those forces of production, including science and medicine. According to this understanding, socialism is needed to fully develop the potential of medicine. The political consequences of this understanding are many. One is that it is in the objective interests of scientists and professionals of medicine, the carriers of science, to ally themselves with the working class in order to be able to better fulfill their commitment to science. Thus the medical profession is viewed as a natural ally of the working class in its struggle for health and better medicine.

Another consequence of this interpretation is an instrumentalist vision of medicine. Socialist medicine is medicine better distributed through the intervention of the state. In this understanding, socialist medicine becomes statist medicine. The social democratic and large sectors of the Leninist tradition have reproduced with their practice this understanding of socialist medicine. It is important to stress that from the very beginning, this understanding of socialist medicine and science has been challenged by other Marxist forces, who have refuted the concept of "neutral" science. Navarro's (1977, 1978a) critiques of the social democratic tradition of the British Labor Party and of the unmodified Leninist practice of the Communist Party of the Soviet Union, for example, are theoretical interventions aimed at questioning the theory and practice of this specific reading of socialism. The struggle for socialism implies not only a change of priorities within medicine and a change in its distribution (that is, the uses of medicine), but also a massive democratization of the process of production of medical knowledge and practice and of the medical institutions. This democratization should take place not only through agencies of representation (indirect democracy) but also through direct forms of participation and control. The centrality of Marxism and democracy has been stressed in this tradition. The political practice derived from this specific Marxist tradition has been discussed by Assenato and Navarro (1980) in the area of occupational health and medicine. It is important to stress that, according to this tradition, the full development of democracy cannot take place under capitalism since the capitalist class remains dominant in that social formation. The National Health Service in Great Britain, for example, is not a socialist island in a capitalist state. It continues to operate under the dominance of the capitalist class and thus with a bourgeois understanding of health and medicine. As a result of this fact, this tradition (as any other Marxist tradition) is aware of the importance of seizing state power as a condition to establishing socialism. This position has been the focus of continuous abusive misinterpretations by liberal and radical authors who wrongly accuse Marxists of believing that "nothing can be changed until the revolution takes place." This accusation is inaccurate on both practical and theoretical grounds. In practical terms, this misrepresentation ignores the fact that many health reforms in the United States have been stimulated and supported by, among other forces, Marxists or groups influenced by Marxism. For example, Marxists were the founders of the Socialist Caucus of the American Public Health Association (APHA—the major public health association in the United States and one of the largest public health associations in the world), the largest caucus in that association and one that has had a considerable influence. The Socialist Caucus was instrumental, for example, in stimulating the commitment of the APHA to a National Health Program, a proposed federally funded and community controlled program with active worker and community participation. Similarly, Marxists were equally influential in changing many of the sections of the APHA (such as the occupational health and safety section) from a pro-business orientation to a pro-labor orientation. Across the country Marxists are involved in many struggles for health reforms.

At the international level, U.S. Marxists have been instrumental in the establishment of the International Association of Health Policy, in which Marxist scholars from Europe (such as Giovanni Berlinguer, Uli Deppe, Finn Diderichsen, Ann Hammarstrom, G. Urban, Lesley Doyal, Malcolm Segall, among others); Latin America (the late Juan Cesar Garcia, Cristina Laurell, Carlos Escudero, Hesio Cordeiro, Jaime Breilh, among others), and other continents have had great influence in redefining the terms of the ideological struggle in those continents, actively intervening in the health development of their own societies. There is a lot that Marxists and other forces can do under capitalism to improve the health of the population.

These social (including health) reforms, to the degree they are democratic reforms empowering the working class and popular forces, can be part of a socialist strategy to transcend capitalism. It is important, however, not to confuse health reforms with socialism. This is the basic distinction between the Marxist tradition, on the one hand, and Fabianism and social democracy, on the other. Socialism is not capitalism with social (including health) reforms. Socialism and its mass democratization require transcending capitalism.

There is not a mass consciousness in the United States for the need to transcend capitalism, which explains why the revolutionary or even prerevolutionary project is extremely limited in the United States. It is important to clarify, however, that the historical record shows that no modern social revolution has ever been made by a unified class demanding a completely new social order. Revolutions have been made when various forces with different immediate reformist demands—peace, bread, land; end of repression; freedom; social security; and so on—have come together to face a divided and weakened bourgeoisie unable to respond to those demands satisfactorily. The continuous demand for these reforms within an order incapable of satisfying all of them has led to the revolutionary transformation of that order. In other words, revolutions are not made by a conscious revolutionary class but, rather, by nonrevolutionary forces who push for the resolution of their demands, even at the cost of breaking and transforming that order. It is the task of the organized socialist forces to stimulate and support these forces and to assist in forging the linkages and unity that will make the project of transformation possible. The increased inability of the current capitalist order to resolve and respond to the increasing demands of the working class and popular forces makes that transformation historically possible today in many parts of the world.

The flexibility of the U.S. capitalist system, however, is still enormous, further augmented by the centrality of the United States within the Western system of power, which adds considerable leverage to the U.S. capitalist class. Nonetheless, the escalation of demands for social and health reforms is an urgent task in the United States, where the welfare state is dramatically underdeveloped (for example, 38 million Americans do not have any form of health insurance). Moreover, the escalation of these reforms heightens the conflict between a system of production based on profit and one based on human needs, including health. The theorization of a socialist strategy in the health sector in the United States, based on the actual practice of the working class and other popular forces, is undeveloped. The enormous theoretical and practical problems are further augmented by the left-wing practices in the United States. It is the only country in the West where the left operates primarily through social movements (labor movement, black movement, feminist movement, ecological movement, and so on). The labor movement does not follow class practices (by law it is forbidden to do so by the Taft-Hartley Act), and there is no political instrument of labor.

Consequently, the U.S. capitalist class is the most powerful capitalist class in today's world. The absence of class discourse and practices by labor and other social movements is the primary source of power of that capitalist class. The underdevelopment of the welfare state in the United States is rooted in this reality.

Underdevelopment does not mean nonexistence, however. The New Deal, the foundation of the welfare state in the United States and a direct result of class mobilizations and practices, triggered most important health and social reforms in this country. However, class practice became replaced by a focus on specific constituencies, leading to the Great Society programs, such as Medicaid and Food Stamps. This disaggregate form of response has made these programs very vulnerable in the current situation of social "austerity" and reaction. There is a great need to rekindle class practices, whose consequences in the health and medical sectors could be of considerable importance. Navarro (1980a), and the several authors of the collection edited by Salmon (1985), represent recent attempts to analyze current practices and to see their relevance for socialist projects in today's United States.

The enormous ideological avalanche from the right in all areas of endeavor, including health and medicine, makes it difficult to see the great potentialities for progressive change that exist in the United States, even today. Marxist analysis, however, can provide what U.S. folk singer Woody Guthrie used to call the new lenses that can help the U.S. working population see light where the reaction wants them to see darkness, to see hope where they want them to see despair, and to see possibilities for change where they want them to get trapped in the shifting sands of continuous pessimism. Demand for these lenses is growing. And never has Marxist theoretical production in the analysis of health and medicine been so abundant and productive as it is now. This chapter has barely touched upon this large production that responds to a growing demand for alternative explanations to the dominant ones, describing and analyzing the unhealthy reality that constrains the healthy and joyful existence of our citizens. Its attractiveness is its threat to the current order. Side by side with other traditions, Marxist scholarship is providing pointers on the road—a difficult road—toward a new, healthy society, a society that would allow for (as Marx and Engels once wrote) "the full expression of the enormous potential of our fellow human beings."

BIBLIOGRAPHY

Alford, R. *Health Care Politics*. Chicago: University of Chicago Press, 1975.

Altman, D. E. "What Americans Really Want." *Health Affairs*, Fall 1984.

Anderson, O. *Health Care: Can There Be Equity? The United States, Sweden and England*. New York: John Wiley, 1972.

Assenato, G., and Navarro, V. "Workers' Participation and Control in Italy: The Case of Occupational Medicine." *International Journal of Health Services* 10 (1980).

Berliner, H. "A Larger Perspective on the Flexner Report." *International Journal of Health Services* 5 (1975).

———. "Philanthropic Foundations and Scientific Medicine." Doctoral Thesis, School of Hygiene and Public Health, The Johns Hopkins University, 1977.

Berman, D. *Death on the Job*. New York: Monthly Review Press, 1978.

Brown, P. *The Transfer of Care: Psychiatric Deinstitutionalization and Its Aftermath*. Boston: Routledge and Kegan Paul, 1985.

Brown, R. *Rockefeller Medicine Men: Capitalism and Medical Care in America.* Berkeley: University of California Press, 1979.

Campbell, C. E. "Nestlé and Breast vs. Bottle Feeding: Mainstream and Marxist Perspectives." *International Journal of Health Services* 14 (1984).

Chavkin, W. (ed.). *Double Exposure: Women's Health Hazards on the Job and at Home.* New York: Monthly Review Press, 1984.

Coye, M. J. "Crisis: Control in the Workplace. A Review of Three Major Works in Occupational Health." *International Journal of Health Services* 9 (1979).

Coye, M. J., and Livingston, J. (eds.). *China: Yesterday and Today.* New York: Bantam Books, 1975.

Crawford, R. "You are Dangerous to Your Health. The Ideology and Politics of Victim Blaming." *International Journal of Health Services* 7 (1977).

———. "A Cultural Account of 'Health' Controls, Release and the Social Body." In McKinlay, J. B. (ed.). *Issues in the Political Economy of Health Care.* London: Tavistock, 1984.

Danielson, R. *Cuban Medicine.* New Brunswick, N.J.: Transaction Books, 1979.

Ehrenreich, B. and J. *The American Health Empire.* New York: Random House, 1970.

———. "Medicine and Social Control." *Social Policy,* May-June 1974.

Ehrenreich, J. "Introduction." In Ehrenreich, J. (ed.). *The Cultural Crisis of Modern Medicine.* New York: Monthly Review Press, 1978.

Elling, R. "Industrialization and Occupational Health in Underdeveloped Countries." In Navarro, V. (ed.). *Imperialism, Health and Medicine.* Farmingdale, N.Y.: Baywood, 1983.

Engels, F. *The Conditions of the Working Class in England.* Stanford, Calif.: Stanford University Press, 1968.

Eyer, J. "Prosperity as a Cause of Death." *International Journal of Health Services* 5 (1975).

———. "Capitalism, Health and Illness." In McKinlay, J. (ed.). *Issues in the Political Economy of Health Care.* London: Tavistock Publications, 1984.

Fee, E. (ed.). *Women and Health: The Politics of Sex in Medicine.* Farmingdale, N.Y.: Baywood, 1982.

Field, M. *Soviet Specialized Medicine.* New York: The Free Press, 1967.

Foucault, M. *The Birth of the Clinic: An Archeology of Medical Perception.* New York: Pantheon Books, 1973.

———. *Surveiller et Punir.* Paris: Gallimard, 1975.

———. *La volonte de savoir.* Paris: Gallimard, 1977.

Friedson, E. *Professional Dominance.* New York: Atherton Press, 1970.

Fuchs, V. "Health Care and the United States Economic System." *Milbank Memorial Fund Quarterly* 50 (1972).

Goldsmith, F., and Kerr, L. E. *Occupational Safety and Health*. New York: Monthly Review Press, 1984.

Gordon, L. "The Politics of Birth Control, 1920-1940." In Ehrenreich, J. (ed.). *The Cultural Crisis of Modern Medicine*. New York: Monthly Review Press, 1978.

Guttmacher, S., and Berliner, H. *Materialist Epidemiology*. Health Marxist Organization Booklets 3 (1974).

Guttmacher, S., and Danielson, R. "Changes in Cuban Health Care: An Argument Against Technological Pessimism." *International Journal of Health Services* 7 (1977).

Himmelstein, D. U., and Woolhandler, S. "Medicine as Industry." *Monthly Review*, April 1984.

Illich, I. *Medical Nemesis: The Expropriation of Health*. New York: Pantheon Books, 1976.

International Conference on Primary Health Care, Alma Ata, USSR, September 6-12, 1978.

Karasek, R. "Job Demands, Job Decision Latitude and Mental Strain: Implications for Job Redesign." *Administration Science Quarterly* 24 (1979).

Karasek, R., Baker, D., Maixer, F., Anders, A., and Theorell, T. "The Decision Latitude, Job Demands, and Cardiovascular Disease: Prospective Study of Swedish Men." *American Journal of Public Health* 7 (1981).

Kelman, S. "Toward the Political Economy of Medical Care." *Inquiry* 8 (1971).

Kotelchuk, D. Special Issue on Occupational Health and Safety. *Health PAC*, 1982.

Marmor, T. *The Politics of Medicare*. Chicago: Aldine Publishing Company, 1973.

McBride, R. B. "Business as Usual: Heroin Distribution in the U.S." *International Journal of Health Services* 14 (1984).

McKinlay, J. "The Business of Doctoring or Doctoring as Good Business: Reflections on Friedson's View of the Medical Game." *International Journal of Health Services* 7 (1977).

________. "On the Medical-Industrial Complex." *Monthly Review*, October 1978.

________. "Towards the Proletarianization of the Medical Profession." *International Journal of Health Services* 15 (1985).

Mechanic, D. *Readings in Medical Sociology*. New York: The Free Press, 1980.

________. "The Transformation of Health Providers." *Health Affairs*, Spring 1984.

Navarro, V. "Health, Health Services, and Health Planning in Cuba." *International Journal of Health Services* 2 (1972a).

________. "Health Services in Cuba. An Initial Appraisal." *The New England Journal of Medicine*, November 9, 1972b.

________. "What Does Chile Mean? An Analysis of the Health Sector Before, During and After Allende's Administration." *Health and Society*, Spring 1974.

________. "The Industrialization of Fetishism or the Fetishism of Industrialization: A Critique of Ivan Illich." *International Journal of Health Services* 5 (1975).

________. *Medicine Under Capitalism*. New York: Prodist, 1976.

________. *Social Security and Medicine in the USSR: A Marxist Critique*. Lexington, Mass.: Lexington Books, 1977.

________. *Class Struggle, the State and Medicine: A Historical and Contemporary Analysis of the Medical Care Sector in Great Britain*. London: Robertson, 1978a.

________. "The Crisis of the Western System of Medicine." *International Journal of Health Services* 8 (1978b).

________. "The Nature of Democracy in the Core Capitalist Countries: Meanings and Implications for Class Struggle." *The Insurgent Sociologist* 10 (1980a).

________. "Workers and Community Participation and Democratic Control in Cuba." *International Journal of Health Services* 10 (1980b).

________. "Work, Ideology and Science. The Case of Medicine." *Social Science and Medicine* 14C (1980c).

________. "The Labor Process and Health: An Historical Materialist Interpretation." *International Journal of Health Services* 12 (1982a).

________. "The Crisis of the International Capitalist Order and Its Implications for the Welfare State." *International Journal of Health Services* 12 (1982b).

________. "Where Is the Popular Mandate?" *The New England Journal of Medicine* 307 (1982c).

________. (ed.). *Imperialism, Health and Medicine*. Farmingdale, N.Y.: Baywood, 1983a.

________. "Radicalism, Marxism and Medicine." *International Journal of Health Services* 13 (1983b).

________. "Determinants of Health Policy: A Case Study. Regulating Safety and Health at the Workplace." *International Journal of Health Services* 13 (1984a).

________. "Medical History as Justification Rather Than Explanation: A Critique of Starr's *The Social Transformation of American Medicine*." *International Journal of Health Services* 14 (1984b).

________. "A Critique of the Ideological and Political Position of the Brandt Report and the Alma Ata Declaration." *Social Science and Medicine* 18 (1984c).

Navarro, V., and Berman, D. (eds.). *Health and Work Under Capitalism: An International Perspective*. Farmingdale, N.Y.: Baywood, 1984.

A New Perspective on the Health of Canadians. Ottawa Health and Welfare, Canada, 1974.

North and South: A Program for Survival. The Report of the Independent Commission of Willy Brandt. Cambridge, Mass., 1980.

Relman, A. S. "The New Medical-Industrial Complex." *The New England Journal of Medicine* 303 (1980).

Renaud, M. "On the Structural Constraints to State Intervention in Health." *International Journal of Health Services* 5 (1975).

Rogers, D., Blendon, R. J., and Maloney, T. W. "Who Needs Medicaid?" *The New England Journal of Medicine* 307 (1982).

Salmon, J. "Monopoly Capital and the Reorganization of the Health Sector." *Review of Radical Political Economy* 9 (1977).

———. "Corporate Attempts to Reorganize the American Health Care System." Doctoral Dissertation, Cornell University, 1978.

———. (ed.). *Alternative Medicines Popular and Policy Perspectives*. London: Tavistock, 1985.

Schumacher, E. F. *Small Is Beautiful: Economics as if People Mattered*. New York: Harper and Row, 1975.

Sidel, R., and Sidel, V. *The Health of China*. Boston: Beacon Press, 1982.

Sigerist, H. *Medicine and Health in the Soviet Union*. New York: Citadel Press, 1947.

Smith, B. E. "Black Lung: The Social Production of Disease." *International Journal of Health Services* 13 (1982).

Stark, E. (ed.). Special Issue on the Political Economy of Health. *Journal of the Union Radical Political Economy* 32 (1978).

———. "Doctors in Spite of Themselves: The Limits of Radical Health Criticisms." *International Journal of Health Services* 12 (1982).

Starr, P. *The Social Transformation of American Medicine*. New York: Basic Books, 1983.

Strelnick, H. "The Sandinista Revolution is Health." *Health Pac* 13 (1984).

Taussig, M. "Nutrition, Development and Foreign Aid: A Case Study of U.S. Diverted Health Care in a Colombian Plantation Zone." In Navarro, V. (ed.). *Imperialism, Health and Medicine*. Farmingdale, N.Y.: Baywood, 1983.

Taylor, R., and Rieger, A. "Rudolph Virchow on the Typhus Epidemic in Upper Silesia: An Introduction and Translation." *Sociology of Health and Illness. A Journal of Medical Sociology* 6 (1984).

Terris, M. "The Contributions of Henry E. Sigerist to Health Services Organization." *Health and Society*, Fall 1975.

Twaddle, A. C. "From Medical Sociology to the Sociology of Health: Some Changing Concerns in the Sociological Study of Sickness and Treatment." In Bottomore, T., Nowak, S., and Sokolowska, M. (eds.). *Sociology: The State of the Art* (International Sociological Association). Beverly Hills, Calif.: Sage Publications, 1982.

Waitzkin, H. *The Second Sickness: Contradictions of Capitalist Health Care*. New York: The Free Press, 1983.

Waitzkin, H., and Modell, H. "Medicine, Socialism and Totalitarianism: Lessons from Chile." *The New England Journal of Medicine* 291 (1974).

Waitzkin, H., and Waterman, B. *The Exploitation of Illness in Capitalist Society*. Indianapolis: Bobbs-Merrill, 1974.

Young, A. "The Relevance of Traditional Medical Cultures to Primary Health Care." *Social Science and Medicine* 17, 1983.

Journals

Health and Medicine. 220 South State, Suite 300, Chicago, IL 60604.

Health PAC/Bulletin. 17 Murray Street, New York, NY 10007.

International Journal of Health Services. Baywood Publishing Company, 120 Marine Street, Farmingdale, NY 11735.

Science for the People. 897 Main Street, Cambridge, MA 02139.

Socialist Caucus Newsletter. APHA, 1032 West Altgeld, Chicago, IL 60614.

8

MARXISM AND COMMUNICATIONS RESEARCH IN NORTH AMERICA

Vincent Mosco

INTRODUCTION: MATERIAL INFLUENCES ON RESEARCH

> We found out and it wasn't years till we did, that all the bread we made for Decca was going into making little black boxes that go into American Air Force bombers to bomb fucking North Vietnam. They took the bread we made for them and put it into the radar section of their business. When we found that out, it blew our minds. That was it. Goddamn, you find out you've helped to kill God knows how many thousands of people without knowing it.
>
> Keith Richard
> The Rolling Stones
> (Chapple and Garofalo, 1977:xi)

What Richard and other media practitioners are coming to recognize is that the media are far from autonomous leisure activities. They are integrated tightly into the wider institutional power structure of capitalism. Over the past fifteen years, communications research has begun to take up the substance and the spirit of Richard's concern. It has begun to draw out the dense web of connections among seemingly unrelated forces in society: Decca and the Indochina War, Gulf+Western's media empire and its labor camps in the Dominican Republic, RCA's space weaponry and the programming of its subsidiary, NBC. By making explicit these connections, Marxist research reveals the systemic nature of capitalism and the critical role of media within that system.

The growth of communications research in a Marxist tradition reflects the growth of communication and information systems in the post-World War II era. Three developments in the wider political economy are especially significant: international business expansion, the spread of mass consumption, and the growth of the state, particularly military growth. In addition, communications research has sprung from the recognition that the means of communication are vital for movements in opposition to capitalism.

Many have written on the widespread impact of business expansion over the past forty years. The merger movement accelerated during this period to the point where most capitalist industries are shaped by vertically and horizontally integrated companies. With production as well as distribution processes embedded in a multiplicity of nations, business is more thoroughly than ever transnational in nature. Among other things, postwar expansion increased the strategic significance of communication and information processing in business. In order to maintain centralized control over the range of activities, transnational enterprises require communication and information systems that are far more extensive, reliable, and cost efficient than have heretofore been available. The international expansion of production facilities and markets has brought about international systems for the production of information and communication. The development of such global, integrated systems and their social, political, and economic consequences have stimulated independent research on the left.

The expansion of transnational business led to global networks of computers, communication satellites, and other sophisticated technologies. So too did the expansion and intensification of mass consumption. Capital had long been interested in the production of mass audiences of consumers. Television provided an efficient and effective vehicle for accomplishing this. It took one decade for television to go from a curiosity piece for the rich (there were just 1 million sets in use in 1948) to a nearly universal staple in living rooms throughout North America (Barnouw, 1975). Capital used television to reshape mass leisure. Advertisers had the opportunity to reach huge audiences regularly and in receptive settings with messages about products and, through these products, about consumption as the centerpiece of the American Way of Life. This acceleration in building mass audiences for mass consumption influenced the direction of communications research in the Marxist tradition.

The expansion in both the production and consumption ends of business helped to bring about a substantial increase in state activity. The state increasingly took on the role of active manager of the conflicts and contradictions in the expanding monopoly capitalist system. State functions required substantial investment in government information and communication systems as well as a regulatory apparatus to oversee the development of private forms of electronic communication. Military requirements generally headed the list of government communication and information priorities. Military expansion required sophisticated intelligence-gathering and rapid, efficient, and secret communication networks worldwide. Fighting wars, whether to stop indigenous revolutions or to prevail in a nuclear confrontation, necessitates extremely complex computer/communications technologies and networks. The growth of the state, particularly the military, is an important theme in critical communications research.

Communications research on the left has also come to recognize the significance of media for struggles to counter capitalism generally and imperialism specifically. The struggles of blacks and women, the peace and environmental movements, all reflect the complex relationships of social struggle to the mass media. On the one hand, these movements learned to use the media, their own and mainstream, to expand the reach of their many messages. However, they also learned that playing to the media invites co-optation and internal disruption. Communications research has also felt the influence of international movements, such as resistance struggles in the Third World that have used media extensively in building the movement and, in the case of some successful struggles, to build socialism. International research has built on the Third World movement to demystify the West's ideological offensive to achieve a "free flow of information." Research has documented how free flow masks Western domination and undermines the cultural sovereignty of the non-Western world. Moreover, this research has supported efforts at the United Nations and elsewhere to build what Third World leaders identify as a New World Information Order.

ADMINISTRATIVE VERSUS CRITICAL RESEARCH

The growth of transnational enterprises, the development of a mass consumption society, the expansion of the state, and the response of mass opposition movements worldwide have all influenced the development of communications research within a Marxist perspective. Nevertheless, forces integral to the production of communications teaching and research in North America have retarded the growth of critical work. Communications programs tend to have a far greater vocational emphasis than programs in economics, political science, history, or sociology. Indeed, schools of communication generally developed outside the liberal arts, with the aim of training journalists, advertising and public relation specialists, video and film makers, and broadcasters. Moreover, with minor exceptions, research within these programs is defined narrowly. On the whole, research means market studies, assessments of advertising campaigns, public opinion polling, content analysis, and the like. In part, this conforms to the vocational thrust of communications programs. Even those who are not identified as media practitioners are schooled in skills that offer job opportunities in the research departments of media companies or, more generally, the marketing and media divisions of large corporations. A less significant but growing variant on this tendency is media policy research. Here researchers are steeped in the legal dimension of state regulation of media with all of the formalistic constraints contained in legal research. For example, one might conduct research on judicial and regulatory definitions of the Fairness Doctrine in broadcasting (Simmons, 1978). Such research wends its way through a thicket of court cases on what constitutes the legal responsibility of a broadcaster to air a variety of views. Again, this variant, itself identified with more progressive communications research programs, would prepare people for careers or consultancies within the legal departments of companies or with any of a number of government regulatory, commerce, or intelligence agencies concerned with media.

Back in 1941, Columbia University sociologist Paul Lazarsfeld identified this conservative tradition as *administrative research*, work in the service of a particular organizational interest. Such work was to be distinguished from *critical research*, which would uncover how and why media serve power. As Lazarsfeld put it in an article coauthored with noted functionalist sociologist Robert Merton:

> But clearly, the social effects of the media will vary as the system of ownership and control varies. Thus to consider the social effects of American mass media is to deal only with the effects of these media as privately owned enterprises under project oriented management.
>
> . . . Big business finances the production and distribution of mass media. And, all intent aside, he who pays the piper calls the tune (Lazarsfeld and Merton, 1949).[1]

Until recently, most communications research ignored this conclusion and pursued an administrative approach. Consequently, the 1950s and 1960s are marked by few isolated examples of critical North American research in the Marxist tradition. These include Smythe's

(1957) work on the political economy and regulation of U.S. media, and H. Schiller's *Mass Communication and American Empire* (1969), a comprehensive analysis of how media companies in traditional (broadcasting) and new technologies (communication satellites) are well integrated into American imperialism, including its political, economic, and military dimensions. Additionally, Guback's *The International Film Industry* (1969) offered a detailed political economic analysis of how the U.S. film industry shapes a global system of production, distribution, and exhibition.

THE GROWTH OF CRITICAL COMMUNICATIONS RESEARCH

The growing awareness that communication and information technology are vital in capital accumulation, mass marketing, and the expansion of the military state certainly has inspired interest in Marxist perspectives on communications research. A further source of inspiration is the growth of critical and Marxist research in Europe and Latin America. Since this chapter examines developments in the United States and Canada, it is inappropriate to report in detail on the growth of European and Latin American research. Nevertheless, the latter has influenced North American work, so it is important to mention a few significant examples. In Europe, Murdock and Golding (1974), Garnham (1979), Hamelink (1983), Nordenstreng (1974), and Mattelart (1979) offer good examples that have influenced the development of a critical political economy in North America. In particular, this European research has emphasized social class, the power of U.S. transnationals, especially financial institutions, the militarization of technology, and contradictions brought about by state control of mass media and telecommunications in Europe. Also in Europe, the work of Williams (1975, 1981), Hall (1982), the Glasgow Media Group (1977, 1980), Mattelart and Siegelaub (1983), and Enzensberger (1974), among others, has influenced the study of media content and impact. This work has led North Americans, in both the Marxist and mainstream traditions, to question content analysis, the established approach to cultural research, which relies on numerical counts of verbal and pictoral information. European research is concerned with the historical forces that shape contemporary content, such as the relationship of nineteenth-century economic depressions to contemporary advertising (Williams, 1980:170-95) or traditions of class struggle to the production of oppositional popular culture (Mattelart and Siegelaub, 1983:11-100). Similarly, North Americans have drawn extensively on the contribution of Latin American scholars in both political economy and media culture. The overwhelming impact of U.S. media companies on mass media in Latin America and subsequent UN attention, particularly in UNESCO, spurred the formation of several centers for media research in Latin America. Notable among these is ILET (the Latin American Institute for Transnational Studies) in Mexico City. Representative work on the political economy of Latin America draws heavily on *dependency* theory. Of particular influence is the research of Beltran and Fox (1979), Janus (1981), Rada (1981), Roncagliolo and Janus (1981), Reyes Matta (1981), Schnitman (1981), and Somavia (1981). Latin American research on mass media culture also takes off from various models of cultural imperialism. Here, Dorfman (1983) and Dorfman and Mattelart (1975) have been especially influential in North American mass cultual analysis in the Marxist tradition. By showing how transnational companies, from advertising to computer firms, have come to dominate Latin American communications, they indicate the enormous transformation required to achieve democratic communications.

There is no ideal sorting device for categorizing North American communications research on the left. A useful, though by no means flawless, division is to distinguish between work that concentrates on the political economy of media and that which focuses on media content and culture. At the risk of oversimplification, the former starts from questions about ownership and control of media institutions, identifies processes of media production, distribution, and reception, and analyzes linkages between media and the wider capitalist system. The latter starts with media content and forms, analyzes the impact of content and form on consciousness and ideological production, and links the production of media to the wider ideological apparatus of capitalist society.

THE POLITICAL ECONOMY OF COMMUNICATION

The Business of Communication

The powerful changes taking place in the world political economy of media and information technology and the contribution by Marxist scholars, principally in Europe and Latin America, have helped North American researchers make substantial contributions to communication scholarship in the Marxist tradition. This is particularly the case in political economic research where several ideas central to a Marxist perspective are reflected in recent research.

A leading point of research here is the influence of successive revolutions in the means of communication on the overall process of accumulation in capitalism. Historical works have shown how capital integrated communication and information technology into the fundamental processes of production to the point where capitalist economies are critically dependent on communication for domestic and international activity. The most substantial historical work has concentrated on the means of mass communication. D. Schiller (1981) and Eisenstein (1979) have shown how the press emerged from the need for reliable business communication—information on prices, markets, commodities, and so on—to become a mass medium directed to a burgeoning working class of consumers. In doing so they identify the press as a major instrument in the creation of a mass consumption society so vital to the absorption of mass production. The press was able to direct its mass circulation audience to products through the development of advertising. Here Stuart Ewen's *Captains of Consciousness* (1976) provides a social history of advertising that identifies the ways media restructured the social relations of consumption, drawing the home into near complete dependency on the capitalist marketplace. Ewen shows how companies wed science and technology to establish systems of public relations and mass marketing to break traditional family and household relations and thereby commodify the home. In essence, capital gives rise to advertiser-supported print media that makes possible the vast expansion of the capitalist mode of production and distribution. Further expansion came with successive waves of mass electronic media, chiefly film, radio, and television.

Guback (1969) and Wasko (1982) have provided detailed analyses of how a few firms with close links to finance capital came to dominate U.S. film production and through complex networks of legal, financial, and political control shaped the global film industry. As a result, transnational companies with complete U.S. government support made Hollywood commercial feature films a world model. For example, in 1918 the Webb-Pomerene Export Trade Act permitted U.S. film companies to combine to fix prices and divide foreign markets, activities that would otherwise violate antitrust statutes. From that time, the Motion Picture Export Association, the government-sanctioned cartel representative, has used the combined economic power of U.S. film production and distribution companies to spread American film worldwide (Guback, 1969). One specific means of doing this takes advantage of an important characteristic in film and video: the ease of reproduction after initial production. After making a profit in the domestic marketplace, U.S. companies have distributed their movies and television programs internationally at well under the costs of production. The result of this form of "dumping" is to stifle sources of indigenous film production that cannot hope to compete with a U.S. film that cost $10 million to produce, but that is made available in the Third World for $1,000. Moreover, U.S. government aid programs support foreign media producers that adopt U.S. models and become regional distributors of U.S. programming or produce programs such as the *telenovela* that mirrors, in this case, the U.S. soap opera (Tunstall, 1977:176-77). Drawing on Barnouw's (1975) important descriptive history of broadcasting, H. Schiller (1969), Smythe (1981), Mander (1978), and Mosco (1979) have shown how the three dominant broadcasting networks and their corporate/state allies built mass market radio and television into the dominant mode of audience production and reproduction in North America. This research shows how successive revolutions in the means of electronic media, from AM radio to color television, were promoted by a small group of large firms, well integrated into monopoly capital. These firms—AT&T, General Electric, Westinghouse, RCA, CBS, ABC, among others—built huge commercial media empires and used close state connections to frustrate successive attempts to build publicly controlled broadcasting stations and networks. The result is a thorough integration of the mass audience commodity into the capitalist system (Smythe, 1981:22-51).

Historical research is not as extensive in telecommunications or such point-to-point systems as postal, telegraph, and telephone communications. It is common for histories of these to be contained within books of wider scope (Smythe, 1981:139-57). Research in this area has focused on the ways these technologies contributed to business expansion, which in turn propelled more intense technological development. Particularly significant here is DuBoff's (1984) research on the relationship of telegraphy to business demand and market structure in the nineteenth century and Danilean's (1939) classic account of AT&T's rise to dominance. Renewed interest in the history of telecommunications has been inspired by the growth of computers and the ability to link telecommunications systems to computers and thereby create powerful *telematics* networks. Telematics systems make possible rapid data processing and communication over vast distances. Noble's work (1984) on the history of computers and related technology identifies the significance, for design and use, of military/corporate control over computer development. The twin goals of extending managerial control and automating warfare continue to shape computer systems (Greenbaum, 1979; Mosco, 1985). Historical research has taken major strides in carrying out a project that Marx identified in *Capital* (1972:106):

> The revolution in the method of production in industry and agriculture, likewise necessitated a revolution in the general conditions of the social process of production, that is to say in the means of communication and transport. In a society whose pivots . . . were, first, small-scale agriculture, with its subsidiary home industries, and, secondly, urban handicraft, the means of communication and transport were utterly inadequate to the requirements of the manufacturing period, with its extended division of social labor, its concentration of the means of labor and of the workers, and its colonial markets; communications and transport, therefore had to be revolutionized, and were in fact revolutionized.

Communications research has focused on another dimension of the Marxist tradition: the process of business concentration resulting in a shift from competitive to monopoly capitalism. Though considerable work remains to be done in this area of political economy, substantial progress has been made over a range of media. Recent research has begun to identify the transition within monopoly capital of control over media firms by transnational conglomerates whose principal business interest lies outside of media. Research on the rise of press conglomerates, director interlocks, and the financial ties of large newspaper firms has demonstrated why "All The News That Fits" is a more appropriate logo for the New York *Times* (Dreier, 1982; Bagdikian, 1983). Though the focus of her research is on the international impact of the advertising industry, Janus (1981, 1984) provides detailed information on the structure of these firms and their links to other elements of capital. Janus shows, for example, that Latin American mass media contain more advertising than anywhere in the developed world. Print and television media devote from 30 to 50 percent of their space and time to advertising. Moreover, greater than 60 percent of women's magazine ads and 80 percent of television commercials feature products promoted by transnational capital: soap, drugs, cosmetics, tobacco, processed foods, and alcoholic beverages. She concludes: "The same firms developing the marketing uses of the new communication technologies control the economies of many Third World countries and dominate their mass media systems" (Janus, 1984:68-69).

Guback's recent research (1982) on the film industry complements his and Wasko's (1982) historical research with detailed financial and structural data on conglomerate control of film. Though much of the research on the recording industry has addressed cultural and ideological issues, Shore's (1983) work offers a thorough consideration of political economic forces that connect record, radio, and video companies in an international network that pipes top-40 music, wire service news, and commercials into homes throughout the world. Smythe (1981), H. Schiller (1976), Gitlin (1981), and Mander (1978) have identified similar processes at work in the broadcasting area.

The political economy of corporate concentration and control has expanded to include the newer technologies built on computer/communication or telematics networks. D. Schiller (1982) and H. Schiller (1984) situate the major participants in business data processing and communication. Mosco (1982) identifies the extent of concentration in the newer mass media technologies such as interactive cable television, teletext, and videotex.

The tendency toward concentration makes possible another tendency, well-noted in the Marxist tradition: the global expansion of monopoly capital and the creation of an international division of labor. Communications research has been particularly extensive here, in part because of the worldwide debate, raised in many international bodies, about media imperialism. Research on the left has demonstrated the widespread penetration of Western wire services (AP, UPI, Reuters, and Agence-France-Press) into mass media throughout the Third World. Similar research on advertising (Janus, 1984; Fejes, 1980), magazines from *National Geographic* (H. Schiller, 1973) to Disney comics (Dorfman, 1983), film (Guback, 1969; Pendakur, 1984), music and radio (Shore, 1983), and television (H. Schiller, 1976, McAnany, 1984) identifies the spread of media from capitalist core to periphery. This is accomplished in a variety of ways, including export of media products, often at well under market costs, establishment of branch plants, media schools (often related to aid programs), the pressures of international advertisers, and the generally strong promotion of Western media models. The latter typically remain when a nation, like Brazil or Mexico, sets up its own national public or private media system (McAnany, 1984). The expansion of mass media firms into the Third World advances the accumulation process in a number of ways. In addition to the obvious addition to the mass audience, there is the significant dimension that media provides, of selling a *way of life* as well as specific products. That way of life includes support for private as opposed to public enterprise, competitive individualism over social cooperation, and the application of sophisticated technology to consumption and leisure as well as to production.

Recent research has identified the application of advanced communication and information technology to the process of worldwide American expansion and the creation of an international division of labor. Computer communications systems give corporations the ability to locate their operations wherever costs are lowest without sacrificing centralized control. As a result, Control Data can hire microelectronics assembly workers in South Korea for $.60 (U.S.) an hour and American Airlines can take advantage of communication satellite links to hire data entry clerks in Barbados at $2.00 (U.S.) an hour. In these and other areas, this same microelectronics technology is used to monitor and measure each bit of work performed, thereby advancing control over an increasingly deskilled labor force (Ehrenreich and Fuentes, 1983; Gregory, 1982; Sussman, 1984).

Much of the political economic research describes the communication/information sector as an industry in its own right and as a major force in the global expansion and centralization of business throughout capitalism (H. Schiller, 1984). More recently, attention has been turning to a major transformation in the product of this new technology—information. Advances in electronics make it possible to divide a message (whether a phone call, a batch of bank check numbers, a set of military codes) into discrete signals or bits. In this electronic bit form, messages can be monitored, stored, measured, manipulated, and distributed more easily and more rapidly than ever before. As a result, information has taken on enhanced value as a commodity. An entire information industry has grown around the ability to package, repackage, buy, and sell information. Moreover, traditional businesses such as banking, insurance, and retailing have established entire subsidiaries and divisions devoted to marketing information produced by the parent company in the course of conducting its established business. Demographic, consumer preference, attitudinal, financial background, and other information can be packaged in forms that make it sufficiently profitable for conglomerates like Citicorp, Sears, and American Express to identify themselves as information businesses. The ability to measure and monitor information transactions makes it possible for telephone, computer, and interactive cable television companies to charge by the minute or the page of information provided on the screen. Similarly, clerical workers in the information industry are now often paid per keystroke or line of information provided.

The other side of the measurement coin is the ability to do detailed monitoring of consumer preferences and work activity. The results are marketable files of information on consumer choices and detailed profiles of worker behavior—both valuable commodities and instruments of social control (Mosco, 1982; Perolle, 1983).

There is substantial work to be done on the nature of the commodity form in communications research. While many focus on content, information, or entertainment as the chief commodity produced in capitalism, others contend that the audience is the principal commodity (Smythe, 1977). The latter theme starts from the practice central to commercial mass media: Program content is built on the practice of marketing audiences to advertisers. The debate over the information and audience commodities is one of the livelier within Marxist perspectives in communications research (Murdock, 1978; Smythe, 1978; Livant, 1979).

Communication and the Capitalist State

Critical research departs from the narrow traditional focus on regulatory behavior to examine the relationship of the state to media and information technology. H. Schiller's early research (1969) identified the significance of communication for state activity in capital accumulation, legitimation, and repression. For example, he shows how the state used its anti-Soviet campaign to fund the space program and turned over much of the technology to private companies such as RCA and AT&T. Moreover, the state has retained enough control over the technology for the development of military communication and surveillance. Schiller further shows how the U.S. government established international bodies such as Intelsat for communication satellites to maintain U.S. government and corporate control of this sector. Specifically, the state did so by setting up a joint government-private corporation, Comsat, which would represent U.S. political and corporate interests in Intelsat. Despite the participation of over 100 nations, voting is based on amount of satellite usage and so control remains in the hands of a small bloc of Western nations, led by the United States, which uses 20 percent of satellite space. Later work has built on this by analyzing the impact of the tight network of relationships between corporate and state elites nationally and internationally. More recently, corporate state and world system perspectives have been used to explain the development and use of new information technologies (Mosco, 1982).

The state is the single largest user of media and information technology. Moreover, state agencies divert resources into corporate development in this area and thereby spur capital accumulation generally (D. Schiller, 1982; Mosco, 1982:16-66). The means of communication are also direct forms of legitimizing state and corporate activity. Research has examined the manifold ways the state has used media to mobilize popular consent and stifle opposition. Haight and Weinstein (1981) show how the state deflected opposition to corporate electronic media by setting up an elaborate regulatory process that consumed the resources and energy of opposition groups, co-opting several in the process. Rips (1981) documents the ways the FBI and other agencies used opposition media, including campus newspapers, radio stations, newsletters, posters, and so on, to undermine and divide radical movements in the 1960s. Recent research examines the ways the U.S. government is using mass media to promote its interests worldwide. Frederick (1984) has documented the Reagan administration's efforts to develop Radio Marti, a high-powered broadcasting system, to blanket Cuba with U.S. propaganda. Moreover, as state oversight and regulation of electronic media in the U.S. have receded, corporations have become more directly involved in the use of media for ideological ends. Examples range from advertisements that identify support for the company or "the American way" as the message to direct corporate investment in news programming, such as Biznet, a national cable television network owned and operated by the U.S. Chamber of Commerce. Media and information technology are also integral to police and military activity. Research here has focused on the connection of media to domestic and foreign intelligence agencies, the use of media to promote militarism, and the indispensable role of computer/communication systems for advanced, including nuclear, weapons systems (Chomsky and Herman, 1979; Bamford, 1982; Mosco, 1985).

Communication and Struggle

Research into the political economy of communications has concentrated on how capital shapes and uses media and information technology to meet its ends. There is less research on the contradictions inherent in that process and outright class struggles over control of the means of communication. Important exceptions include Gitlin's (1980) work on media and the student movement in the 1960s and Demac's (1984) research on conflicts over the Reagan administration's efforts to control the flow of government information. Gitlin uncovers the contradictions inherent in mass electronic media by showing how a radical student movement was able to perform in such a way as to attract widespread television coverage and thereby spread its message. Moreover, Gitlin is particularly effective in showing how reliance on established media led movement leaders to bend their strategies to a medium that called for increasing levels of radicalism to justify coverage. As a result, groups like SDS (Students for a Democratic Society) declined as they mistook media attention for popular support.

The research emphasis on developments outside the United States results from the influence of U.S. media worldwide and the conflicts between international and national capital that such influence regularly brings about. Moreover, outside the United States, historical struggles have left a complex mix of private and public communication institutions that are the site of struggles for control (Mosco and Wasko, 1984). These struggles include the trade union movements within these institutions (Mosco and Wasko, 1983). Smythe (1981) and Freiberg (1981) have identified these contradictions and conflicts in Canadian and French media, respectively. Mattelart and Siegelaub (1983) have done so for the Third World.

Communication and Culture

There is an extensive and growing body of research on the content and form of communication. This research is linked to three themes in the Marxist, particularly Western Marxist, analysis. The first considers the relationship of major or hegemonic ideas to the interests of the ruling class. North American research here has flowed from two general directions: an interest among political economists in the production of dominant class ideology and the work of the structuralists, particularly Althusser (1971) and Habermas (1973). A second major theme identifies the ways a ruling ideology opposes movements of social change. This work reflects an interest in broadening the scope of analysis to account for counterhegemonic culture. Finally, some have focused directly on the media and movements of those opposing capitalism and struggling to use media in the process of building socialism.

Most work on media content starts from the premise that the ruling ideas are those of the ruling class. H. Schiller's *The Mind Managers* (1973) offers an early model of this research for North American scholars. In this work, he ranges widely over advertising and public relations, Disney Productions, the *National Geographic*, and other cultural and informational media to suggest how images of private property, free enterprise, individual acquisitiveness, militarism, and racism are spread in light, attractive, and generally accessible packages throughout the world. A number of research projects follow directly from this perspective. Ewen's analysis (1976) of how the advertising and public relations business spread the gospel of mass consumption and thereby reshaped family/gender relations within capitalism is a good example. Within this historical framework, Rosenberg (1982) examines the ways business and government joined to spread these values throughout the world. Her work is unique in that it situates the establishment of a global communications infrastructure of technology (undersea cable, telegraphy, telephony, and radio) and of government bodies (for example, the United States Information Agency, Voice of America) within the general structure of what she calls the Promotional State. Similar analyses of ideological production are provided by Mander (1978) for television; Real (1977) and Gruneau (1983) for sports and spectacles; and Goodman (1979), Allen (1985), Butsch (1985), and Toles (1985) for games. There is also considerable research on the ways news media content directly reflects a class ideology. Most of this work concentrates on coverage of international media generally. Good examples are Chomsky and Herman (1979) on coverage of Third World revolutions, Leggett (1978) on New York *Times* coverage of Allende's downfall in Chile, and Chorbajian (1985) on coverage of Olympic Games boycotts. This work has been particularly useful in unmasking the established media's claim to objectivity. Instead it leads one to the conclusion that objectivity is a set of social practices or ceremonial rituals that provide strong protection for underlying political ends. Research has begun to look at the presentation of class in American mass media (Butsch and Glennon, 1983). Of particular interest here is research that grows out of trade union struggles, which suggests that the sheer *absence* of the working class and particularly of trade unions in mass media is as significant in maintaining stereotypes and diminishing consciousness as their misrepresentation (Rollings, 1983; Knight, 1982).

Another group of works within the ruling ideology perspective is set apart by its strict concern for uncovering the meanings revealed in the form and content of the specific medium. This interest in a close textual analysis draws heavily on the work of structuralism and semiotics. The emphasis here is less on the social relations of media production and reception and more on how form and content structure hegemony. Leading work here includes Dorfman (1983) on children's stories, Buxton (1985) on popular music, Nichols (1981) on film, Bathrick (forthcoming) on monuments to women, Goldman (1982) on popular television, and Slack (1983) and Finlay-Pelinski (1983) on technology and policy. For example, Dorfman starts from the notion that childhood can be looked on as a form of underdevelopment, literally in the individual sense and metaphorically in a social sense. He takes this idea and considers the ways popular culture reflects it in form and content. The Babar stories evoke increasingly sophisticated portrayals of coming to consciousness in the dual sense of person and society. Similarly, Disney stories and the Lone Ranger succeed in packaging the values of greed, individualism, and the authoritarian state in attractive comic and dramatic forms. Furthermore, *Readers Digest* extends the infantilization of the reader into adult life. Dorfman sandwiches his stories about stories within a discussion of struggles, his included, to subvert these forces in the process of building socialism in Chile.

A second theme of research on content and culture draws more explicitly from a concern for social and class struggle. While the emphasis remains on hegemonic ideology, that ideology is situated in struggles with competing movements and ideologies, most of which are distinctly anticapitalist. Paradigmatic here is the work of Stuart and Elizabeth Ewen (1982), which identifies class struggles over dominant images and modes of expression (official language versus vernacular) historically and in our time. Their essay, "The Bride of Frankenstein," identifies several of the struggles that derive from the overwhelming force of technology over the last three centuries. Official language is reflected in both the word, such as the *Bible*, and the machinery exhibited in regular celebrations of capitalist power such as the Philadelphia Centennial Exposition of 1876. Together these comprise a "technology of discourse," "the imperative to develop a means by which the law, knowledge, information, transactions, and priorities of an expanding world market economy could be disseminated and controlled" (1982:16). In essence, Dr. Frankenstein promises freedom from want but delivers domination. But out of this domination grows opposition in the form a vernacular print tradition represented in the pamphlets of Gerrard Winstanley and Thomas Paine. The Ewens conclude by suggesting how contemporary movements, awash in a sea of mass commercial media, can recapture that vernacular spirit. Slack (1984) and Meehan (1984) take up the issue of ideology and technology in the modern setting—the debate over the so-called Information Society. Several works address the issue of media and information in social struggle: Gitlin's *The Whole World is Watching* (1980) examines the relationship of media to the student movement, particularly Students for a Democratic Society, in the 1960s; Raboy (1984) does the same for the independence struggle in Quebec; Douglas (1983) assesses the unique efforts of U.S. workers to use established media to build a trade union; and Salter (1980) and Gandy (1982) consider the role of media in several movements to change social policy.

Closely tied to the theme of media in social struggle is research that looks to the contradictions within hegemonic ideology and within the processes of transmission and reception of that ideology. Much of the recent work on television, particularly on the presentation of class on TV, identifies contradictory themes that open the possibility for different class readings of themes (Kellner, 1982; Newcomb, 1982).

Finally, there is a growing body of research that identifies the relationship of communications workers to their product. Bernard's (1982) research on telephone workers in British Colombia examines the struggles that are common to trade unionists and unique to communications workers. Her description of the successful takeover of the offices of British Colombia Telephone, a subsidiary of the U.S. giant GTE, offers excellent insight into the problems of trade unions in a business undergoing the rapid technological change particularly prominent in the communications industry. Neilsen's (1983) research on film unions and Wasko (1983) on unions in broadcasting identify similar conflicts as unionists struggle to build solidarity in the face of technological change.

A third area of research on content and culture is the development of distinctly anticapitalist and socialist media. Some of this research undoubtedly grows out of a concern with social class struggle; but it departs from the previous theme in its focus away from capitalist media and directly on oppositional and alternative media. Though most of the readings are outside the North American context, the starting point for any analysis of oppositional media is Mattelart and Siegelaub's collection *Communication and Class Struggle. Vol. 2: Liberation, Socialism* (1983). Downing's (1984) *Radical Media* provides a detailed analysis of anticapitalist and socialist media in the recent experience of the United States, Portugal, Italy, and Eastern Europe. Most North American research on the use of media in socialist struggles focuses on Latin America, with work on Chile, Cuba, and Nicaragua of particular interest (H. Schiller, 1976:98-109; Bresnahan,

1985). Research on anticapitalist and socialist media is especially concerned to raise questions about the degree to which one should use capitalist media, particularly advanced technology, how one should relate to pervasive ideologies such as formal press freedom, and the opportunities for democratizing media by turning it over to full popular control.

CONCLUSION—A GROWING NETWORK AND SEVERAL CHALLENGES

Over the past ten years, research on communication in the Marxist tradition has grown considerably. What was once the purview of a handful of individual scholars is now the work of entire groups of teachers and researchers across North America. Certain institutions such as Hunter College in New York, the University of California at San Diego, the University of Texas, and Simon Fraser University in British Columbia are places identified with critical communications research. Nevertheless, many more programs now contain courses on critical, including Marxist, research in communication. In addition, the Union for Democratic Communication, a national association of critical and Marxist teachers, writers, and media practioners, provides a good ground for sharing research as well as media productions. Moreover, publications like the *Critical Communications Review* offer an annual research forum for work in the Marxist tradition. Mainstream communications research has begun to notice the growth of this work. The *Journal of Communication* devoted a double issue in 1983 to what it called the "Ferment in the Field." The Speech Communication Association has sponsored a new journal, *Critical Studies in Mass Communication*.

Much remains to be done. On the research side, it would be useful to promote more discussion between political economic and cultural analysts. This would help us to address better such questions as the implications of ownership patterns for specific forms and content of media and the ways media texts relate to specific ongoing social struggles. Critical communications research would benefit from a closer reading of recent developments in Marxist theory and particular work on the labor process, the state, and new forms of imperialism. Moreover, we need closer ties between the research community and those who are directly involved in the production of media and information technology, including workers, their trade unions, artists, and activists who make extensive use of media. Finally, Marxists generally need to pay closer attention to mass media and information technology. For some, the field remains peripheral, buried somewhere in the superstructure, if not simply a blindspot (Smythe, 1977). To the contrary, communication is integral to accumulation, legitimation, and repression in capitalist society. Indeed it is vital to transformations taking place within capitalism today. More attention to research in communication and information technology would help us to understand the nature of these transformations and their powerful implications.

FOOTNOTE

1. These two articles pretty well exhaust what Lazarsfeld and Merton have had to say about critical research. This contrasts with their shelves of work on public opinion, advertising campaigns, the impact of propaganda—all administrative research.

BIBLIOGRAPHY

Allen, Jeanne. "The Industrialization of Culture: The Case of the Player Piano." In Mosco, Vincent, and Wasko, Janet (eds.). *The Critical Communications Review. Vol. 3: Popular Culture and Media Events*. Norwood, N.J.: Ablex, 1985.

Althusser, Louis. "Ideology and Ideological State Apparatuses." In his *Lenin and Philosophy and Other Essays*. London: New Left Books, 1971.

Aronowitz, Stanley. *The Crisis in Historical Materialism*. New York: Praeger, 1981.

Bagdikian, Ben H. *The Media Monopoly*. Boston: Beacon Press, 1983.

Bamford, James. *The Puzzle Palace*. Boston: Houghton Mifflin, 1982.

Barnouw, Erik. *Tube of Plenty*. New York: Oxford University Press, 1975.

Bathrick, Serafina. *Monumental Women*. Madison: University of Wisconsin Press, forthcoming.

Beltran, L. R., and Fox, E. "Latin America and the United States: Flaws in the Free Flow of Information." In Nordenstreng, Kaarle, and Schiller, Herbert (eds.). *National Sovereignty and International Communication*. Norwood, N.J.: Ablex, 1979.

Bernard, Elaine. *The Long Distance Feeling*. Vancouver, B.C.: New Star Books, 1982.

Bresnahan, Rosalind. "Mass Communication, Mass Organizations, and Social Participation in Revolutionary Cuba and Nicaragua." In Mosco, Vincent, and Wasko, Janet (eds.). *The Critical Communications Review. Vol. 3: Popular Culture and Media Events*. Norwood, N.J.: Ablex, 1985.

Butsch, Richard. "The Commodification of Leisure: The Model Airplane Hobby and Industry." In Mosco, Vincent, and Wasko, Janet (eds.). *The Critical Communications Review. Vol. 3: Popular Culture and Media Events*. Norwood, N.J.: Ablex, 1985.

Butsch, Richard, and Glennon, Lynda M. "Social Class: Frequency Trends in Domestic Situation Comedy, 1946-1978." *Journal of Broadcasting* 27:1 (1983).

Buxton, David. "Rock Music, the Star-System, and the Rise of Consumerism." In Mosco, Vincent, and Wasko, Janet (eds.). *The Critical Communications Review. Vol. 3: Popular Culture and Media Events*. Norwood, N.J.: Ablex, 1985.

Chapple, S., and Garofalo, R. *Rock N Roll is Here to Pay*. Chicago: Nelson-Hall, 1977.

Chomsky, Noam, and Herman, Edward. *The Political Economy of Human Rights*. 2 Vols. Boston: South End Press, 1979.

Chorbajian, Levon. "Mass Media Coverage of Olympic Boycotts." In Mosco, Vincent, and Wasko, Janet (eds.). *Critical Communications Review. Vol. 3: Popular Culture and Media Events*. Norwood, N.J.: Ablex, 1985.

Danilean, N. R. *The AT&T*. New York: Vanguard, 1939.

de la Haye, Yves (ed.). *Marx and Engels on the Means of Communication*. New York: International General, 1979.

Demac, Donna. *Keeping America Uninformed: Government Secrecy in the 1980s*. New York: Pilgrim Press, 1984.

Dorfman, Ariel. *The Empire's Old Clothes*. New York: Pantheon, 1983.

Dorfman, Ariel, and Mattelart, Armand. *How to Read Donald Duck*. London: International General, 1975.

Douglas, Sara. "Organized Labor and the Mass Media." Doctoral Dissertation, University of Illinois, Urbana-Champaign, 1983.

Downing, John. *Radical Media*. Boston: South End Press, 1984.

Dreier, Peter. "The Position of the Press in the U.S. Power Structure." *Social Problems* 29:3 (1982).

DuBoff, Richard. "The Rise of Communications Regulation: The Telegraph Industry, 1844-1880." *Journal of Communication* 34:3 (1984).

Ehrenreich, Barbara, and Fuentes, Annette. *Women in the Global Factory*. Boston: South End Press, 1983.

Eisenstein, Elizabeth. *The Printing Press as an Agent of Change*. Cambridge: Cambridge University Press, 1979.

Enzensberger, Hans Magnus. *The Consciousness Industry*. New York: The Seabury Press, 1974.

Ewen, Stuart. *Captains of Consciousness*. New York: McGraw-Hill, 1976.

Ewen, Stuart, and Ewen, Elizabeth. *Channels of Desire: Mass Images and the Shaping of American Consciousness*. New York: McGraw-Hill, 1982.

Fejes, Fred. "The Growth of Multinational Advertising Agencies in Latin America." *Journal of Communication* 30:4 (1980).

Finlay-Pelinski, Marika. "Technologies of Technology: Social Discourse on New Communications Technology." McGill University, Graduate Program in Communications, Working Paper Series, Winter 1983.

Flora, C. B. "Contradictions of Capitalism: Mass Media in Latin America." In McCormack, Thelma (ed.). *Studies in Communication*. Greenwich, Conn.: JAI Press, 1980.

Frederick, Howard. "La Guerra Radiofonica: Radio War Between Cuba and the United States." In Mosco, Vincent, and Wasko, Janet (eds.). *The Critical Communications Review. Vol. 2: Changing Patterns of Communication Control*. Norwood, N.J.: Ablex, 1984.

Freiberg, J. W. *The French Press: Class, State and Ideology*. New York: Praeger, 1981.

Gandy, Oscar. *Beyond Agenda Setting: Information Subsidies and Public Policy*. Norwood, N.J.: Ablex, 1982.

Garnham, Nicholas. "Contribution to a Political Economy of Mass Communication." *Media Culture and Society* 1:2 (1979).

Gitlin, Todd. *The Whole World is Watching: Mass Media in the Making and Unmaking of the New Left*. Berkeley: University of California Press, 1980.

________. "Media Sociology: the Dominant Paradigm." In Wilhoit, G. C., and de Bock, H. (eds.). *Mass Communication Review Yearbook*. Vol. 2. Beverly Hills, Calif.: Sage Publications, 1981.

________. "Prime Time Ideology: The Hegemonic Process in Television Entertainment." In Newcomb, Horace (ed.). *Television: The Critical View*. 3d ed. New York: Oxford, 1982.

Glasgow Media Group. *Bad News*. London: Routledge and Kegan Paul, 1977.

________. *More Bad News*. London: Routledge and Kegan Paul, 1980.

Goldman, R. "Hegemony and Managed Critiques in Prime-Time Television." *Theory and Society* 11:3 (1982).

Goodman, Cary. *Choosing Sides: Playground and Street Life on the Lower East Side*. New York: Schocken, 1979.

Gouldner, Alvin W. *The Dialectics of Ideology and Technology*. New York: Oxford University Press, 1982.

Greenbaum, Joan. *In the Name of Efficiency*. Philadelphia: Temple University Press, 1979.

Gregory, Judith. "Technological Change in the Office Workplace and Implications for Organizing." In Kennedy, Donald, Craypo, Charles, and Lehman, Mary (eds.). *Labor and Technology: Union Responses to Changing Environments*. Department of Labor Studies, Pennsylvania State University, 1982.

Gruneau, Richard. *Class, Sports and Social Development*. Amherst: University of Massachusetts Press, 1983.

Guback, Thomas. *The International Film Industry: Western Europe and America Since 1945*. Bloomington: Indiana University Press, 1969.

_______. "Theatrical Film." In Compaine, Benjamin et al. (eds.). *Who Owns the Media?* 2d ed. White Plains, N.Y.: Knowledge Industries Publications, 1982.

Gurevitch, M., Bennet, T., Curran, J., and Woolacott, J. *Culture, Society and the Media*. London: Methuen, 1982.

Habermas, Jurgen. *Legitimation Crisis*. Boston: Beacon Press, 1973.

Haight, Timothy R., and Weinstein, Laurie R. "Changing Ideology on Television by Changing Telecommunications Policy: Notes on a Contradictory Situation." In McAnany, Emile G., Schnitman, Jorge, and Janus, Noreene (eds.). *Communication and Social Structure*. New York: Praeger, 1981.

Hall, Stuart. "The Rediscovery of Ideology: Return of the Repressed in Media Studies." In Gurevitch, M. et al., 1982.

Hamelink, Cees J. *Cultural Autonomy in Global Communications*. New York: Longman, 1983.

Janus, Noreene. "Advertising and Mass Media in the Era of the Global Corporation." In McAnany, Emile G., Schnitman, Jorge, and Janus, Noreene (eds.). *Communication and Social Structure*. New York: Praeger, 1981.

_______. "Advertising and the Creation of Global Markets: the Role of the New Communication Technologies." In Mosco, Vincent, and Wasko, Janet (eds.). *The Critical Communications Review. Vol. 2: Changing Patterns of Communication Control*. Norwood, N.J.: Ablex, 1984.

Kellner, Douglas. "TV, Ideology, and Emancipatory Popular Culture." In Newcomb, Horace (ed.). *Television: The Critical View*. 3d ed. New York: Oxford, 1982.

Knight, G. "News and Ideology." *Canadian Journal of Communication* 8:4 (1982a).

_______. "Strike Talk: A Case Study of News." *Canadian Journal of Communication* 8:3 (1982b).

Lazarsfeld, Paul. "Remarks on Administrative and Critical Communications Research." *Studies in Philosophy and Social Sciences* 9:1 (1941).

Lazarsfeld, Paul, and Merton, Robert K. "Mass Communication, Popular Taste and Organized Social Action." In *The Communication of Ideas*. New York: Institute for Religious and Social Studies, 1949.

Lazere, Donald (ed.). *Entertainment as Social Control: Left Perspectives on American Mass Media*. Berkeley: University of California Press, 1985.

Leggett, J. et al. *Allende: His Exit and Our Times*. New Brunswick, N.J.: New Brunswick Cooperative Press, 1978.

Livant, Bill. "The Audience Commodity on the 'Blindspot' Debate." *Canadian Journal of Political and Social Theory* 3 (1979).

Mander, Jerry. *Four Arguments for the Elimination of Television*. New York: Morrow, 1978.

Mansell, Robin. "The 'New Dominant Paradigm' in Communication: Transformation Versus Adaptation." *Canadian Journal of Communication* 8:3 (1982).

Marx, Karl. *Capital*. Vol. 1. London: Everyman's Library, 1972.

Mattelart, Armand. *Multinational Corporations and the Control of Culture*. Atlantic Highlands, N.J.: Humanities Press, 1979.

Mattelart, Armand, and Siegelaub, Seth (eds.). *Communication and Class Struggle. Vol. 1: Capitalism, Imperialism*. New York: International General, 1979.

________. *Communication and Class Struggle. Vol. 2: Liberation, Socialism*. New York: International General, 1983.

McAnany, Emile G. "The Logic of Cultural Industries in Latin America: The Television Industry in Brazil." In Mosco, Vincent, and Wasko, Janet (eds.). *The Critical Communications Review. Vol. 2: Changing Patterns of Communication Control*. Norwood, N.J.: Ablex, 1984.

McAnany, Emile G., Schnitman, Jorge, and Janus, Noreene (eds.). *Communication and Social Structure*. New York: Praeger, 1981.

Meehan, Eileen R. "Towards a Third Vision of an Information Society." *Media Culture and Society* 6 (1984).

Melody, W. H., Salter, L., and Heyer, P. (eds.). *Culture, Communication, and Dependency*. Norwood, N.J.: Ablex, 1981.

Mosco, Vincent. *Broadcasting in the United States: Innovative Challenge and Organizational Control*. Norwood, N.J.: Ablex, 1979.

________. "Critical Research and the Role of Labor." *Journal of Communication* 33:3 (1983).

________. *Pushbutton Fantasies: Critical Perspectives on Videotex and Information Technology*. Norwood, N.J.: Ablex, 1982.

________. "Star Wars/Earth Wars." *Radical Science Journal* 17 (1985).

Mosco, Vincent, and Wasko, Janet (eds.). *The Critical Communications Review. Vol. 1: Labor, the Working Class, and the Media*. Norwood, N.J.: Ablex, 1983.

________. (eds.). *The Critical Communications Review. Vol. 2: Changing Patterns of Communcation Control*. Norwood, N.J.: Ablex, 1984.

________. (eds.). *The Critical Communications Review. Vol. 3: Popular Culture and Media Events*. Norwood, N.J.: Ablex, 1985.

Murdock, Graham. "Blindspots About Western Marxism: A Reply to Dallas Smythe." *Canadian Journal of Political and Social Theory* 2:2 (1978).

Murdock, Graham, and Golding, Peter. "For a Political Economy of Mass Communications." In Miliband, Ralph, and Saville, John (eds.). *Socialist Register*. London: Merlin Press, 1974.

Neilsen, Mike. "Toward's a Worker's History of the U.S. Film Industry." In Mosco, Vincent, and Wasko, Janet (eds.). *The Critical Communications Review. Vol. 1: Labor, the Working Class, and the Media*. Norwood, N.J.: Ablex, 1983.

Newcomb, Horace (ed.). *Television: The Critical View*. 3d Edition. New York: Oxford, 1982.

Nichols, William J. *Ideology and the Image*. Bloomington: Indiana University 1981.

Noble, David. *Forces of Production*. New York: Knopf, 1984.

Nordenstreng, Kaarle. *Informational Mass Communication*. Helsinki: Tammi, 1974.

Nordenstreng, Kaarle, and Schiller, Herbert (eds.). *National Sovereignty and International Communication*. Norwood, N.J.: Ablex, 1979.

Pendakur, Manjunath. "United States-Canada Relations: Cultural Dependence and Conflict." In Mosco, Vincent, and Wasko, Janet (eds.). *The Critical Communications Review. Vol. 2: Changing Patterns of Communication Control*. Norwood, N.J.: Ablex, 1984.

Perolle, Judith A. "Computer Technology and Class Formation in the World System." Paper presented at the 1983 Conference on Communications, Mass Media and Development, Northwestern University, Chicago, 1983.

Raboy, Marc. *Movements and Messages: Media and Radical Politics in Quebec*. Toronto: Between the Lines, 1984.

Rada, Juan F. "The Microelectronics Revolution: Implications for the Third World." *Development Dialogue* 2 (1981).

Real, Michael A. *Mass-Mediated Culture*. Englewood Cliffs, N.J.: Prentice-Hall, 1977.

Reyes Matta, Fernando. "A Model for Democratic Communication." *Development Dialogue* 2 (1981).

Rips, G. "The Campaign Against the Underground Press." In Janowitz, A., and Peters, N. J. (eds.). *Unamerican Activities*. San Francisco: City Light Books, 1981.

Rollings, Jerry. "Mass Communications and the American Workers." In Mosco, Vincent, and Wasko, Janet (eds.). *The Critical Communications Review. Vol. 1: Labor, the Working Class, and the Media.* Norwood, N.J.: Ablex, 1983.

Roncagliolo, Rafael, and Janus, Noreene. "Advertising and the Democratization of Communications." *Development Dialogue* 2 (1981).

Rosenberg, Emily S. *Spreading the American Dream.* New York: Hill and Wang, 1982.

Salter, Liora. "Two Directions on a One-Way Street: Old and New Approaches in Media Analysis in Two Decades." In McCormack, Thelma (ed.). *Studies in Communications.* Greenwich, Conn.: JAI Press, 1980.

Schiller, Dan. *Objectivity and the News.* Philadelphia: University of Pennsylvania Press, 1981.

________. *Telematics and Government.* Norwood, N.J.: Ablex, 1982.

Schiller, Herbert I. *Mass Communication and American Empire.* Boston: Beacon Press, 1969.

________. *The Mind Managers.* Boston: Beacon Press, 1973.

________. *Communication and Cultural Domination.* White Plains, N.Y.: International Arts and Sciences Press, 1976.

________. *Who Knows: Information in the Age of the Fortune 500.* Norwood, N.J.: Ablex, 1981.

________. *Information in the Crisis Economy.* Norwood, N.J.: Ablex, 1984.

Schnitman, Jorge. "Economic Protectionism and Mass Media Development: Film Industry in Argentina." In McAnany, Emile G., Schnitman, Jorge, and Janus, Noreene (eds.). *Communication and Social Structure.* New York: Praeger, 1981.

Shore, Larry. "The Crossroads of Business and Music: The Music Industry in the United States and Internationally." Doctoral Dissertation, Stanford University, 1983.

Simmons, Steven J. *The Fairness Doctrine and the Media.* Berkeley: University of California Press, 1978.

Slack, Jennifer D. *Communication Technologies and Society.* Norwood, N.J.: Ablex, 1983.

________. "The Information Revolution as Ideology." *Media Culture and Society* 6 (1984).

Smythe, Dallas W. *The Structure and Policy of Electronic Communications.* Urbana: University of Illinois Press, 1957.

________. "Communications: Blindspot of Western Marxism." *Canadian Journal of Political and Social Theory* 1:3 (1977).

_______. "Rejoinder to Graham Murdock." *Canadian Journal of Political and Social Theory* 2:2 (1978).

_______. *Dependency Road: Communication, Capitalism, Consciousness and Canada*. Norwood, N.J.: Ablex, 1981.

Somavia, Juan. "The Democratization of Communications: From Minority Social Monopoly to Majority Social Representation." *Development Dialogue* 2 (1981).

Sussman, Gerald. "Global Telecommunications and the Third World: Theoretical Considerations." *Media Culture and Society* 6 (1984).

Toles, Terry. "Videogames and American Military Ideology." In Mosco, Vincent, and Wasko, Janet (eds.). *The Critical Communications Review. Vol. 3: Popular Culture and Media Events*. Norwood, N.J.: Ablex, 1985.

Tran van Dinh. "Nonalignment and Cultural Imperialism." In Nordenstreng, Kaarle, and Schiller, Herbert (eds.). *National Sovereignty and International Communication*. Norwood, N.J.: Ablex, 1979.

Tunstall, Jeremy. *The Media are American*. New York: Columbia University Press, 1977.

Wasko, Janet. *Movies and Money: Financing the American Film Industry*. Norwood, N.J.: Ablex, 1982.

_______. "Trade Unions and Broadcasting." In Mosco, Vincent, and Wasko, Janet (eds.). *The Critical Communications Review. Vol. 1: Labor, the Working Class, and the Media*. Norwood, N.J.: Ablex, 1983.

Williams, Raymond. *Television, Technology and Cultural Form*. London: Fontana, 1975.

_______. *Problems in Materialism and Culture*. London: Verso, 1980.

_______. *Culture*. London: Fontana, 1981.

9

SOCIAL WORK AS A NATURAL HARBOR FOR MARXIST THOUGHT

Philip Lichtenberg
Howard Raiten

INTRODUCTION

Social workers in the United States organize, develop, promote, and render human services in a capitalist society. They do their work in the private sector and in the public sector, confronting the contradictions of capitalism directly in their practice on every front. The range of human services is enormous, stretching across the life span from prenatal care to work with the elderly, across the disabilities from physical ailment to mental illness, across social problems from criminality to abandoned children, reaching into every corner where human concerns can be found. Social workers are in migrant labor camps, in the offices of legislators, organizing in neighborhoods, staffing settlement houses, welfare agencies, and government bureaucracies. There are social workers in the private practice of psychotherapy and in the planning centers of modern society.

Wherever they are, social workers focus on human beings as ends in themselves, as persons with dignity, as individuals in the community of all humanity. This is the first contradiction social workers face: They put the well-being of the individual first, without regard to the needs of capital. Contending with this contradiction, this fact that their work is embedded in a social order that negates their value system is a major problem for social workers.

There is a second contradiction that rivals the first: Social work is a profession, which means that it survives in being practical. To be practical, social work must come to terms with, must accommodate to, things as they are. Whether done in the private or public sector, social work is dependent upon support in the form of resources or social legitimation. To function it must be sanctioned. While social workers must make their peace with the ruling powers and principles in the society, to implement their rules they must help bring about change in the individual, the group, the neighborhood, the laws, and indeed the whole society. Social work in all its facets is a social change enterprise. Thus, social workers must both gain acceptance from the forces representing the status quo and, at the same time, try dramatically to change the way things are. In the 1960s, for example, social workers, under the auspices of the Ford Foundation and the U.S. government, were demanding citizen participation and power in the running of cities. The outcome was easy to foresee. Fearing the mobilization of revolutionary forces, the support for these programs was soon withdrawn.

It is Marxist social workers, with their sense of the dialectic, who openly acknowledge and address these contradictions. The welfare state is both attacked and defended by Marxist social workers, attacked for being used to undergird and protect capitalist society, to serve the accumulation process; but it is also supported for being the achievement of the demands of the working class and the dispossessed, an achievement wrested from the ruling powers by unceasing struggle. Neighborhood organizing is encouraged in activating citizens to struggle on their own behalf and is criticized for developing reforms that serve to keep the system intact. Family care and psychotherapy are condemned for adjusting families and individuals to the status quo, and praised for liberating people from the chains of unconscious internalized oppression. It is through such dialectical understanding and analyses that Marxist social work academics part company with liberals and conservatives in the profession.

Marxist social workers contend with one another over how to understand these contradictions and what to stress in them. Is social work simply an institution of the capitalist state that exists only to enable the continued functioning of the capitalist system? Does neighborhood organizing inevitably lead to safe reforms if done under the leadership of professional social workers rather than political party representatives? Is clinical social work a mystifying force in its very nature? Can the state be used to support radical political education? Should Marxist social workers address legislative issues or concern themselves only with mobilization of the masses? These and related differences will be examined in the review that follows.

EARLY MARXIST WRITINGS

Marxism was a lively force in social work circles in the 1930s; it faded in the 1950s and surfaced again in the 1970s. In the days of the depression, as Jacob Fisher has recorded in *The Response of Social Work to the Depression* (1980), there were Mary van Kleeck, Harry Lurie, Jacob Fisher (who edited the journal *Social Work Today*), Bertha Reynolds, Ira Reid, and members of the Rank-and-File Movement who gave voice to Marxist thought. Mary van Kleeck, for example, distinguished between two views on the nature of government. One "saw government as independent of the conflicting interests of society, as arbiter in effect among these interests, and dedicated to the greatest good of the greatest number." The second, which she favored, viewed "government as dominated by the strongest interests and, because of the nature of the American economy, tending to protect property rather than human rights" (Fisher, 1980). Whether the state is essentially a neutral arbiter or biased on behalf of the capitalists remains a central issue and is the major question dividing Marxist from liberal camps in the social work academy.

Bertha Reynolds, probably the most memorable figure from the left social work movement of the 1930s, was active in joining Freud and Marx in her personal life, as revealed in her autobiography, *An Uncharted Journey* (1963), and in her professional life, as when she introduced social services to a union setting (*Social Work and Social Living*, 1951). Her commitments to the self-determination of clients, democratic supervision in social work practice, and enhancement in the power of practitioners are common themes among Marxist social workers today.

The Marxist social work tradition from the 1930s was ravaged by the events of the 1940s and early 1950s. *Social Work Today* ceased publishing after taking its readers on the roller-coaster ideological rides of the times: uncompromising antifacism followed by justification of the Nazi-Soviet pact, followed in turn by calls for aid to the Soviet Union after Hitler's invasion. Also, social workers of a Marxist bent had joined left-wing unions, and when the union movement in the 1940s turned upon these groups, social workers were isolated and in retreat. What did not arise from disillusion with party-line dictates and from the counterrevolutionary actions of the AFL-CIO to push Marxist ideas from the social work scene was accomplished by McCarthyism. Like others on the left, social workers were hounded and hurt and finally withdrew from open Marxist activity.

CONTEMPORARY MARXIST SCHOLARSHIP

The recovery of the left tradition from the 1930s has been one of the aims of social work thinkers in the past decade. In addition to Fisher's book, much attention has been paid to Bertha Reynolds (for example, Alexander, 1976; Schwartz, 1981; and Cullen, 1983), to *Social Work Today* (Alexander and Lichtenberg, 1978), and to the Rank-and-File Movement (Leighninger and Knickmeyer, 1976; and Spano, 1982). While not directly on social work, Paul Lyons's (1983) study of Communist Party activists of the 1930s, in which he elaborates the social and personal conditions that underlay their long-term involvement in basic social change, is also very relevant.

The revival of interest in Marxism by social work academics has run parallel to the significant expansion in scholarly endeavors associated with increased doctoral education in the field. With the spread of social and behavioral sciences into social work came Marxist criticisms of these developments, and beginning in the 1970s several major works summarizing Marxist thought in social welfare appeared. From Great Britain came *Radical Social Work* (Bailey and Brake, 1975), *Radical Social Work and Practice* (Brake and Bailey, 1980), and *Social Work Practice Under Capitalism: A Marxist Approach* (Corrigan and Leonard, 1978); and from the United States came two books by Jeffry Galper, *The Politics of Social Service* (1975) and *Social Work Practice: A Radical Perspective* (1980), and most recently Ann Withorn's *Serving the People: Social Services and Social Change* (1984). These six books encompass the major concerns and offerings of Marxist thinkers in the field of social welfare, including the most significant debates and differences in perspective that enliven the field. Galper's books especially, because they are meant to be used as textbooks in social work education, are comprehensive, far-ranging, and rich in their references to other works.

In *The Politics of Social Services* Galper makes the case for a socialist analysis of the social welfare system. Early in the book he criticizes common conceptions of the welfare state, arguing, as van Kleeck had done, against the liberal view of the state, and noting that social work has adopted this liberal view as its own. According to Galper (1975:22), "liberalism's assumptions that institutions of the welfare state modify and humanize capitalist processes and that competitive individualism is an appropriate base from which to maximize individual and social well-being do not survive close scrutiny." Included in his "scrutiny" is an assessment of the views of human nature contained in welfare state ideology, particularly its emphasis upon competitiveness and bourgeois individualism. In a chapter on the political functions of the social services, he deals with the conformity and conservatism that are fostered in both clients and workers. Welfare clients, for instance, are required to seek regular work; day care is organized in ways that depend upon the requirements of the labor market; Social Security controls retirement age, and so on. He then analyzes social work as a "conservatized version of social reform," and interprets community organizing and casework as methods for the "containment of change." Professionalism, functional specificity of competence, emotional neutrality, service to others without regard to the self, and impartiality mark the conservatizing side of social work practice. Community organizing and casework bring reforms that do not challenge the capitalist system as a whole but rather shore it up, and, as such, represent acts of containment. Galper concludes this book by counterposing a radical position that would transform all the arenas in social work, from welfare theory and policy to clinical casework, into places and occasions for radical political activity.

In his second book, *Social Work Practice* (1980), Galper revises and enlarges upon the last sections of his first book. In particular, he expands his analysis and recommendations for an openly socialist social work practice. Part I, "Theoretical Foundations," defines what radical social work is and is not, describes processes of socialist transformation, analyzes, again, social welfare in capitalist society, and provides connections between the social services and socialist transformation. In this section of his book, Galper is critical of those reformers and revolutionaries who segregate the personal and political, who denigrate the role of casework, and who minimize transformations of consciousness in the revolutionary process. In Part II, "Applying Theory to Practice," he explores a series of issues related to radical social work practice, such as "primitive rebellion," the dialectic of meeting individual needs in services while also building a revolutionary movement, and how radicalism plays itself out in community organizing and in direct casework service. There are chapters also on unionism, working from within to change social service agencies, research and writing in social work, and schools of social work as arenas for socialist struggles.

Both for their range and how they combine an acceptance of the power of social work with a negation of its limitations, Galper's books represent the state of the art in the field.

The two books by Bailey and Brake are edited works that are more loosely organized and less comprehensive in their coverage. The two most notable chapters in the first volume (Bailey and Brake, 1975) by Richard Cloward and Frances Fox Piven and by Peter Leonard, and the chapter by Bailey and Brake in the second volume (Brake and Bailey, 1980), are also the most general in treating social work as a field. Other chapters tend to focus on specific issues, such as community development, homosexuality, feminism and social work, and racism, or on bringing particular sociological concepts into social work. Cloward and Piven detail the harm-producing, citizen-pacifying aspects of social welfare institutions and call for resistance to these institutions. Like a number of other left-wing thinkers in the social work academy, they concentrate on the underside of social work organization and practice in the welfare state, sometimes to the exclusion of its positive contributions.

But social work is not all bad. Leonard (in Bailey and Brake, 1975: 22) is more dialectical:

> In capitalist society, social work operates as part of a social-welfare system which is located at the centre of the contradictions arising from the dehumanizing consequences of capitalist economic production. Social workers, although situated in a largely oppressive organizational and professional context, have the potential for recognizing these contradictions and, through working at the point of interaction between people and their social environment, of helping to increase control by people over economic and political structures.

Relying on the work of Paulo Freire, Leonard suggests that the context of social work provides an opportunity for enhancing the creative, determining potential of people. The individual client is to be empowered, treated as a creative agent in life, helped to become someone who can determine his or her own fate. At the point of contact between social worker and client, this enabling, facilitating, educating role is ever available. He notes that the relationship between people and the various social systems that comprise their environment is dialectical, and, like Galper, Leonard sees systems as both oppressive and supportive. He insists that we must take account of individual consciousness, and in particular what any situation means to a person, if we are to play a role in transforming the passive, oppressed client into an actor on the social and political scene. One aspect of radical social work practice is consciousness-raising, more particularly, class consciousness-raising.

Bailey and Brake lean upon the theories of Antonio Gramsci in calling social workers to think about their profession as part of the working class struggle. For instance, they speak to the issue of excessive individualism in social work practice, of the ideology of the welfare state as defined by the ruling class, and of not using vulnerable and oppressed people in ways that defeat them even while mobilizing them for social struggle. Their main call is for social work to collectivize its own practice as a radicalizing endeavor.

In *Social Work Practice Under Capitalism: A Marxist Approach*, Corrigan and Leonard (1978) are deeply respectful of the practical lives of social workers, as other left theorists sometimes fail to be. They introduce a series of problems that often face social workers, contrasting a typical assessment of each situation with a Marxist analysis. One example is that of a family conflict in which a fifteen-year-old girl is brought to a social worker by her mother. Typically the social worker sees the girl as victim and the mother as victimizer, whereas a Marxist analysis would entertain the idea that the adolescent girl may be as oppressive and chauvinist as her mother. Further, the whole family and all the individuals in it would be seen in their relationship to capitalist production and the necessary reproduction of the social relations of capitalism. Thus mothers are to be seen as women, as workers, and also as mothers with all that this entails.

In the second half of their book, Corrigan and Leonard explain the theory they have used in its own terms. Here they take up Marxist notions of production and reproduction, the concept of class, the state and its relationship with the ruling class, individual consciousness (and the need for a Marxist psychology that can take account of the limitations of psychoanalysis without losing its contributions), and the family. In the chapter on the state, they take up such questions as the specific ideological functions of the welfare state (for example, to engineer consent), the relationship of the state to the ruling class and to the working class (for example, the state reflects *struggle* as well as *status quo*), and social workers as state employees. Their chapter on individual consciousness takes up the cult of individualism, the objection of Marxism to the notion of a "basic human nature," the absurdity of an unconscious that is detached from reality, and the dualism in psychoanalysis that separates mental from material existence. They end the book with a call for the union of social workers with others who are working for revolutionary change, arguing that Marxist social workers alone cannot carry out their noble intentions within a bourgeois social welfare system.

In another work from Great Britain, Pritchard and Taylor (1978) contrast "democratic socialist" and "Marxist" views on the ideology and place of social work in society. While both authors are committed to socialism and the effort to achieve it, Pritchard takes the democratic socialist perspective and Taylor the Marxist one in a debate. Does social work contribute most to radical change when it adopts a reformist or a revolutionary perspective? Pritchard aruges that the welfare state and the Labour Movement can be used to create reforms that will lead to a socialist society of a democratic sort and that Marxist revolutionary actions, both in theory and as realized elsewhere, must fail because they are invariably antidemocratic. He believes that piecemeal welfare reforms are important, current political parties can be instruments of fundamental social change, revolutions always throw up authoritarian leaders, and Marxism has failed to find democratic methods for controlling such leadership. Taylor counters that reforms merely shore up the capitalist state, that alternative institutions must be built within capitalist society, and that only revolutionary means will achieve a socialist society. He suggests that in building new vehicles for socialist change, social work, especially community work, has a crucial role to play since it can create new tenant groups, neighborhood organizations, and so on, which can become revolutionary instruments. He decries the association of Marxism with Stalinism in Pritchard's argument and claims a commitment to decentralization as basic to Marxism. They agree that conflict and struggle will be necessary to achieve socialism and that social work has a role to play in that struggle.

Ann Withorn's *Serving the People* (1984) also deals with the conflict between radicals and social workers concerning the role of services in social change endeavors. Withorn, who came into social work from a radical background, argues forcefully that social services can be used in revolutionary struggle, that they have been so used in the past (for example, Workmen's Circle, IWW) and that social work can be adapted to radical social change. The left is short-sighted in ignoring the potential of social services as an instrument of change just as social work is limited when it fails to be radical. She is especially articulate in relating her own experience and the relevance of joining the personal with the political that highlighted the 1960s. Her assessment of the problems that professionalism poses for social workers is thorough and subtle, and she encourages deprofessionalization, so that clients are considered as equals and possible comrades in social struggle. She also examines some of the problems involved in working for bureaucracies while maintaining an orientation to fundamental social change.

The Marxist view of social work, albeit somewhat less general and theoretical, can also be found in two other collections of articles: *Welfare in America: Controlling the Dangerous Classes* (1975), edited by Betty Reid Mandell, and a special issue of *The Journal of Sociology and Social Welfare* called "The Political Economy of Social Work" (1983), edited by Michael Reisch and Stanley Wenocur. The Mandell book deals critically with such key topics as work and manpower programs, social security programs, birth control and abortion, medicine and social control, and the criminal justice system, which serves the rich and punishes the poor. Unlike most of the books presented thus far in this review, however, there are few creative suggestions for alternatives.

In the Reisch and Wenocur volume, Harold Lewis treats social services as a commodity and, from this perspective, develops principles for guiding social welfare in the 1980s. He directs his attention to the most disadvantaged, unlike David Gil who, as we will see, focuses on provision of services for everyone. Abramovitz and Hopkins document the weakening of the welfare state that is occurring simultaneously with the intensification of poverty, unemployment, and inequality under the Reagan administration. Other pieces in this special issue concern political aspects of mental health care, organizing in communities, and political issues in the profession and among social service workers in agencies.

In social work education and scholarship three areas are usually kept distinct: social welfare history, philosophy, and policy; contributions from the social and behavioral sciences; and social work practice (which recently has included policymaking, program development, administration, community organizing, and clinical social work). Marxist thought has penetrated most deeply into the domains of welfare policy and practice. While social workers have applied Marxist ideas in their field, the results of their activities do not seem to have affected the development of Marxist theory. An exception is *Psychoanalysis: Radical and Conservative* by Lichtenberg (1969), where an attempt to construct a Marx-Freud connection is carried beyond the discussions found in the general books reviewed above. In this work, Lichtenberg shows that Freud developed two psychologies: one a liberal-oriented view, the other a radical one compatible with Marx's conception of alienation and open to radical social thought in general. He examines these contrasting psychologies as they apply to such central psychoanalytic issues such as anxiety, narcissism, sense of reality, melancholia, and the role of satisfaction in growth and development.

Welfare Policy and History

The most prolific Marxist writers on welfare policy and the history of social work are Frances Fox Piven and Richard Cloward and David G. Gil. The books by these authors have captured a lot of attention and stirred up considerable controversy both within the discipline and among the general public. Some observers have questioned how "Marxist" they are, but we have chosen to take a broad, nonpurist view of our subject and so have no difficulty including them in this review.

In *Regulating the Poor* (1971), Piven and Cloward assert that social welfare policies, far from being benevolent responses to demands from below, are chiefly designed to serve the needs of the ruling class. Social unrest and the market's need for labor are the primary grounds for the implementation of welfare programs. With more unrest and diminished need for labor, the welfare rolls expand and, conversely, with less unrest and when the demand for labor increases, welfare recipients are pushed off the welfare rolls. Welfare policy protects the market economy by controlling those who might organize to oppose it. In *Poor People's Movements* (1977), these authors assess some of the most important mass actions in this century (by the unemployed in the 1930s, the industrial workers during this same period, the Civil Rights movement and the welfare rights movement more recently). They conclude from these studies that it was mass defiance, not formal organizations, that won the reforms in the 1930s and 1960s. Indeed, whatever formal organization these movements achieved served to blunt their militancy. In *The New Class War* (1982), they claim that the crises faced by corporations in the 1970s led to a two-front attack against labor and welfare recipients. To increase the profitability of investments, taxes were reduced. This led to reductions in the welfare budget and to removing previously eligible people from the welfare rolls. This, in turn, put more people into the labor market, intensifying the downward pressure on wages, and increasing in still another way the profitability of investments. Despite their rather bleak assessment of the current situation, they expect major outbreaks of mass protest in the near future.

David Gil, who has created a Center for Social Change Practice and Theory at Brandeis University, has written several works from what he calls a "radical humanist or humanist-Marxist perspective." Egalitarianism is a major theme in this perspective. In *Unravelling Social Policy* (1981b), Gil puts forward a conceptual model for the analysis and synthesis of social policy and political action "aimed at structural social change toward an egalitarian, humanistic social order." He explores this model in respect to Mothers' Wages Policy. Radical changes in society, he suggests, are more likely to come from policies that serve directly all population groups (a universalist orientation) rather than from those directed at particular disadvantaged groups, where means-testing and other forms of inequality prevail.

In *The Challenge of Social Equality* (1976), Gil examines the systemic roots and dynamics of social problems found in child abuse and in institutions set up to serve children in need. He articulates again what he means by a humanistic and egalitarian perspective. The same line of thought is carried further in *Beyond the Jungle* (1979). In a recent article, Gil (1984c) studies the institutional context of human abuse. He connects different manifestations of abuse (verbal, physical, psychological) with diverse contexts (interpersonal, institutional, societal) and argues that these cannot be understood apart from one another. He further notes the relation of human abuse in these forms and contexts to social, economic, and political dynamics "rooted in particular societal structures" and in the value systems and ideologies that correspond to these structures. Human abuse, he demonstrates, also varies with resource management, the nature of work, the legal system, and so on. By placing the issue of human abuse in a much larger framework than is customary in conventional thought, Gil illuminates the problems involved in a dramatic fashion.

Allan Moscovitch (1980:94) analyzes the "boundaries of social welfare policy" in a typically Marxist manner. He concludes:

> All of these [social welfare] policies have the same basis: insuring continued existence of a relatively healthy, relatively disciplined labor force, a labor force which is available when needed to produce the goods and services in our society. These are the goods and services, in turn, which provide for the continued existence of that labor force and for the continued existence of those who own and control the tools with which they work.

Keefe (1978) uses the historical-materialist perspective to predict the changes in social work practice and in social welfare policies that are bound up with developments in our capitalist society. Unlike many Marxist thinkers, he does not devalue casework services to individuals. He notes two traps common in therapeutic practice: viewing the client as the sole cause of his or her problems, and making the client simply a dependent victim of circumstance. The client may be both a carrier of his or her problem and also a victim of circumstance, and is never simply one or the other as is frequently asserted. Keefe also claims that social workers are not simple change agents or control agents, again as so many have suggested, and that social work practice can be of service both in times of change and in the socialist society to come. Clearly, he argues more dialectically than many theoreticians in the field.

In a critique of the American welfare state, DeJong (1978) challenges the values and assumptions of the free-market-pluralist ideology that underlies it. Analysis of health care and institutional social services care shows the destruction not only of individuals but also of community. A major conclusion of DeJong's essay is that groups and whole communities should have a more meaningful role in determining how public services are rendered. This call for people to actively participate in determining their fate and their social world appears often in the writings of radical social workers.

Paul Adams (1978) sees cutbacks in welfare benefits as attacks on social wages for all members of the working class and is critical of theorists who see the welfare state primarily in terms of social control. The performance of the Carter and Reagan administrations would seem to support his thesis. In an essay calling upon human service workers to fight for their programs in the 1980s, Withorn (1982a) examines the tactical and other weaknesses of welfare proponents: overpromising, believing that they have influence as individuals, leading the attacks on their own programs, excessive professionalism, and aiming services only toward the poor and most disadvantaged rather than toward the whole population. She calls for a militant stance in actively promoting as well as defending social welfare activities.

Finally, in respect to welfare policy as an area, Marlene Webber (1980), an ex-social worker, in a stinging article sets herself apart from much of the work that is considered radical in our discipline. She believes most of this work is more social democratic than Marxist, that it represents a "mystified understanding of the state" by obscuring its class nature, and that such illusions must be overcome. She asserts that so-called radicals in social work underestimate the class consciousness of workers in society, overestimate their own consciousness, and arrogantly believe they must impart political awareness to clients. She attacks the tendency to assign to personal transformation a key role in progressing toward a new society, referring to the call for individual change as part of the revolutionary agenda as a "most pernicious suggestion." (We are reminded of Marx's central notion that it is not the consciousness of men that determines their being, but their social being that determines their consciousness.) She is critical of radicals in social work who fear social revolution (that is, violence) and who systematically choose reformism over revolution. She is also scornful of those social work thinkers who would fight against social welfare programs, thereby increasing the pain of workers, on the grounds of speeding up the engine of revolt.

Social Work Practice

When we turn to the practice areas of social work, we see that a lot of work on the policymaking process (for example, Gil, 1981, Galper, 1980) has already been dealt with as part of our discussion of welfare policies. Two other areas merit attention: community organizing and clinical social work, once known as social casework. The field of community organizing was treated in some detail by Galper in his books, and it has been, of course, a major interest of New Left activists who are not professional social workers. For many years the work of Sol Alinsky has had a dominant place in the teaching of community organizing in social work schools. Recently the most prominent scholarly contribution to this subfield has come from Steve Burghardt (1982) in his book *The Other Side of Organizing*.

Using Paulo Freire along with Marx, Burghardt is as concerned with the more personal side of life and work as with the political nature of practice and the political forces that influence practice. His goal is a politics of self-determination that will contribute to our resistance against the conservative forces that are so dominant today. Promoting a dialectical practice, Burghardt argues that the caseworker who attends to the social context as part of a client's care is "more *politically engaged* than the top-down organizer" who ignores others' personal needs and concerns in pursuit of political goals. Similarly, the organizer who engages the personal reactions of fellow activists during the course of political work is more personally relevant than the caseworker who avoids social realities in the life of the client in order to emphasize psychodynamic factors. The organizer should facilitate the expression of the personal in political action, but must be careful that it does not become dominant. Burghardt explores a broadened use of self (an old casework idea) as essential both to organizing the oppressed and to preventing burn-out of the social worker. Borrowing heavily from Freire, he examines leadership in community organizing and points toward methods for developing broad critical consciousness as an alternative to the typical training of leaders.

The contradictions involved in racist, sexist, and classist practice, one's own as well as that of others, are also discussed. Unless social workers are fully committed to the resolution of racism, sexism, and classism in their own lives and not just in the lives of others, they will not be willing to put up with the pain involved in trying to solve these problems in society. Making such a commitment enriches one's life and makes whatever pain is felt secondary to the rewards derived from this effort.

Further on, Burghardt examines the encroachment of capitalism into social welfare organizations and the class position of social workers. Following recent Marxist writings on class in modern American capitalism, he points to the disparity between the economic and ideological positions of social workers: Though they have little control over social welfare as a system, they have some degree of control in their immediate work activities and, thus, are in a position to subvert bourgeois ideology. That there is considerably more potential for social workers to use their work in a more revolutionary way than is currently being done seems to be an important message in his writing. This book offers what is probably the most complete statement of the integration of the personal and the social in social work practice. Informed throughout by a keen dialectical sensibility, Burghardt's work succeeds in opening possibilities for radical action in a time of political conservatism.

Shaffer (1972), in a posthumously published paper on "Community Organization and the Oppressed," also draws upon the consciousness-raising work of Freire.

After establishing that all social change efforts are purposive, John Else (1977) examines, from a Marxist perspective, some of the organizational issues that confront social change organizations such as The Southern Conference Educational Fund and The Oakland Economic Development Council, Inc. His two major conclusions are that power in social change organizations is most effectively implemented in informal ways (formal power, if too prominent, suggests problems in the organization) and that process concerns as well as product concerns are important to the best management of such organizations.

Too often on the left, process concerns have been relegated to the background to the detriment of the long-term working of the group. Interpersonal relationships in the group, for example, must be attended to when people are intensely involved in dangerous and personally frightening work. People involved in such activities need support and failure to provide it often comes from neglect of process concerns.

Clinical Social Work

Turning to the clinical side of social work, we are faced with a choice. Stemming partly from the work of the New Left, partly from social work itself, and partly from self-help groups in the community, there arose in the 1970s a radical therapy approach (really, alternative) to social work that based itself on egalitarianism, democracy, and antiprofessionalism. This radical therapy movement joined with other alternative services to compete with establishment mental health endeavors and spurred controversies reminiscent of the "red" versus "expert" debates of an earlier time (and of other places). Located somewhere between this grouping and professional social work there arose also the feminist therapy movement Given the special concerns of this chapter, we have decided to restrict ourselves to work in radical therapy that was done within the field of social work.

Lichtenberg (1977) has reviewed his experience with a group that offered "responsible therapy" to movement personnel. He notes issues that come up in therapy when a worker is involved in left-wing politics, such as positive transference coming from shared political orientations. Clients' ambivalence with respect to their political activity may also become troublesome to the therapist, since there may be occasions in which a client needs to withdraw from political engagement, and therapy must help this come about. Acceptance of the conservatism in each of us who have grown up in capitalist society is also a challenge to the therapist with a political purpose.

Caspary (1980) assesses four common views of the relationship of psychotherapy to politics: psychotherapy has nothing to do with politics; psychotherapy adjusts people to the status quo and is a negative force; psychotherapy, like other countercultural influences, can liberate people without political action being required; and there can be a radical therapy, informed by the politics of class, race, sex, age, corporate power, and so on. He then tries to synthesize the best wisdom from each of these views.

Gil (1976) notes that the objectives of clinical and political practice are complementary and can inform each other. Were clinical social workers to adopt human self-actualization as the goal of practice, he suggests, they would necessarily be rejecting the dominant therapeutic model that implicitly affirms the established social order. He urges clinicians to accept instead an alternative therapeutic model that helps individuals to trace the causes of suffering and ill-health to the existing social order (its pressures and reactions to these pressures), and that helps them transcend a consciousness shaped by the system.

Observing that "social casework seems always in tension between some inherent tendency to be radical in a social and political way and a comparable drive to hold on to the established modes of life that are conventional and conservative," Lichtenberg (1976b) studies the radical and conservative tendencies in casework and proposes four ways in which radicalism can affect practice: revision of goals from individualistic well-being to social and personal involvement; patterns of selecting clients that are purposive in promoting radicalization; including work life, political engagement, and so on, as subject matter of therapy; and giving special attention to cooperative egalitarianism in the relationship of client and therapist. Daphne Statham (1978) combines alternative services, social work, and political activity in a different way. She calls for the informing of social work practice by experiences in political movements without a major revision of casework itself.

Social Work Education

Marxist scholars have also attended to social work education. Many social work educators, especially those who have engaged in group work, community organization, or clinical social work, apply their experience in the field to work in the classroom. Thus, many social work educators include both radical content and radical process in their work as teachers. Examples of concern with course content, other than those cited above, come from Longres (1981b), Gil (1981a), Galper (1976), and Lichtenberg (1976a), and range from social welfare policy and social analysis to psychological concerns.

The works of Paulo Freire (1973a and b) have proven to be of particular relevance to many Marxist social work educators, especially his view of education as a potentially empowering process. Freire contrasts his empowering and liberating "problem posing" or "dialogic" method of education to the oppressive "banking" approach. One supporter, Norman Goroff (1982), asserts that "a pedagogy for a radical social work practice should provide opportunities for persons to critically examine and analyze the knowledge that is put forth as 'the truth,' and to develop relationships which are egalitarian, cooperative and collectively oriented." He sets no requirements for his students (he calls them colleagues), though he clearly sets standards and demands for himself. He believes that establishing requirements for others defines them as incapable of establishing their own. Because he claims not to know what is best for others, he must trust these others to know what is best for themselves.

Further support comes from Reisch et al. (1981), who argue that the teacher-student relationship (a hierarchical form) must be avoided and replaced by an educational-political process in which all parties grow. Social work education directed at empowerment "re-presents" existing dilemmas (as students experience and describe them) not in the form of lectures by a teacher, but as problems that require collaborative efforts toward resolution.

While such views are widespread, there is considerable diversity of opinion on how to educate in a Marxist way, that is, using Marxist process. Moreover, it is only fair to note, many liberal and humanist social work educators also teach in an egalitarian and liberating manner. Social work has been self-conscious about its teaching for many years and is far in advance of most other disciplines in its pedagogical practice.

Journals

Readers should note that two journals, frequently referred to in this chapter, are particularly oriented toward Marxist scholarship in social work and social welfare: *Catalyst: A Socialist Journal of the Social Services*, which began in the late 1970s, and *The Journal of Sociology and Social Welfare*, which is somewhat older. *Social Policy* is another journal that publishes a lot of work in this area by the left academy.

CONCLUSION

Social workers have been involved in left-wing activities for many years, both inside and outside of the academy. They have brought to community and political organizing their experience and knowledge as professionals; and they have brought back into the profession the lessons they have learned by their work with others in the community and political spheres. As their attention to scholarship expands, so do their offerings to the field and to the left academy at large. It is a modest, hard-working profession, with more intellectual substance to offer than is commonly recognized. We commend it to our sisters and brothers in the academy.

BIBLIOGRAPHY

Abramovitz, Mimi. "The Conservative Program is a Women's Issue." *Journal of Sociology and Social Welfare* 9 (1982).

_______. "Everyone's On Welfare: The Role of Redistribution in Social Policy: Revisited." *Social Work* 28 (1983).

Abramovitz, Mimi, and Epstein, Irwin. "The Politics of Privatization: Industrial Social Work and Private Enterprise." *Urban and Social Change Review* 16:1 (1983).

Adams, Paul. "Social Control or Social Wage: On the Political Economy of the 'Welfare State.' " *Journal of Sociology and Social Welfare* 5:1 (1978).

Adams, Paul, and Freeman, Gary. "On the Political Character of Social Service Work." *Catalyst: A Socialist Journal of the Social Services* No. 7 (1980).

Alexander, Leslie. "Organizing the Professional Social Worker: Union Development in Voluntary Social Work, 1930-1950." Unpublished Ph.D. Dissertation, Bryn Mawr College, 1976.

Alexander, Leslie B., and Lichtenberg, Philip. "The 'Casework Notebook': An Analysis of Its Content." *Journal of Sociology and Social Welfare* 5:1 (1978);

Bailey, Roy, and Brake, Mike. *Radical Social Work*. London: Edward Arnold, 1975.

Beverly, Creigs C. *Community Services in the Ghanaian Context*. Medina, Ghana: Ministry of Labour and Social Welfare, 1984.

Brake, Mike, and Bailey, Roy. *Radical Social Work and Practice*. Beverly Hills, Calif.: Sage, 1980.

Brigham, Thomas M. "Liberation in Social Work Education: Applications from Paulo Freire." *Journal of Education for Social Work* 13:3 (1977).

Burghardt, Steve. *The Other Side of Organizing*. Cambridge, Mass.: Schenkman, 1982.

_______. *Organizing for Community Action*. Beverly Hills, Calif.: Sage, 1982.

Carniol, Ben. "The Social Action Process." *The Social Worker* 44:2-3 (1976).

_______. "A Critical Approach in Social Work." *Canadian Journal of Social Work Education* 5:1 (1979).

Caspary, William R. "Psychotherapy and Radical Politics." *Catalyst: A Socialist Journal of the Social Services*, No. 7 (1980).

Corrigan, Paul, and Leonard, Peter. *Social Work Practice Under Capitalism: A Marxist Approach*. London: Macmillan, 1978.

Cullen, Yvonne Taylor. "An Alternative Tradition in Social Work: Bertha Capen Reynolds, 1885-1978." *Catalyst* 4:3 (1983).

DeJong, Gerben. "A Political Economy Critique of the American Welfare State." *Journal of Sociology and Social Welfare* 5:1 (1978).

Else, John F. "Purposive Social Change from a Radical Humanist Perspective: Conceptual and Organizational Issues." Ph.D. Dissertation, Brandeis University, 1977a.

______. "Radicalizing Our Organizations and Our Operating Styles." *Social Development Issues* 1:2 (1977b).

Epstein, Irwin. "Organizational Careers, Professionalization and Social-Worker Radicalism." *Social Service Review* 44:2 (1970).

Farris, Buford. "Social Work as a Foreign Body in Late Capitalism." *Journal of Applied Behavior* 18:1 (1983).

Findlay, Peter. "Critical Theory and Social Work Practice." *Catalyst: A Socialist Journal of the Social Services* 1:3 (1978).

Fisher, Jacob. *The Response of Social Work to the Depression*. Cambridge, Mass.: Schenkman, 1980.

Freire, Paulo. *Education for Critical Consciousness*. New York: Seabury Press, 1973a.

______. *Pedagogy of the Oppressed*. New York: Seabury Press, 1973b.

Galper, Jeffry H. *The Politics of Social Services*. Englewood Cliffs, N.J.: Prentice-Hall, 1975.

______. "Introduction of Radical Theory and Practice in Social Work Education: Social Policy." *Journal of Education for Social Work* 12:2 (1976).

______. *Social Work Practice: A Radical Perspective*. Englewood Cliffs, N.J.: Prentice-Hall, 1980.

Gil, David G. "Practice in the Human Services as a Political Act." *Journal of Clinical Child Psychology* 3:1 (1974).

______. *The Challenge of Social Equality–Essays on Social Policy, Social Development and Political Practice*. Cambridge, Mass.: Schenkman, 1976.

______. "Clinical Practice and Politics of Human Liberation." *Catalyst: A Socialist Journal of the Social Services* 1:2 (1978a).

______. "Parents' Wages in the Context of Meaningful Work and Adequate Income Policies." In Banks, Sheila, and Bryce, Marvin (eds.). *Home-Based Services for Children and Families: Policy, Practice, and Research*. Springfield, Ill.: C. C. Thomas, 1978b.

_______. *Beyond the Jungle–Essays on Human Possibilities, Social Alternatives, and Radical Practice*. Cambridge, Mass.: Schenkman, and Boston: G. K. Hall, 1979.

_______. "Social Sciences and Human Liberation." Paper presented at Annual Meeting of the Association for Humanist Sociology, 1981a.

_______. *Unravelling Social Policy: Theory Analysis and Political Action Towards Social Equality*. 3d enlarged ed. Cambridge, Mass.: Schenkman, 1981b.

_______. "Dialectics of Individual Development and Global Social Welfare." In Mohan, Brij (ed.). *New Horizons on Social Welfare and Policy*. Cambridge, Mass.: Schenkman, 1984a.

_______. "The Ideological Context of Child Welfare." In Laird, Joan, and Hartman, Ann (eds.). *A Handbook of Child Welfare*. New York: Free Press, 1984b.

_______. "Institutional Abuse: Dynamics and Prevention." *Catalyst: A Socialist Journal of the Social Services* 4:4 (1984c).

_______. "Reversing Dynamics of Violence by Transforming Work." *Journal of International and Comparative Social Welfare* 1:1 (1984d).

Goroff, Norman N. "Ideology, Sociological Theories and Public Policy." *Journal of Sociology and Social Welfare* 1:1 (1973).

_______. "A Pedagogy for Radical Social Work Practice." Paper presented at the Annual Program Meeting of the Council on Social Work Education, New York, March 1982.

Gottschalk, Shimon. "Toward a Radical Reassessment of Social Work Values." *Journal of Sociology and Social Welfare* 1:2 (1974).

_______. "Thinking About Aging–A Critical Assessment of the Social Meaning of Growing Older." *Gerontology* 23 (1983).

Keefe, Thomas. "The Transition: An Historical-Materialist Perspective on Social Welfare and Social Work Practice." *Journal of Sociology and Social Welfare* 5:5 (1978).

_______. "Alienation and Social Work Practice." *Social Casework* 65:3 (1983).

Knickmeyer, Robert. "A Marxist Approach to Social Work." *Social Work* 17:3 (1972).

Leighninger, Leslie, and Knickmeyer, Robert. "The Rank and File Movement: the Relevance of Radical Social Work Traditions for Modern Social Work Practice." *Journal of Sociology and Social Welfare* 4:2 (1976).

Lewis, Harold. "Morality and the Politics of Practice." *Social Casework* 53:7 (1972).

_______. "The Battered Helper." *Child Welfare* 54:4 (1980).

———. "The Social Work Commodity in a Period of Inflation." *Journal of Sociology and Social Welfare* 10:4 (1983).

Lichtenberg, Philip. *Psychoanalysis: Radical and Conservative*. New York: Springer, 1969.

———. "Introduction of Radical Theory and Practice in Social Work Education: Personality Theory." *Journal of Education for Social Work* 12:2 (1976a).

———. "Radicalism in Casework." *Journal of Sociology and Social Welfare* 4:2 (1976b).

———. "Therapy Within a Radical Political Context." *Social Development Issues* 1:2 (1977).

Longres, John F. "Social Change Needs of Chicanos: A Radical Perspective." In Sotomayor, M., and Ortega y Gasca, P. D. (eds.). *Chicano Content and Social Work Education*. New York: Council on Social Work Education, 1975.

———. "From John F. Longres, A Response." *Social Work* 26 (1981a).

———. "Social Work with Racial Minorities: A Study of Contemporary Norms and Their Ideological Implications." *California Sociologist*, Winter (1981b).

———. "Marxist Theory and Its Applications for Social Work Practice." Paper read at the 25th Anniversary Celbration of the Doctoral Program in Social Work and Social Science, University of Michigan, 1982.

———. "Alienation Among Social Service Workers and Integration into the Social Services." *Journal of Sociology and Social Welfare* 10:4 (1983).

Lyons, Paul. *Philadelphia Communists, 1936-1956*. Philadelphia: Temple University Press, 1982.

———. "Ideology in Social Welfare Policy Instruction: An Examination of Required Readings." *Journal of Sociology and Social Welfare* 10:3 (1983).

Mandell, Betty Reid (ed.). *Welfare in America: Controlling the "Dangerous Classes"*. Englewood Cliffs, N.J.: Prentice-Hall, 1975.

Mohan, Brij. "Social Revolution and Need for Reorienting Social Work Education, with Particular Reference to Indian Position." *Social Democracy* 2:2 (1971).

Moscovitch, Allan. "The Boundaries of Social Welfare Policy." *Catalyst: A Socialist Journal of the Social Services*, No. 6 (1980).

Piven, Frances Fox, and Cloward, Richard A. *Regulating the Poor*. New York: Vintage, 1971.

———. *Poor People's Movements: Why They Succeed, How They Fail*. New York: Pantheon, 1977.

_______. *The New Class War: Reagan's Attack on the Welfare State and Its Consequences.* New York: Pantheon, 1982.

Prigoff, Arline. "Social Work Practice and Class Struggle in the United States: Dilemmas and Opportunities." *Catalyst: A Socialist Journal of the Social Services*, No. 4 (1979).

Pritchard, Colin, and Taylor, Richard. *Social Work: Reform or Revolution?* London: Routledge and Kegan Paul, 1978.

Rein, Martin. "Social Work in Search of a Radical Profession." *Social Work* 15:2 (1970).

Reisch, Michael, Wenocur, Stanley, and Sherman, Wendy. "Empowerment, Conscientization and Animation as Core Social Work Skills." *Social Development Issues* 4:4 (1981).

Reisch, Michael, and Wenocur, Stanley (eds.). *The Political Economy of Social Work.* Thematic issue of *Journal of Sociology and Social Welfare* 10:4 (1983).

Reynolds, Bertha Capen. *Social Work and Social Living.* New York, Citadel, 1951.

_______. *An Uncharted Journey.* New York: Citadel, 1963.

Richan, Willard C., and Mendelson, Allan R. *Social Work: The Unloved Profession.* New York: New Viewpoints Press, 1973.

Schulman, Ken. "Radical Social Work: a Beginning Bibliography." *Catalyst: A Socialist Journal of the Social Services* 4:3 (1983).

Schwartz, William. "Bertha Reynolds as Educator." *Catalyst: A Socialist Journal of the Social Services*, No. 11 (1981).

Shatz, Eunice O. *The Defense of Socially Structured Inequality: A Theoretical Analysis.* Ann Arbor, Mich.: University Microfilms, 1973.

_______. "Teaching and Learning Radical Social Work." *Social Development Issues* 1:3 (1977-78).

Shaffer, Anatole. "Community Organization and the Oppressed." *Journal of Education for Social Work* 8:3 (1972).

Sherman, Wendy R., and Wenocur, Stanley. "Empowering Public Welfare Workers through Mutual Support." *Social Work* 28:5 (1983).

Spano, Rick. *The Rank and File Movement in Social Work.* Washington, D.C.: University Press of America, 1982.

Sparks, Anne. "Radical Therapy: A Gestalt Perspective." *Catalyst: A Socialist Journal of the Social Services* 1:1 (1978).

Statham, Daphne. *Radicals in Social Work.* London: Routledge and Kegan Paul, 1978.

Terrell, Paul. "The Social Worker as Radical: Roles of Advocacy." In Weinberger, Paul E. (ed.). *Perspectives on Social Welfare*. New York: Macmillan, 1974.

Van Kleeck, Mary. *Creative America. Its Resources for Social Security*. New York: Covici, Friede, 1936.

Webber, Marlene. "Abandoning Illusions: The State and Social Change." *Catalyst: A Socialist Journal of the Social Services*, No. 6 (1980).

Wenocur, Stanley. "The Social Welfare Workers Movement: A Case Study of New Left Thought in Practice." *Journal of Sociology and Social Welfare* 3:1 (1974).

Withorn, Ann. "Surviving as a Radical Service Worker: Lessons from the History of Movement-Provided Services." *Radical America* 12:4 (1978).

________. "Beyond Realism: Fighting for Human Services in the Eighties." *Catalyst: A Socialist Journal of the Social Services* 4:2 (1982a).

________. "Helping Ourselves–The Limit and Potential of Self Help." *Social Policy* 11:3 (1982b).

________. *Serving the People: Social Services and Social Change*. New York: Columbia University Press, 1984.

INDEX

ABOUT THE EDITORS AND CONTRIBUTORS

Frank Bonilla is Director of the Centro de Estudios Puertorriqueños at Hunter College of the City University of New York and Professor of Sociology and Political Science, CUNY doctoral programs.

Ricardo Campos is a political scientist and research director of the History and Migration Task Force of the Centro de Estudios Puertorriqueños at Hunter College of the City University of New York. Together with Frank Bonilla he is coauthor of numerous publications on migration, including *Labor Migration under Capitalism: The Puerto Rican Experience*, and articles in *Daedalus, Review*, and *Contemporary Marxism*.

Lucie Cheng is a Professor of Sociology and Director of the Asian American Studies Center, University of California, Los Angeles.

Estevan T. Flores is Assistant Professor of Sociology and Director of Mexican American Studies at Southern Methodist University. His publications have appeared in the *Houston Journal of International Law*, the *Hispanic Journal of Behavioral Science, Historia y Sociedad*, and most recently in *International Migration Review*. He is also Vice-chair of Dallas's "Hispanic Issues Forum."

Juan Flores is Associate Professor of Sociology at Queens College of the City University of New York and a Research Associate of the Centro de Estudios Puertorriqueños at Hunter College. He has written widely on Puerto Rican culture and related issues in culture theory and change. He is author of a prize-winning monograph, *Insularismo e ideología burguesa*, and articles in *Daedalus* and other journals.

David F. Greenberg is Professor of Sociology at New York University. An alumnus of the University of Chicago, as well as of the Civil Rights, antiwar, and prisoners' rights movements, he is now a member of Democratic Socialists of America. He is the author, coauthor, or editor of *The University of Chicago Graduate Problems in Physics with Solutions, Struggle for Justice, Mathematical Criminology, Corrections and Punishment, Crime and Capitalism*, and *Linear Panel Models*, and is completing a comparative and historical study of perceptions of homosexuality.

Philip Lichtenberg is Professor of Social Work and Social Research at Bryn Mawr College and is on the faculty of The Gestalt Therapy Institute of Philadelphia. His interests currently are in connecting insights from clinical work with social struggles. He is a practicing psychotherapist. He has published *Motivation for Child Psychiatry Treatment, Psychoanalysis: Radical and Conservative, Cognitive and Mental Development in the First Five Years of Life,* and *Lectures in Psychoanalysis for Social Workers*.

John M. Liu is an assistant professor in the Program of Comparative Culture, University of California, Irvine, and associate editor of *Amerasia Journal.*

Manning Marable is Professor of Political Sociology and Director of the Africana and Hispanic Studies Program of Colgate University, Hamilton, New York. He is the author of six books, including *How Capitalism Underdeveloped Black America*; *Race, Reform and Rebellion*: *The Second Reconstruction in Black America*; *Black American Politics*: *Volume I Race, Politics and Power*; and the forthcoming *W.E.B. Du Bois*: *A Critical Study*. His syndicated political column, "Along the Color Line," appears in over 140 newspapers in the United States, the Caribbean, England, and India.

Vincent Mosco is Associate Professor of Sociology at Queen's University, Kingston, Ontario, specializing in the political economy of mass media and information technology. He is author of *Broadcasting in the United States, Pushbutton Fantasies*: *Critical Perspectives on Videotex and Information Technology*, and articles on the commercialization and militarization of information technology. He has edited four books with Janet Wasko on labor and media, international media power struggles, popular culture, and Latin American media. He is currently studying the impact of new technologies on telecommunications workers and the relationship of new media to social class and state conflicts.

Vicente Navarro is Professor of Health and Social Policy in the School of Hygiene and Public Health of the Johns Hopkins University. He is a founder and past president of the International Association of Health Policy and founder and editor of the *International Journal of Health Services*. He is the author of *Medicine Under Capitalism*; *Social Security and Medicine in the USSR*: *A Marxist Critique*; *Class Struggle, the State and Medicine*: *An Historical and Contemporary Analysis of the Medical Sector in Great Britain*; *Crisis, Health, and Medicine* and has edited *Health and Medical Care in the U.S.*: *A Critical Analysis*; *Imperialism, Health and Medicine*, and, with Dan Berman, *Health and Work Under Capitalism*: *An International Perspective*.

Bertell Ollman is Professor of Politics at New York University. He is the author of *Alienation*: *Marx's Conception of Man in Capitalist Society* and *Social and Sexual Revolutions*: *Essays on Marx and Reich*, co-editor of *Studies in Socialist Pedagogy*, and the creator of "Class Struggle," a Marxist board game. His most recent book is *Class Struggle is the Name of the Game*: *True Confessions of a Marxist Businessman*.

Howard Raiten is on the faculty of the Chinese University of Hong Kong and is a doctoral candidate at Bryn Mawr College. He is a clinical social worker and his dissertation is on the state of radical social work education in the United States today.

Edward Vernoff is a teacher of history and the editor of the *Dictionary of Twentieth-Century Biography*.

Lise Vogel teaches in the Sociology Department at Rider College, Lawrenceville, New Jersey. Her research interests include women's and family history, the sociology of work, and feminist and Marxist theory. She has published articles on women textile workers in the early nineteenth century, family transformation in the transition to capitalism, and socialist-feminist theory. Her book, *Marxism and the Oppression of Women: Toward a Unitary Theory*, appeared in 1983. Her current research focuses on the dynamic and uneven coexistence of distinct cultural concepts of women's equality in industrial societies.